echos

Published by:
Actar D
440 Park Avenue South, 17th Floor
New York, NY 10016, USA
T +1 212 966 2207
salesnewyork@actar-d.com

First Edition

SAIDechoƨ

Echoƨ Journal 1

Produced through the Office of the SAID Directors –
Edward Mitchell , William Williams, and Michael McInturf –
and the graduate seminar course of Mara Marcu; SAIDinPrint

Many thanks to the School of Architecture and Interior Design
in the College of Design, Architecture, Art, and Planning
at the University of Cincinnati.

Editor: Mara Marcu
Student Editors: Kyle Winston, Alan Alaniz, Chas Wiederhold,
Christina Tefend, Jamie Kruer, John Meyer, Anjana Sivakumar,
Erin Klein, Daham Marapane, Michael Sullivan, Brady Ginn, Seher
Hashmi, Gael Perichon, Farshad Khalighinejad,
Kristin Moreno, and Garcia Ghislaine
Editorial Board: Edward Mitchell, Udo Greinacher,
Elizabeth Riorden, Edson Cabalfin
Graphic Design: Mara Marcu with Student Editors
Copy Editor: Gabriela Sarhos

Echoƨ graphic & all type set in Akzidenz-Grotesk
Library of Congress Publication Data: 2018942687

Echoƨ Journal –1st ed.
406 p. 6.50 x 8.25 in.
ISBN 9781948765046
1. "Echoƨ" by Mara Marcu – 2 . ANXIETY by Peter Zellner –
3. PRAXIS by Victoria Meyers – 4. TROPE by Aaron Betsky–
5. CHREOD by Edward Mitchell – 6. UTOPIA by Peter Waldman

All contents produced from the students, faculty, and guests at
the School of Architecture and Interior Design in the
College of Design, Architecture, Art, and Planning at the
University of Cincinnati.

This is the first publication of student work from the School of Architecture and Interior Design (SAID) in the College of Design, Architecture, Art, and Planning at the University of Cincinnati.

First and foremost, our sincere gratitude to former SAID Director William Williams for initiating the effort, to former SAID Interim Director Michael McInturf for his continued support, and to present SAID Director Edward Mitchell, who through his generous time dedication, multiple edits and invaluable feedback has made this all possible.

We would also like to thank the Christopher Earls Family Endowment, The Modern Sustenance Research Fund, the contributors to the SAID Discretionary Funds, and to Dean Robert Probst for his support.

Special acknowledgments to SAID graduate Kyle Winston, who profoundly impacted the identity of the publication and to the following students who have, with much dedication, carried the initiative further – through interviews, documentation, and laborious editorial decisions: Alan Alaniz, Chas Wiederhold, Christina Tefend, Jamie Kruer, John Meyer, Anjana Sivakumar, and Erin Klein. Others include: Daham Marapane, Michael Sullivan, Brady Ginn, Seher Hashmi, Gael Perichon, Farshad Khalighinejad, Kristin Moreno, and Garcia Ghislaine.

Last, but not least, many thanks to our copy editor, Gabriela Sarhos, and to the following SAID faculty for their guidance: Udo Greinacher, Elizabeth Riorden, and Edson Cabalfin.

SAID

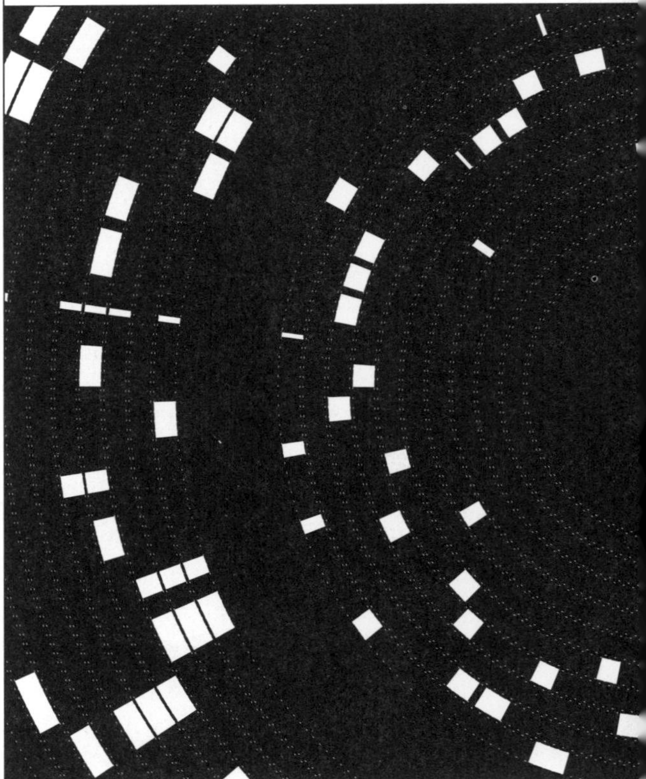

Echos

Mara Marcu

Assistant Professor,
University of Cincinnati
School of Architecture
and Interior Design

1. Wikipedia. (n.d.). "Echos". Accessed Feb 18, 2018. https://en.wikipedia.org/wiki/Echos. *Echos* (Greek: ἦχος [ˈixos] "sound"; pl. *echoi* ἦχοι [ˈiçi], Old Church Slavonic: гласъ [glasŭ] "voice, sound") is the name in Byzantine music theory for a mode within the eight mode system (oktoechos), each of them ruling several melody types, and it is used in the melodic and rhythmic composition of Byzantine chant ("thesis of the melos"), differentiated according to the chant genre and according to the performance style ("method of the thesis"). It is akin to a Western medieval *tonus*, an Andalusian *tab'*, an Arab *naġam* (since 1400 "*maqam*"), or a Persian *parde* (since 18th century *dastgah*).

e·chos
noun \ ˈi-(.)kōs \

2. Merriam-Webster. (n.d.). "Echos". Accessed Feb 18 2018. https://www.merriam-webster.com/dictionary/echo. Plural of *echo*, also *echoes.*

e·cho
noun \ ˈe-(.)kō \

1 a : the repetition of a sound caused by reflection of sound waves
  b : the sound due to such reflection
2 a : a repetition or imitation of another : reflection
  b : repercussion, result
  c : trace, vestige
  d : response
3: one who closely imitates or repeats another's words, ideas, or acts
4: a soft repetition of a musical phrase
5 a: the repetition of a received radio signal due especially to reflection of part of the wave from an ionized layer of the atmosphere
  b(1): the reflection of transmitted radar signals by an object
  (2): the visual indication of this reflection on a radarscope

In general, the term *echos* means sound or voice. In music, the concept refers to a chant sang in dialogue by a choir. This melodic structure has specific hierarchy, notes, and intonations. Although not as popular, *echos* has also become an increasingly accepted plural form of the noun *echo*. The spelling *echoes* is however more commonly found.

The publication ECHOS synthesizes the work done at the University of Cincinnati, School of Architecture and Interior Design, marked by moments of compression and release in our curriculum, which revolves around traditional semester-long sessions and co-op (curriculum-based paid internships) semesters. Though intentionally dissonant at times, our program reinforces the relentless belief that the profession and academia do not need to build on one another in redundancy to reinforce each other. This publication provides an intimate look at our students' intricate path at the School of Architecture and Interior

Design, emphasizing our unique approach to research and practical experience. Co-op semesters at firms including Studio Gang, DIGSAU, MAD Architects, Kennedy Violich Architects, SOM, Gensler, Eisenman Architects, and OMA weave with a year round schedule of highly theoretical, experimental, and consequently research based courses. All of our top-ranked interior design and architecture undergraduate and graduate programs complete a thesis or capstone research project, giving each student the opportunity to develop an intimate body of work.

Indexing student and faculty work, co-op stories, and snapshots from several events, the book places the reader in the midst of Peter Eisenman's famous Grand Staircase, the living room of the Aronoff Center for Design and Art, where the many student and faculty voices form a multilayered chorus of one of the most vibrant and diverse design schools in North America. Part of the College of Design, Architecture, Art, and Planning, the program benefits from its affiliations with industrial design, fashion design, communication design, art, landscape architecture, and urbanism. The opportunistic dialogue that inevitably influences the studio environment happens irrespective of disciplinary boundaries. This relaxes what might become an otherwise dogmatic curricular agenda, breeds new taxonomies and asks questions such as Amanda Lo's thesis – "Do buildings dream of swallowed futures?". In this way we elicit a ludic, nevertheless investigative attitude towards architecture and education.

Events like the ACADIA 2015 conference transform the city in an architectural hub to include notable speakers like Nader Tehrani, amid.cero9, KieranTimberlake, Achim Menges, Francois Roche, and Branko Kolarevic. Lectures with important architects like Neil Denari or Craig Dykers add to our discussion. The chance for students to exhibit work outside the school at SOFA Chicago or the ICFF, and study abroad in Paris, Turkey, India, and China help perpetuate an international dialogue.

The SAID faculty is composed of diverse scholars whose research spans across sustainability, design-build, digital fabrication, community outreach, computation, architectural robotics, history, archeology, and theory. The unique environment in which our school is set, including its award winning architecture campus, is a crucible for architectural discourse that contains a multiplicity of academic possibilities.

Various constellations chart our diverse academic and social interactions that revolve around the book's five main themes: *anxiety, praxis, trope, chreod*, and *utopia*. Introduced by a series of analytical diagrams which are paired up with essays by lead figures in the discipline who have critically shaped the school at some point in time, the themes expand on the issues of theoretical anxiety, architectural discourse, practice, typology, analogies, and *ad hoc* morphologies inherent to research. Flux and reflux return each disruption to a steady trajectory similar to the academic cycle of compression and release generated by the real world realties of the co-op program and the fictitious and idealistic nature of the academic studio.

Anxiety, introduced by Peter Zellner, collects and synthesizes multiple contradicting theories that entertain with equanimity various solutions to design problems. *Praxis*, introduced by Victoria Meyers, looks at outcomes—physical, prototypical, digital or analog, multi-dimensional and multi-media, spoken, written or unwritten—as well as working methodologies that shape design thinking. *Trope*, introduced by Aaron Betsky, maps out trends, emergent ideologies, and design expressions. *Chreod*, introduced by Edward Mitchell, documents and interprets field conditions, rule-based processes, issues of transgressions, non-smooth and nomadic entities that cut across arbolic-like divisions. *Utopia*, introduced by Peter Waldman, while suspending various otherwise necessary constraints, allows for an euphoric and unapologetically optimistic view of the world, with the goal of envisioning daring possibilities otherwise unimaginable. *Utopia*, therefore, prefigures all other themes and is the ambition and imaginary locus of the multiple programs and opportunities at the School of Architecture and Interior Design at the University of Cincinnati.

Photography Credits / **JOSHUA ANDERSON**

BSARCH

BSINTD

SAID 1001: Design Lab 1
SAID 1011: Communication Skills 1
SAID 1031: Human Dimension of Space
ENGL 1001: English Composition
Free Elective: Elective

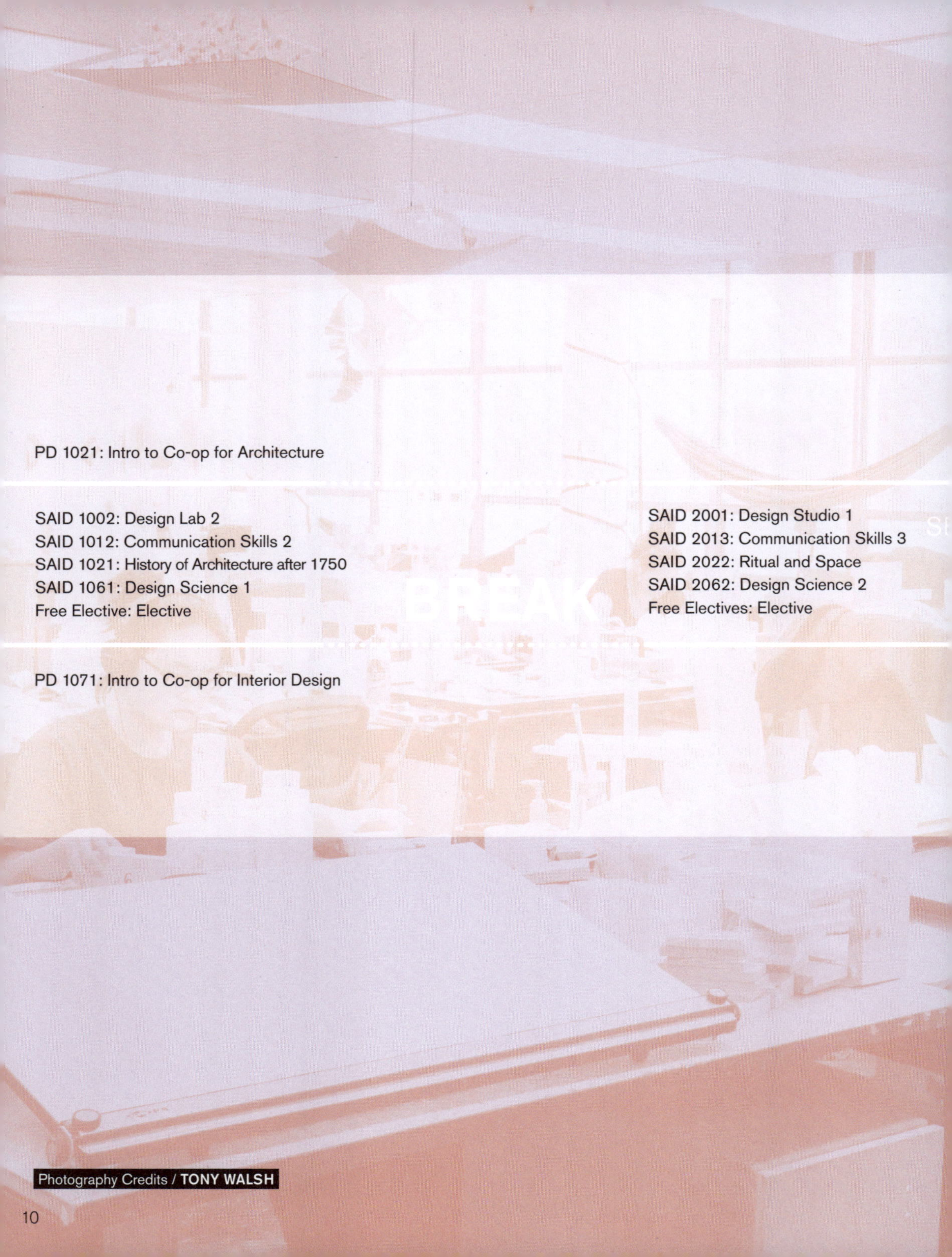

PD 1021: Intro to Co-op for Architecture

SAID 1002: Design Lab 2
SAID 1012: Communication Skills 2
SAID 1021: History of Architecture after 1750
SAID 1061: Design Science 1
Free Elective: Elective

BREAK

SAID 2001: Design Studio 1
SAID 2013: Communication Skills 3
SAID 2022: Ritual and Space
SAID 2062: Design Science 2
Free Electives: Elective

PD 1071: Intro to Co-op for Interior Design

Photography Credits / **TONY WALSH**

ARCH 2003: Architecture Studio 1
ARCH 2004: Architecture Studio 2
ARCH 2023: Classical Tradition in Architecture
Free Electives: Elective

CO-OP

SAID 2063: Design Science 3

INTD 2002: Interior Design Studio 2
INTD 2031: Professional Practice 2
INTD 2061: Materials and Fibers /Construction
ENGL 2089: Intermediate Composition

ARCH 3001: Architecture Studio 3
ARCH 3014: Digital Media Skills
ARCH 3071: Structures
ENGL 2089: Intermediate Composition
Free Electives: Elective

ARCH 3001: Architecture Studio 4
Free Electives: Professional Elective
Free Electives: Elective
Free Electives: Elective
Free Electives: Elective

CO-OP

INTD 3001: Interior Design Studio 3
INTD 4022: History Theory Criticism 2
Free Electives: Elective
Free Electives: Elective

INTD 4001: Interior Design Studio 4
INTD 4022: History Theory Criticism 2
Free Electives: Elective
Free Electives: Elective

MARCH

ARCH 7001: Order/Tectonics in Architecture
ARCH 7012: Design Visualization 1
ARCH 7021: History of Architecture to 1600
ARCH 7061: Construction Technology

Photography Credits / **JOSHUA ANDERSON**

ARCH 4002: Building Design Studio
ARCH 4051: History and Theory of Cities
Free Electives: Professional Elective
Free Electives: Elective
Free Electives: Elective

CO-OP

CO-OP

INTD 4081: Interior Lighting
INTD 5001: Senior Capstone Studio 1
INTD 4031: Professional Practice 3
Free Electives: Elective
Free Electives: Elective

ARCH 7002: Civic Realm + Public Context
ARCH 7013: Design Visualization 2
ARCH 7022: History of Architecture 1600 to present
ARCH 7081: Environmental Technologies 1

ARCH 7014: Design Visualization 3
PD 7022: Practitioner-Led Seminar Series for Master of Architecture CO-OP
ARCH 7081: Environmental Technologies 1

ARCH 7004: Advanced Building Design Studio
ARCH 7062: Integrated Technologies
ARCH 7072: Structures 2
PD 7021: Introduction to Master of Architecture COOP
Free Electives: Elective

MSARCH

ARCH 8091: Colloquium 1
Quantitative Research Methods
ARCH 9021: Advanced Theory 1
Ancient to Modern
ARCH 8012: M.S. Research Methods
Free Electives: Elective

MINTD

INTD 5002: Senior Capstone Studio 2
Free Electives: Elective
Free Electives: Elective

INTD 7001: Graduate Studio 1
INTD 7021: History, Theory, and
Criticism in Interior Design
INTD 7031: Research Methods 1
INTD 7081: Colloquium 1
PD 7001: Professional Development

CO-OP

CO-OP

ARCH 7005: Advanced Integration Studio
ARCH 7035: Architecture Theory 2
Thematic Overview 20th century to present
ARCH 7051: Site Systems
ARCH 7082: Environmental Technologies 2
Free Electives: Elective

Photography Credits / **TONY WALSH**

ARCH 8092: Colloquium 2
M.S. Teaching + Pedagogy
ARCH 9022: Advanced Theory 2
Contemporary Architecture Theory
Free Electives: Elective
Free Electives: Elective

BREAK

ARCH 8093: Colloquium 3
M.S. Research + Inquiry
ARCH 9023: Advanced Theory 3
Global Perspectives
ARCH 8013: M.S. Thesis Writing
Free Electives: Elective

CO-OP

INTD 7002: Graduate Studio 2
INTD 7022: Graduate Seminar 2
INTD 7032: Research Methods 2
INTD 7061: Illumination, Energy and Sustainability
Free Electives: Elective
Free Electives: Elective

INTD 8001: Thesis Studio 1 - Research
INTD 8021: Thesis Development Seminar 1
INTD 8081: Colloquium 2
Free Electives: Elective

CO-OP

ARCH 8001: Building Design Studio
ARCH 8012: M.S. Research Methods
ARCH 7054: History + Theory of Cities
Free Electives: Elective

ARCH 8009: Thesis Studio 1
ARCH 8041: Professional Practice/Ethics
Free Electives: Interior Design Elective
Free Electives: Elective

ARCH 8094: Colloquium 4
M.S. Teaching + Pedagogy
ARCH 8014: M.S. Thesis
Free Electives: Elective

INTD 8002: Thesis Studio 2
Free Electives: Elective
Free Electives: Elective

PHDARCH

ARCH 9021: Theory 1
ARCH 9093: Colloquium 1
ARCH 8012: Research Methods
Free Electives: Elective

ARCH 8009: Thesis Studio 2
Free Electives: Elective
Free Electives: Elective

Photography Credits / **VINCENT SANSALONE**

ARCH 9022: Theory 2
ARCH 9094: Colloquium 2
Free Electives: Elective
Free Electives: Elective

BREAK

ARCH 9023: Theory 3
ARCH 9095: Colloquium 3
Free Electives: Elective
Free Electives: Elective

ARCH 9024: Theory 4
ARCH 9096: Colloquium 4
ARCH 9011: Qualifying Paper
Free Electives: Elective

BREAK

ARCH 9013: Minor Exam
ARCH 8018 Teaching Practicum
Free Electives: Elective

Photography Credits / **BENJAMIN BLAKE, MICHAEL FERGUSON, LAURA KENNEDY, CALEB LANG**

ARCH 9014: Major Exam
ARCH 9012: Dissertation Proposal

BREAK

ARCH 9091: Field Research 1

BREAK

ARCH 9092: Field Research 2

ARCH 9015: Dissertation 1

Photography Credits / **TONY WALSH**

ARCH 9016: Dissertation 2

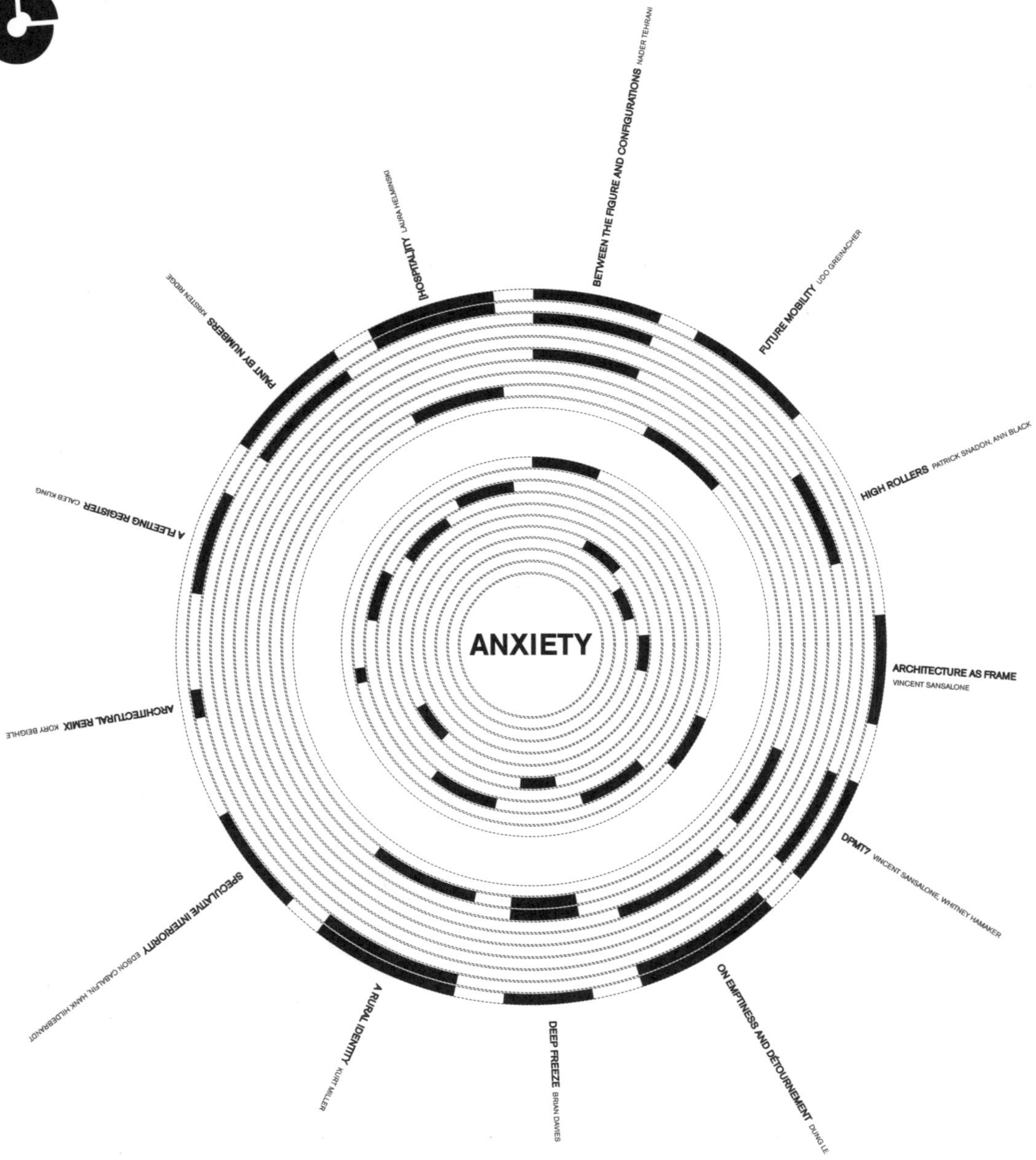

LEGEND:

1. OUTER SECTOR = ID
2. INNER SECTOR = LEVEL
3. WIDTH = SCALE

1. *From Outer Ring to Inner Ring:*
Design Thinking
History/Theory
Material Investigation
Branding
Design Build
Digital Craft
Computational Design
Fabrication
Sustainability
Public Interest

2. *From Outer Ring to Inner Ring:*
Professional
PhD
Graduate 3rd Year
Graduate 2nd Year
Graduate 1st Year
Undergraduate 5th Year
Undergraduate 4th Year
Undergraduate 3rd Year
Undergraduate 2nd Year
Undergraduate 1st Year

3. *Width of Black Poché:*
Scaleless
Object
Furniture
Body
Room
Building
Cluster/Complex
City/Region

ANXIETY

Permanent Crisis

The American City seems to exist now in a state of permanent crisis that is a self-renewing state of emergency driven by multiplying acts of violence directed against civilians by officers of the peace, and more recently, by civilians against officers of the peace. Recent acts of seemingly retaliatory counter-violence have raised the possibility that our cities may become settings for persistent urban confrontations pitting civilians against the police, the very branch of local government retained to maintain a civil society.

This crisis may be tied to the rolling back of the idea of the historical American City as a space of free political expression and, more directly, to the dismantling of the project of civil rights and individual freedoms since 9/11. The impact of this crisis on architecture and city design remains largely unexamined.

The City State

The city, Michel de Certeau tells us, might be best understood as an operational or functionalist concept founded on the constructing of space "on the basis of a finite number of stable, isolatable, and interconnected properties" [1]. These stable properties extend the rationalization of space (city design let's say) to the replacement of a "synchronic" and "flattened" structure (the feudal system for instance) for various urban resistances that align with the creation of a universal and anonymous subject. This subject might be, perhaps, substituted for a democratic citizen while the rationalization of space might be understood as an urban scheme (grids, blocks, tracts and communities for instance.) Lastly, in De Certeau's notion of indeterminable and stubborn resistances, we might find the conception of free and democratic assembly and protest being a welcome byproduct of a civil society.

As an administrative construction, however, the city must also be seen as dualistic structure: both an autonomous utopian object (More) and a correlated political project (Hobbes). Therefore, the City's well being always remains liminal, somewhere between an idea and a political reality, depending largely on the successful coordination of its various managerial mechanisms, physical assets, and populations. The management of the City's various physical infrastructures (roads, sewers, power, airports, ports, and communication networks) is directly connected to the larger problem of serving its economic goals and providing for its constituents' well-being. The City, then, is both an idea and an object, and its protection has been historically tied to the administration of laws, the protection of its citizens, the safe policing of its spaces and boundaries.

Polis/ Police

Polis, the Greek notion of the City State, shares an etymological connection to the term Police, linked via the Greek concept of politeia: administration, polity, and citizenship. *Polis* is connected to the concept of the common good and to the idea of the commons as both a physically and metaphorically shared space.

The City and its police forces emerged in parallel, both formations being directly tied to the Hellenistic ideals granted to the free citizen: the right to free speech, the right to free congregation, and the right to free public exchange. Not coincidentally the Greek City-State's first police force was made up not of freeman but of Scythian slaves, and not coincidentally, our own urban civil rights movement have been led, mainly but not exclusively by the descendants of slaves. Urban civil rights imply or even demand not only freedom from enslavement but also a civil space, meaning that the City must provide a space for individuals and groups to equally participate in civil life without fear of repression, reprisal or violent threat by its agents and agencies. Civil and political rights in North America extend to the right to due process and a fair trial, and these functions, managerially, have fallen to law enforcement agencies and the criminal justice system. Rarely do they extend to the Right to the City described by Henri Lefebvre, in his 1968 book *Le droit à la ville*, as the right to "urban life, to renewed centrality, to places of encounter and exchange, to life rhythms and time uses, enabling the full and complete usage of moments and places" [2].

The work of maintaining the tenuous and delicate relationship between policing urban populations and administering justice connects physical and lived space to bureaucratic space, and it is in this zone that the police and police work lies: in the streets of the City, within its communities, and between the lines of the City's codes, rules, regulations and civil laws. Consequently without civil space, the enterprise of City making (politeia) is threatened, and without a City (polis) there is no Police, no need to secure what has been made permanently insecure, and in turn this leaves possibility of another condition, namely civil war.

The American City, Destabilized

After many organized national protests (notably Ferguson, Cleveland, and elsewhere) around police-related deaths in communities of color and the killings of police officers that followed in Dallas and Baton Rouge in 2016, the idea of the post-war American City as a stable expression of governmental space seems threatened by the very administrative systems, organizations, and bodies that were established to serve its universal and anonymous subject, the citizen. And, while the public reply to police related deaths has been organized, largely peaceful public resistance, the counter response from a now militarized police force is mutating the City from a space of democratic exchange into a theater of intimidation and violent conflict between mostly unarmed individuals, public groups, and heavily armed civil officers.

The conflict could not be more starkly outlined as each week or month another police-related death incites a community to protest, with often very tragic consequences for both the public and the police. However, as Michel Foucault submitted, in the modern state "power is less a confrontation between two adversaries or the linking of one to the other than a question of government." Government, Foucault asserts, refers not only "to political structures or to the management of states; rather it designate[s] the way in which the conduct of individuals or of groups might be directed…not only…the legitimately constituted forms of political or economic subjection, but also modes of action, more or less considered and calculated, which were destined to act upon the possibilities of action of other people" [3].

The City as a State of Anxiety

If the City in/as a state of anxiety originates with the expectation that the application of force, or power, against the notion of citizenry, civil life, and civil rights will continue or extend beyond individual incidents, then the City is moving towards the concept of a total Polizeistaat (von Mohl). While this theory runs entirely against the evolution of the American urban situation—from self-liberating 18th century colonial outposts, to emerging 19th century industrial, cultural and economic hubs, to 20th century urban/suburban agglomerations—what is clear is that our crisis of government has enabled a national furor over the deaths of Philando Castile not only to go unanswered but to exacerbate a national crisis of confidence very organs of justice that uphold out cities.

"To govern," Foucault asserts, "is to structure the possible field of action of others." The construction of the city in relationship to "power would not therefore be sought on the side of violence or of struggle…but rather in the area of the singular mode of action, neither warlike nor juridical, which is government" [4]. When civil administration of the city is replaced by the arbitrary and violent control of urban populations by a militarized police force, then the space for these confrontations must be examined in terms of the degrees to which power is either reaffirmed through the maintenance of stable administrative structures or unleashed through radicalized communal action within those spaces. Therein lies the challenge to the status of the modern City as a democratic and free space: once the specter of state-sponsored police control has been summoned, we raise the very possibility of totalitarianism and with it the return to idea of the American city as a failed project.

Fuck the Polis?

The ancient Greek concept of *topos* referred to both a physical place, like a city, and a space of social, philosophical or poetic exchange. *Topos* expressly connected space to the notion of free public exchange through *topoi* (rhetorics). The formation of free public exchange was reinforced by the conception of civic and civil space as a nominally shared or neutral territory, neither private nor official.

Safely securing the zone between private zones (commercial or residential) and sanctioned spaces (religious, administrative, or military) lies at the heart of the City's stability, of the due democratic right to assemble freely. This is one of the key functions of government, specifically of the police, and important source of the City's democratic vitality.

In crushing the very resistances and subjects formed within the rationalized spaces of civic and civil life, our unbridled urban and suburban police forces—understood here as the City's frontline administrative and managerial agents—have accelerated the process of dismantling the City as our most visible expression of a free and democratic culture.

The Architect's Crisis

The architectural profession's largely self-imposed disconnection from both centers of administrative power and the larger community invokes in many architects something like a crisis of conscience. As it as has been noted elsewhere [5], most North American architects have been largely silent about recent civil unrest, and this is perhaps because contemporary architecture has an uncomfortable if not oblivious relationship to power. Stubbornly rooted for decades in largely meaningless debates around minor academic, artistic or technical dilemmas, the architectural discipline stands witness to a crisis beyond the reach of its current theoretical, formalist, or materialist discourses.

The appropriation of the City as the stage for the violent conflict indirectly implicates architecture and city design, if only because architects steadfastly refuse to acknowledge the stage they always set for power in the design of the city and its architectural components. Despite the architect's anxieties about the political moment she/he finds herself in, the profession has been, of late, passively observing the devolution of the City, the very source and subject of the profession's existence some might say. North American architects and urbanists, never entirely functionaries of the state nor players wholly detached from the market, operate today in a nebulous arena: somewhere between advocating for the open construction of civic space and ignoring the more obvious manifestations of violent authoritarianism at work in our cities.

This situation defies the discipline to find some authentic form of professional expertise that might be applied to the problems of maintaining the sorts of civil space that promote architecture's relevance. At the heart of this challenge is the true source of the architect's anxiety: it is that the discipline's academic and professional bodies have resisted examining the unspeakable relationship between urban or architectural form and the degree to which it has delayed, aided, or abetted the abuses of power.

Yet, if architects do suffer from a state of professional anxiety around not only our relevance but more largely around the entire project of the modern City, to date there has been little debate or conjecture within either our academic or professional communities about how a more engaged role in the life of our cities might be invented to confront or even radically resist what is beginning to seem more and more like state-sanctioned urban violence against a civilian population, paralleled by a domestic cultural and political war being waged against the civic, civil and cosmopolitan culture that forms the core of the modern democratic City.

Notes:

[1] Michel De Certeau. *The Practices of Everyday Life.* Trans. S. F. Rendall. Berkeley: University of California Press, 1984.

[2] Henri Lefebvre. "Le droit à la ville" in *Société et Urbanisme*, 1, Paris : Anthropos, 1968, 1.

[3] Michel Foucault. *Discipline and Punish: The Birth of the Prison.* Trans. Alan Sheridan. New York: Pantheon, 1977, 215.

[4] Michel Foucault. Ibid. 215.

[5] Mimi Zeiger. (2014). "Koolhaas may think we're past the time of manifestos, but that's no reason to play dumb." *DEZEEN*, 12 December 2014. Web. 23 Mar 2017. < http://www.dezeen.com/2014/12/12/mimi-zeiger-opinion-urban-unrest-police-violence-race-architecture-urbanism-ferguson/>. "Architecture as a practice sits at the juncture of hegemonic structures and the community it serves. It's an uncomfortable position and architecture's social agenda is often viewed as a failure when compared to its formalist counterpart."

UDO GREINACHER

FUTURE MOBILITY

Fourth Year Architecture Capstone Studio
Haiti / New Orleans, Louisiana, USA / Zaatari Refugee Camp, Jordan

For the last two hundred years, nothing has influenced our way of life and altered the places in which we live as drastically as advances in transportation. In the United States, inlets and rivers originally determined our settlements. Railroads helped push settlements westward and made, or in the case of Cincinnati, doomed cities. Streetcars triggered the first ring of suburbs, while the automobile led to urban sprawl. Digitization weakens the link between object and place further by drastically increasing the speed of movement. Each of above advances has altered shape, type and use of our homes, workplaces and civic communities. What's next?

How will we move in the future? Will we be shuttled in self-driving zip-cars? Will drones deliver our purchases? Will all physical movement cease while our thoughts connect in cyberspace?

The Future Mobility Studio generated several probable scenarios for 2050 that informed diverse sets of building types and programs.

Project 1 used traditional forecasting methods that assume the future will be a continuous development of the past, with a 10% variance in either direction.

We entered the results to the "Cities of Our Time" competition and were rewarded with the first prize and numerous honorable mentions.

Project 2 based the designs on student-developed scenarios that included uncertainties as game changers.

Project 3 tested the prototypes developed in Project 2 by entering them into a variety of competitions. The results were not yet available at the time of publication.

LEX COLTON / rendering

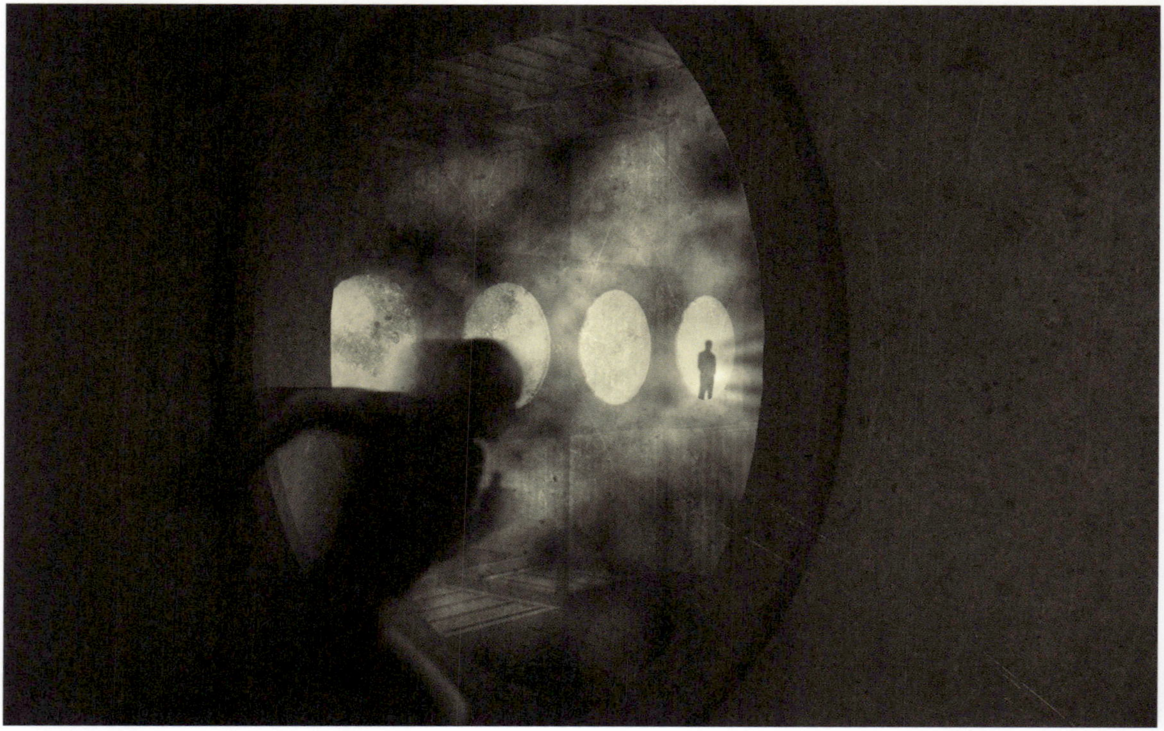

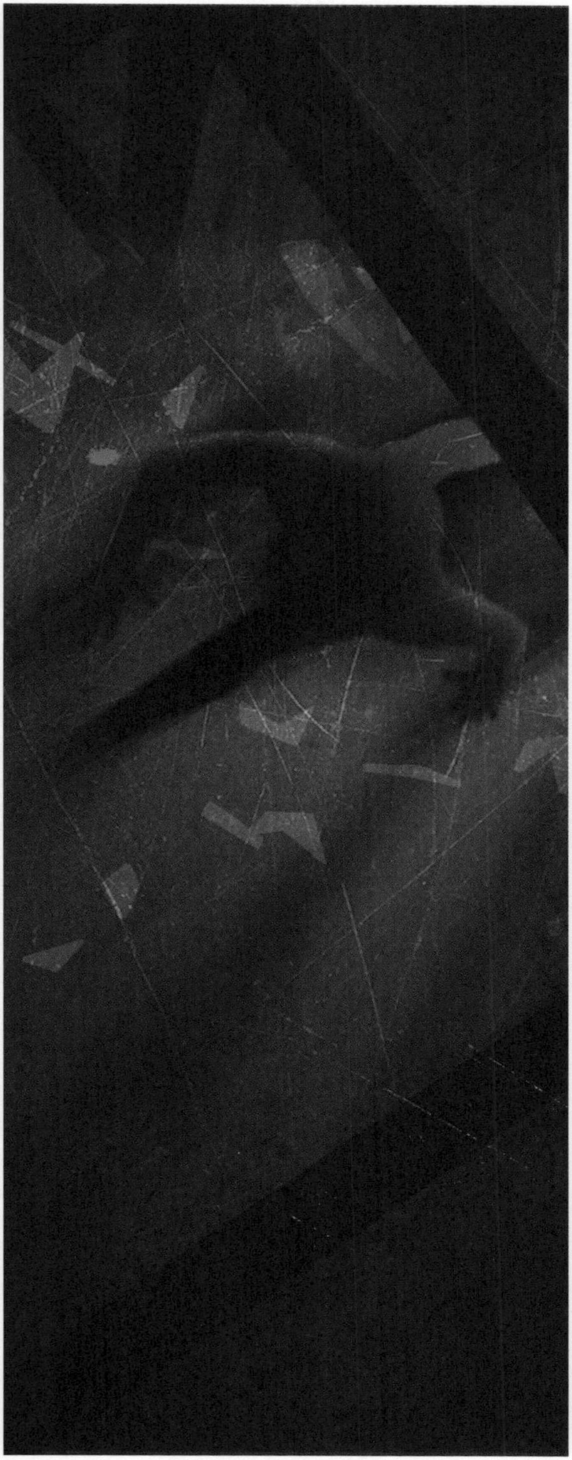

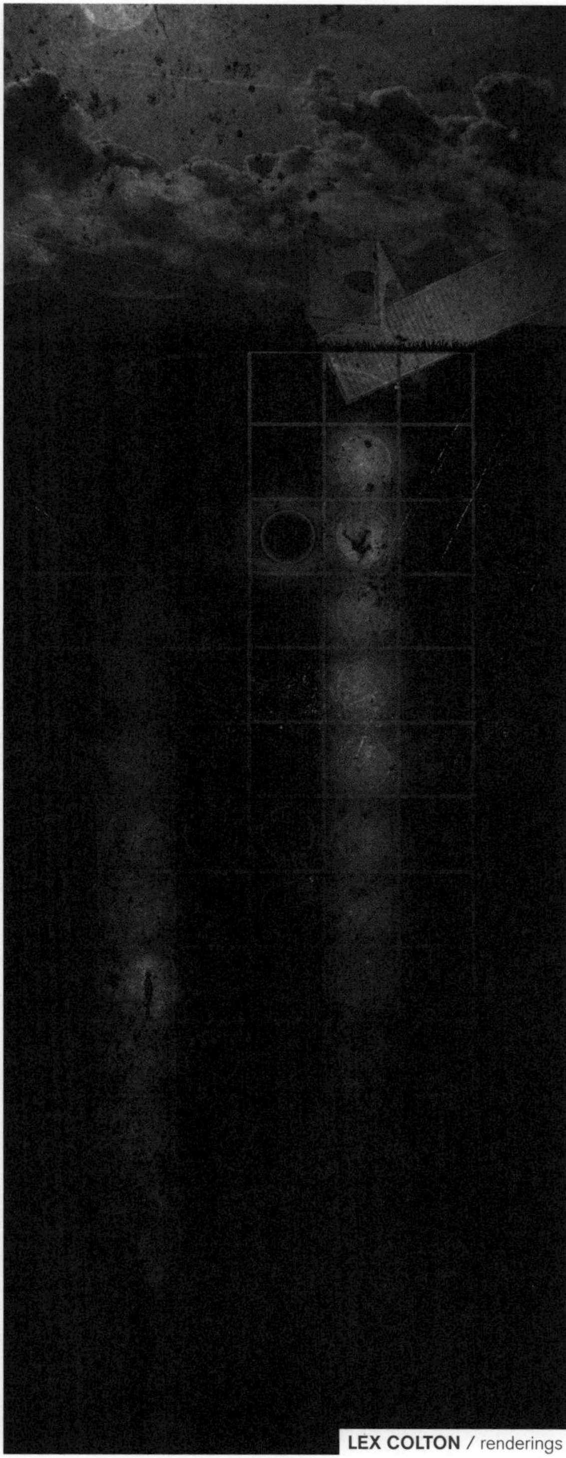

LEX COLTON / renderings

PATRICK SNADON, PH.D.
ANN BLACK

HIGH ROLLERS LAS VEGAS SUITES

Undergraduate Interior Design, Hospitality Studio
Las Vegas, Nevada, USA

The third year hospitality design studio focuses on the impact of interpersonal and social relationships on space, particularly human-behavior, socio-cultural dynamics, and meaning and placemaking. Additionally, a strong emphasis is placed on the development of concept and "brands" and translating those from idea to three-dimensional spatial solutions. Questions of "What is a brand and how do brands differ?" and "How is a brand communicated?" are explored. Understanding the user, competition within the sector, and future trends are all considered in this studio.

Las Vegas has been the playground for the wealthy for years. Persons with expendable wealth travel there to spend money gambling and shopping. Lavish suites and unparalleled service are the trademarks of the hotels along the Strip. Today's high rollers range from couples looking to escape their routine lives to groups of friends who want to stay together and party until all hours of the morning.

Because many hotels provide dedicated floors of suites for the exclusive use of "High Rollers," this third year hospitality studio focused on the meaning of designing for luxury and opulent services. The wealth of each type of user—whether a product of a privileged class, or valued based on social capital, or "earned" by virtue of skill/ expenditures—its impact on their hypothetical expectations became a framework for comparison. Teams of three students each designed a lobby space. Individually, each student designed a suite for a targeted user group: a couple with "old money," a couple with "new money," or a couple with an entourage of friends who travel together.

The ability to forge social connections became a common thread in many of the projects. While some individual student designers chose to focus on the ways in which technology could enhance the physical experience of space in the suites, others projected the impact of physical traits such as color, material and texture to attract groups of people and to encourage engagement with one another.

interior living area

HANNAH CLARK / interior bar rendering

interior rendering

studio unit

master suit

section

interior cocktail area

Whether facilitating intimacy or collaboration, students explored how the spirit of a place such as Las Vegas, with its legendary cultivation of fantasy, can contribute to the design of memorable and meaningful interiors for persons who seek the most in life.

One student focused on technology, branding the suite "Virtual Vitality". Using the latest trends in technology, this student provided the users with an out-of-body experience. The users would theoretically be able to socialize through technology and develop closer relations with the world, with Las Vegas, and with each other.

Another student emphasized the concept that the more occupants and activity in the suite, the more colorful the space became through dramatic lighting techniques.

VINCENT SANSALONE

ARCHITECTURE AS FRAME: THE OBJECTIVITY OF THE SUBJECT

Fourth Year Architecture Capstone Studio
Building Design Studio

This studio is interested in the question of frame and the image of the 'canvas.' It was a way into a painting; focusing the view. A frame can inform meaning, and still today in some cases can mean 'this is art.' A frame is a threshold between a painting and a wall, just as aperture is a frame between one space to another. In psychological terms, it is the spatial structure that acts as wayfinding in the understanding of the performative nature of place. Through the perceptual, physical, and spatial frame, a cognitive map may occur through singular and multiple frames–think of a frame in a film–in the end a completed, self-directed work.

ZACH SCHOLL / question of homelessness

KYLE WINSTON / circuit proposed rendering

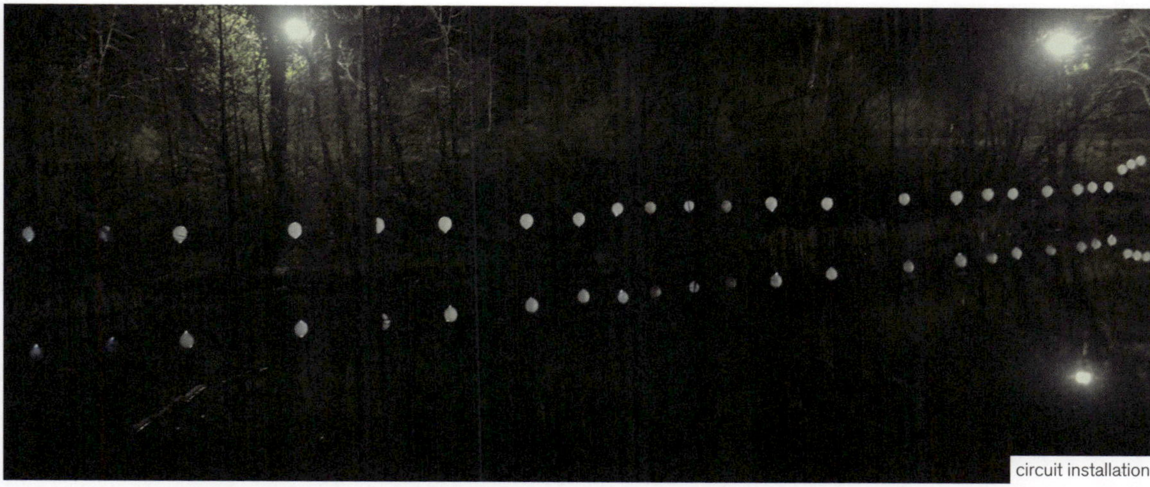
circuit installation

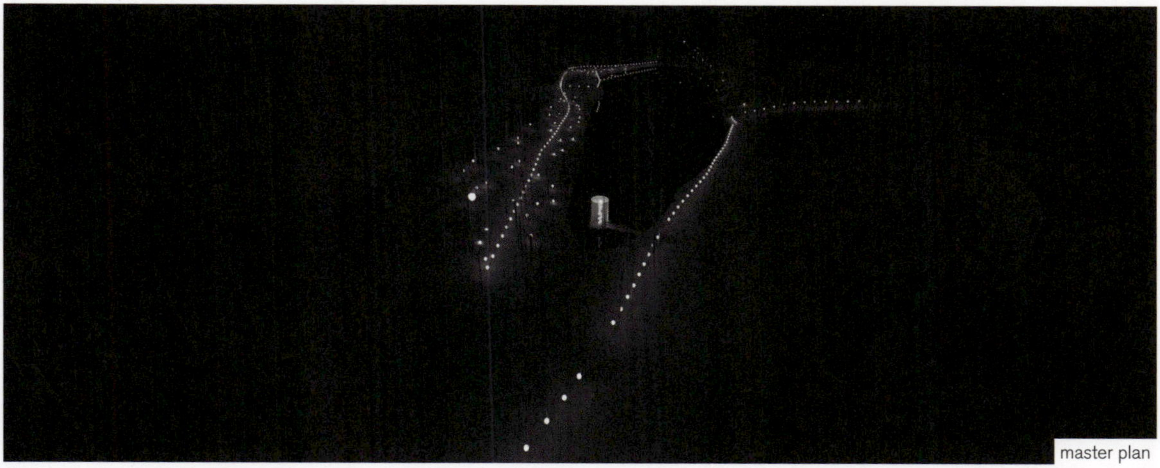
master plan

KYLE WINSTON / circuit installation

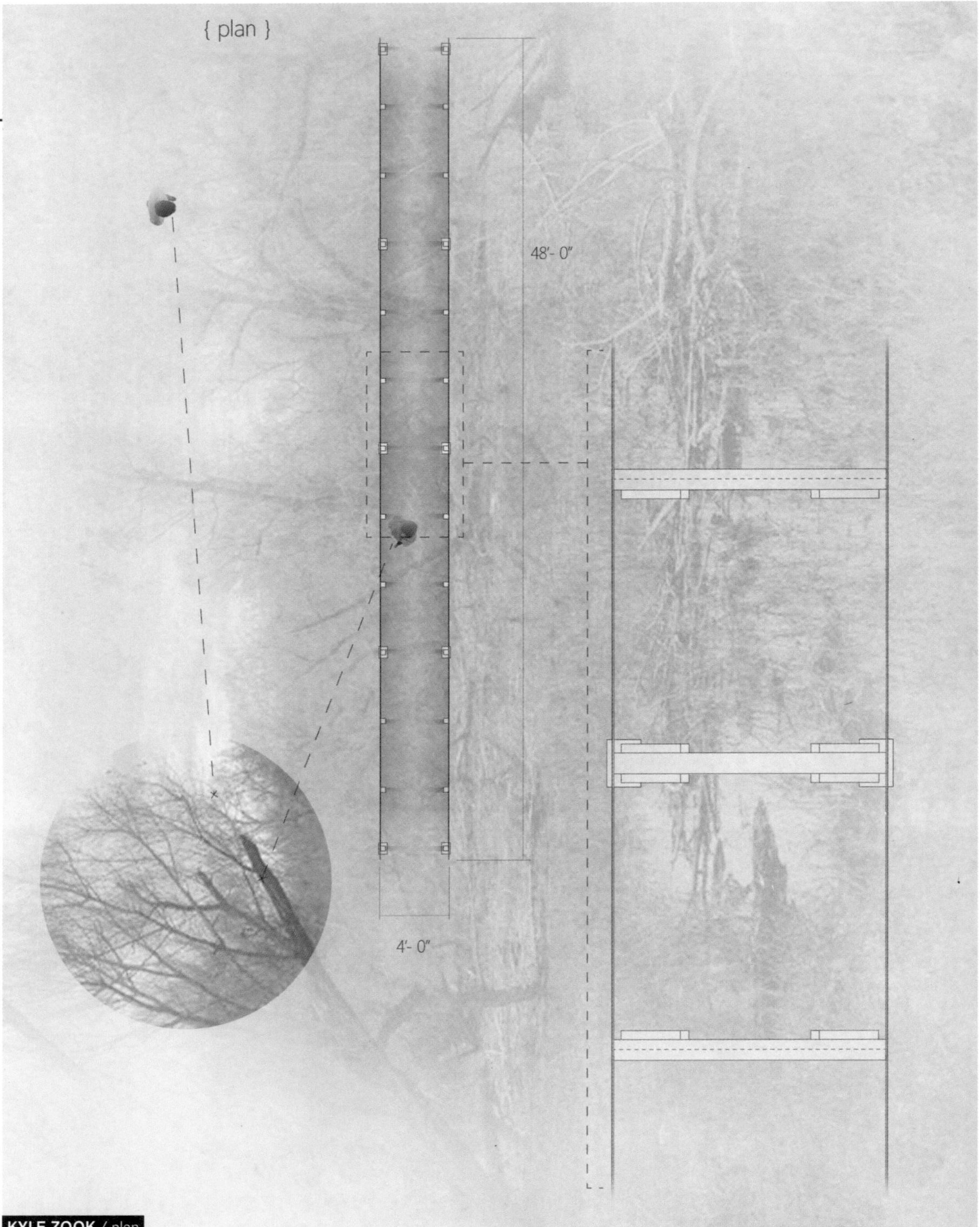
{ plan }
48'- 0"
4'- 0"

rendering

section perspective

KYLE ZOOK / rendering

VINCENT SANSALONE
WHITNEY HAMAKER

DPMT7

Cincinnati, Ohio, USA

Welcome to our world of experiencing the (k)new–a web of material structure, forming a textured space of solitude where the distinctions between past, present and future are a persistent illusion. The eye moves interrupted by image constructing form; a square, a collage of sequential vignettes of (the) everyday, an operatic insight of thought. The "constructions" are isolated curiosities; but through an iterative process of re-imagining and conversation develop into a rich spatial collage of the seemingly banal.

The process grows in a naïve and organic manner, cultivated by a given prompt and constrained though a determined rule-set, pulled directly from the surrounding context, history, and the frame of the post-industrial landscape. We utilize the ready. Made to facilitate: a bricolage of experience, fabrication, or place creating a critical feedback. Iterative processes facilitate a performative quality to each moment, not as a definitive conclusion but rather as a line of argument in a continuing conversation; a palimpsest of investigation and expression. Moving around, through a tunnel of light washed over by the sirens towards the materiality of the Stelae–a quiet memorial to a seemingly insignificant place, object, or person that we have known, worth considering and celebrating–16 figures in assemblage watched over by a vision form vectors, threads of a collective tapestry. The tangible becomes intangible.

A view of the past feeds the present. An ephemeral foundation of ceaseless activity, a new presentation of the (w)hole, grounds the structure above. A construct, formed in time - Are the sixteen one or eight visions? This is for the individual to conclude not a conscription of thought but a moment of new perspective. One descends into a moment that slips through the light between memory and the present, into a space of another; sound is quieted by silence and the images of the other appear. Presenting: An apparatus of thought and experience.

Crevalcore model/ Weston Art Gallery, Cincinnati, OH (photo credit: Tony Walsh)

Un Teatro Del Nuovo, cyclorama model iterations/ Weston Art Gallery, Cincinnati, OH (photo credit: Tony Walsh)

Untitled, 4' x 8' chalk on plaster by Vincent Sansalone in the Un Teatro Del Nuovo exhibition/Weston Art Gallery, Cincinnati, OH.

'Stelae' exhibition, Vincent Sansalone + Whitney Hamaker/ Birmingham Bloomfield Art Ceter, Birmingham, MI

Cyclorama, Un Teatro Del Nuovo/ Weston Art Gallery, Cincinnati, OH.

Crevalcore model being positioned during the install of the Un Teatro Del Nuovo exhibition/ Weston Art Gallery, Cincinnati, OH.

DUNG LE
AARATI KANEKAR, PH.D. (chair)
ELIZABETH RIORDEN (member)

ON EMPTINESS AND DÉTOURNEMENT

A Spectacle of the Architectural Köans
Master of Architecture Thesis
Geylang,Singapore

This thesis critiques and analyzes the persisting issues of modern life as they impact architecture based on *The Society of The Spectacle* by Guy Debord. *The Society of The Spectacle* made such a profound impact on French society in the 1960s that it aided in the creation of the avant-garde social movement dubbed Situationism. The Situationists strongly believed that by constructing different actions within the city fabric, spectacle could actually create a more meaningful urban experience.

Seeing the similarities between Situationism and Mahayana Buddhism in their ultimate quest to cease human suffering, this thesis then argues that the architectural significance of the idea of Emptiness in Mahayana Buddhism holds the answer to the 'Grand Spectacle' proposed by Guy Debord and the Situationists.

Through an in-depth study and analysis of the Situationist's *Dérive* and *Détournement* as the means of production, the thesis aims to create an architectural state of Emptiness at the Geylang Neighborhood of Singapore, commonly known as the Red Light District. This project can be categorized into two stages based on the scale of intervention into the existing urban texture. At the urban scale, the project would propose a number of conceptual *Dérive* and *Détournement* pathways to connect between human scale insertions. These urban interventions encourage the spectators to deviate from the ordinary and emerge into the unexpected.

The building called Käla consists of Moon Space and Sun Space, which are tilted at a five degree angle against each other in elevation to resemble the movement of the Sun and the Moon as observed by the human eye. In Moon Space, the mirror clad oculus is pointed towards the location of the full moon in the night sky every lunar month of July, which is also the festival of compassion. The prism oculus in Sun Space is aligned to the location of the Sun at noon at the Spring Equinox. At this moment of the year, daylight will be split into moving color spectrum washing against the entrance wall of Sun Space. The interweaving set of stairs placed at the interstitial space between the two structures represent the eclipse, when the notion of day and night, darkness and light, is in a state of discombobulation.

Käla

The Oculus on Mid-Autumn Festival

Moon Space

The Oculus on Spring Equinox

Sun Space

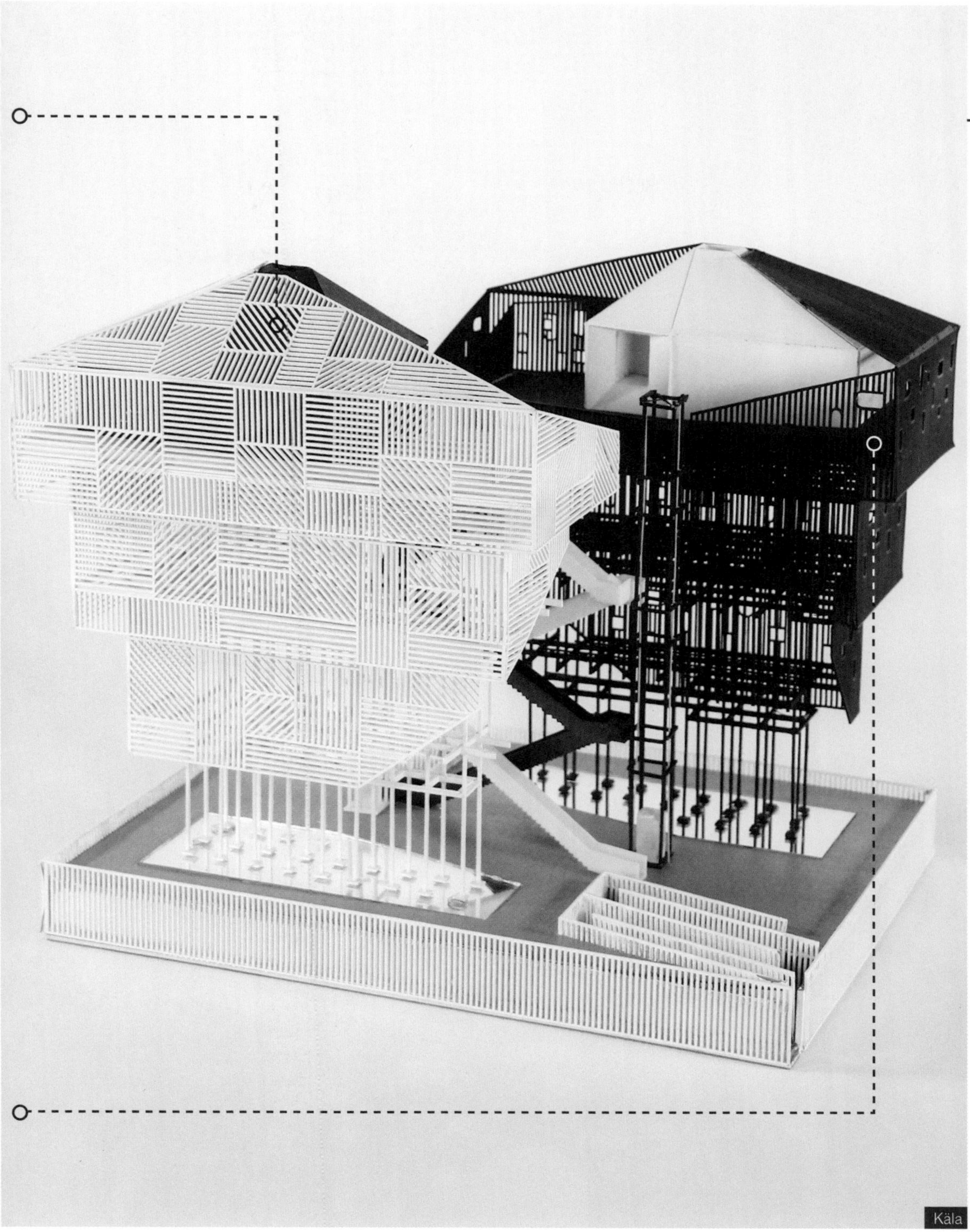

Käla

Inside the Mirror Chamber

The architectural insertion called Dukkha is situated along the street frontage of Geylang Road, the main street of the red light district. Dukkha consists of a gilded circular ramp that leads up to the Kaleidoscopic Chamber on the third floor.

The interior of the Chamber is clad with mirror with randomly situated apertures that take the form of the existing shophouse windows. Walking inside the Kaleidoscopic Chamber, one sees daily life being reflected in infinity.

BRIAN DAVIES

D.E.E.P. FREEZE

Undergraduate Interior Design Research
Design Enabling Science
Indian Himalaya, Florida Keyes, USA

The most beautiful, the most powerful, and the most desperate places are all equally vulnerable to natural disasters [1]. As humankind's aspirations for exploration increase, so do the risks and strains on human support needs. Engineering has been the dominant discipline in designing for extreme environments. Interior design, and its purpose to simply enhance life in environments—extreme or otherwise [2]—can play a key role in inhabiting nontraditional territories.

The Design for Extreme Environments Project [DEEP] at the University of Cincinnati strives to enable research and education platforms through the development of human support systems that mediate adverse conditions of extreme environments, such as atmospheric content and pressure, gravitational force, spatial constraints, and confined personal dynamics. DEEP endeavors to lend the perspective of humanistic design in support of the physiological and psychological well-being of future explorers, field reseachers, and displaced persons to supplement the accomplishments of engineering and science.

DEEP was initiated in Spring 2008 to extend the capabilities of students beyond the assimilation of existing knowledge, enabling them to envision innovative future solutions. In situ problem solving and cross-disciplinary interactions are structured to equip students to consider future built environments through a global lens, while anticipating the changing conditions of the natural environment. With the global population tripling since 1950, extreme environments have experienced increasing stresses as people live closer to these realms. Many of these extreme environments are experiencing the greatest negative impact associated with human-induced climate change.Therefore, there is increasing need to be able to live and research in extreme environments to understand the nature and dynamics of environmental change, with much at the current data collection for climate change predominately gathered in extreme environments, such as Aquarius Reef Habitat, Antarctic Research Station, and glacial environments [3].

The condition of these environments strain research efforts as outdated human support practices are employed in supporting advanced scientific discovery. The researchers' environmental exposure limits the amount and quality of data gathered. DEEP unites design, geology, and engineering experts in supporting human performance under inhospitable conditions in the service of science to innovate collectively.

Notes:

[1] Slaughter, S. and B. Davies. (2014). "Out of Failure: Disaster Relief and Digital Fabrication," *102nd ACSA Annual Meeting Proceedings, Globalizing Architecture/ Flows and Disruptions*, 87-93.

[2] "Underwater Studio, Extreme Environments Design Class." *Archinect*. 8 Sept. 2008. Web. 14 May 2015. <http://archinect.com/features/article/77867>.

[3] Benn, D. I. and L. A. Owen. (1998). "The Role of the India Summer Monsoon and the Mid-latitude Westerlies in Himalayan Glaciation: Review and Speculative Discussion." *Journal of the Geological Society* 155: 353-63.

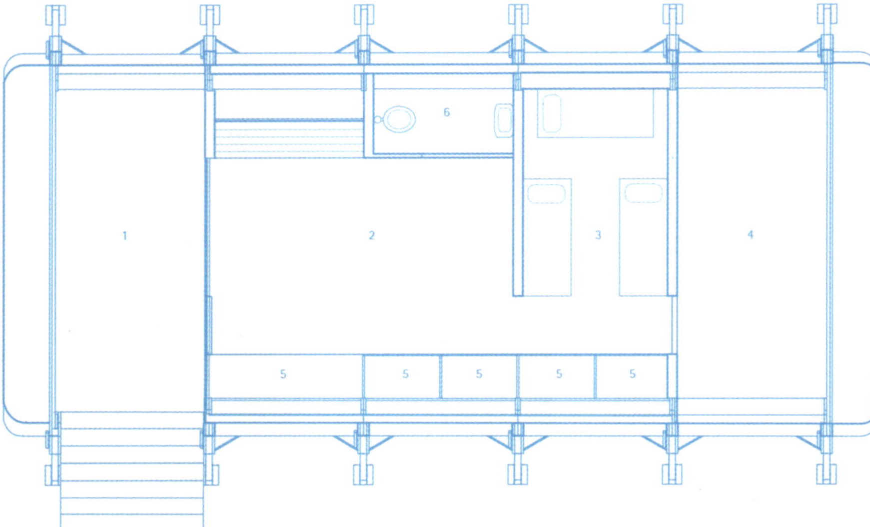

exterior renderings and floor plan

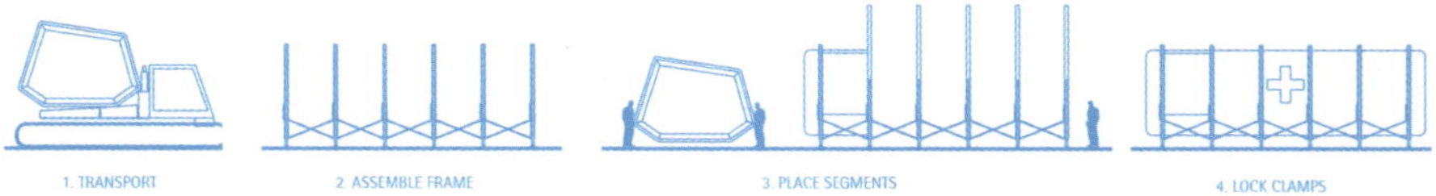

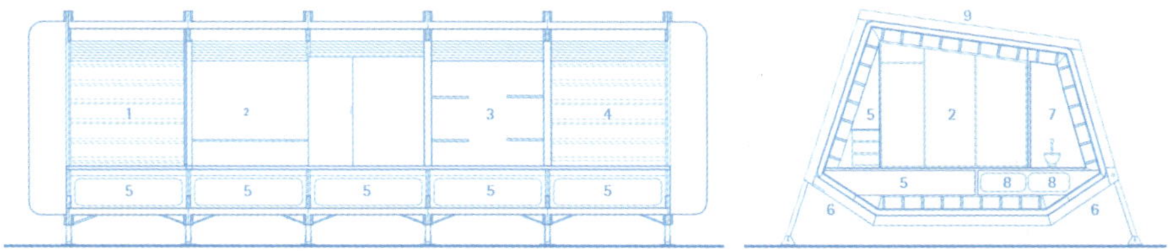

REUBEN ALT / interior rendering and sections

KURT MILLER
JOHN ELIOT HANCOCK (chair)
MICHAEL MCINTURF (member)

A RURAL IDENTITY

Master of Architecture Thesis
Cincinnati, Ohio, USA

Contemporary rural architecture, particularly of rural midwestern Ohio, produces uninspiring, abject, and cheap architectural solutions that become universally accepted, yet ignore the depth and complexity of meanings and particularities of place inherent in their geographic, cultural, and historic relationships. Through a hermeneutic and phenomenological enrichment of Critical Regionalist theory and practice, this thesis develops an architectural design process for Saint Henry, Ohio and the surrounding midwestern Ohio region that reveals the subtle architectural and cultural regional identities.

Critical Regionalism, as explored by Kenneth Frampton, works within the mediation of technological universality and traditional regionality to produce architecture that poetically engages specifics of its time and place. These well-known ideas are deepened through a phenomenological understanding of experience as ongoing interpretation of already existing traditions, meanings, and relationships.

Specifically understood through five relationships of geography and place; history and time; culture and identity; material and "presencing" (or foregrounding); and tectonics and engagement, this thesis will develop a Town Hall and Square for St. Henry, Ohio through a process of reading regional particularities. As a result, the town hall typology will enhance a sense of place through architectural intervention, specifically, a presencing of meanings and relationships already latent in the cultural and built environment.

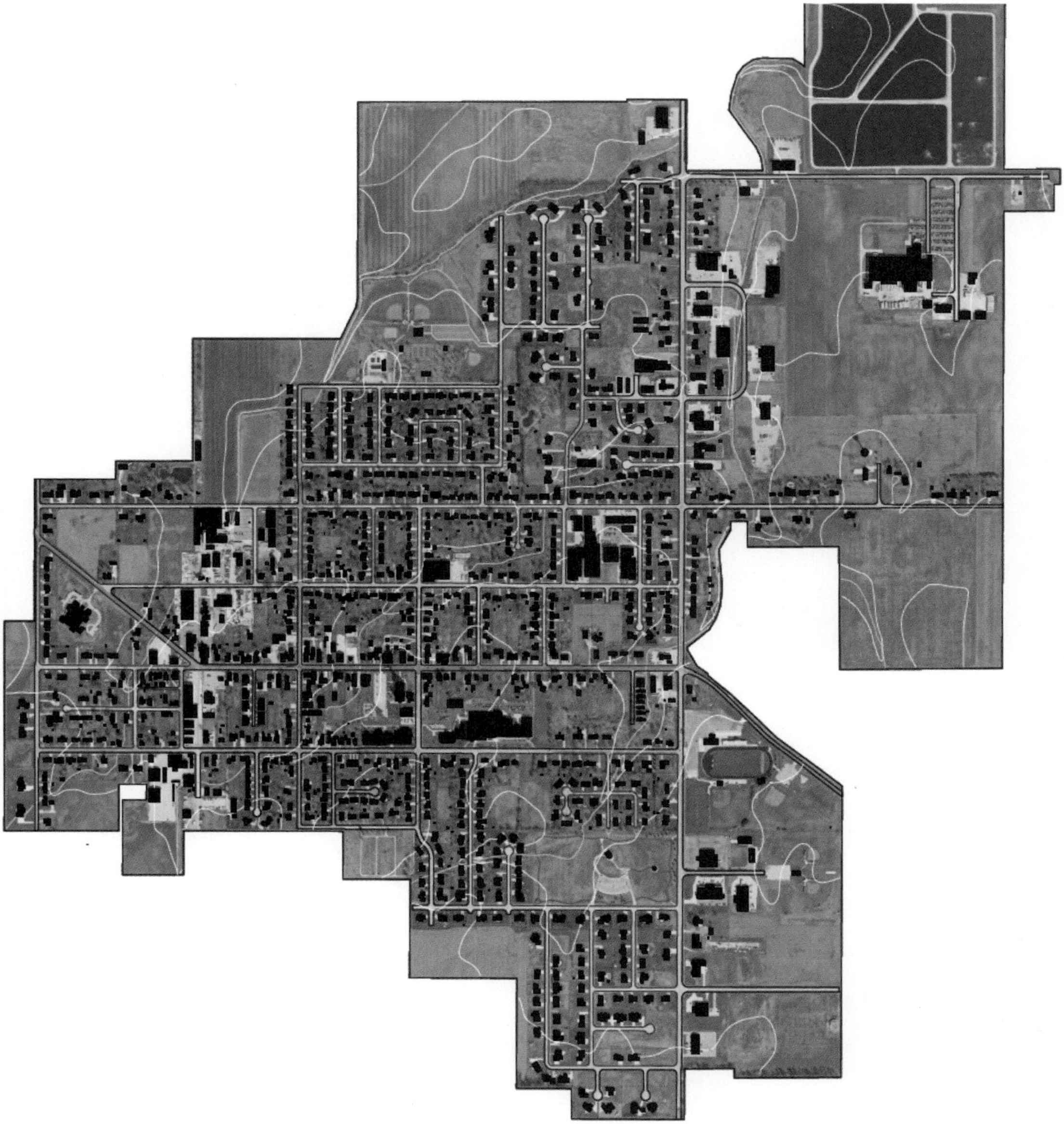

urban fabric and views

geography / place
The geographic conditions of the region work to shape the character of the region's sense of place. Natural features play a large role in shaping human development, which in turn influence the particularities of place.

history / time
The relationship between history and time can be understood through the analysis of the process of development of the built environment of the region. Key historic influences help reveal an understanding of a current ongoing, lived tradition.

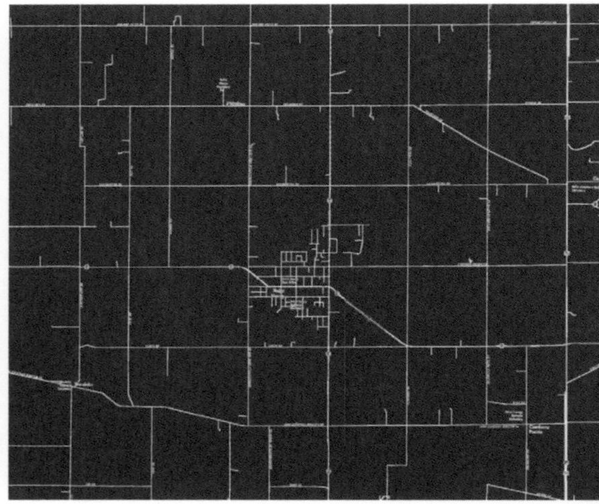

culture / identity
The relationship between culture and identity can be understood through the analysis of the process of tradition and how individuals can relate to the past as tradition through the presencing of the everyday activities within individual communities as well as the Midwestern Ohio Region overall.

material / presencing
tectonic / engagement
The final two relationships are developed through the design process of the St. Henry Town Hall and Town Square. This relationship will inform how architecture ultimately presences and engages the community through materiality, tectonic expression, and construction.

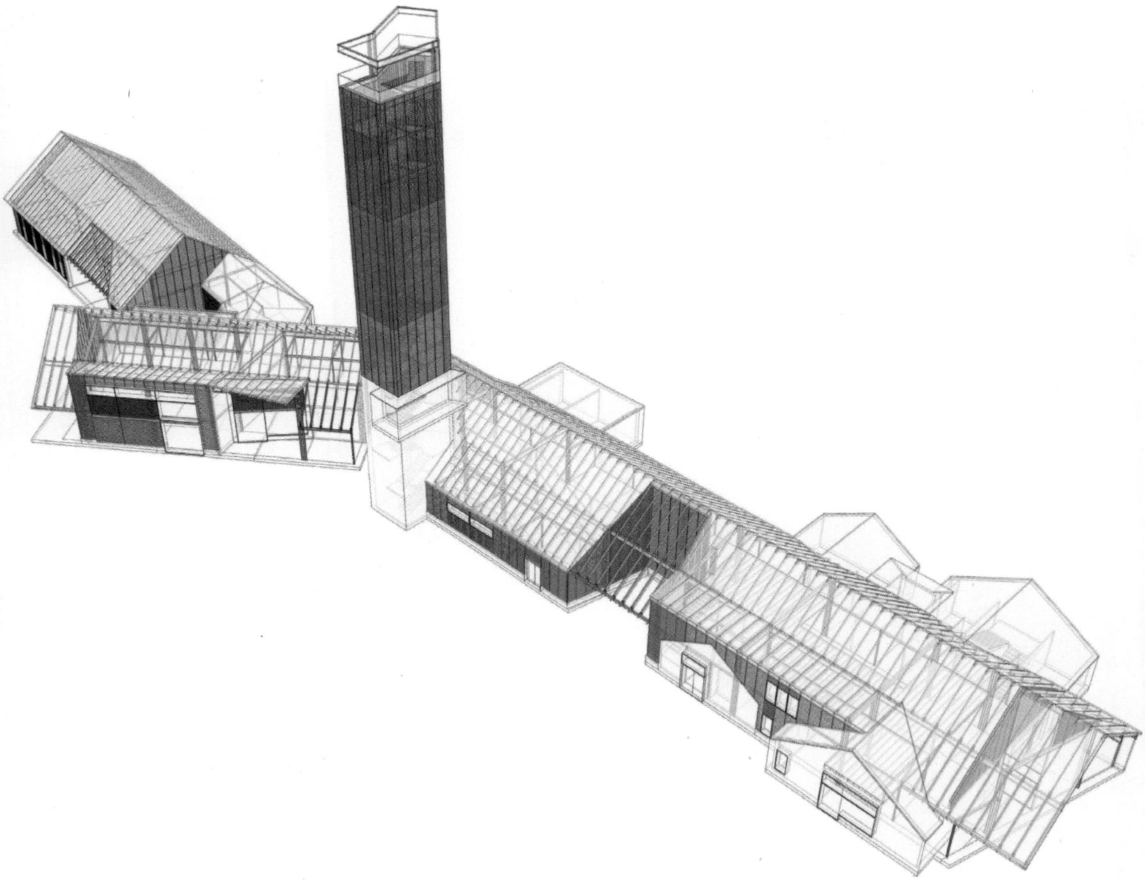

axonometric construction

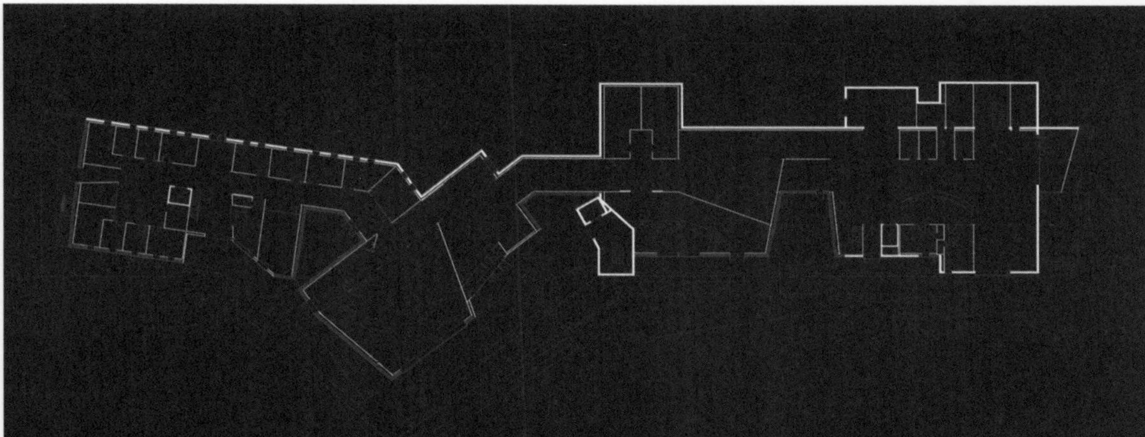

floor plan

urban fabric

approach

aerial

approach

entrance

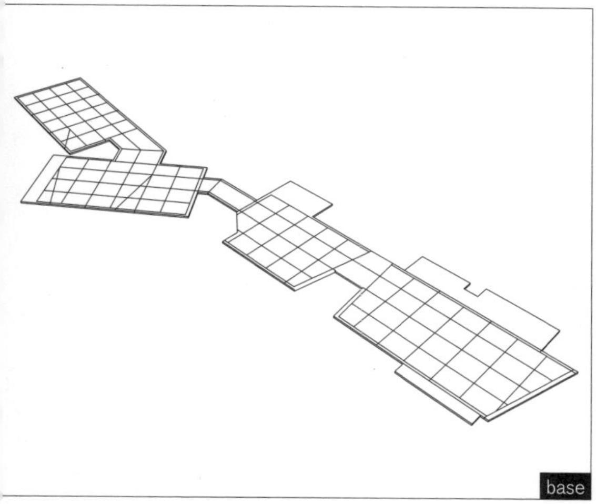
base

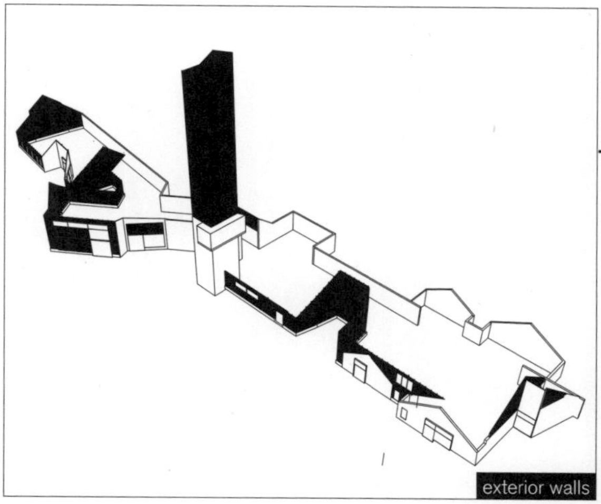
exterior walls

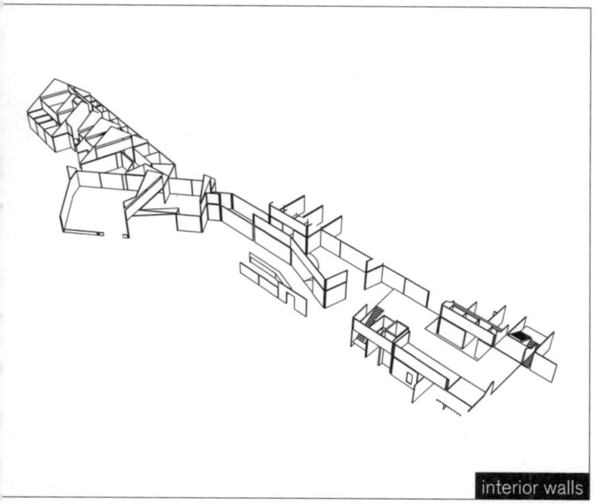
interior walls

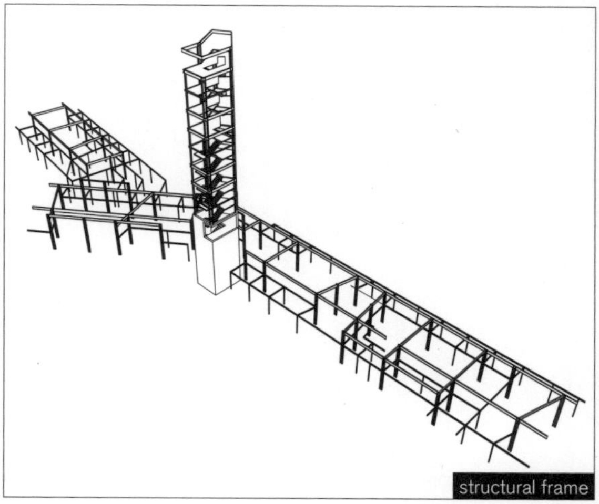
structural frame

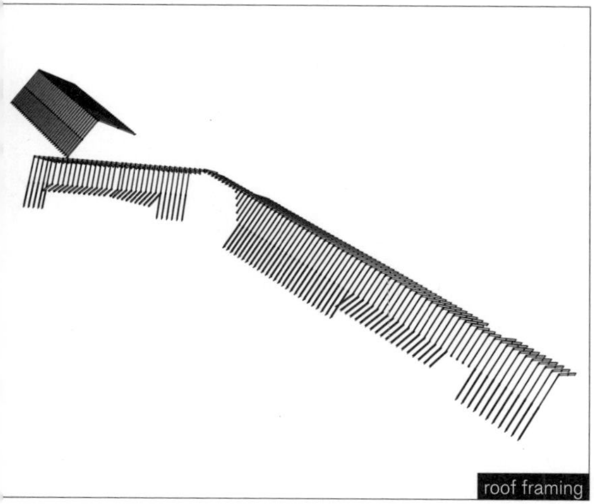
roof framing

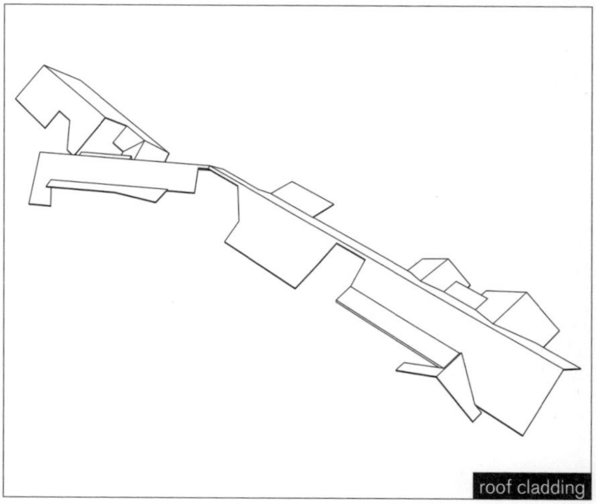
roof cladding

KIM BURKE
EDSON CABALFIN, PH.D. (text author)
BRIAN DAVIES
HANK HILDEBRANDT (coordinator)

SPECULATIVE INTERIORITY

Undergraduate Fifth Year Interior Design
Research Driven Capstone Project
Cincinnati, Ohio, USA

According to a 2001 study by the U.S. Environmental Protection Agency and University of California at Berkeley, the average American spends 93% of their time indoors. This revealing statistic forms a fundamental impetus to reconsider the role of interior design in the shaping of human experiences. While the impact of the designed interior environment is unquestionably important, the challenge as to how we can begin to reconsider future possibilities for interior design becomes a significant challenge for the design profession.

The two-semester senior capstone project addresses this challenge by speculating on the promises of interiority, its inextricably intertwined relationship with architecture, and the advancement of a discourse of experience. Interiority here is defined as a reconceptualization of interior space through a diverse set of modalities and perspectives. Interiority is not diametrically opposed to the exteriority, but rather elucidates the inevitable collusion of the human experience in a totality of the environment. Interiority is not only a condition of boundary, (e.g. limited by the existence of walls, ceilings and floors), but is also a heightened awareness of the human capacity to intervene in the environment. Thus, interiority as a concept expands on the notion of the practice of interior design as simply a decorative or ornamental collage, but rather advocates for a concept of dynamic creativity in the shaping of interior phenomenon.

The questions posed by the studio run a gamut of issues: fast fashion and the impact on the retail experience, disaster recovery and evacuation centers, revitalizing a historic hotel, experiential storytelling in restaurants, cancer recovery for women, utilizing the Cincinnati subway, redefining subcultures, healthy eating and food retail, among others. Still others investigate the connection between history and interiors, women's health and mobile centers, art and the city, and electronic dance music and the immersive experience.

MARY WAGNER/ String Theory, a String music center

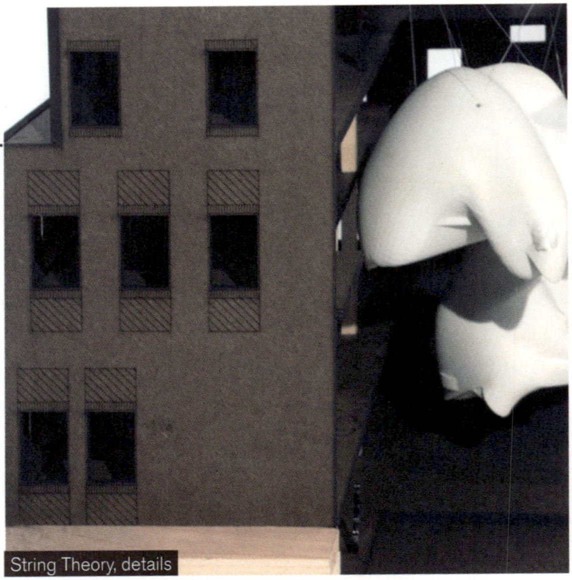

String Theory, details

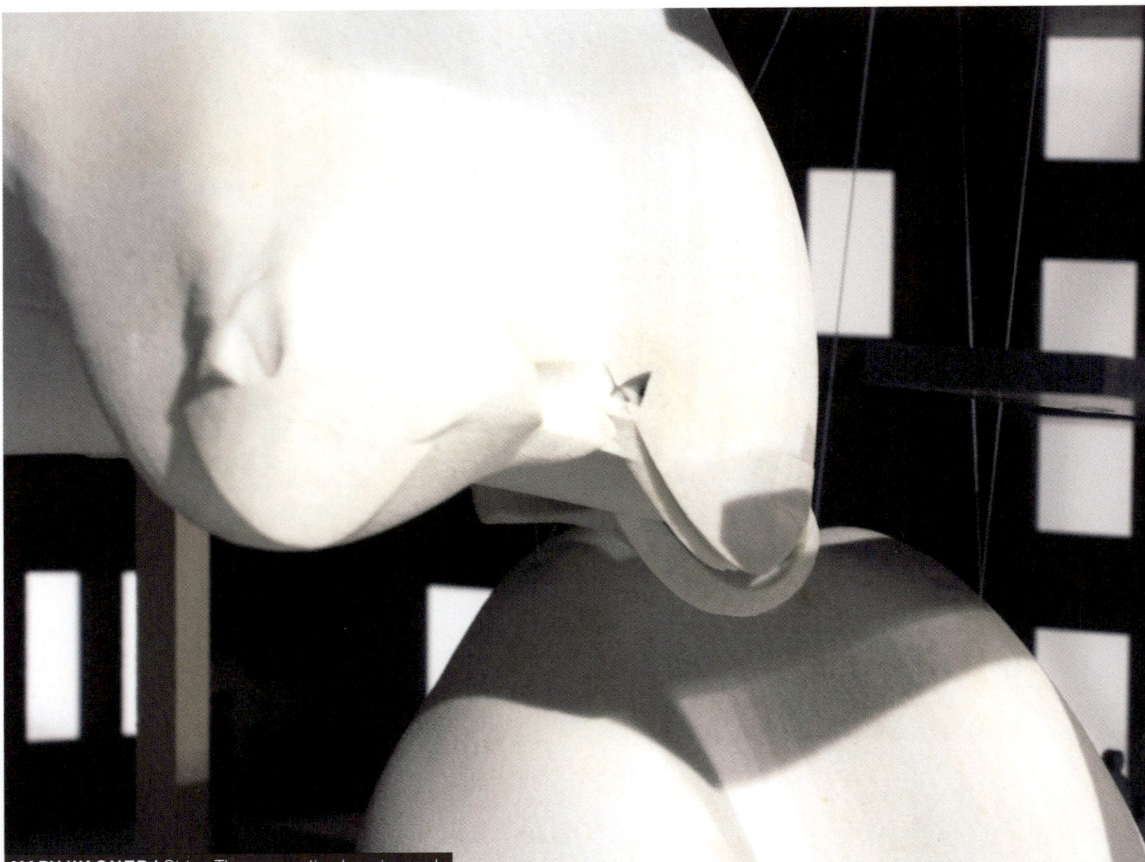

MARY WAGNER/ String Theory, practice hanging pods

OLIVIA HENNESSY/ Lightbourne Spa, model

OLIVIA HENNESSY/ Lightbourne Spa, model

Build space

Create space

Discover space

Community space

exterior rendering

interior hallway

KATIE MERRILEES/ An After School Center in Over-the-Rhine, section

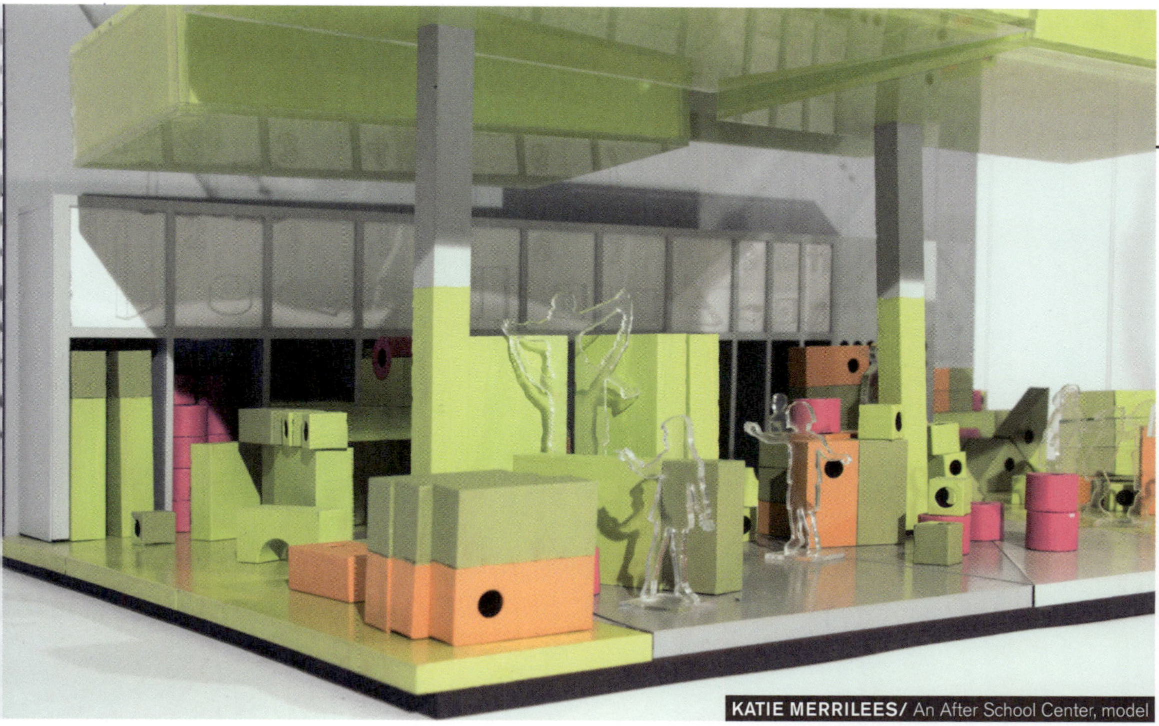

KATIE MERRILEES/ An After School Center, model

KATIE MERRILEES/ An After School Center, detail

KORY BEIGHLE
AARATI KANEKAR, PH.D. (chair)

ARCHITECTURAL REMIX

Cincinnati, Ohio, USA

We exist in the context of a digital revolution and the accelerating growth of vast communication networks, a landscape comprised of an incalculable number of new and emerging disciplines. As early as the late 1970s, the postmodern condition of our contemporary age had been described and activated by Jean-François Lyotard, who defined the postmodern condition of knowledge within the context of these expanding networks as one of transformation and unsettlement.

The technological transformations of the late twentieth century radically altered the dynamics of knowledge, specifically its two primary functions—evolution through knowledge production and dissemination. As Lyotard writes in his work *The Postmodern Condition: A Report on Knowledge*, "the nature of knowledge cannot survive unchanged within this context of general transformation." The point Lyotard makes is quite similar to the thesis Maryanne Wolf presents in her book, *Proust and the Squid: The Story and Science of the Reading Brain*. Wolf's argument contends that human existence and interaction with the digital age is fundamentally altering the way our minds are organized and consequently, how our being and its relationship to knowledge are altered.

If one accepts the contention that the digital age is in fact affecting a great change within the fabric of humanity and even altering the core of human structures of knowledge within a new paradigm, it stands to reason that disciplinarity, which has customarily been the factory, storehouse and distribution platform for this knowledge, should also be on notice. Interestingly, many traditional disciplines, be they rooted in the arts, the sciences or the humanities, have and continue to question both their own validity as singular mediums of expression as well as their relationships to the vast array of other language-mediums emerging within the postmodern. One of the principal ways these questions have been explored in this context of collisions is through a wide-spread emphasis on interdisciplinary, cross-disciplinary and transdisplinary studies. Such studies constitute a remixing of the architectural language through processes of appropriation,

reorganization, representation, and ultimately translations between various disciplinary language-mediums.

So how has the momentum of this transformation reframed more traditional understandings of architectural disciplinarity? How is the way we define architectural knowledge changing? How can we define architectural knowledge? What is the margin or limit of architectural? How is architectural knowledge created and disseminated (produced and consumed)?

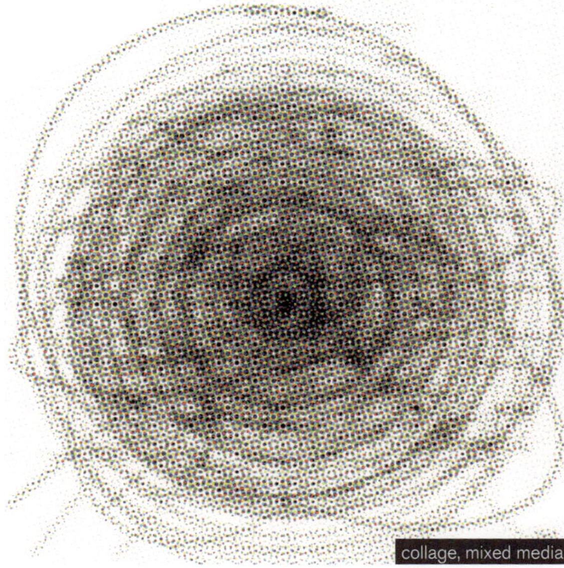

collage, mixed media

It is the contention of this exploration that knowledge production and consumption in the context of our digital epoch has changed to an inherently more connected landscape of collisions, which simultaneously flatten deep space and inject depth into flattened (spatialized) planes, forcing knowledge into a more ambiguous, liminal category. As a means of engaging works in this landscape, architectural disciplinarity has developed a sense of itself in this new context by beginning to enact an alchemic process of collaging the architectural language within this kaleidoscopic framework. Within these explorations, the technique of collage, understood broadly, extends beyond the limit of procedure to an alchemic paradigm similar to verbal translation between disparate languages in which indirect, yet equivalent exchange occurs despite superficial differences. This new paradigm represents a reframing of our field and beyond, to the core of being (designer, architect, human)...

After decades of participating in this process of questioning, the field of architecture continues to be steeped in uncertainty and self-doubt; immersed in the postmodern condition of the late twentieth century; the limit of architecture—its disciplinary boundary—has experienced numerous expansions, contractions and / or intersections through these alchemic processes. The work of architectural thinker-makers such as Charles and Ray Eames, Peter Eisenman, and John Hejduk laid the ground work for contemporary praxis through their contribution of certain and varied insights into this development, albeit from a wide range of perspectives. Taken individually their works introduce new ways of seeing the problem of architecture, prototyping certain enigmatic tools that have been and continue to be exploited within the language medium; taken together as a coherent movement, their work hints at a larger, kaleidoscopic trend the world over.

This study carries the narrative of this historical development and the production of these enigmatic tools through the frame of the contemporary design firm of Diller Scofidio + Renfro, whose work collapses, re-interprets and re-presents these enigmatic tools for our contemporary milieu.

This study proposes to begin processes of remixing the architectural discipline through four forms of examining, articulating, reorienting and operationalizing the enigmatic tools discussed for the architectural discipline, its borderlands and beyond.

First, in order to examine the spatial-temporal development of the discipline over the course of the recent past, subtle lines of flight will be highlighted within a web of discourse. Secondly, a series of iterations will attempt to articulate this web in order to uncover the subtle and nuanced themes of visuality and the operationalizing tools that support them. DS+R will serve as the vehicle for examining these themes and tools. Third, these issues will be reoriented through a process of unpacking potential theoretical positions in the context of more broad ranging meta-narratives of being in our contemporary age, albeit in a necessarily generalizing way. Finally, through actualizing these concepts into an applied research methodology, this study proposes to operationalize and extend the articulation of research from a traditional, textual documentation to a spatial-visual-textual, corporeal embodiment of a collapsed act of knowledge production-consumption. The goal of this fourfold process is to attempt to engage more effectively in this landscape of collisions.

The study closely examines the margin or limit of disciplinarity in this new context of interconnection and collision, but that does not mean the work is marginal. It is important to note that the proposal made here is not in search of an overcoming of the status quo or "convention" as such, but rather an undergoing of these contexts. On one level, the pursuit of such an overcoming is not possible, because it relies upon the definition of an alternative model to be defined in advance and enacted. There is no institutional understanding of what constitutes a unified center of architectural culture, and so the definition of any alternative becomes undefinable, even outside of language. Instead of overcoming so-called conventions through alternative practice, a process of undergoing, as advocated here, engages in a feedback loop of evolution—a constant remixing—allowing new models to emerge in a perpetual process of re-creation and re-framing.

It is not enough to merely understand these trends. Actualizing movements must be rendered, and a sense of agency must be cultivated. One must go to the works themselves: experiencing the works as they are (or have been) in their totality (built, drawn, written, etc.); exploring their contexts; and examining their patterns of convergence and divergence from existing codes. Somewhere between these connective engagements, a layered reading of architectural works begins to emerge. By activating as many of the layers presented as possible, whether they be "spatial," "visual," "written" or otherwise, this consideration of the late avant-garde's collision with the limit of architecture might begin to encounter a limit of its own through acts of translation; as the inevitable gaps of the in-between are carried forward, decentralization of the discipline will accelerate, flowering into new models for our contemporary age. These processes of translation expose this liminal space, allowing the interpretive acts to inform the process of inquiry for the architectural discipline, its borderlands and beyond, engaging more effectively and affectively in this broader landscape of collisions.

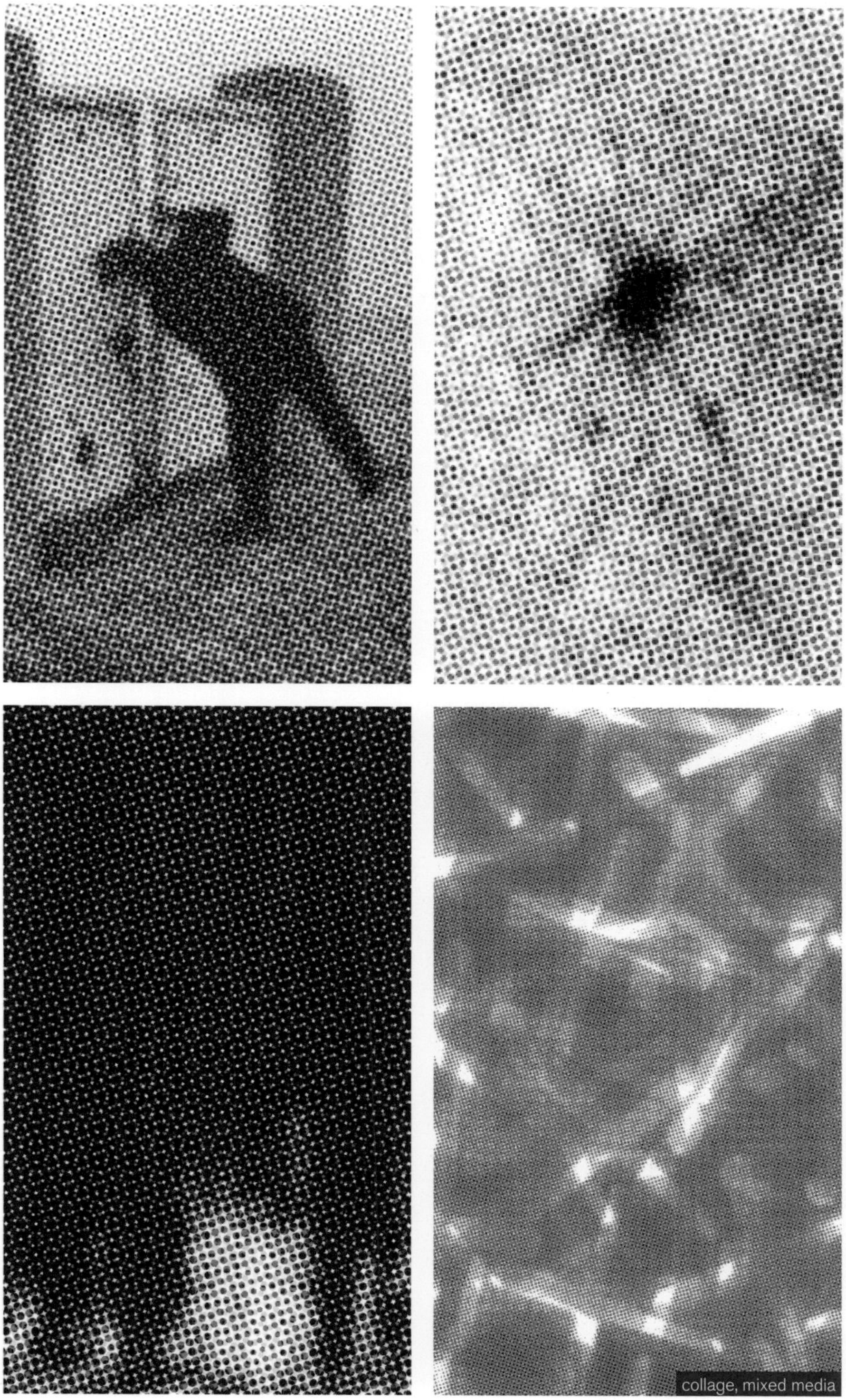

collage, mixed media

CALEB KUNG
AARATI KANEKAR, PH.D. (chair)
MICHAEL MCINTURF (member)

A FLEETING REGISTER

Master of Architecture Thesis
Hong Kong Special Administrative Region of the People's Republic of China

The world is accelerating; the rapid change that transforms entire cities and landscapes, and inevitably their inhabitants and culture, is precipitating a phenomenon of disappearance that renders the city volatile and elusive. Hong Kong is one such place where many factors have collided to create a semi-autonomous political entity that struggles with its social, even spatial, identity. The effects of colonialism, the development of the Eastern Hemisphere's busiest trade port and economical hub, and more recently the return of sovereignty to the People's Republic of China contribute to a disappearance of culture that has within a generation's time metamorphosed into a culture of disappearance.

This thesis attempts to analyze the causes and processes of disappearance in Hong Kong, borrowing from the process of film construction, primarily Wong Kar-Wai's 2046, in an attempt to develop an approach towards the design of space that at once participates in and documents the progress of the phenomenon of disappearance.

Embedded within film are several concepts relevant to the discussion on disappearance: **speed, composition and focus, real time, representative time and representative space**.

A film addresses speed on multiple levels: the speed of images, the subject within the images, the camera that is representative of the viewer. Composition and focus pertain to the images themselves, their choice of subjects, contexts, and the relationship between them. Real time concerns the film's relation to the viewer's own time beyond the screen. Finally, representative time and space, usually brought out by plot in cinematography, is the internal content of the film that at the same time obliges the film to exist in its own reality.

cast adrift

CALEB KUNG / caught in drift

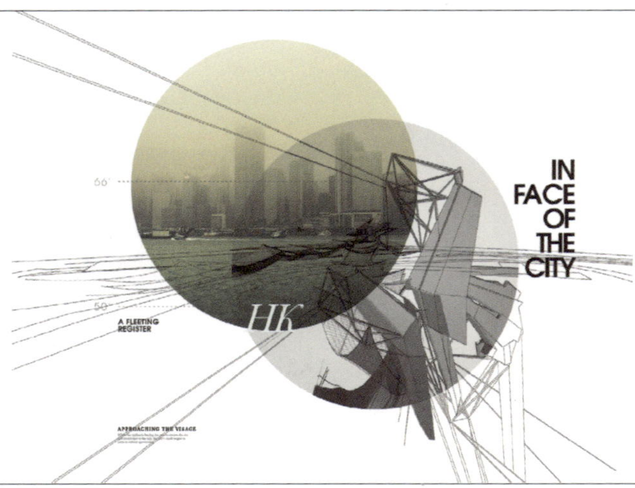

approaching the visage

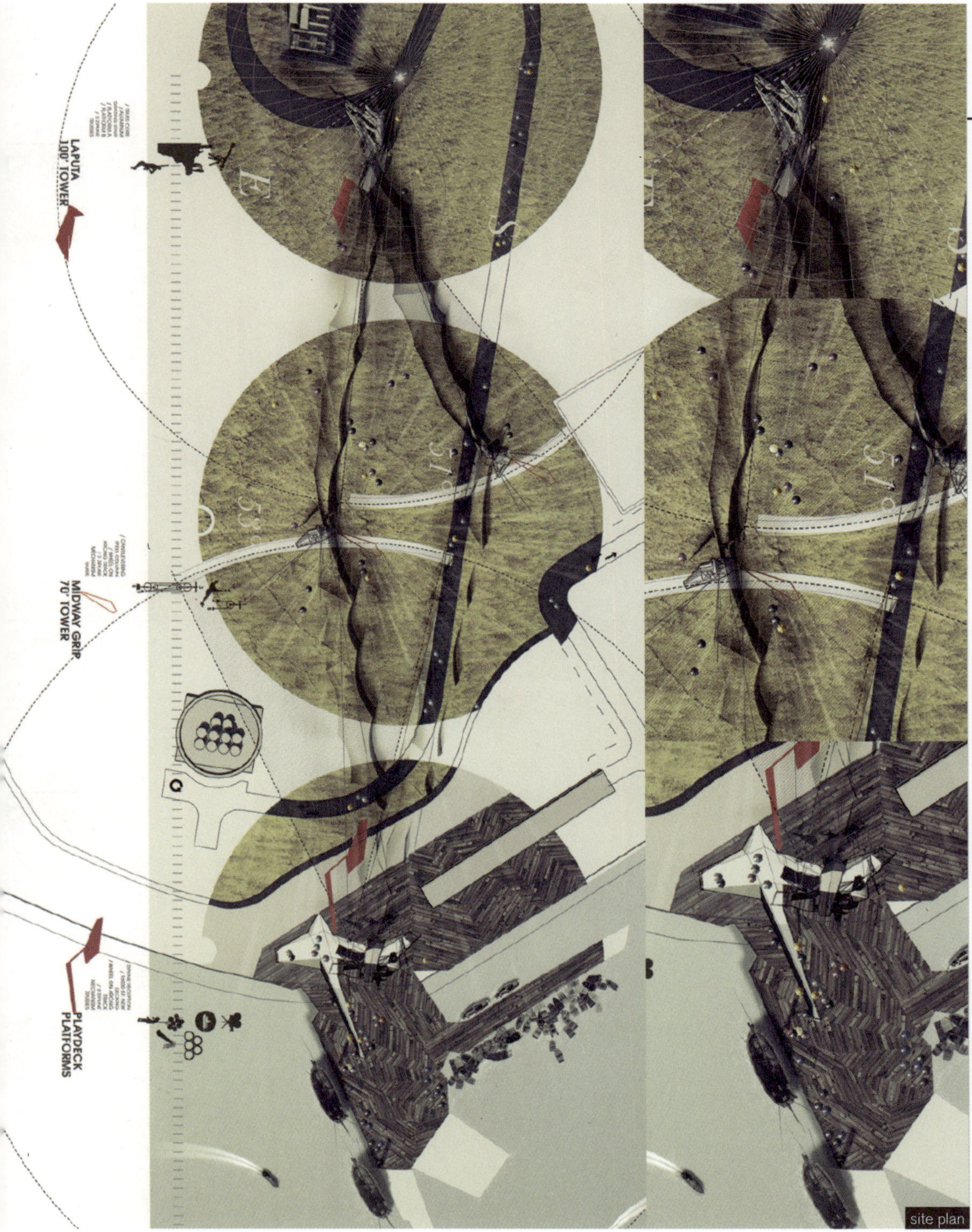

site plan

KRISTIN RIDGE
PAINT BY NUMBERS

My heart was set on Philadelphia. I wanted to be on the East Coast, but I didn't want to be as mainstream as New York. I wanted to be off the traditional cosmopolitan grid. My dreams were shot when Kieran Timberlake did not hire any students for the semester. Determined, I did a side search. Google's "related to Kieran Timberlake" searches produced DIGSAU. Looking at their website, I was sold and basically harassed them until they hired me. I was very persistent to say the least. It was well worth the persistence because it was my favorite internship.

DIGSAU is composed of former associates from KTA, so in a way I had the Kieran Timberlake education. They had all worked there, they all had stories about working there. They were all stylistically similar to them, but they just wanted to do their own thing. DIGSAU broke off and started their own firm a block away.

The office is young, fun, and hip, even the "Old Guys". Their offices are in an old loft-style building. They gave me freedom to work on whatever projects I wanted. Going to my supervisor and saying "I need construction administration hours!" the next week he'd put me on a job site. I was largely in charge of operating the laser cutter, which I had never done before. I learned how to calibrate and operate the machine on my own. I was in my own world in the model shop, operating laser cuts and having total freedom.

My first day at DIGSAU they asked "We just got asked to do this project. You wanna jump in and learn more about it?" I was involved from the beginning stages of the Miquon School in Conshohocken, Pennsylvania—a Quaker philosophy school where kids attend classes in cabins in the woods. It's an experiential learning environment for pre-K through sixth grade where during play time they wander into the wilderness. As an old campus unchanged since the '50s they received a grant for a new library and fourth grade building. The campus was arranged in such a particular way that our new design had to be sensitive to the context. From the beginning stages of the project into Schematic Design, I was there.

There were a lot of iterations of hand models. I had to build a large site model, go back and forth between sketching and the computer, iteration after iteration after iteration. Just throwing something on the board, sketching on it, coming back. In one respect it was really refreshing to observe and reflect on a different design approach, and in

a way they were holding my hand through the whole process, exactly what I needed. In school you juggle so much that you can't devote your attention to learning a new skill well. You get so lost in your own work that your project doesn't even make sense anymore. When you can step away and really focus on something on an internship, it's like starting with paint by numbers and slowly learning the concepts of composition and finer strokes and line weights until you can venture further into improvisation.

I don't think I ever worked on a weekend when I was in Philadelphia. My roommate at the time was a real estate developer and he was working on his own software that would leverage the real estate market. He had graduated from Penn and many of my co-workers went there as well, so I was kind of involved in their culture. I visited the campus multiple times during the semester going with my roommate or my co-workers, visiting events. I became interested in technology through the influence of my UPenn friends and my roommate building software.

They took me to an event called PennApps where aspiring developers gather and compete in creating different apps. I spent my off time with local Philadelphians and getting involved in their lives. I lived directly above a coffee shop so I was constantly downstairs working on building my own website. The weekends were dedicated to regrouping and discovering new things about the city. I ran the half marathon, so I spent a good portion of every Sunday running along the breathtakingly beautiful Schuylkill River. Some might say that Philadelphia isn't as "vibing" as New York would have been but that's why I loved it. It was a slower pace, I could be in control of where I was going and how I was getting there and how much money I was going to spend.

I learned Rhino. At my previous internship I didn't work on anything new or different but when I got to DIGSAU, I was thrown into the deep-end. I had to learn Rhino I had to learn how to operate the laser cutter and all of these things that I used to have to ask for help on. That's the time I needed to really focus on learning.

LAURA HELMINSKI
JOHN HANCOCK (chair)
MICHAEL MCINTURF (member)

[HOSPITAL]ITY

Master of Architecture Thesis
"Hospitable Hospitals: A Place of Healing"
Sylvania, OH, USA

In all of its complexity, hospital architecture is merely a shell constructed around the scientific knowledge of human bodies and the technological instruments required to care for them. The traditional approach to hospital design has become so utilitarian that it has resulted in a loss of intimacy between humans and their environment and community, evoking moods of inhospitable estrangement and isolation. Governed by global economics and modern technology, the current mega-hospital model neglects the invisible foundation of human relationships and intuitive background experiences within the everyday lived world, explained by Heidegger as "the loss of nearness."

This thesis offers a more poetic language of hospital architecture, in order to turn our attention away from the utility of medical equipment and instead foreground the lived world around us with sensual experiences and sharpened understanding of the spiritual intimacy and layers of meaning inherent in life and death. The design of a small suburban hospital for seniors in Sylvania, Ohio mediates between the objective world that science measures and the inexhaustible lived world of experience and traditions. This project explores the positive effects that comforting, intimate, and sensually engaging environments can have on the healing process of patients, seeking a welcoming embrace for the human spirit.

The syncretic design deploys allegorical tectonics, poetic materiality, meditative lighting, invigorating landscapes, and intuitive wayfinding, creating meaningful environments that will restore the human need for placefulness, sensuality, and intimacy. A truly healthful and hospitable hospital must embed the factual objectivity of medical science within the patients' and visitors' truthful and subjective experiences of being.

approach

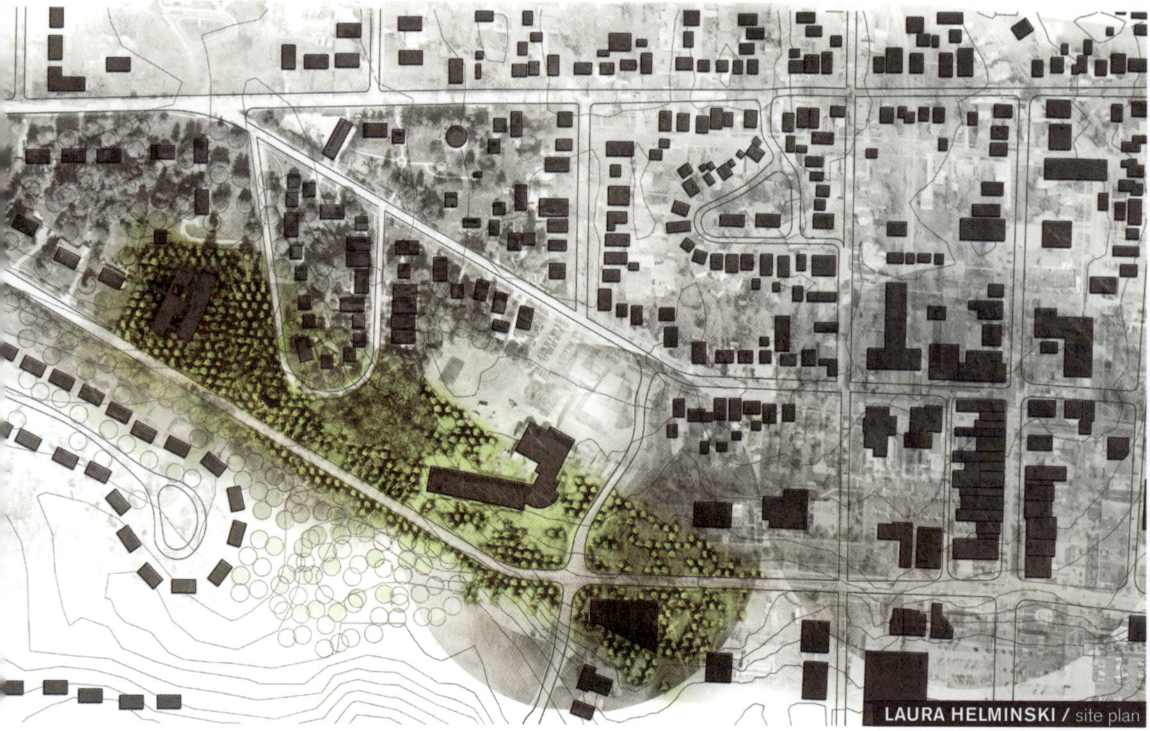
LAURA HELMINSKI / site plan

LAURA HELMINSKI / entrance

elevations

street view

winter

NADER TEHRANI

Between the Figure and Configurations

SAID Interview
Conducted by Christoph Klemmt
Edited by Mara Marcu

Nader Tehrani is Dean of The Irwin S. Chanin School of Architecture at The Cooper Union and principal of NADAAA, a practice dedicated to the advancement of design innovation, interdisciplinary collaboration, and an intensive dialogue with the construction industry.

Christoph Klemmt: There is a long list of very creative and beautiful projects that you have completed and among them are many highly complex free-form geometries. However, it appears that your recent work has become significantly more straight and orthogonal. Is architecture's blob and parametric movement coming to an end?

Nader Tehrani: My interest, over the years, has not been in complex free-form geometries, per se, but rather the role of "figuration" in architecture. The presence of the 'figure' can be seen in the Tavolone, in Casa La Roca, or MOMA Fabrications: the first example entails orthogonal elements, the second features ruled surfaces on the garden wall, and the latter is composed of facets which are seen as flat from a certain perspective, but in fact is quite complex three dimensionally. My interest in the figure is three-fold: the ability of form to perform from a structural point of view (Casa La Roca and its serpentine organization), for it to release sematic affiliations (Tavolone and the 'table' as allegorical figure), or for it to establish a critical relationship with representation itself (MOMA Fabrications and its anamorphic projection). To this end, the figure plays on multiple levels of architectural culture, and is not invested in geometry as the sole basis for engagement.

This intellectual project has more recently extended itself into both Dortoire Familiale and the NH House, both of which have clear typological roots, while also transformed spatially, geometrically and morphologically in substantially complex ways. This is also true for the roof of the Daniels Building, whose figure is brought together by the confluence of structural, hydrological and daylighting considerations. Other projects like the MSD suspended studio, Entrelac in Amman, and the Catenary Compression installation in Boston involve complex arrays of figural engagements that fulfill geometric, structural and integrative commitments.

I am not a devotee of the blob, nor parametricism, but both have been absorbed sufficiently into architectural culture to the point that they have become conventionalized, maybe to the limits of banality. For this reason, we need to pose questions of architecture that have a wider and more complex conceptual reach.

As architects we become mediators between aesthetic considerations and our client's needs and budget, while in our education we are encouraged to develop our own identity and style that a building should reflect. How are you managing to achieve this so well in your projects?

I am not certain I agree with your characterization of the dichotomy between professional and academic commitments. I do not necessarily see client considerations of budget or aesthetics as a liability, nor the desire for an architect's identity/style as relevant.

Our process of design engages the particularities of client culture, the local construction industry, and economic forces as a central part of our research – I hope in a speculative way that advances the intellectual project of architecture. For this reason, you can see many different material explorations, spatial and typological configurations, as well as an array of iconographic commitments in the work. I do not think our work requires a stylistic consistency, or a singular authorship, as such; maybe what comes through is a 'sensibility' that is driven by some of our intellectual biases – the very things that sponsors our research agendas.

If, at the end, we are able to overcome the apparent dichotomies between the professional and academic world, then it might be because we do not set them in opposition to begin with: we see an imperative to construe budgets as the basis for invention, as much as we see the conceptual aspects of academic advancement conversant with the political context within which they become relevant.

What role does contemporary architectural theory play for the profession? Are our academic endeavors still relevant?

There are many platforms for ideas today, and maybe what characterizes theory in this day is the sheer proliferation of ideas, debates and discourses. The academic platform is particularly relevant today because of the means through which individual voices have gained a wider audience through the Internet. Students and young architects have gained unprecedented intellectual range due to their access to information and knowledge, and in turn, they have developed their agency as a result of the very same means. My particular interest is in the way in which material explorations–in the academy–have impacted the means and methods of construction, bottom up, in the construction industry; our ability to restructure innovation in the building industry is a result of this process. We have seen analogous advances in other academics' work, whose research is beginning to impact practice: Laura Kurgan and her work on data research and mapping, David Benjamin and his work at the intersection of biology and material sciences. To this end, we might consider what constitutes theory today, which theory, whose theory, and what its relationship is to intellectual practices beyond the terms of its own realm.

The dream of Modernism to change our society through architecture is mostly regarded as unsuccessful. Should we stop to try to solve the world's problems and instead concentrate on being an art form and a service industry?

I am not sure it is productive to argue for architecture as an art form, nor a service industry. Invariably, the discipline, and its practices bring both into conversation, among a range of others issues, which involve community engagement, the redefinition of the public realm, the infusion of invention (from the academic realm) back into practice. The question is not whether we should 'dream to change society through architecture', but the fact that it is inevitable: the conceptualization and construction of our environment is a central aspect for what forms our consciousness as beings, and in turn, it is also the very phenomenon that has led us into the age of the Anthropocene. If we begin to accept our accountability on the one hand, and gain our agency on the other, it can only thicken the plot of what it means to be an architect.

In a lecture of yours at the University of Cincinnati you talked about the development of ornament and structure in traditional Iranian architecture and how the ornament lost its non-aesthetic functionality over time. What do you think is the relationship between structure and ornament in architecture today?

In my lecture, I mapped out the transition between structure and ornament from the Seljuk to the Safavid and the Qajar periods. By the Qajar period we witness the emergence of tile work, which is completely dis-engaged from the structural core that we see in the prior periods. Though unrelated, by extension, what is maybe the most radical shift in recent history is the evolution of the 'rain screen' system of waterproofing, which has effectively disengaged the elemental functions of roofs, drainage systems, walls and sills from their traditional vocation of having to repel water in varied ways. In the rain screen system, all the technical function is suppressed to the realm of an underlay, such that the expression of the outer skin may play out its tectonic representation in accordance with alternative narratives, outside of any faithfulness to their discrete function.

Once we are able to 3-d print varied materialities in a thickened wall section–effectively to overcome the laminar wall section that currently characterizes the discrete differences between insulation, sheathing, vapor barrier, and external skin–we can yet imagine a completely different conceptual approach to the question of structure and ornament.

The question of structure and ornament remains somehow relevant if seen against the backdrop of a certain ethic in architecture: the reciprocity between the interior and exterior, the representational commitment to integration, and the discipline of part to whole thinking, all of which produce substantial challenges to the architect. But without this type of 'friction', I would say the relationship between structure and ornament becomes somewhat of a moot issue.

In our highly globalized society, what role does an architect's cultural background play?

Neither our local or global identity can guarantee the relevance of our instrumentality. The architect's ability to channel irreducible forms of intelligence we bring to the equation is what is at stake. We tend to see things from a different vantage-point, to the extent that forms of representation, or generative thinking, can visualize different types of questions that cannot be posed through words alone. That is the cultural backdrop we bring to society–something that others cannot.

You are not only very successful as a practitioner but also in academia as the Dean of Cooper Union's School of Architecture. Do you think our education does justice to the needs of the profession and to the continuous development of the building industry?

Insofar as education can provide for a space of learning that is speculative, critical and open to transformation, we can continue to imagine the function of a school to achieve more than preparing students for skills that are on the verge of obsolescence. Our relevance can be measured, in part, on how our agency becomes central to the evolution of the policies that guide our environment. For this reason, I think of the educational environment as a space of play, to some degree, to tease out ways of thinking, such that we may pose questions of the world that others may not be able to visualize. The building industry plays only one small part of that equation.

You mentioned at a lecture at the University of Cincinnati how you struggled at the beginning of your career to start your architectural office. What are your recommendations for today's graduates that find themselves in the same situation?

Today's graduates have a very different environment from which to launch their careers. Technologies of varied kinds gives them an entirely different reach as basis for a launch. My recommendation for graduates today might be to define their 'project' with clarity, and then have the courage to take a risk for it.

When we launched our careers, we did not have the financial stability of a back-up system. Nor did we have any special cultural connection to the United States. We had the wealth of education, and just enough confidence to allow failure as basis for the launch.

I was curious if you would like to recommend to our readers an architect, an author, a musician or similar who you value highly but who you think is not recognized as much as he or she should be?

Protagonists of various kinds come and go in and out of focus, and some come back again for reconsideration. My current preoccupation is with Italian architect, Luigi Caccia Dominioni (well known in Milano, but lesser known internationally), with the writings of Robin Evans which remain as relevant today as when we were students, and the emerging work of composer Suzanne Farrin.

Photography Credits / **JOSHUA ANDERSON**

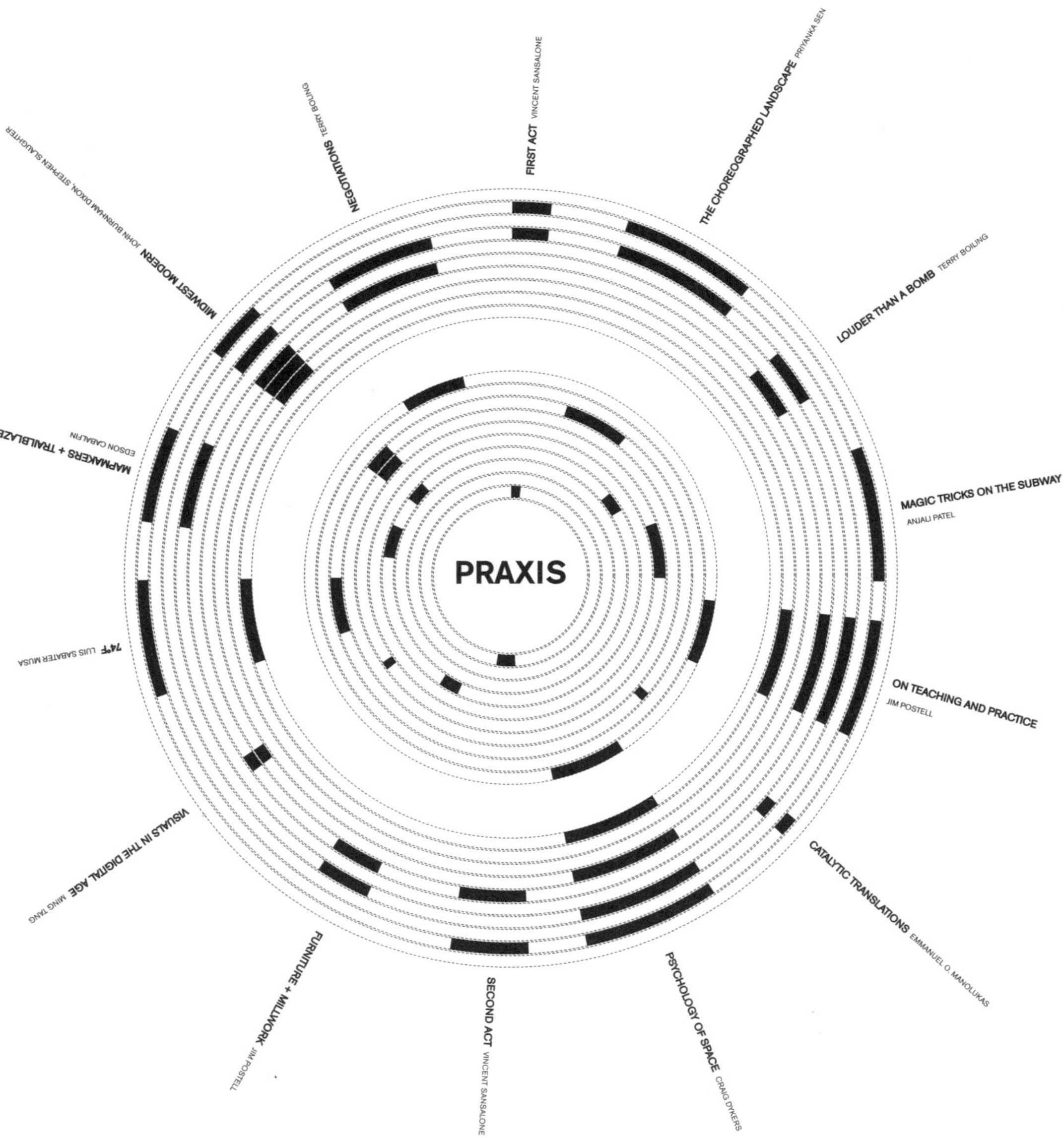

LEGEND:

1. OUTER SECTOR = ID
2. INNER SECTOR = LEVEL
3. WIDTH = SCALE

1. *From Outer Ring to Inner Ring:*
   Design Thinking
   History/Theory
   Material Investigation
   Branding
   Design Build
   Digital Craft
   Computational Design
   Fabrication
   Sustainability
   Public Interest

2. *From Outer Ring to Inner Ring:*
   Professional
   PhD
   Graduate 3rd Year
   Graduate 2nd Year
   Graduate 1st Year
   Undergraduate 5th Year
   Undergraduate 4th Year
   Undergraduate 3rd Year
   Undergraduate 2nd Year
   Undergraduate 1st Year

3. *Width of Black Poché:*
   Scaleless
   Object
   Furniture
   Body
   Room
   Building
   Cluster/Complex
   City/Region

PRAXIS

The Oxford English Dictionary defines *praxis* as 'that through which *theory* or *philosophy* is transformed into (a) practical… activity.' In architecture, *praxis* refers to the practice of making buildings in critique with theory and the history of ideas. *Praxis* in architecture refers to a practice that builds with the integrity of theory behind every detail.

If you are an architect and practice, your work encompasses ideas, philosophies of making, and research. I separate the notion of a studio or atelier, from that of an 'office'. An office references an architectural practice that intersects with commercial interests. Studio or atelier references a more elevated idea of practice as a philosophical and theoretical critique of building, or *praxis* (Image 1).

Building, Teaching, Writing: The Mirror

As an architect who builds, teaches, and writes, I see architecture as a finely calibrated mirror. Architecture as *praxis* is akin to building the opposite side of our selves. By opposite, I refer to architecture as a critical operation: a mold or mask that allows us to see ourselves—as a reflection—similar to the 'oppositional writing' of Leonardo da Vinci. Architecture, by this definition, is similar to the butterfly's cocoon or the Halloween reveler's mask—a formal registration of our selves, at any given moment in time (Image 2). By 'selves', I refer to the common identity of a larger group of citizens of a broader culture, and not to the singular person.

hMa: Practice, Teaching, Thinking

As a practitioner, I have an architectural practice, hMa, that is a reflection of my own mind, calibrated by a partner—Thomas Hanrahan, Dean the of Pratt School of Architecture. I teach and am actively involved in architectural education. Until 2005 I was the core-coordinator at Columbia's GSAPP; more recently I was the David Niland Chair at the University of Cincinnati; previously, I was a professor at Cornell's School of Architecture.

Professional schools of architecture cannot operate successfully without architectural practitioners, both as tenured and part-time faculty—due to the necessary requirements of *praxis*. Without practicing architecture, it is impossible to understand how or what should be emphasized in the instruction of students of architecture. *Praxis* involves practice, teaching, and research.

Architects build things. Beyond studying the history of architecture and doing an apprenticeship with a licensed architect, architects learn their craft by going into the field and making things. Architecture is critiqued in the public realm. Until a graduate of architecture has that experience, she or he cannot understand the process of *praxis*.

Mathematics, Geometry, Form and Physical Science

Architecture involves a series of mathematical equations that make space. At hanrahan Meyers architects, we build projects, including *Infinity Chapel*, as reflections of human knowledge and aspirations (Image 3). *Infinity Chapel* presents a series of ideas about light, shadow, mathematics, and reflection. Mathematics and the properties of light include $E = mc^2$, Albert Einstein's equation establishing equivalencies between mass, light, and energy.

Infinity as Architecture

Infinity Chapel is an homage to Albert Einstein. Einstein's work was an overview and logical sequence of thought about the nature of the universe, and had extraordinary influence over science, the fine arts, and architecture. Einstein's equation for the equivalency between energy and mass was a capstone of twentieth century thought. It was a singular achievement — akin to Newton's Laws explaining most of the West's contemporary ideas about gravity and planetary orbits — and had a profound effect on society, the arts, and architecture.

Infinity Chapel was an attempt to apply contemporary ideas about space, energy form, and matter within the design of a building. We began our work on the Chapel as a concept about space and light. During the design of the project, hMa carried a series of discussions about energy and light with Harvard physicist Dr. Lene Hau. In the process of producing a book about light in architecture—*Designing with Light* (Abbeville Press, 2004)—I spent time in Dr. Hau's laboratory in Cambridge, Massachusetts, discussing her work using lasers to control the speed of light, which has been foundational in research for optical computers. At hMa's *Infinity Chapel*, light-wells frame the walk from an entry at MacDougal Street, through a reading room, a chapel, and to an outdoor garden (Image 4). *Infinity Chapel*'s light-wells—holes cut through the Chapel's concrete floor—manifest as rectangular wood objects of varying heights and shapes at the ground-floor level of the building. The light-wells frame tubes of light that mark the path from street to garden on the ground floor. In the Sunday school below, light-wells appear as illuminated squares and lines in the ceiling. *Infinity Chapel* uses energy waves of light and sound to create a calibrated experience of church by relating ideas about physics, light, time, and movement: this is an example of *praxis*.

DWi-P: Sound, Architecture, and Landscape
hMa's DWi-P (*Digital Water i-Pavilion)* is a community center in New York City, opposite the World Trade Center Memorial site (Image 5). *DWi-P*'s main façade is an east-facing glass wall embedded with a frit pattern representing a sound-score titled *WaTER* by New York composer Michael J. Schumacher. *DWi-P* is dedicated mostly to swimming and offers other community activities including dance, basketball, fitness, and classrooms.

DWi-P's largest public space is its pool-room facing the building's primary east façade, a 550-foot long glass wall. The pools are visible from the Ballfields to the east, and, from the west through windows that overlook the pools one story above, the *DWi-P* site has an eight foot drop from North End Avenue to the Ballfields. Visitors enter *DWi-P* from North End Avenue that also meets the ground level of *DWi-P*'s green roof, the Ballfields Terrace park. In the entry lobby, floor-to-ceiling glass overlooks the pools, underlining water's central role in the project. *DWi-P* is a culmination of hMa research into sound and its role in generating and interacting with spatial form. For the project, hMa studied sound as an energy wave capable of changing the perceptions of space, as made evident in the east facing glass wall that is itself an embodiment of sound embedded with the *WaTER* score (Image 6).

Victoria Meyers

Founding partner, hMa, hanrahan Meyers architects; architect, writer, lecturer, educator

1.

2.

3.

A key aspect of hMa's sound research includes collaborations with sound artists including Stephen Vitiello, Max Neuhaus (thanks to Silvia Neuhaus), and Michael J. Schumacher. hMa sound research is cataloged in my 2014 book, *Shape of Sound (SOS)* that studies sound in architecture, urban design, and landscape. *DWi-P* is hMa's first major built proposal that makes sound the generative aspect of a public pavilion's formal design, as well as a formal arc that frames a large-scale public park in New York City, the Ballfields.

Space Measured through the Human Body
Part of what defines us as human is how we move our bodies through space. Contemporary marathons attest to the human capacity to out-run prey in the distant past by sustaining a slow, steady run, for days. There are connections for all of us between walking, thinking, and speaking. As a species, we move through space, and this is partly how we develop and maintain our brains. *DWi-P* facilitates walking, moving and thinking, through a sound-score; *Infinity Chapel* does so through light. *On/In Landscape*, an hMa collaboration in process with visual artist Bruce Pearson, is a garden folly that invites visitors to walk through a maze and be surrounded by the text *contains real hard won insight*.

By understanding the human walk and limitations of movement, students learn how to detail and create space (Image 7). The human walk has a certain length, width, and depth. These dimensions determine the basic aspects of building design, including the proper sizing of stairs, openings, and landings. It comes down to the scale of the human body. This sounds mundane. In reality, it is the basis of ephemeral creations, and *praxis*.

***On/In Landscape*: Collaborating with New York Artist Bruce Pearson**
In addition to studies of human movement, light, and sound, hMa pursues the concept of 'writing' on/in buildings (Image 8). Text on buildings captures ideas for future generations. The concept of 'writing on the building' partly determines the details of hMa's glass wall at *DWi-P*, and the use of light at *Infinity Chapel*. hMa's most recent application of writing on/in built form is our collaboration with the artist Bruce Pearson on his constructed text sculpture: *contains real hard won insight (crhwi)* (Image 9). hMa's application of a sound-score to the façade at *DWi-P*, the use of light at *Infinity Chapel*, and literal text in *contains real hard won insight*, are examples of *praxis*.

Duchamp, Cage, Arvo Part, and Dr. Lene Hau
hMa's pursuit of praxis includes homage to the ideas of Marcel Duchamp and John Cage. hMa's works—cataloged in my book, *Designing with Light (DWL)*—connect with the concept *praxis* through works that focus around physics, time, and space. *DWL* pays homage to the oeuvre and writings of John Cage, Marcel Duchamp, and contemporary composers and artists, including Arvo Part. Similarly, *Shape of Sound*, published in 2014, chronicles hMa collaborations and discussions with sound artists and colleagues, including Stephen Vitiello (Image 10), Eric Howeler, and João Onofre. Sound compositions, like architecture, reflect changing cultural memes. hMa uses sound, light, and text as secondary 'mirrors'—or filters—for the architectural process, and we see these mirrors or filters, as part of our application of *praxis* to architecture.

Praxis
The curriculum in schools of architecture lays the foundation for future architects. *Praxis* is an inherent aspect of the discussion within any school of architecture. A depth of thinking and intellectual discourse acts as a scaffold for architectural education. Remove the practitioners or the theory, and there is no *praxis*.

An abbreviated list of studios I have taught cover topics investigated in hMa's work: *Line*; *Library of the Spoken Word*; *Time/ PassageWay*; *S o U n d* (Image 11). My design studio programs present a catalog of ideas, tested in the academic environment, and applied to built works in hMa's studio. For any architectural work to be a serious discourse, it must be pursued as *praxis*: built work grounded in the history of ideas, theory, and philosophy.

I would like to end with a quote from Robert Frost, as we reflect on the notion of praxis, and how it relates to education and architectural practice: **"Education is the ability to listen to almost anything without losing your temper, or your self-confidence."**

The two greatest architects of the twentieth century, Le Corbusier and Frank Lloyd Wright, never graduated from schools of architecture. Le Corbusier's PhD dissertation was *Villa Savoye*. Frank Lloyd Wright's

PhD dissertation was *Falling Water*. They both followed
ι tradition of learning architecture that has existed at
east since the 11th century, when architecture was
passed from generation to generation, through the
guild'—an on-site learning experience in real time.

n the 11th century there were no schools of architecture,
/et the guild passed knowledge to generations of builders
architects) by seeing, doing, and making. This includes
extraordinarily complex building forms, including
gothic cathedrals.

see myself as part of that guild, having started my work
n the field as a 16-year-old apprent ce, in the office
of a local architect in a small town in Pennsylvania.
At the time, I was appreciative of the opportunity and
eager to get my architectural degree. In retrospect, I
see those early days working in a traditional firm as
ny entry into the guild, and feel fortunate to have had
that opportunity, in addition to every moment I have
spent on any job site, giving direction, and overseeing
the production of the spatial construction of ideas.

would like to end by giving a special thank
/ou to Professor Mara Marcu, whose serious
and astute study and production in architecture
provides an excellent example of *praxis*.

mages:
1. hMa (hanrahan Meyers architects),
2. Untitled (Stairs), Rachel Whiteread
3. Infinity Chapel, hMa
4. Sequence of Sound + Light, Infinity Chapel, hMa
5. DWi-P (Digital Water i-Pavilion), hMa
6. DWi-P (Digital Water i-Pavilion), hMa | Nude Descending a Staircase, Marcel Duchamp
7. Animal Locomotion, Plate 163, Eadweard Muybridge
8. DWi-P (Digital Water i-Pavilion), hMa
9. Contains Real Hard Won Insight, Bruce Pearson with hMa
10. All those vanished Engines, Stephen Vitiello, MASS MoCA
11. Project from V. Meyers Graduate Advanced Studio: Time Passageway, Fall 1999. Studio investigation by students applying contemporary construction techniques to the study of Time as it relates to space, form, and materiality to Einstein's equation $E = mc^2$.

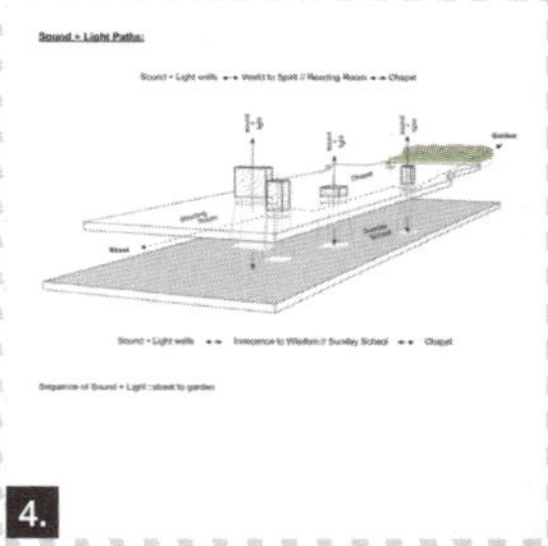
4.

5.

6.

7.

8.

9.

10.

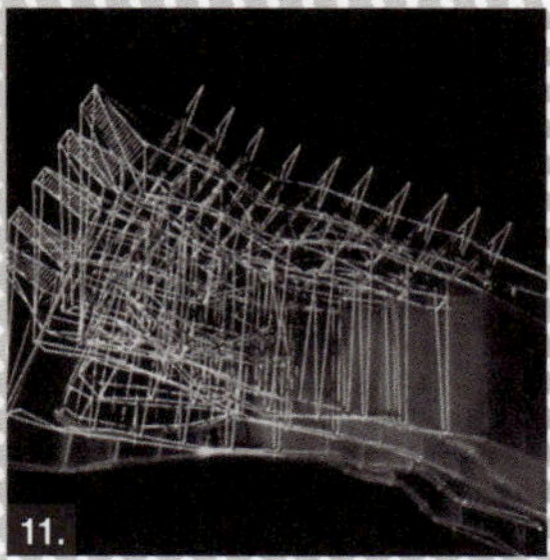
11.

RYAN BALL
SEAN COTTENGIM
WHITNEY HAMAKER
MEGHAN MINTON
ANA OZAKI
VINCENT SANSALONE (coordinator)
MELANIE SWICK

FIRST ACT

First Year Architecture and Interior Design Foundation
Cincinnati, OH, USA

As first year faculty, coming with diverse voices and unique pedagogical agendas, but all with a clear desire to foster young minds, we lead approximately 150 students in the processes of educating themselves in both making and applied visual thinking sited within the historically essential elements of the plastic arts. We believe in inquiry as the core component of students' foundational experience. Inquiry is the notion whereby people reenvision the world around them and possess the ability to critically change it. We premise that the pursuit of inquiry will inculcate students with a desire to become active participants in visual cultural production, leaders in global innovation, and theorists who confront and solve the most pressing problems of the world. Nevertheless, to be clear, this is not only a first year strategy but part of a vertical approach where the tactics learned in first year play throughout students' tenure at the school. The protagonist in this play is the humanist mind and the critic or foe is the job. Here the poetics of the script dates back to Aristotle and his writing on observation.

Following in the rigorous tradition of the Bauhaus and Black Mountain with a nod to the MIT Media Lab, this Foundation program yearns for trans-disciplinary thinking to the sound of 'Take Five'. Accordingly, students go beyond representation, both in theory and practice to an outline for thinking that investigates the ideas of the past, critiques and deepens current best practices, but dares to suggest a future that propels SAID into the forefront of preparing students to become cultural leaders.

This sequence hopes to show how this constructivist pedagogy weaves a new fabric of thinking and working. The opening line of the story may start with "line, plane, volume" propped with materiality; but it is staged in the theatre of ethics on the scale beyond the ivory tower.

First-year students learn core principles, but more importantly, question and transgress tradition. The curriculum places a heavy emphasis on self-awareness. In other words, it requires students' constant consideration and incorporation of physical scale—the set of physical qualities, and quantities of information that characterize motor, sensory, social, and mental capabilities. Over the course of the semester, the program(s) unfolds in a series of projects developed to teach the principles of composition, form, and materiality through an acute understanding of the hand and making via iteration, craft, scale, and questioning.

The first act or the first semester.

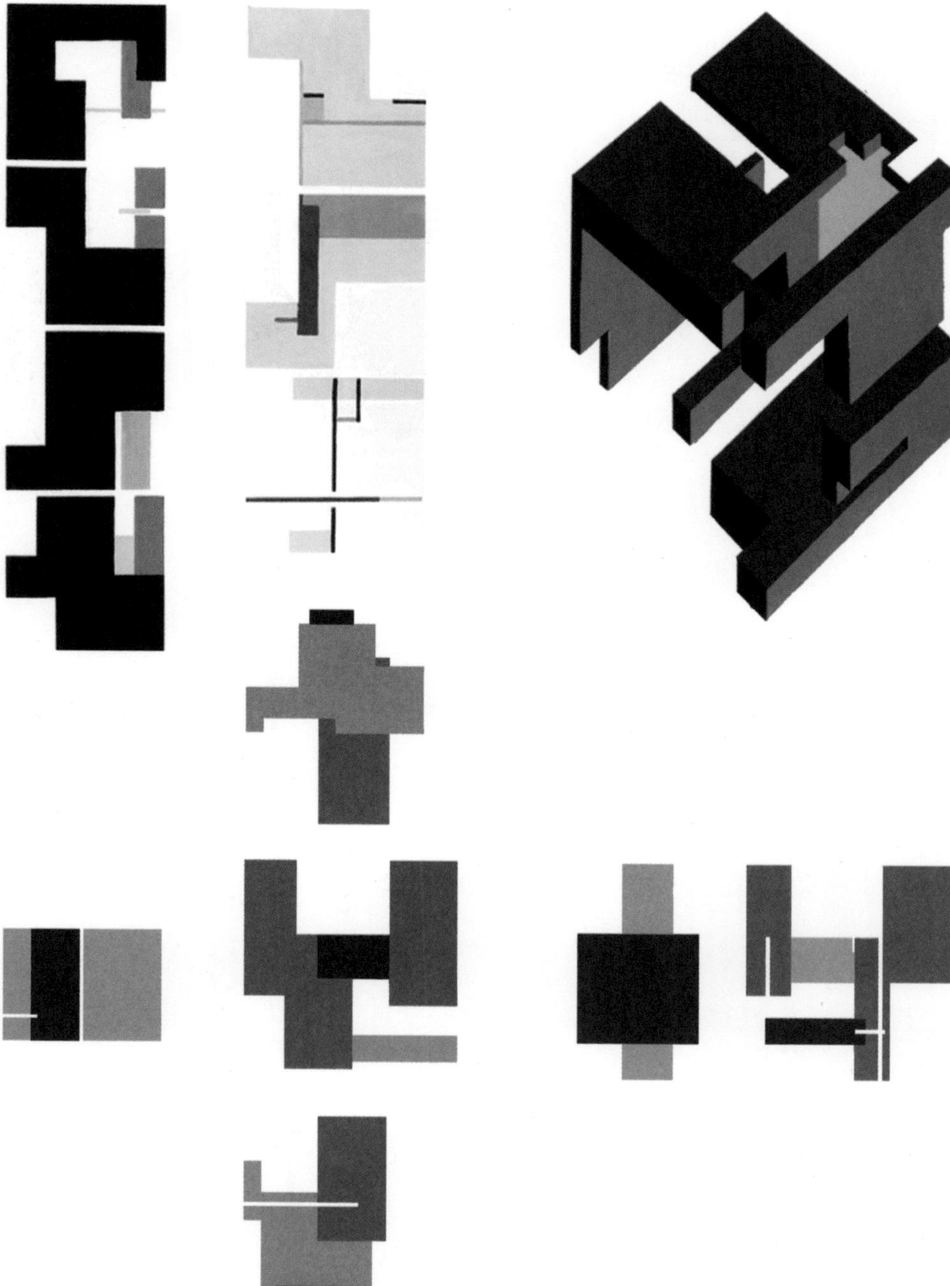

MATTHEW KLUMP / gouache orthographic projections

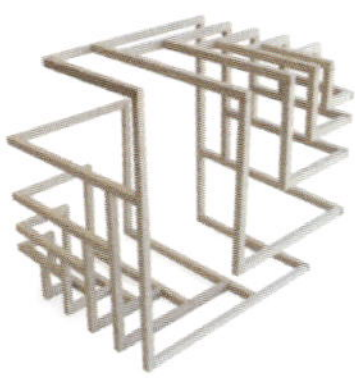

JACOB ANDERSON

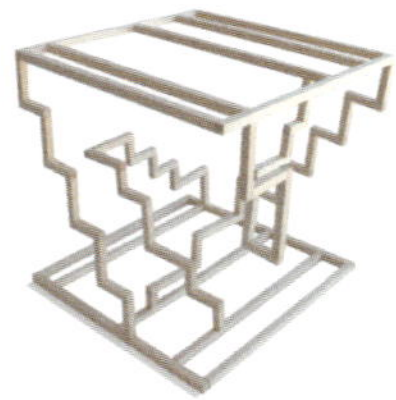

NATALIE STEIMER

SARAH SHEDLOSKI

YAN JIAXI

LILLIAN ACREE

MACKENZIE FORD

ALEXIS GAUSS

SISI ZHANG

LILLIAN ACREE

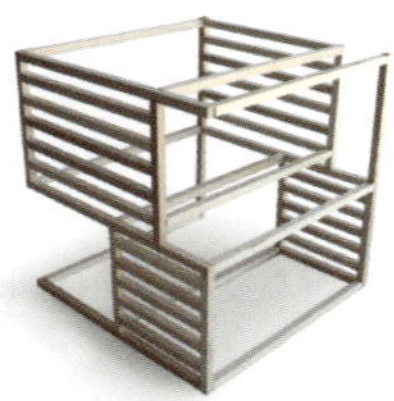

MACKENZIE FORD

ALEXIS GAUSS

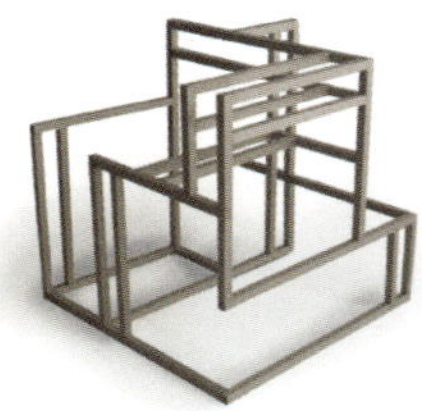

BEN FLESCH

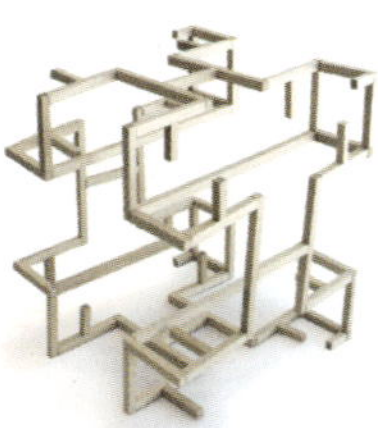

GABRIELA ZAVALAGA

AMY ZYLKA

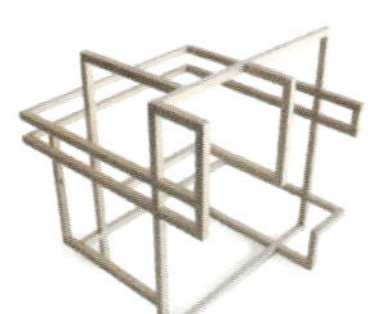

PETER FOSTER

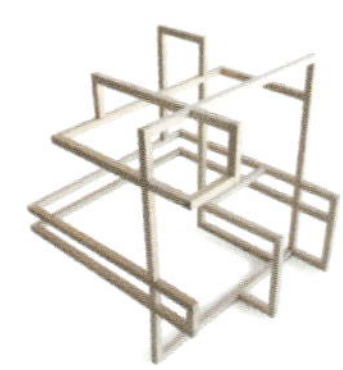

PETER FOSTER

ELEANOR GREEN

ALAN BOSSMAN

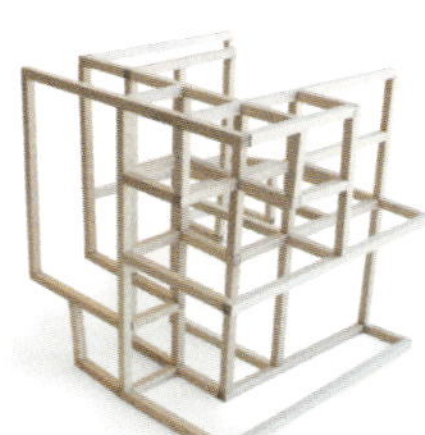

ALAN BOSSMAN

SHION IWAIZUMI

TRANG LE / armature

ABBY GOLDEN / armature

EMMA WEAVER / armature

KYLE MOLL /armature

line vocabulary

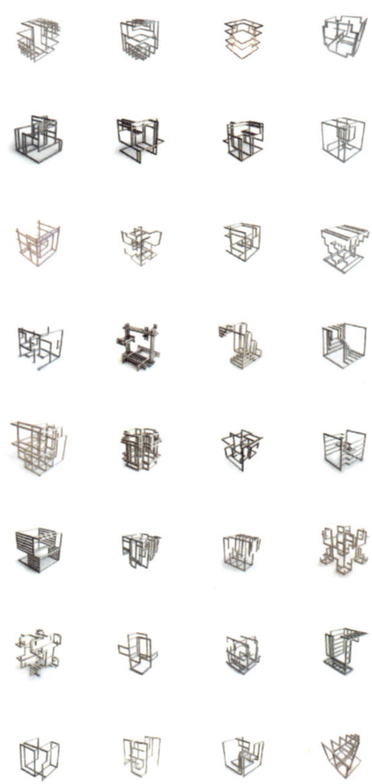

line clusters

plane vocabulary

cube armature

plane clusters

line/plane vocabulary

cast volume

cube cluster

armature

Foundation, exhibition

100 + 1

Alice F. and Harris K. Weston Art Gallery

PRIYANKA SEN
AARATI KANEKAR, PH.D. (chair)

CHOREOGRAPHED LANDSCAPE

Master of Architecture Thesis
Performance at the Queensgate Railyard

The translation of one medium to another symbolizes the transfer or crossover of implications, consequences, and therefore, meaning. In Walter Benjamin's essay "The Task of the Translator," the original translation is no longer as important as that of its "afterlife"—in which the reproduction and reincarnation of the translation becomes all-encompassing. The act of translating allows for a further and deeper understanding and interpretation of a relatively autonomous entity. Architecture and several other media, including music and art, possess a rich kinship to one another, but the relationship between architecture and choreography remains finite and tepid. This thesis seeks to interrogate the intersection between the two disciplines through translation in order to explore and engage new interpretations and associations between the two disciplines. The site of the Queensgate Rail Yard in Cincinnati, Ohio becomes the mediating force of the translation between these two entities, capturing the essence of a choreographed landscape that ultimately lends itself to architectural interventions. Each component possesses its own feature: the landscape as spectacle, the rail yard as stage-space for performance, and the design structures as observational points.

The relationship created between the two disciplines exists with the establishment of the frontal proscenium, generating a barrier between the audience and the performer, the viewer and the viewed, the spectator and the spectacle. The industrial corridor of "events" at Queensgate coalesces into a larger spectacle landscape with choreographed components, both existing and new, throughout the site. Here, the rail yard acts as both spectacles of body and of landscape.

The theoretical framework of this thesis utilizes Bernard Tschumi's 1981 Manhattan Transcripts as a foundation, specifically in his discussion of space, event, and movement and Guy Debord's seminal 1967 text The Society of The Spectacle to create the underlying frame of reference for the landscape spectacle site of Queensgate.

PRIYANKA SEN / contour diagram

Utilizing the methodology of mapping through collage and montage allows for a new perspective on site potential, excavating hidden meaning and moments throughout the site. These series of analytical layered drawings dissect the site, recording pertinent existing information, such as train/traffic movement, sound, rail pathways, and rail yard switches, while also extracting inherent movement within the site. These methods of mapping, in addition to dance movement notation begin to represent the dynamism inherently engrained within Queensgate that become the catalyst for architectural interventions.

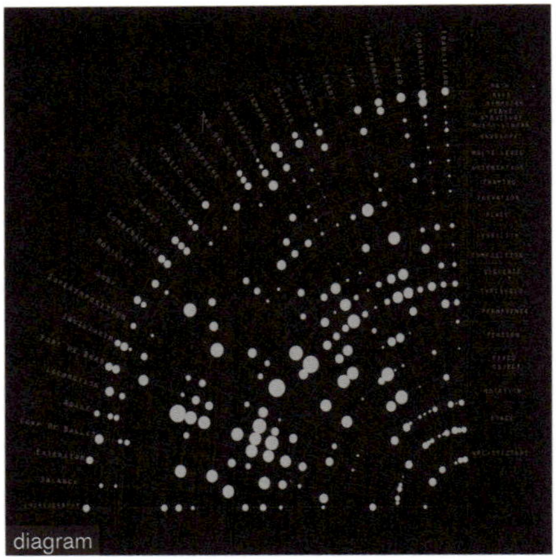
diagram

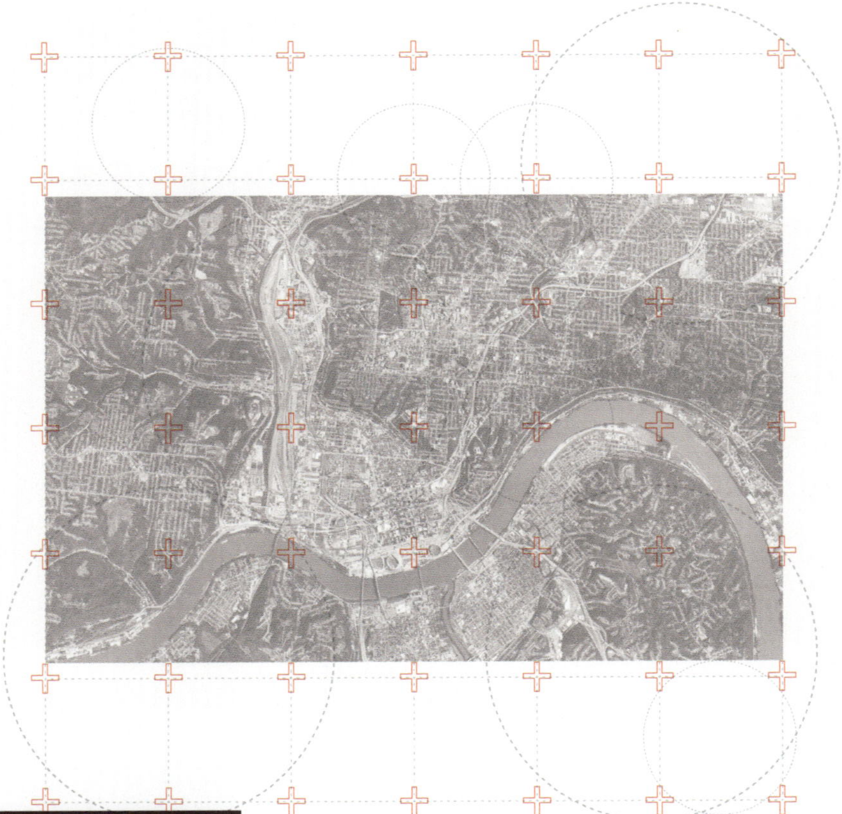

PRIYANKA SEN / methodology

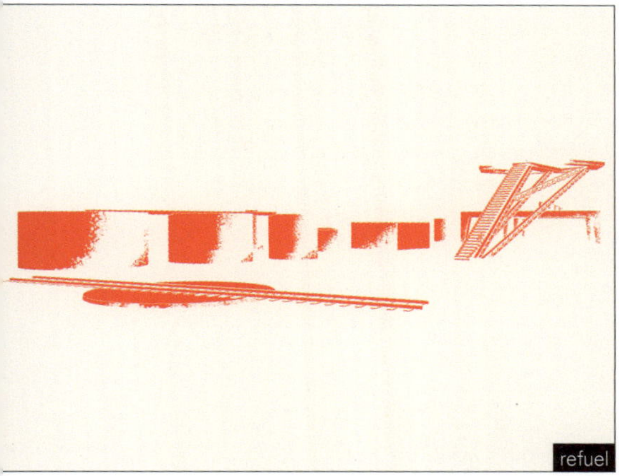
refuel

silo

arches

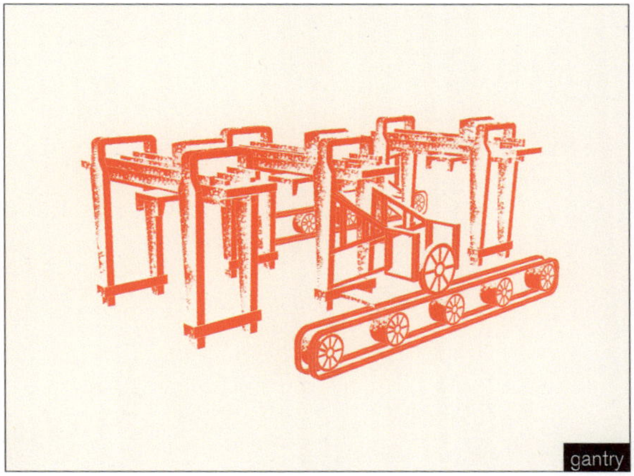
gantry

By tracing the combinatory trajectories of architecture and choreography, a deeper understanding of how composition, as defined through dance methods and terminology, can begin to influence and inform architectural interventions at the site. Developing historian Mitchell Schwarzer's discussion and notion of the rail yard in his book Zoomscape, a conceptual design for a series of structures, sited from the mappings, will engage with ideas of movement, sequence, and framing of the choreographed, spectacle rail yard.

These movements take inspiration from the existing machinist language of the site and its combination with mechanical dynamism. In addition to these observation points, a series of nodal coordinates are interspersed throughout the landscape and possess a dualistic function: to act as superimposed moments throughout the site, allowing for a specific engagement of a varieties of movements as defined by the role of dance, and to record the overall choreographed composition for the future.

PRIYANKA SEN / railway maps

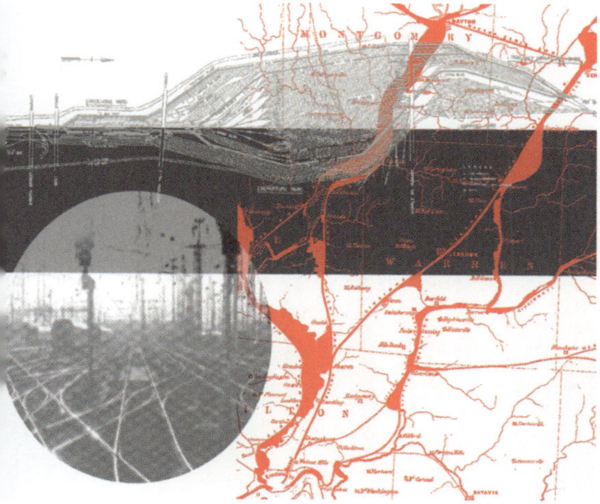
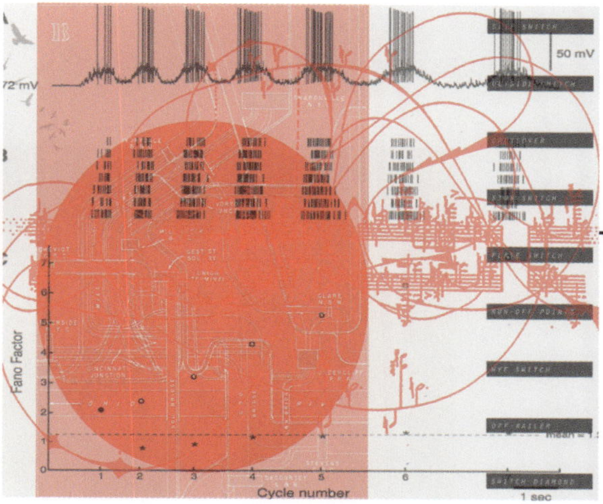
50 mV
Fano Factor
Cycle number
1 sec

CITY OF CINCINNATI.
RAPID TRANSIT RAILWAY.

gantry, model

silo, model

refuel, model

PRIYANKA SEN / arches, model

TERRY BOLING

LOUDER THAN A BOMB

Undergraduate Architecture
MetroLAB
Cincinnati, OH, USA

UC MetroLAB is a Design / Build / Research program within the University of Cincinnati School of Architecture and Interior Design (UC SAID) that engages students and faculty from both SAID and across UC with local, national, and international communities.

Louder Than A Bomb is a youth poetry festival designed by the Young Chicago Authors organization in 2001 to be a platform that not only gives youth a voice, but gives them a chance to share their stories, learn from each other, and find common ground. Since its founding, it has become the largest youth poetry festival in the world, and has spawned competitions in urban areas throughout the country.

MetroLAB teamed up with the local Louder Than A Bomb organization to create a series of performance and exhibition environments for the 2015 Finals held at the Harriet Tubman Theater in the Cincinnati Freedom Center. For fifteen weeks, the students collaborated with more than twelve academic and community organizations and sponsors, including Elementz, a non-profit hip-hop youth arts organization, Wordplay, a local nonprofit literacy group, and the Taft Research Center. We worked with local high school student teams to design and construct portable, prefabricated performance environments (platforms, walls, seats, lighting, etc.) for the competitors to use during their preliminary and final performances. The fabrications were intended to support the young poets and not distract from the performances. The materials needed to be easily assembled and disassembled, inexpensive, durable, and performative in their own right. The working prototypes were designed to be re-purposed for subsequent competitions and exhibitions.

The students worked exclusively at full scale in the studio on material investigations, trying to uncover attitudes or strategies that could inform the performance environments. They worked with inexpensive and readily-available materials and techniques that they hoped would somehow connect to the particularities of the event, namely the rough, raw, and beautiful poetry to which they were exposed.

ALEX NYKTAS
ALLIE VANDERBURGH
ANH TRAN
BRANDON DALESSANDRO
CALEB HERRICK
CAROLYN LINDGREN
DANIEL KRUK
EVAN SOLIC
JOHN ELLIOTT
LEX COLTON
LUKE SHERRON
MARGARET FRANK
MEGAN GOTSCH
MICHAEL KAUFMAN
NIKKI WEITZ
SHAY MYERS
/ MetroLAB team

Four primary materials—newspaper, wooden pallets, steel, and acrylic—were subject to operations like bending, burning, cutting, laminating, etching, and sanding, with the goal of transforming them from something banal into something unexpected and precious, a kind of alchemy. The objectives of these operations were to re-inscribe value and meaning to material through a process that is not industrialized, but crafted.

This definition of craft is not simply the consequence of skilled labor, but results from a convergence of intellectual and physical operations, leaving indelible traces of processes, techniques, and humanity embedded in the work itself.

"Our collaboration with the poets offered a very unique and personal opportunity to think about a project within the context of our own city, allowing us to witness how the final fabrication of our designs empowered and inspired this incredible community of artists."

***Nikki Weitz**, 4th year architecture student*

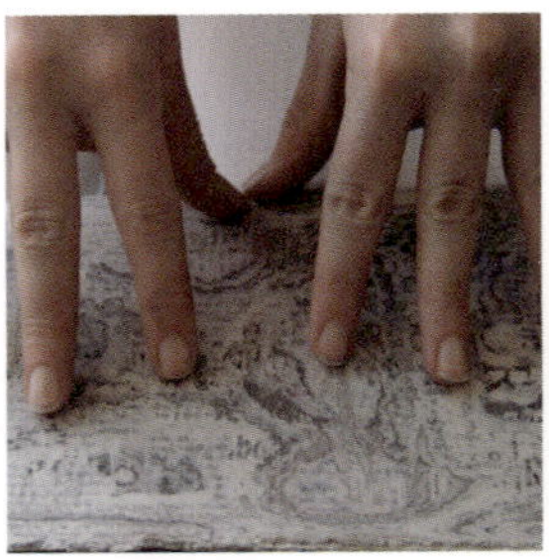
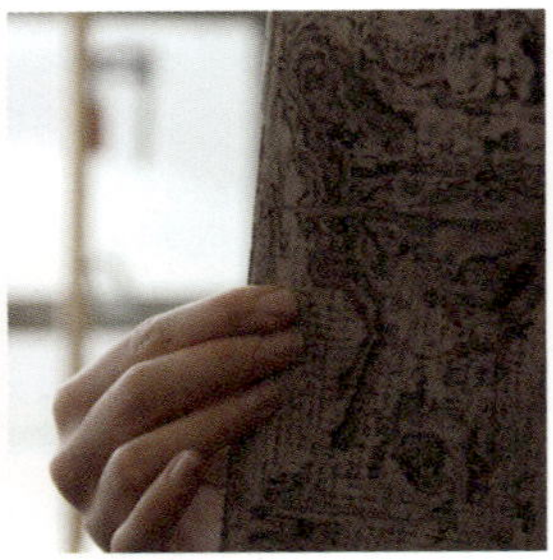

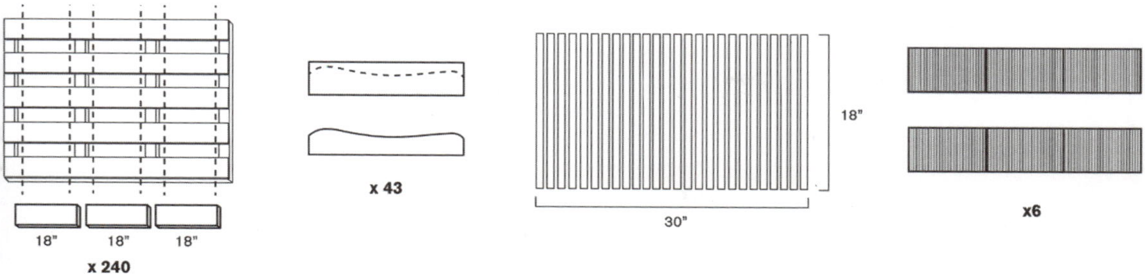

process and final details

METRO LAB TEAM / dj booth and fold taxonomy

ANJALI PATEL

MAGIC TRICKS ON THE SUBWAY

In Spring of 2014 Kohn Pedersen Fox (KPF) was working on the master plan for Hudson Yards. I worked on Tower A and the podium of the Hudson Yards project. We designed two buildings that swayed away from each other. One was in the construction phase, the other was still in schematic. I worked on the taller, schematic phase building. I actually thought the other was more interesting because it engaged the High Line and the schematic building did not. The third building was the podium which was in between the construction phase and schematic buildings. I spent most of the time working on the exterior and producing renderings.

While I worked long hours, I would take every chance I could to go out in the city. I saw Sou Fujimoto speak at Columbia University and completely geeked out. I had the chance to talk to him and I just swooned. I'd attend similar lectures as often as possible. During the week I'd go try and go to shows in different venues all over the city. It was cool to see the different crowds that would convene in these different places. The performances all had an indie bend because that's my kind of music, but I went to the Output and some funkier shows. It was interesting to see how people engaged with space in the different venues. Some were just like theater spaces, intensely lit and with little tables arranged for standing and sitting. Other venues were more like a party—designed for the crowd to do whatever they wanted. I visited Beacon, New York and appreciated the opportunity to get away from the city— there's no way I could live in Manhattan. The daily commute was something that I loved. On the commute, I met a magician! I was reading this book on memory, just sitting there, reading, and I saw this guy practicing sleight of hand tricks. This normal-looking, kind of urban guy, and I said to myself, "Oh my god this is my chance to get a card trick out of this guy!" I thought to myself, "I've gotta be pretty sly to make this happen...." So I walked over to him and said, "Do you know magic?" and then we proceeded to talk about all these magic movies we saw and all these venues where we saw magic. Then he asks, "Would you like to see a magic trick?" and I screamed "Oh my God yes!"

He showed me this awesome card trick right before I got off the train. He says, "You know what? You have a nice life!" and I was like, "You too, man!" He didn't hit on me, it wasn't weird it was just a moment that two people experienced in a moment that I don't think happens that often, especially in New York. That's what made it so great. I'd have strange conversations and I know people would say, "Of course, Anjali, you would be the one to have a conversation on a train," which is fair, but I feel like that's what makes

New York awesome. There's this part in *Waking Life* where they say "We're all just ants we go from point A to point B and we kind of miss the in-between," and I think that's kind of why I fell in love with New York and why I'm going back.

I feel that once you work at KPF you can work anywhere. I became the graphic guru of my team. It was nice to be working for my director, Marianne, because no one ever quits her team, and I was also lucky to work for a woman at KPF: she's the nicest boss in the world, and she's a genius. They taught me how to make effective diagrams and graphics, and I ended up making hand models because some of the machines were broken sometimes. There was this time when an entire room was filled with just my work. Of course I didn't present it but it was just cool to see "Hey! This is my room." I worked very hard, a ton of hours. I think the latest I came home once was 4:30 in the morning just to return at 9:30 to put final touches on the presentation. After the meeting Marianne told me "Anjali! It went so well!" but I was almost too tired to react.

Working at KPF was insane but I needed the insanity. Before I'd get distracted from my work, and now when I sit and focus, I actually sit and focus and that's what KPF taught. My co-workers were so awesome they even looked at my portfolio and marked the entire thing up. They talked me through their thesis and told me why they said what they said. We regularly had deep conversations. Skill-wise the firm taught me to focus and get my work done. Even though a project will take a significant amount of time, I know I can finesse and make the final product better. Bill Pederson would come and talk about my drawings. He would say, "this one's my favorite!" It was like a confidence booster because it was my first co-op, and I was nervous wondering if I was going to be up to par. Pedersen's praise was kind of a validation I guess that I could do well at school and work too. It gave me more confidence to talk about my ideas.

ON TEACHING AND PRACTICE

Cincinnati, OH, USA

Designs and projects in both studio and practice result from collaborative work. After years of teaching undergraduate studios and practicing as a sole proprietor, design-fabrication processes began to inform the pedagogy of studio instruction and professional practice.

Teaching

As an educator, I am a generalist with specific knowledge in areas of furniture design, interior design, sustainable design, materials, craft, ergonomics, and human factors. I view teaching as the ability to transfer concepts, specific skills, cultivate critical thinking, and foster the student's ability to exercise judgment, as designers rely upon their intuition and design judgment in practice, on a daily basis.

Working within a larger curriculum and with students is my primary commitment, focusing on the ideal of integrating space and form with design intent; integrating aspects of making; material properties; cross-cultural communications; and human factors. Teaching and practice often intersect, and through the process they can enrich one another.

Teaching is collaborative and dynamic. As a teacher, I strive to weave group and individual learning dynamics in my classes. Innovative instructional methods include forming dynamic partnerships and student-group organizations, interdisciplinary learning opportunities, and design-build opportunities, arranged to maximize long-term learning outcomes for students.

An epistemological core in my approach to teaching, actively seeks opportunities for "structured play" emphasizing exploration and learning through doing. I find strength in a performance-based and a phenomenological approach in teaching students about architecture and interior design. Embracing a phenomenological view underpins the importance of measurable and haptic experiences in design. In a manner similar to the Montessori approach (learning through doing), coupling the mind with motor skills takes most students further when folded within a rationalist foundation of reading and research (theory). It is rarely a case of "either - or"; rather it is often an "and - both" polemic. I am passionate about building and making, but realize the need and value for research and theory in design.

Jimmy's buffet, overall

Alverno Salon and Spa, front screen

Holy Family Church, Altar

Holy Family Catholic Church, Ambry

Practice

In 2010, Studio 161 was launched as a design-fabrication practice, engaging students and faculty in collaborative professional work. Studio 161 seeks client and industry relationships and offers design solutions for a variety of project types. To date, we have completed projects in furniture design, interior design, and architecture and have worked on hospitality, institutional, liturgical, residential, and workplace environments. The practice considers issues of making and current building practices early in the design process and balances design aesthetics, material research, fabrication methods, and programmatic needs into integrated design solutions. Because of the long-standing connection to the School of Architecture and Interior Design at the University of Cincinnati, Studio 161 seeks opportunities to integrate teaching and research activities within its mission.

The practice was initially based upon an applied knowledge of furniture design, a working relationship with a local woodworking company, and an awareness of societal and liturgical shifts in contemporary places of worship. Over time, work expanded in scope and social-use and now focuses upon design and fabrication processes utilizing hand and digital technologies. Design leads to production. Construction and fabrication are fundamentally linked activities where intention is transcribed through workmanship. Correlations between ideas and built-form, people and place, process and product result from the realization of design ideas. Correlations between designing and making are significant because, through production, one begins to understand architecture and interior design in both holistic and technical dimensions. To this point, working with students is especially gratifying when making is part of the process of learning. This notion underscores my engagement with design-build projects through professional practice and involving students and faculty in the process of design and construction solutions.

I place significant weight upon commitment, passion, and the idea of ethos within all action-based activities. As a practitioner interested in the human dimension, "craft", ergonomics, proxemics, function, and programming have significant value and shapes design work.

Alverno Salon and Spa, hair cutting stations

How does the process of making influence the final result of design? What are the connections between conceptual ideas and the spatial-physical properties of built-form? What cultural or societal aspects give shape to form and spatial order? What correlations exist between form and function, between material and production, between space and human perception? These questions are raised and explored through teaching and practice.

Teaching is my primary vocation, practice comes naturally, and writing is difficult but something that I enjoy immensely. In recent years, writing and publishing have evolved as significant venues. The benefit of pursuing one activity in conjunction with the other is synergetic. Teaching benefits by experiences gained through practice and research.

My professional work can be organized in four categories. The first category focuses upon thinking about the making of architecture and interior design.

Wohl Chapel at Wise Center, Liturguical Furnishings and Bema

Studio 161 in winter

view to the north

There is an on-going and conscious effort to link thinking with making, drawing with building, teaching with practicing. "Construing and Constructing" describes an effort to narrow the gap between design ideas and construction realities, to reconsider the relationships between "head and hand."

The second category embraces transformative and life-style aspects engaged through projects designed for the domestic landscape, which I refer to as "The Furnished House." Collectively, residential renovations and additions, more often than not, place emphasis upon societal and cultural aspirations. Spatial transformation, along with custom furnishings and built-ins are lead musicians in an architectural minuet, often conceived in parts.

The third category, "Altars, Ambries and Ambos" places focus upon the design and location of custom liturgical furnishings within the context of transformed architectural space. Through the work, a broad series of formal and spatial constructs arise from social and liturgical shifts in the way people worship and pray. Sister Margaret Carney, OSF and current President of Saint Bonaventure University in New York, helped open my eyes to the vast intellectual and spiritual depth within many religious communities. Never before had I experienced such a close working relationship with a group of caring, thoughtful, and creative individuals. It was an early experience working with clients, specifically religious communities that fostered a pedagogical core in my professional work and initiated a series of liturgical projects, completed over the past twenty years.

The fourth category, "Frame + Imprint" underscores ideas of containing and being contained, addressing the physical and spatial transformation of site and context. Building and interior projects illustrate how metaphor and allegory can underpin spatial transformation.

upper deck from below

detail

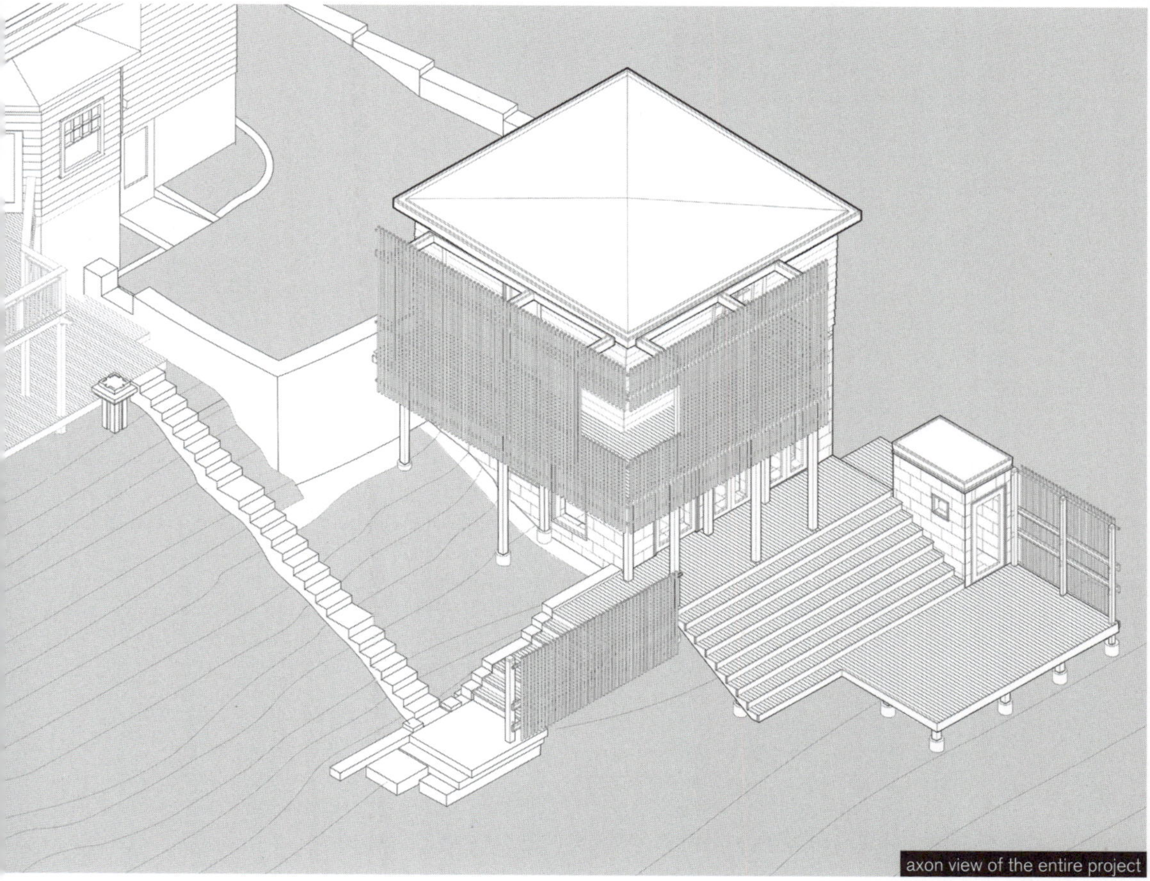
axon view of the entire project

EMMANUEL O. MANOLUKAS
UDO GREINACHER (chair)
AARATI KANEKAR, PH.D. (member)

CATALYTIC TRANSLATIONS

Master in Architecture Thesis
Architectural Assemblage through Methods of Printmaking
Cincinnati, OH, USA

Catalytic Translations explores the notion of 'process' defined by physical and chemical manipulation within the visual art of printmaking to formulate translations into the medium of architecture. The analysis seeks to challenge the influence of the autonomous technological designer and restore meaning into the connections and tectonic realities that architecture can spatially share with disciplines of the hand.

Catalytic Translations is a journey of exploration and process that moves across the boundaries of different media, attempting to discover meaning where few have thought to look. This journey unfolds with, first, the conversation of translation: a verb that describes the movement of ideas from one form of expression to another. Walter Benjamin describes translation as "finding the particular intention toward the target language, which produces in that language the echo of the original."

As a response to potential consequences of digital automation a project was formed which takes direct inspiration from the work of Brodsky and Utkin [1]. Using a similar approach, a prospective future is portrayed: the environment defined by current social and technological trends. The key feature of this future is the neurological integration of the human brain with the digital realm. The prevalence of cell phones is now replaced with a Nano-biological neural insert that expands and connects the human brain directly to a digital network.

This future provides the framework for the ideas explored in this thesis to be exemplified in the form of a monument towards the dissolution of the printed image. The monument is sited near the Google headquarters in San Jose, California and is the embodiment of the process and history of the printed image. The design is the expression of various translations of the etching process that are implicitly and explicitly embedded into the experience.

Woodcut Prints

Investigation began with woodcuts. Carved patterns are informed from classical stereotomic forms such as coffered cathedral ceilings. This is an expression of architecture that becomes unified in its application as both a structural element and decorative feature through the use of relief. The bronze casting becomes a three-dimensional representation of the woodcuts using simple geometry with a method that has analogous characteristics to printmaking.

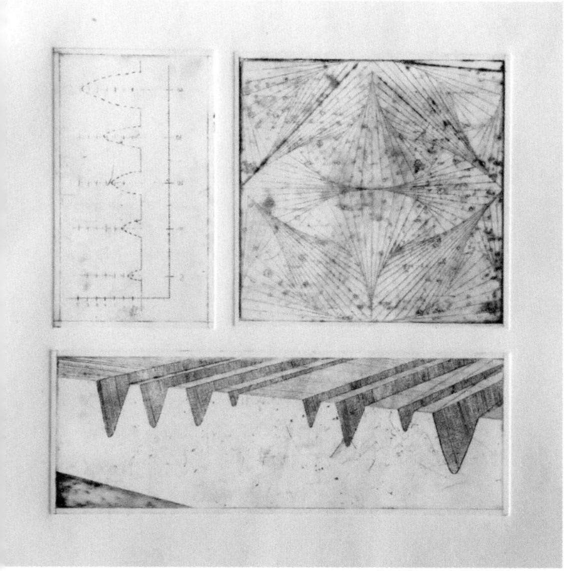

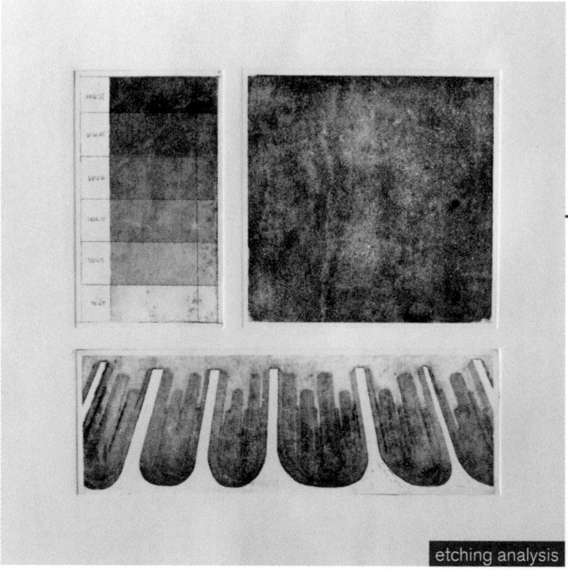

etching analysis

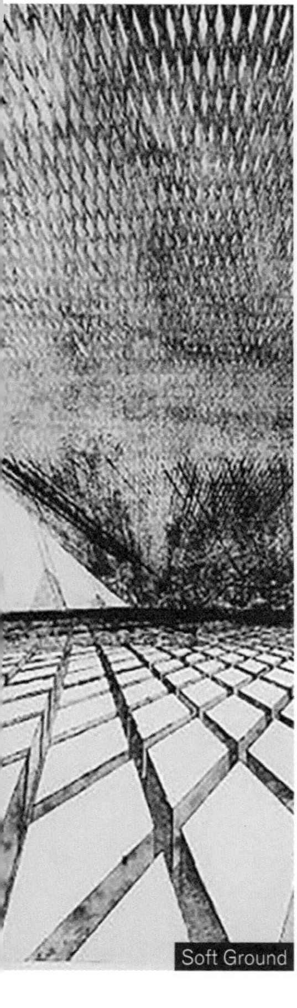

Soft Ground

Pressure Printing

Line Etch

Aquatint

Etching Prints

The concept is structured according to the sequential processes of etching in its application towards the printing of an image. The four sequences are: Line Etch, Soft Ground, Aquatint, and Printing. Each sequence expresses an architectonic translation of the technical steps in a symbolic and representational manifestation of architectural form, correlating the nature of the architectural element to the etching technique.

The breaking down of hierarchical sequence of process in both acid etching and relief printing are the basis for methodology and dissection. The analysis of the resulting artifacts provides both a macro-tectonic understanding towards qualities of plate, ink, and paper and a foundational concept for understanding the intersection features and principles of printmaking to those of architecture. These intersections serve as the drivers that guide the manifestation of an architectural assemblage that translates the nature of the sequential printmaking process into a symbolic spatial experience.

model

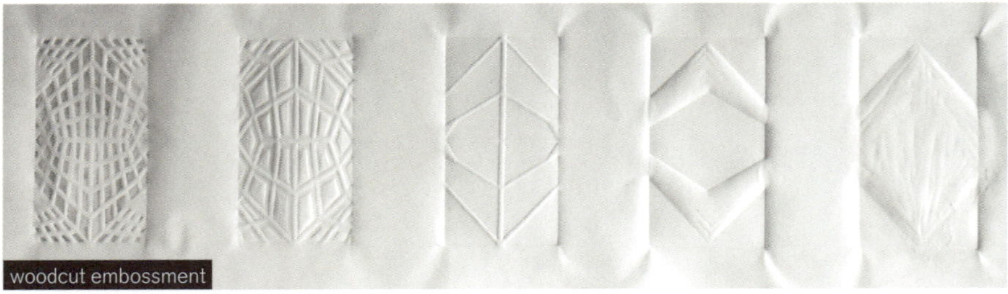

woodcut embossment

woodcut ink

Aquatint

Line Etch

bronze cast

bronze cast

Notes:
[1] Nesbitt, Lois, Brodsky & Utkin: *The Complete Works.* New York, NY: Princeton Architectural Press, 1991.

CRAIG DYKERS, FRIBA, FRSA, RAAR

Psychology of Space

SAID Interview Excerpt
Conducted by Kyle Winston
Edited by Chas Wiederhold

Craig Dykers is founding partner of Snøhetta, a multidisciplinary firm providing architecture, landscape, interior design, and branding services. With offices in Oslo, New York, and San Francisco, Snøhetta's work has been widely published and has received numerous international awards.

Kyle Winston: You are an accomplished designer and you sometimes teach. What are your thoughts on architectural education today?

Craig Dykers: I have to say that my view of architectural education is kind of bleak. I see many challenges when we hire people today. I feel there are often misplaced interests. Not that people aren't intelligent—a lot of intelligence, a lot of great thinkers, a lot of very creative people, in one way or another—that's not necessarily the issue. There tends to be a disassociation with the world around them. I think architecture, as a profession, has grown more and more segregated from society. Architects lost a lot of power over the years. After WWII, engineers did most of the building. Buildings had to be built fast in the west, or in areas affected by WWII. Architects began to come back but they were overly heroic in th 1950's, the 1960's. Their buildings didn't hold up ver well. Architects were losing control of the process. So project managers were invented. Architects have tried to have significance in society and, for quite sor time before the rise of the "starchitects," architecture was more or less off the radar. In this time, architects created their own language. They created everything about themselves that others wouldn't necessarily be able to understand unless they went through the same process of learning it in school. As a result you find words that are only used by the architectural profession that no one else understands. Even the architects have variations in definitions of those same words. There is an inability for most architects graduating from school, and even in the profession, tc understand what the actual needs are, not only of the people who are going to use their buildings, but of the society that has to interact with it. As long as it fulfills the needs of the architectural profession, this means that it is good in most architects' eyes. Architecture faces a pretty big challenge unless schools find a way to reconnect and not be embarrassed by the idea that we are in fact a service industry.

How do you approach the problem of architectural education with your teaching today?

I don't often teach, as I'm pretty damn busy. When I do teach I try to create an alternative method of creating a studio. I try to get everybody interacting. I try to get students to talk to each other as much as possible. I try to really rip apart the whole problem of self-authorship. It's a big issue, you know. I understand that there is a problem if you don't have some degree of self-authorship. It's hard for professors to grade you. A good teacher should be able to give you a grade by following your work without necessarily seeing a project that is only done by you.

I try to do lots of group work. I also try to have jury reviews that aren't a line of professors and critics and everyone else dead silent and asleep in the back. I try to force students to sleep the night before presentation. In general, I try to get people to work normal hours and focus their work. I try to have presentations that are off the regular grid of showing graphic or three-dimensional imagery. I've had presentations where I put students' drawings and models in a separate room from the jury. The jury is only allowed to listen to the student present their work verbally. Then the jury has to go into the other room and try to match the projects to the verbal description and then make a final judgment.

What kind of forces developed this anti-ego-that-is-all-so-common-in-architecture attitude I am picking up on?

My beginnings were not in architecture. I wanted to be a fashion designer. That didn't work out and after not getting anywhere with fashion, I ended up in medical school. My parents said, "Do something serious with your life." And I don't know why—I guess I watched Marcus Welby as a kid—God knows what, but I said okay, and somehow they accepted me. The school where I was had an amazing tradition for teaching. You weren't just graded on your test scores or only on your classroom skills, but you also had to turn in your notebooks at the end of the quarter. They would go through your notebook and see how you took notes and score you. I thought that was pretty neat. They basically told me at the end of the semester that my scores and tests were okay, but they weren't great. I could speak reasonably well, but I wasn't likely going to be good doctor material. However, they said that my notebooks were the best they had ever seen. I had made a lot of sketches. They told that I should become a medical illustrator—you know, draw one-celled animals and stuff. So I took to the art school, and the art school was a revelation for me.

I called up my father, who I was really close with, and said, "Hey Dad, I want to be an artist." And he said, "Well, you're not getting help from me." That didn't sound like him because he loves art. He continued, "Well, son, if you were really going to become a great artist you would never call up your father and ask him what he thought of about it, you would just do it. So now that you've called me up this just proves you'll never be a great artist." He mentioned that I should take architecture.

I suppose the short answer to your question is that I have learned enough things, I went through enough avenues of exploration, that by the time I got to architecture I could see it in the context of the rest of the world. Architecture in and of itself is useless. It is a worthless thing. It has no value unless it has fuel. It needs fuel and the fuel does not come from architecture, it comes form everything else around it. The more you are aware of what's around, the better your architecture will be.

You were born in Germany. Your father was in the U.S. Army. Did you grow up in the United States?

I'm 53 and I've lived 33 years in Europe. I was in Germany until I was 17 with a little stint in Texas. I went back to Texas and then I went to Norway. I met my colleagues, who together started Snøhetta, in 1989 in Los Angeles when we decided to work on the Alexandria Library. We designed the competition in a place we could rent for $50 a month. It was in a hospice, where people go to die. Someone had died, and they had it open for two months. I'll never forget that because it was the best thing that could have ever happened to all those people in the hospice. We were young kids and they would come over and see our progress and bring us cookies. We finished it, sent it off, and we won. It was an open and international competition. It's not every day that at twenty-eight you have a three hundred and fifty million dollar job thrown at you. We had to reconsolidate. We created our company and it was best to do that in Norway. There were some Norwegians there who had a little studio. We could have chosen many places. Norway had a lot of interesting characteristics. Politically it was in alignment with our beliefs. The Norwegians who had families there obviously wanted to be there. Though, the landscape of architecture really hadn't arrived. I remember I used to tell people, "If you really want to make good architecture you have to run away from it about as fast as you possibly can and go to the furthest place on earth where you won't find it" and at that time, Norway was basically it. Magazines weren't there, the famous people weren't teaching there. It was just this architectural wasteland. As a result you had to make your own world. You had to make your own space.

How do a bunch of guys in their 30's make a three hundred and fifty million dollar project happen?

I remember the first time the client wanted to visit us we had to ask our friends to sit in the office so it would look like we actually had an office. We told our friend, "Just move this around." We were just too embarrassed. Fortunately, all of us had done quite a lot of previous work. Even though we were young, I had worked in Los Angeles on one of the most complicated theaters in the US still to this day. My partners had all worked on other interesting projects. We weren't new to complex projects, we were just new to doing it on our own. We were very honest with ourselves as to what our faults and weaknesses were. I think that's why we won. When the competition was released, over 1400 people registered. 700 delivered. 500 were judged. That's a lot of people. And of that 500, a large percentage of them were very small operations, one or two people. Everyone in our group said, "we can't do this alone, we have to be a group. If we're going to win this, we'll have to work with solidarity and move as a much bigger force than as an individual." It changed our sensibilities. Once we won we immediately said, "We are too stupid to do this," and it's a good thing we acknowledged that because anyone smarter would have just walked away from the job because it was crazy to build that kind of building in Egypt at that time. We assembled a stronger team. Honestly, doubt is a powerful tool.

Do you seek out competitions?

A lot of people ask me about this very hot topic. It's an especially hot topic now. There's a question as to what value competitions have because for the most part they are treated like bids which means you work for free. Why would an architect want to work for free? I have to agree, that is very strange. On the other hand I throw two things out there: architects constantly ask contractors to work for free. They ask them all to put in bids, and they all put in bids and they don't get paid to put in bids. You can't have a double standard. You either get paid yourself and you pay everybody else or nobody gets paid. That's my first point. The second is that different kinds of competitions can be useful, and there are many types of competitions. One good thing about a competition is that when you win the design is there. Everyone can focus on it and say: this is the design. We're going to build it. It won. It's great. When you don't have a design competition, you have to build the design consensus through a longer process and people can have louder mouths than others. You get people coming in and saying, "No I want it with gargoyles because I like Gothic," and they're the loudest in the room, and they are going to get their gargoyles no matter what. There are competitions where there's no design, just strategy. There are paid competitions and there are unpaid ones. They all have value. We are far enough along that we don't do many unpaid competitions anymore, but when we were younger we did them a lot, and it was our only avenue. You don't have that opportunity in the US. The US is basically a monopoly or a mafia situation, and it's getting worse; it's getting MUCH worse. For example, to do certain kinds of buildings, you have to have completed, if its public work, five buildings of the same type before you can even qualify to be in a competition. So let's just say, the competition is a 2,500-seat opera. I've been working for 30 years. I've done one of those and it might have won every award in the book, but I've only got one. That's why companies are buying out other companies now. You have these big companies that can afford to buy small companies. They buy five companies that have done an opera and suddenly they've got the experience; really bad logic. I could go on.

Students are so ingrained with thinking about competing in competitions. They must be busy, they must get our work out there, they must fill their portfolios with competitions. How do students keep up in a country where the climate for architecture is getting worse and worse?

Competitions are still available for young people. When I did the Alexandria Library the climate was not much different than it is now. There are opportunities with low pay. It's not about the money. Obviously you need to be able to buy yourself a cup of coffee. You just have to look really hard. I found the Alexandria Library competition sitting in L.A. None of my American friends knew about it because they only read Architectural Record and their only source was the AIA. The Alexandria Library was a UIA (*L'Union Internationale des Architectes*) competition. America is a giant one-way mirror. Everyone can see in and no one can see out. I left the US and thought that never in a million years would I come back. I won a competition. My boss, a good architect, was pretty busy. We were invited to compete for the American Pavilion at the Seville Expo 1994. We won and I was super excited, and two months later Congress voted the money out. They voted the money out. They said, "Why do we need to showcase US culture to the world? Everyone knows what it is anyway. They can go to the movies." One of them said, "Where the hell is Seville anyway?" and the project was dumped. After that, I thought that there wouldn't be any way for me to work [in the US]. So I left with my colleagues to Norway. I desperately was seeking something to leave. Once I left I thought I would never come back. After a while you start to change. You loose a little bit of your radicalism. So I stopped myself. I'm an American citizen; I can't just sit around and pretend like it's not there. I can't complain all the time. I'm going to come back and I'm going to see what I can do and I'm going to see if I can make a difference, even if it is a small difference. I treated America kind of like a third world country that was embattled and maybe there is some way to help the natives.

Did you come to that realization when you entered the competition for the World Trade Center Museum?

The World Trade Center was an interesting story. Of course there was the terrible tragedy that occurred, which was one month before we were supposed to open the Alexandra Library. My first reaction wasn't how to participate as an architect, but some other way of helping. I didn't want to be an architect there. There were enough architects in New York; it's better that they take care of it themselves. To think about architecture felt like being an ambulance chaser. I started getting calls from people, "Oh, we think you could be a fresh voice. Maybe you could help here." And "No, no, no" I said. Many times I said no to participating. I just kept saying no. A friend of mine sent me an RFP, a request for proposals, for the World Trade Center Museums that were to be built on site. I just read the first paragraph; I didn't bother to read the whole thing, and called him back and said no. He encouraged me to read it again. He called me back five times, and I finally read it and I realized they were going to put a museum on the Trade Center site. On the actual grounds themselves—which is unheard of anywhere in the world. If you go to places around the world and look at memorials, there will be the place that was damaged and then the museum would be over in the distance. Never on the place of the tragedy.

People always leave that alone. The challenge of constructing a museum on a memorial is... it's too weird. It's the contemporaneous and the existential. The two don't mix. It's like bringing fantasy and reality together. It doesn't always match. I thought that that was brave. It looks like it is useful. I could be a part of this.

Specifically with that project, what was your relationship with Michael Arad or Daniel Libeskind?

I actually am starting to tell people now, because that is a common question too: the site is not complete. It's still under construction—most people don't know that. On September 11, 2011, ten years later, every critic was writing about the World Trade Center site. They had to have this story, and they drove me crazy. The damn thing was still half under construction. Nothing was there. It was like walking into a construction site without even knowing what the designs are and trying to understand what it's going to be like, and then writing about it saying that it doesn't seem right. Well yeah, it doesn't seem right because it is not there yet. And it's still not there. I think we really need to wait at least until the Calatrava building is finished and the two streets are completed before heavy critique. We might not have all the skyscrapers there yet and that's fine because not all places need to be finished before you can understand them. The ground plane needs to be finished. You can't even walk over one third of the site cause it's off limits as a construction site. The area that is closed down right now is the primary route that most people will take to visit the site: 85% [of people] will come from the northeast, and you can't visit the site from the northeast today. Today you have to walk around a bunch of alleys and you have to walk up from the south. Meander through this weird little corridor, and it does not make sense. I think when you see, you'll be able to see how well we worked together or how we didn't work together. I can't say that we were all holding hands and drinking beer together and going on camping trips with one another or sharing LSD or something like that. It wasn't like that. I wish we would have talked more in some cases, and I wished we had talked less in other cases. Despite it all, you'll find that there is going to be relevance between the projects.

Some dissonance, which I think is important. Our project is about dissonance. In other words, it is not supposed to be exactly perfect or comfortable. Some parts of the project look at the past, some parts look at the future and some parts look at the present. You'll feel all three of those things there... when it's finished.

What a relief it was when they finally took the gates down. Speaking of that, you are also working on Times Square, still dealing with the ground plane. All of your projects have a specific focus on culture. Have you always been interested in cultural projects?

We are landscape architects and architects working together in one studio, never segregated. Interior architects came later, and now we have branding and graphic design. Remember how I said we respect where we're stupid—most architects think that they can do everything. We don't think that way. Working side by side allows us to discuss context and the conditions in which we build better. We allow landscape architects to push us. We open ourselves up to be pushed, and likewise they open themselves up to be pushed. One mistake people make about our work is they think we're about merging architecture with the landscape. We want to have a dialogue with the landscape. Sometimes it's about being friendly and sometimes it's about being mean. Sometimes you have to be mean to make a point. Maybe you rip the landscape up or you expose it in a way that is radical. People see it and they get it. We do not want to be complacent about the landscape.

Can you think of a time where there was push back or resistance to a design?

Times Square was a challenge. The Public Design Commission, which we had to have approval from, was overly concerned that we would design too much. They didn't understand our method of thinking. In order to get people to move appropriately in a place like Times Square, which is one of the most densely visited touristic sites in the world, you really need to manage people almost like domestic livestock. You can't just rely on the way things look only. We put impediments in the way because, for various reasons that we knew, those impediments would shift people's direction. They wouldn't let us go as far as we wanted. We actually wanted to make the ground in Times Square slightly bumped in places, and they wanted it to be absolutely flat. We did the best we could through by the arrangement of the benches we've created. The scale of the benches—they're fifty feet long—is gigantic. There was reluctance. You wouldn't believe how political landscape design is. I've been in interviews where I've said, "I want to use a dogwood tree here" and dogwoods trees are beautiful and there will be one person who will go "I had a dogwood once in my backyard and it leafed everywhere and I hate that and I hate you." "Ma'am, it's just a dogwood. We can use a pecan tree." "Pecans, I hate pecans." Everybody has some kind of vegetative political side to them. Sometimes more political than architecture.

You mentioned livestock briefly; it reminded me of this New Yorker article talking about a story where you talked about dog herding people. I thought that was a great analogy. I guess it speaks to your theme, the psychology of space, dealing with the unconscious things people do. Could you deliberate on that?

I am basically saying what many other people do, and that is that your unconscious controls a considerable amount of your daily activities. We like to think that our conscious controls because we have an ego and we have an id that needs to be fed. Consciousness at a certain level is almost like an emotion. The more conscious you feel, the more control of your life you feel, the more superior your feel to everything else around you. Sense of superiority is one of the things that humans are certainly not lacking. There is a challenge to that, and that is that we are incredibly adept in our conscious patterns and our cognitive skills. Our life is not about that. It's about reacting to things without really knowing it. Your body memory is almost better than your actual memory. Dancers will tell you that. Actors will tell you that. Just doing something a few times gets you into a better understanding of that motion. In our work, in architecture, we design things that dull the unconscious senses often because we are providing routine and patterns. That's what they teach you in school. You have to have a methodology and that methodology has to be a logical methodology, and it has to be able to be understood and carried out and you have to quantify its results. If you don't have quantifiable results, then it's clearly not of any value because everyone is trying to create models of behavior. Any scientist will tell you that there is no such thing as a universal model. It does not exist. That's certainly true of human behavior. Any time you find a model for human behavior, it might work 90% of the time, but that 10% where it doesn't work is often where the value is. Can we break routines? Can we allow the unconscious to be segregated, separated, and allow ourselves to be more cognitive about what we are doing? You could make a door hard to open, for example. Making a door hard to open breaks the rhythm. Everyone will tell you: "A door should be easy to open. They should have nice comfortable handles and they should swing nicely." If every door is nice to open, you're just being built into that sense of security. Sometimes you make things that are not functioning well. We made some tables for the Oslo Opera that were just big enough to put one wine glass on. Two things would happen. If you were with someone, which you normally are at a social event, you'd have to share the table because it only holds one glass. Second of all, it looked scary; even if you put your wine glass on the table it looked like it was going to fall. So everybody was a little more civil to that situation. It broke the rhythm and got you into a different frame of mind. We made bridges that are too narrow like we did in the opera where you have to rub shoulders. We are always trying to put comfort zones into retrograde.

RYAN BALL
SEAN COTTENGIM
WHITNEY HAMAKER
MEGHAN MINTON
ANA OZAKI
VINCENT SANSALONE (coordinator)
MELANIE SWICK

SECOND ACT

First Year Architecture and Interior Design Foundation
Cincinnati, OH, USA

The ways in which foundational disciplines are historically taught and thought (praxis as theorypractice) have an influence on the philosophical dispositions faculty relay to their students. By using the vast body of pedagogical research on teaching arts and humanities, the proposed program can avoid teaching practices that hinder foundational understandings and research, and connect with the goals of the integrated set of capabilities we seek to instill into our students, i.e. students out of the seats. In this way, we seek the stage of Third-Space, a place of exploration of object, context and the interstitial space of possibility.

A disciple simply parrots knowledge and relies on dogmatic thinking to continue to solve the same problem with the same solutions. While this might work in some fields, SAID discipline(s) require inquiry. Inquiry is a description of the dispositions required to explore the world nondogmatically and foster specific skill sets needed to generate knowledge free from constraints. In addition, critical thinking, knowledge of history, and an experimental mindset are the hallmarks of inquirers. For architecture and interior design this is found in the full scale experience of body and space.

The first-year faculty, a merry band of full-time professors and adjuncts, reject passive, talk-at-you lecture-style teaching. Rather, on all levels we embrace dynamic practices and kinesthetic engagement. Knowledge is disseminated in a process similar to the solo in free jazz: an improvised style characterized by the absence of set timing or chord patterns. The lecture, as improvisational solo, is expressed in the vein of John Coltrane's performance in Ascension, with the sound of Eddie Floyd; while the band, or in our case, the first-year faculty, carries the form of the work.

It is with this that we believe the students are aware of what is good today can be better tomorrow. Simply what we do is inspire. We do not teach design, we give the tools to make the world of the mind. This is not a TV sound bite, it is a way of living today and tomorrow.

MDF and sheet metal prototypes

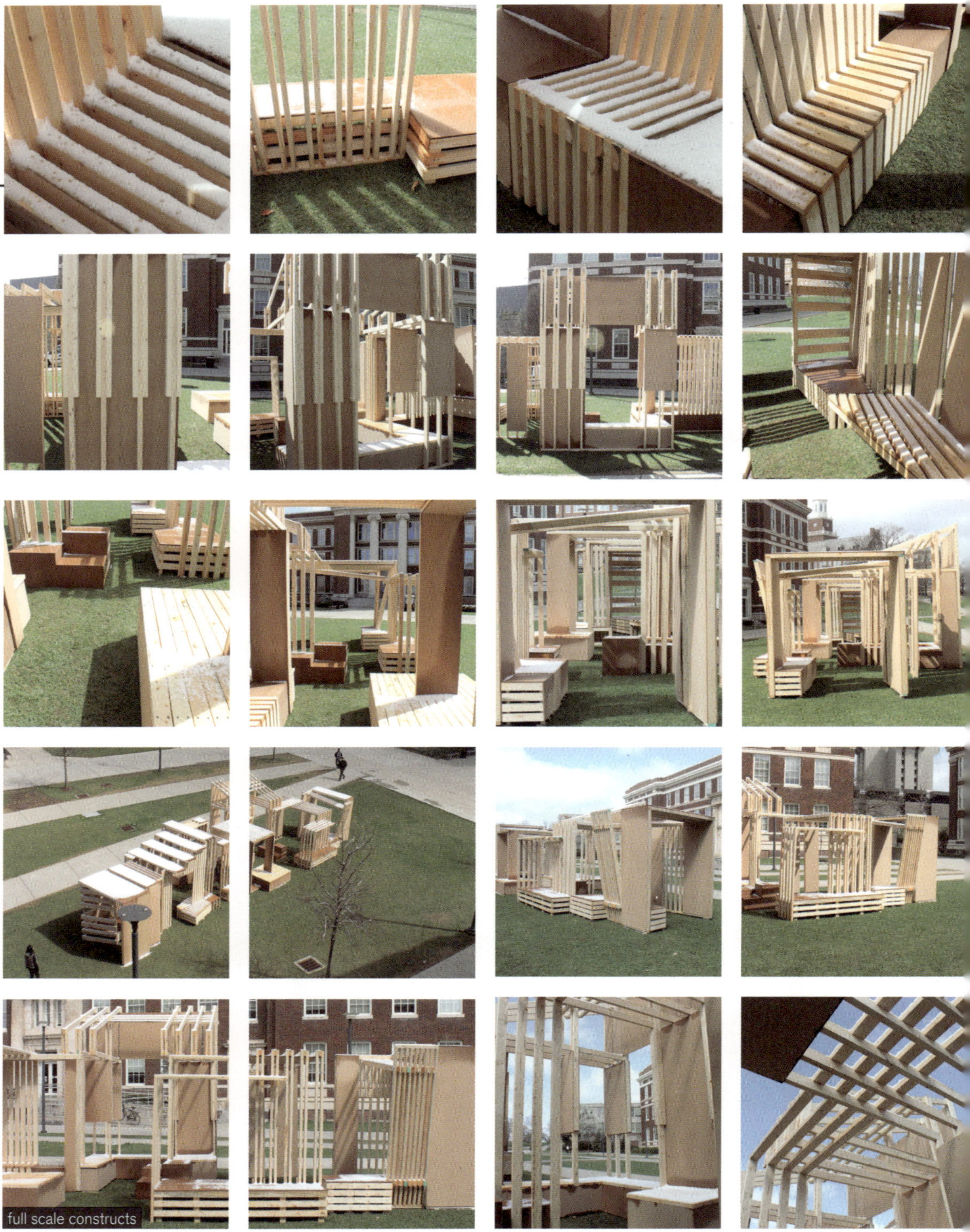

full scale constructs

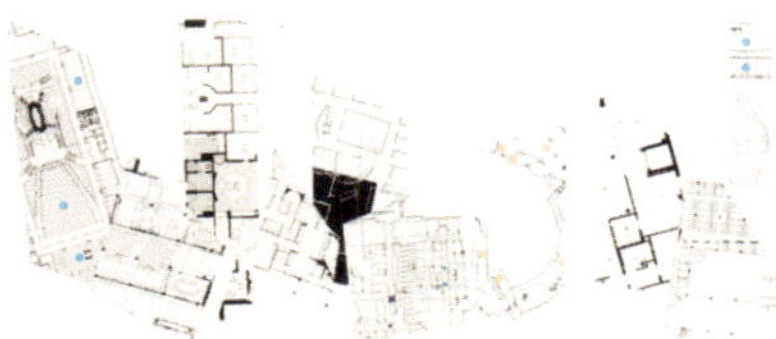

generative collages

JIM POSTELL

FURNITURE + MILLWORK

Undergraduate Interior Design Seminar
Cincinnati, OH, USA

The reality behind fabricating something is that it brings to the forefront design considerations like nothing else can, such as – use, structural integrity, material integration, detail, finish, cost, and resources.

Directing or choosing to design and fabricate a furniture piece from one of four furniture types is a way to focus upon design and rapidly jump into the learning process. In the first week of class, students are asked to select one piece of furniture from the following four types: Human Body Support (chair, bench, or stool, etc.); Storage / Display Unit(modular unit(s), shelving system, etc.); Table / Desk / Work Surface (coffee table, display table, dining table, buffet, desk, etc.); Spatial Partition (screen, privacy panel, etc.).

The first assignment entails making a full size mock-up of the furniture piece with little time to draw. It has to do with size and form. This is a deliberately quick and challenging assignment, one in which material and joinery are intuitively addressed. The totality and immediacy of the process helps students form linkages between something and how it might be made. Because of the process, students tend to work inductively and intuitively, which tends to direct design decisions toward tectonic considerations rather than preconceptions about what the piece should look like.

By the second week of the semester, students are asked to complete a second, full-size prototype. The second prototype offers refinement to aspects of size and form while enabling further consideration about structural considerations. Detail, joinery, and material considerations begin to surface. The idea is that thinking and making, detailing, craft and technique all come together in a more integrative manner when inductive, deductive, and abductive modes of working are synthesized, and in order to obtain a greater sense of synthesis, students need to allow material and fabrication techniques inform design decisions, and vice versa.

A secondary portion of the course focuses on the interior environment millwork, particularly related to the design, specification, and joinery of dissimilar materials for casework. The content of this portion of the course includes standard and custom cabinetry, material specification, hardware and finishes.

LEXIE GAUSS

LEXIE GAUSS

JACKIE REQUEIMA

CLAIRE WETTA

CLARK SABULA

TIA MILLER

BENJAMIN GILLES

MARIELLE JURLINA

NAGARAJAN KAAVLYAA

MING TANG

VISUALS IN THE DIGITAL AGE

Graduate Architectural Skills

Visuals in the Digital Age **closely examines the language of architectural form, allowing students to explore the methods, techniques, and critical principles of graphic representation in architecture and interior design. By doing so, students are able to experiment through analog and digital means, including freehand sketching, drafting, modeling, and a variety of rendering methods.**

Despite the increasing dependency of architecture on digital media, sketching will always be critical in the design process. As design field progresses, so do the implications of software. By learning a variety of design skills, students are able to make thoughtful design judgments and synthesize processes of conceptualization. Drawing on skills from allied design fields, students expand and question various representational techniques.

Today, powerful modeling and rendering software allows us to directly manipulate digital images, and create complex forms and photorealistic renderings without thinking of how to realize it in the physical world. Realizing the importance of materiality and tangible form provokes a question that is vital to the field of design.

The objective of this course is two-fold. First, the course closely examines the language of architectural form and covers a wide range of techniques for analyzing and representing it, including freehand sketching, drafting, painting and different means of rendering. It approaches drawing as a tool for thinking as well as for representation. It is a comprehensive look at representation techniques (digital and analog) and methodologies as they influence the design process.

Second, this course discusses the distinction between developing representation and the act of making itself. Representation such as sketch, rendering, and construction drawing are just the representation of the actual form, where valuable information is stored or released within each of the drawings. However, realizing the building information in the physical world develops new situations where information is no longer just represented but now processed through various pipelines that all differ from each other.

The course discusses the necessity of expanding from representation skills to incorporate craftsmanship and digital craft. In our approach, the consideration of fabrication and assembly process creates a feedback loop with drawing. The results are valued for the process of making, integration of fabrication/material parameters, and the engagement with the tangible world.

SAID 2013 + ARCH 7012 STUDENTS

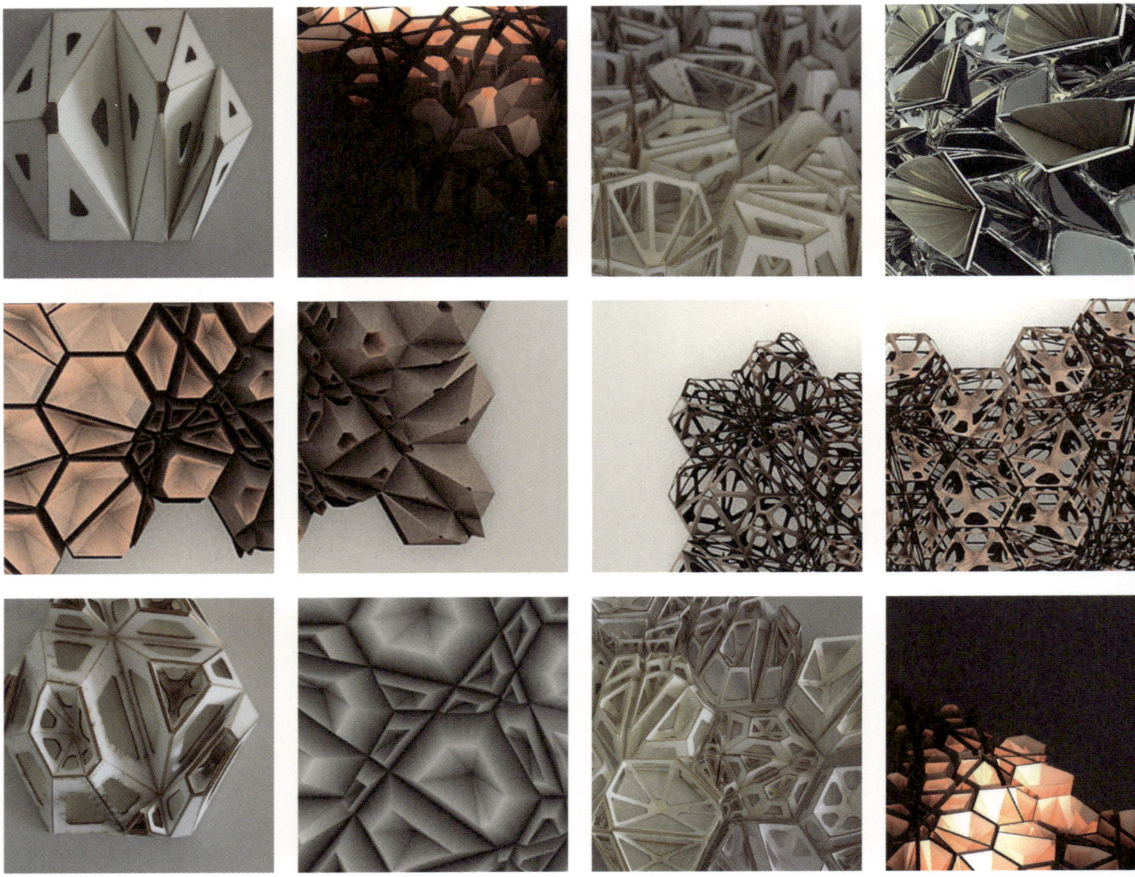

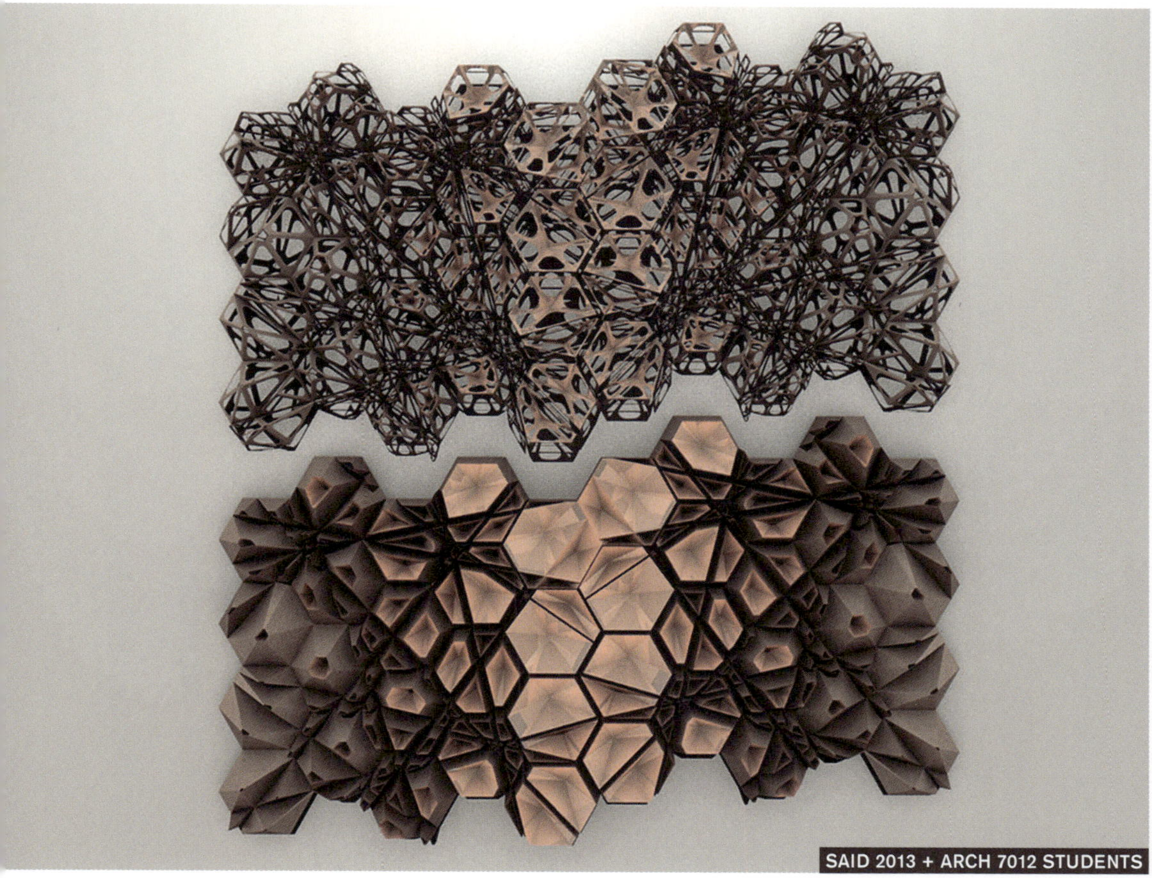

SAID 2013 + ARCH 7012 STUDENTS

LUIS SABATER MUSA
ELIZABETH RIORDEN (chair)

74°F

Master of Architecture Thesis
Thermal Performance in Hot, Humid Climates
Santo Domingo, Dominican Republic

Current design and construction practice in Santo Domingo has not adapted to recent climate change. Local construction technology is oriented around concrete and its derived products despite its poor thermal performance in the hot-humid climate. Although this happens largely due to availability and low labor costs, the strongest reason is cultural; people see concrete as a symbol of safety and progress. Furthermore, the architecture profession has little climate-responsive education, and there are no official energy codes nor guidelines to address. In view of this, this research intends to better understand known materials and strategies in order to provide an appropriate architectural response in Santo Domingo which could lead to thermal comfort.

The project studied both a building and a unit within it. The building was expected to simulate the construction possibilities in Santo Domingo if these were to split from the limitations of current practice. The unit was the DNA, embodying an idea that could be transferred to other high rise projects in the region.

The design challenges the current paradigm based on inappropriate learned concepts. Throughout the investigation, the proposed design redefines what the hot-humid dwelling space could be. The groundbreaking idea proposed a shift in the proportions of open versus enclosed space, offering a unit that behaves as a outdoor space, fully ventilated and flexible enough to adapt to its users' needs.

LUIS SABATER MUSA / schematic design rendering

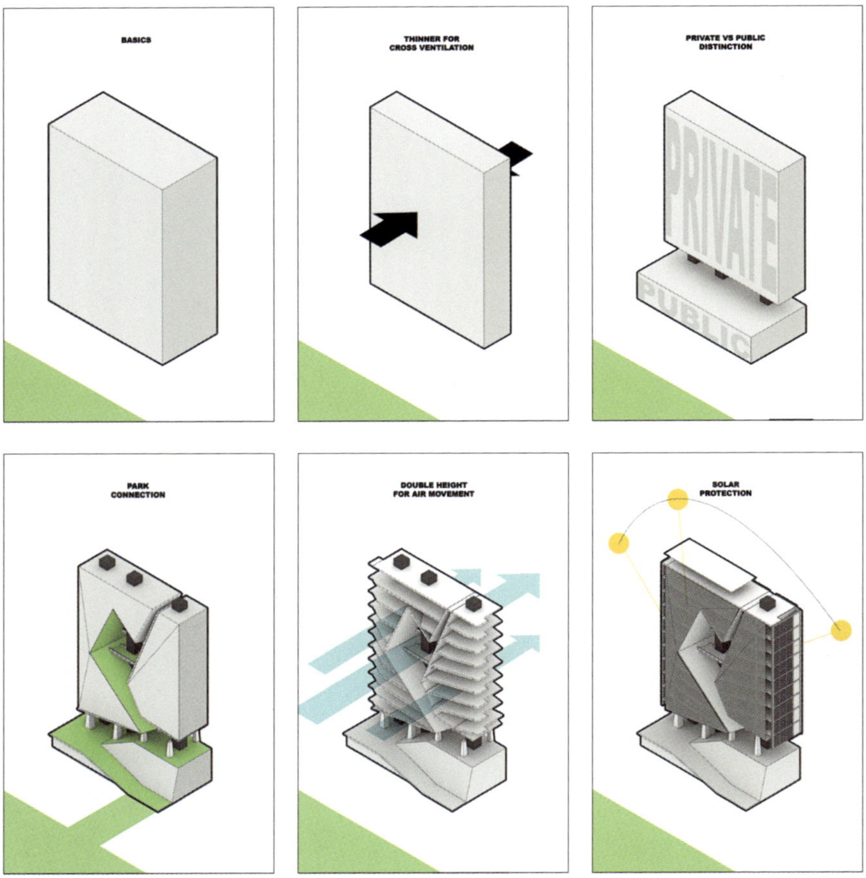

LUIS SABATER MUSA / building diagrams

integrated systems

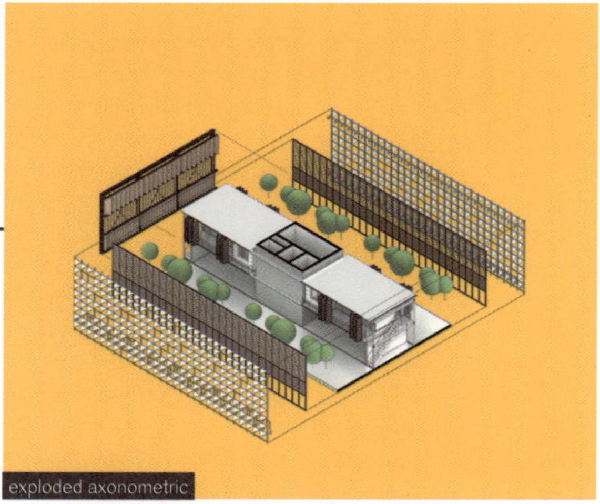

exploded axonometric

LUIS SABATER MUSA / apartment rendering

model

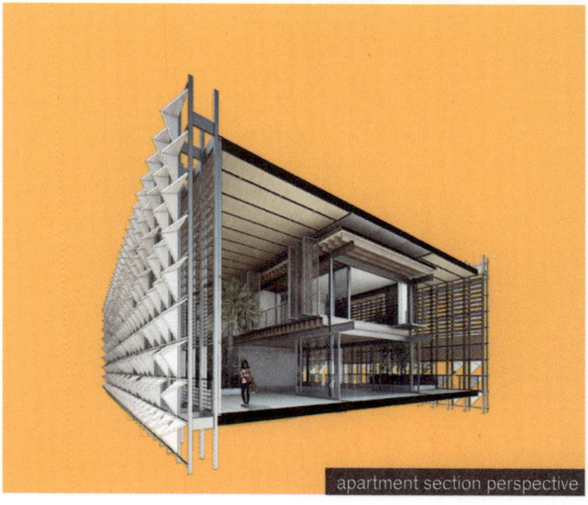
apartment section perspective

EDSON CABALFIN, PH.D.
BRIAN DAVIES

MAPMAKERS + TRAILBLAZERS

Undergraduate Fourth Year Interior Design
Shop-in-Shop Experience Design
Cincinnati, OH, USA

Mapmakers + Trailblazers **creates a new innovative and inspirational camping retail department for the existing REI customer, while attracting a younger demographic: active milennials. The design of the department contains three novel shop-in-shop experiences while maintaining a solid connection to the overall look and feel of the camp department. Connection of the new camp department to the common space is encouraged, along with a connection to the store entry to create a strong first impression of the space.**

The designs engage customers in a meaningful way by implementing a new marketplace concept for the REI brand. The marketplace idea allows for a flagship store to hone in on what makes the city unique, embracing its surroundings and company philosophies and using them to deliver an authentic, experiential shopping adventure that keeps the customer responsive to the brand.

By focusing on the city, people, and adventure, the designs emulate both the District of Columbia and the nature contained within it, creating a balance between existing customer expectations and new customer desires, and embodying the REI brand through the incorporation of the adventurous spirit of each REI customer.

Emphasis has been placed on creating a more intimate relationship between brand and consumer by engaging users in an immersive environment that connects people to experiences through product. Base Camp, Camp Life, and Camp Survival merge together to foster an embedded community space that unites the shop-in-shops within the camping department. Modular system components are layered to form a continuous landscape that spatially defines and conforms to create unique spaces.

** This is a PAVE (Planning and Visual Education/ paveglobal.org) competition sponsored by Sephora and REI.*

interior perspective, rendering

KATIE COSTA/ interior rendering

KY O'KEEFE / exterior rendering

HANNAH CLARK / interior rendering

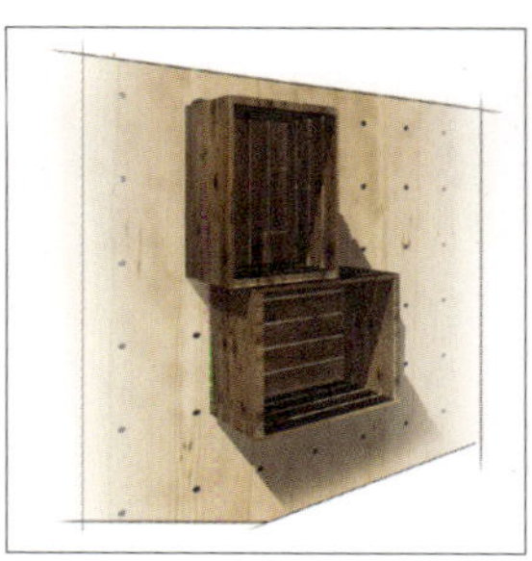

fixture renderings & shelving sketches

IRA SHIBAEVA / interior rendering

GABRIELLE ENZWEILER / fixture renderings

KAYLA REINBOLD / interior renderings

JOHN BURNHAM DIXON
STEPHEN SLAUGHTER

MIDWEST MODERN

Undergraduate Industrial Design and Architecture Collaborative
Product Design + Architecture
Cincinnati, OH, USA

In the spring of 2017 Assistant Professor of Practice John Dixon, and Assistant Professor Stephen Slaughter co-taught a collaborative studio that paired students from the School of Design with students from the School of Architecture and Interior Design. Its mission was to produce work – furniture, houseware, an exhibition environment – and a social and multi-media campaign for a hypothetical brand that would eventually be exhibited the following semester at the International Contemporary Furniture Fair in New York. The identity of the brand was born out of extensive research into Shaker, Scandinavian, Japanese, and Mid-Century Modern design, focusing on the historic connection between Nordic and Mid-American arts and crafts, and its translation into contemporary culture. As the studio moved from research into production a series of internal design charrettes and competitions were held to determine the material, color palette, and graphic, formal, and morphological character of the brand, culminating in products designed within the constraints of readily available and locally sourced materials and technologies.

The work and campaign was completed during the spring semester and was packed, transported, and set up in the Jacob K. Javits Convention Center for the 29th Annual International Contemporary Furniture Fair in New York. North America's premier showcase for contemporary design, ICFF gathers more than 750 international exhibitors to display furniture, seating, carpet and flooring, lighting, outdoor furniture, materials, wall coverings, accessories, textiles, and kitchen and bath designs for residential and commercial interiors. This showcase represents the world's finest, most innovative, and original avant-garde home and contract products.

The exhibition, "Section_001: Midwest Modern," was met with critical acclaim and won the coveted Editor's Choice Award. The ICFF Editors' Awards judging committee and five leading design industry media figures selected University of Cincinnati for the best exhibition in the School category.

Midwest Modern, scene

ICFF/ "Section 001: Midwest Modern" Exhibition

Midwest Modern, scene

ANDREW BIRKHOFF
THEO BONNER
HANNAH DAHL
MADELINE DEATON
ARDEN DRULEY
BRIAN KOVESCI
DANIELLE LANGLOIS
MARY CATE MCINTYRE
POOJA MEHTA
ABBIE MILLER
ELISABETH MORRIS
HAYLEY OLSEN
SAMANTHA PERRY
RYAN PFLAUM
ZOEY PHELPS
TYLER SHANNON
AUDREY TORRENCE
JOSH TRANSUE
NATHALIEVAN DEN BERG
EVAN VERILLI
DAN WHITSELL
JOHN ARNAUD
ANUSHA ALAMGIR
KATY BOHURJAK
NATE LAUX

Midwest Modern, scene

Midwest Modern, overall

NEGOTIATIONS

Cincinnati, OH, USA

"Essentially design is nothing else but the encounter with given realities (actualities, situations, circumstances, conditions, or experiences) in terms of their transformative possibilities and potentialities. Design opens up these possibilities through initiating a process of negotiation with the given which extends the boundaries of the previously possible." — Clive Dilnot

For the past fifteen years I have simultaneously practiced and taught architecture. Teaching and practicing for me are inexorably connected—problems in practice are brought into studio settings for further contemplation, and discoveries in the academic environment are continually tested in practice. My interest in bridging the gap between practice and academia began in the late 1980s when I was a student of architecture, comfortably enveloped in the seductive veil of architectural theory and representation that defined many architectural schools at that moment. Discovering the work of Steve Badanes and Jersey Devil, Michael Cadwell, and shortly thereafter Dan Hoffman, had an enormous impact on me. Their work posited an alternative to the detached, academic provocations I was taught and instead embraced construction, craft, and place, as the true content of architecture.

Of particular interest for me was the shift in emphasis from the abstractions of drawing to the constructed fact. In describing his own passion for making, Michael Cadwell lamented the lack of meaning in the conventions of plans, sections, and elevations, as he no longer knew what the abstractions stood for, yearning for what he called "sensual knowledge" that embraces the tactile and the temporal [1]. Much like a musical score or a recipe, an architect's work is primarily abstract and meant to be interpreted by someone else, a unique combination of words, graphics, and numbers used to accurately fix location and relationships of constituent components—"a set of instructions for realizing a building"[2]. Robin Evans, in Translations from Drawings to Buildings, recognizes the distinct problem of representation for architects: that the work of an architect is always through an intervening medium, most often the drawing, while artists and sculptors work directly on their objects.

Jenco Brothers Candy interior

interior

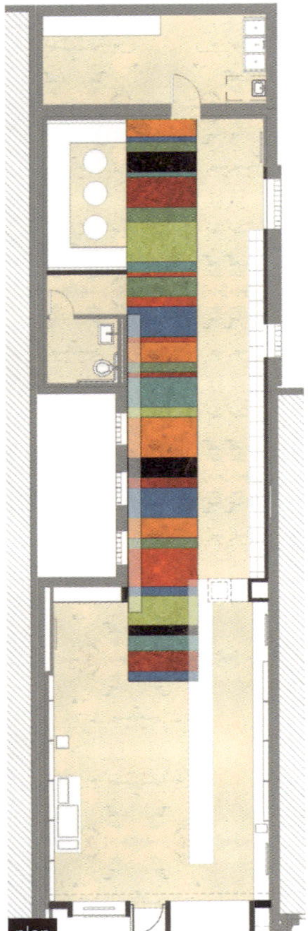

plan

Evans notes that perhaps the real potential of the medium of drawing in architecture is actually in its difference to the thing it is representing rather than in its similarity [3]. The ephemeral qualities of drawing stand in stark contrast with the corporeal properties of the things made. Evans suggests that architects might use the "transitive, communicative properties of the drawing to better effect" [4]. Instead of a one-to-one relationship between drawing and building, new relationships can be constructed that critically interrogate drawing as a generative tool in the process of design. This notion of the expanded role of drawing seems especially clear in the work of Carlo Scarpa, whose drawings were never hollow instructions for making, but mediated between descriptive geometry, perspective, analysis, and technical detail all in the same space, presenting manifold possibilities and readings rather than one fixed and complete representation of an a priori idea [5].

Jenco Brothers Candy

Artichoke

Scarpa's re-working of the conventions of drawing might encourage us to similarly position a way of thinking and constructing that also breaks out of the rigid confines of representation. This might be akin to sketching with material—working at full scale, responding to the conditions, resistances, and tolerances of actual materials, searching for the latent and serendipitous rather than being bound by an abstract set of explicit instructions. Must a constructed architectural artifact always be the material consequence of a pre-determined idea—fixed and delineated by someone and then constructed by someone else—or can the act of making itself be generative, exploiting the dense fertile ground of difference that Evans is implying and that Scarpa demonstrates in his drawings?

exterior strair

column detail

Worthington House

I propose a way of building that uses the transitive power of iterative prototyping to advance the tectonic [6] qualities in the work. This is not simply to say that the architect's direct involvement in the work is any guarantee of success, but to suggest that the gap between the abstraction of drawing and the constructed outcome has been neglected as a source of inspiration and meaning. A robust period of material and assembly explorations, full-scale prototyping, testing for fit on site, all combined with simultaneous refinements and modifications—negotiations—constitute a significant part of a holistic and empathetic design process that has somehow disappeared in the work of many architects.

This is a difficult proposition today, as the days of the master builder are well behind us. Our current academic, professional, and legal constructs make very clear distinctions between intent, which is the architects' charge, and means and methods, which have been disconnected from the architect and have become the responsibility of the builder. The absurdity of this separation is brought to light by Nader Tehrani in the foreword to Michael Cadwell's book *Strange Details*: "How can one not, for instance, differentiate between a cast-in-place concrete wall and a precast one, without simultaneously broaching significant material and philosophical questions? Severing the architect from the means and methods of construction is somewhat like permitting the writer to use a certain vocabulary, but disassociating it from the very alphabet from which the text emerges"[7]. Architecture and building industry, as well as other highly specific offshoots such as construction management, product design and development, and materials science, are now all defined as separate and distinct professions, each having their own education, licensing, and legal ramifications. As a result of these fractures, many architects have been marginalized as image-makers, steadily losing control of the increasingly complex outcomes of the design and construction process.

The bifurcation of idea and its subsequent manifestation in architecture is nothing new. Although the rift between draftsmanship and craftsmanship began during the Renaissance, the digital age has served to make the separation even more pronounced. As digital technologies replace manual ones, it also appears that the interpretive or transitive possibilities in the design process have been diminished completely. Building Information Modeling allows the entire building to be constructed virtually, composed of individual components embedded with information pertaining to their structural properties, performance specifications, and costs. Our ability to virtually define forms and surfaces quickly with multiple-decimal-point accuracy is increasing exponentially, yet our intimate knowledge about materials, construction, and assembly has continued to atrophy. While not longing for a nostalgic return to craft, we must know much more about the behaviors and latent qualities of materials and processes if we intend to orchestrate them—through architecture—in a meaningful and critical manner.

Notes:

[1] Caldwell, Michael. (1996). *Pamphlet 17: Small Buildings*, 4. New York: Princeton Architectural Press.

[2] Allen, Stan. (2009). "Notations + Diagrams: Mapping the Intangible" in *Practice: Architecture, Technique, and Representation*, 41. New York: Routledge. Nelson Goodman's distinction between the allographic and autographic arts is introduced here to explain the unique role of drawing in the making of architecture. The autographic arts are characterized by a direct relationship between author and object, while the allographic primarily involves notation.

[3] Evans, Robin. (1997). *Translations from Drawing to Building*, 154. Cambridge: MIT Press.

[4] Evans, Robin. (1997). *Translations from Drawing to Building*, 160. Cambridge: MIT Press

[5] Frascari, Marco. (1981). "The Tell the Tale Detail" in *Via 7: 30*. Philadelphia: University of Pennsylvania.

[6] Sekler, Eduard F. (1965). "Structure, Construction, Tectonics" in *Structure in Art and in Science*, ed. G. Keppes, 89. New York: George Brazziler. The word tectonic here refers to Sekler's definition as what "... cannot be described by construction and structure alone. For these qualities, which are expressive of a relation of form to force, the term tectonic should be reserved," as distinguished from a Semperian understanding of tectonics as pertaining exclusively to the frame and lightweight linear construction.

[7] Tehrani, Nader. (2007). "A Murder in the Court" in *Strange Details* by Michael Cadwell, vii-xi. Cambridge: MIT Press.

Photography Credits / **TONY WALSH**

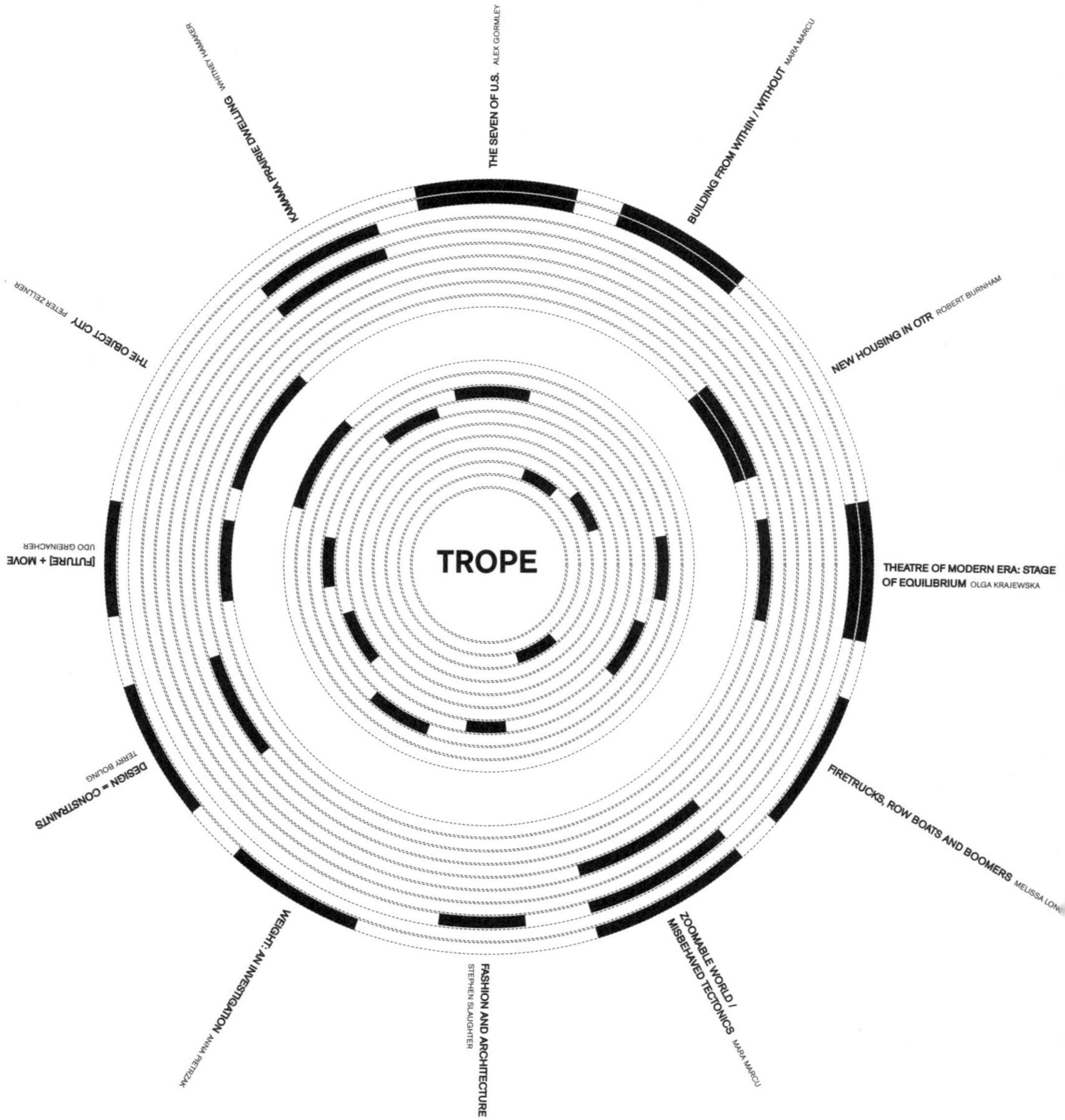

LEGEND:

1. OUTER SECTOR = ID
2. INNER SECTOR = LEVEL
3. WIDTH = SCALE

1. *From Outer Ring to Inner Ring:*
Design Thinking
History/Theory
Material Investigation
Branding
Design Build
Digital Craft
Computational Design
Fabrication
Sustainability
Public Interest

2. *From Outer Ring to Inner Ring:*
Professional
PhD
Graduate 3rd Year
Graduate 2nd Year
Graduate 1st Year
Undergraduate 5th Year
Undergraduate 4th Year
Undergraduate 3rd Year
Undergraduate 2nd Year
Undergraduate 1st Year

3. *Width of Black Poché:*
Scaleless
Object
Furniture
Body
Room
Building
Cluster/Complex
City/Region

TROPE

There are no tropes in building.

I have never heard a building speak. I have never read a building. It is very easy for architects and architecture critics to slip into the use of literary tropes to try to describe the elements of their creations, but it is wrong. Architecture is not a language. It is a three-dimensional representation that also shelters human activities and creates a framework in and through which we can enact our relations to each other and the world around us. It is not a book. It is mute.

There is, of course, a long tradition of architects trying to adopt aspects of language in their work. The most obvious of these are the attempts to create an "architecture parlante," in which the use of metaphors, similes, and even direct references would somehow give architecture a voice. At times, architects have even tried t make their buildings look like or have aspects of books; th most notable example is Henri Labrouste's Bibliotheque S Genevieve (1850), which is not only an extended metaph for the history of books, but also clads itself in images of such artifacts and writing.

Others have tried to develop a "grammar" or even a "language" of architecture. Owen Jones' 1856 attempt to create a lexicon of ornamental motifs and their possible combinations was actually more indexical than it was literary, but Charles Jencks' 1977 argument that architecture was a form of communication that should wo harder to have itself understood correctly by a variety of users and viewers (or readers) certainly marked the high point in the articulation of this argument. Peter Eisenman's willful misinterpretations during the 1980s and 1990s of techniques of deconstruction in literature through the application of its techniques to buildings might mark the low point of this self-destructive tendency, in which buildings try to bury themselves in external tropes.

TROPE

Aaron Betsky

Aaron Betsky is a critic and author of more than a dozen books on art, architecture, and design. Trained at Yale, Betsky has worked as a designer for Frank O. Gehry & Associates and Hodgetts + Fung, taught at SCI-Arc, and served as the director of the 11th Venice International Architecture Biennale. Previously Professor at the University of Cincinnati SAID, he is currently Dean at the School of Architecture at Taliesin.

I would note here that I purposefully confuse makers and interpreters. You could make an argument that tropes are not inherent to buildings, but appear in interpretations of buildings occurring in a culture in which the production of meaning occurs almost exclusively on a literary base. The notion that there might be a visually-based knowledge that could offer an alternative structure of representation is one difficult to argue without having recourse to this word-based toolbox. The making of architecture, as opposed to buildings, is, after all, an attempt to do something with the act of buildings or built facts that communicates or represents the material facts of shelter, enclosure, and framing through drawings, facades, or interpretations. It is meta-building, not a metaphor.

This is where tropes sneak in. It is the critics and viewers who create tropes in architecture. As they attempt to infuse the dead and mute matter out of which we construct our buildings with the life of architecture—as I am doing now—they almost inevitably have recourse to the full array of metaphors, allegories, metonyms, synecdoches, and even oxymorons, to name but a few of the possibilities tropes offer, in order to make buildings speak.

But, buildings don't speak. Architects, architecture critics, and the machinery they lay over buildings do. Architecture lies like a veil over buildings, coloring, obscuring, and intimating at its forms. Lift that veil, and you will find a corpse, not an orating actor.

You find a rise in the ground, two meters long and one meter wide, heaped up in a rough pyramid shape, then you turn serious, and something inside you says: someone lies buried here. That is architecture.
—Adolf Loos

RYAN BALL
KIM BURKE
BLAKE LANE
MARA MARCU (coordinator)
RENEE MARTIN
MEGHAN MINTON
JOHN STOUGHTON
MELANIE SWICK

BUILDING FROM WITHIN / WITHOUT

Undergraduate Second Year Architecture and Interior Design
Cincinnati, OH, USA

***Building from Within / Building from Without* offers, as resolution to the inside/outside dichotomy, a third condition: the state of being hidden. The latent disclosure of what connects the unapologetically transparent to the purely opaque demands spatial secrecy and utmost discretion. The Secret Room silently guides the pilgrim through what would be an otherwise indecipherable, impossible and impenetrable labyrinthine construct.**

We start from the very small elements of architecture—the ones situated in the immediate vicinity of the body—and use the hand as a lens for our discovery. We then use the body as a means to understand medium elements that surround the body and are partially accessible to the hand. Last we arrive at larger architectural elements that connect bodies together and house communities.

In this way, we make a transition from the composition-oriented foundation studios and anticipate the extra-large elements of architecture that structure urban settings. The first two exercises serve as collective research towards the third and final exercise.

Design problems are taught by means of anomalies while employing spatial grammar [bend, skew, expand, extrude, merge, yield, twist, interlock, lift, carve, fracture, shear, embed, puncture] in order to build the narrative.

Sampling becomes the tool used to negotiate between unique site conditions and their implicit constraints. Close attention is paid to apertures with their implied, yet absent, volumes that become part of the fluid circulatory device. While isolating specific variables in the design process, questions are approached with myriad external information at the detriment of having no internal knowledge. Consequently, the lens of discovery shifts from visible analogies and opens up possibilities of endless spatial permutations.

RIFFLE
Copy and Paste study by Maggie Ming
Canonical Architecture:
Ford House by Bruce Goff
Key Verbs:
Scale, Intersect

SHIQI MING / matted plan

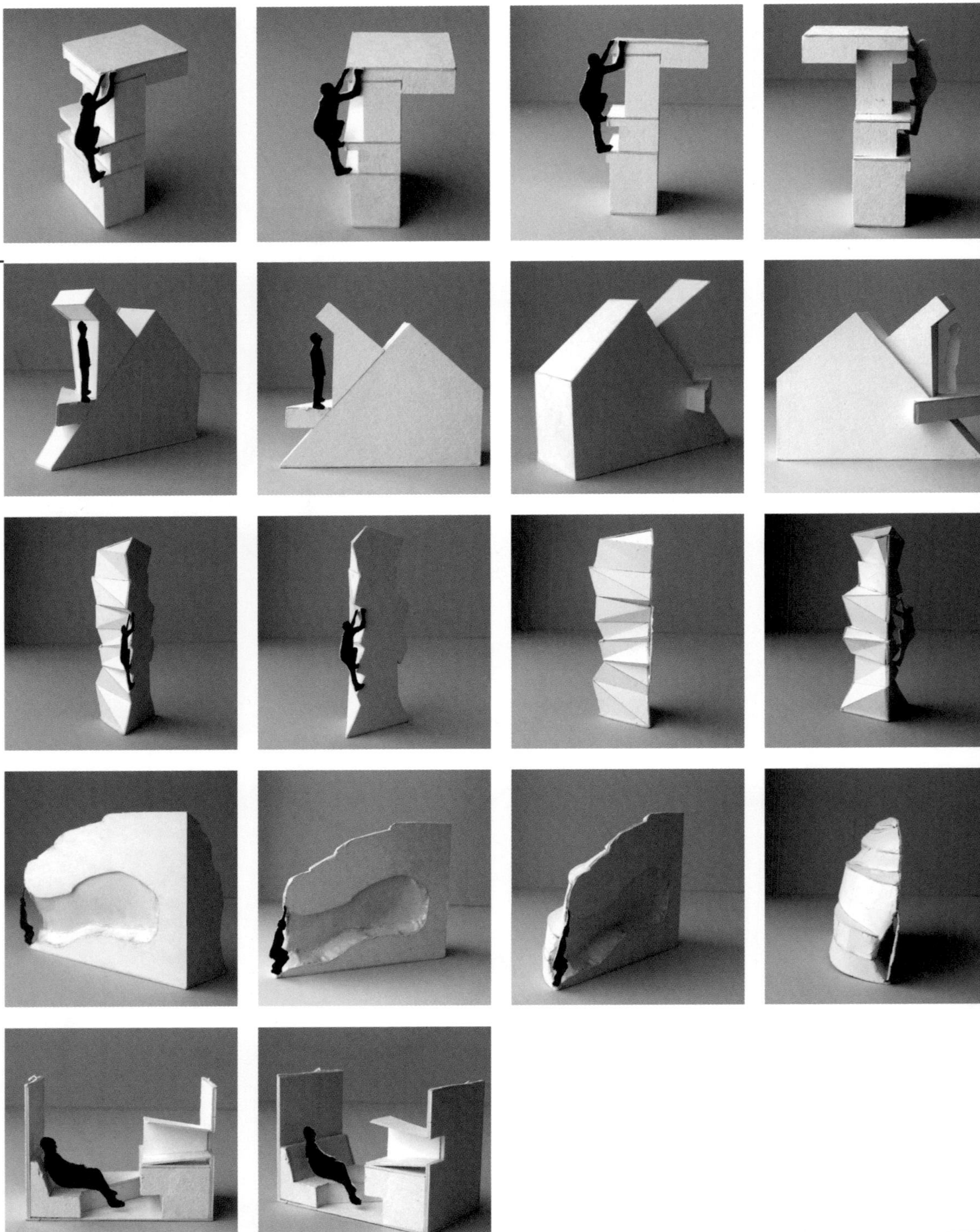

KYLE CANTRELL / Intimate Modulor Permutation

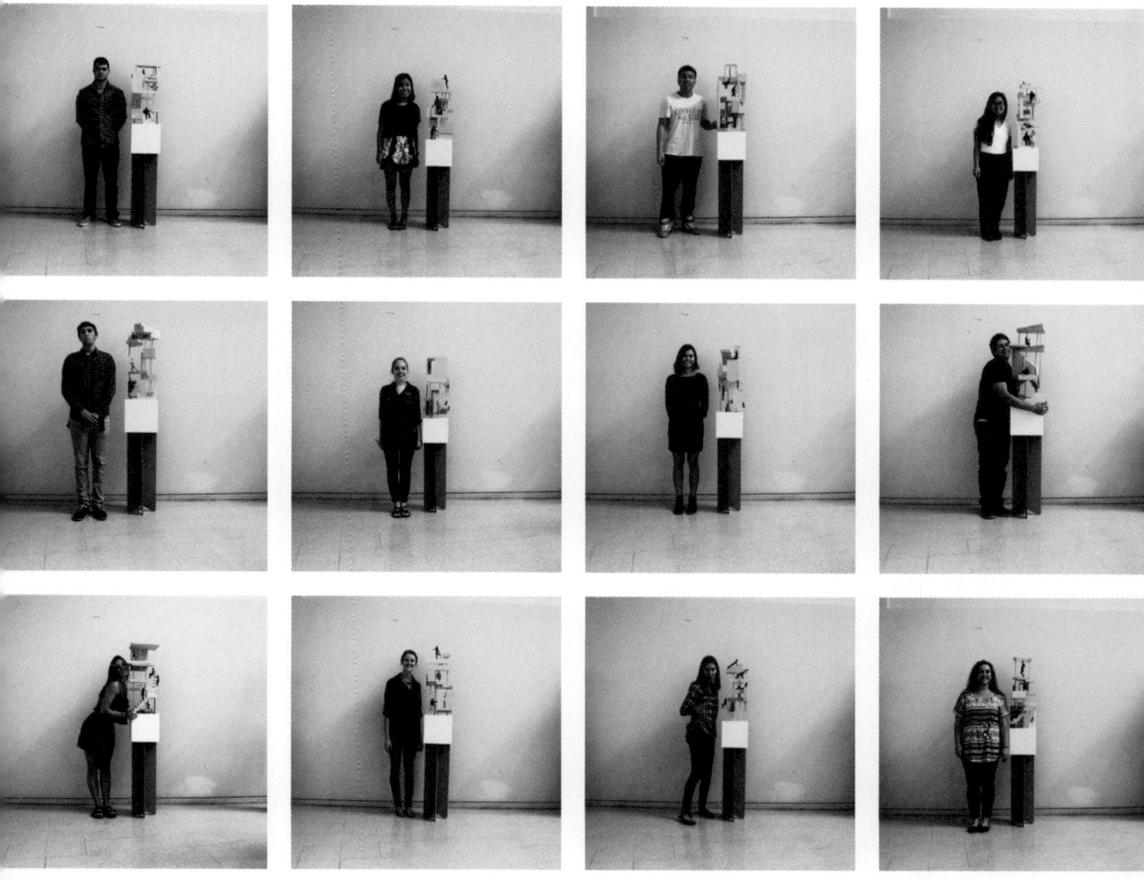

ANALISA BIXLER, MATTHEW BRUBAKER, SHUYANG CHEN, ANGELO DEBLASE, ABIGAIL GOLDEN, ELEANOR GREEN, LOGAN HALTERMAN, KIMBERLY KACHMAR, TRANG LE, MOLLY LOFTSPRING, EMILY LOOMIS, SEAN MCDERMOTT, ANTHONY MILANO, JACQUELINE REQUEIMA, CLAIRE WETTA, XINFANG ZANG / Intimate Modulor, students stand along side models designed to their own body proportions.

longitudinal section

typical plan

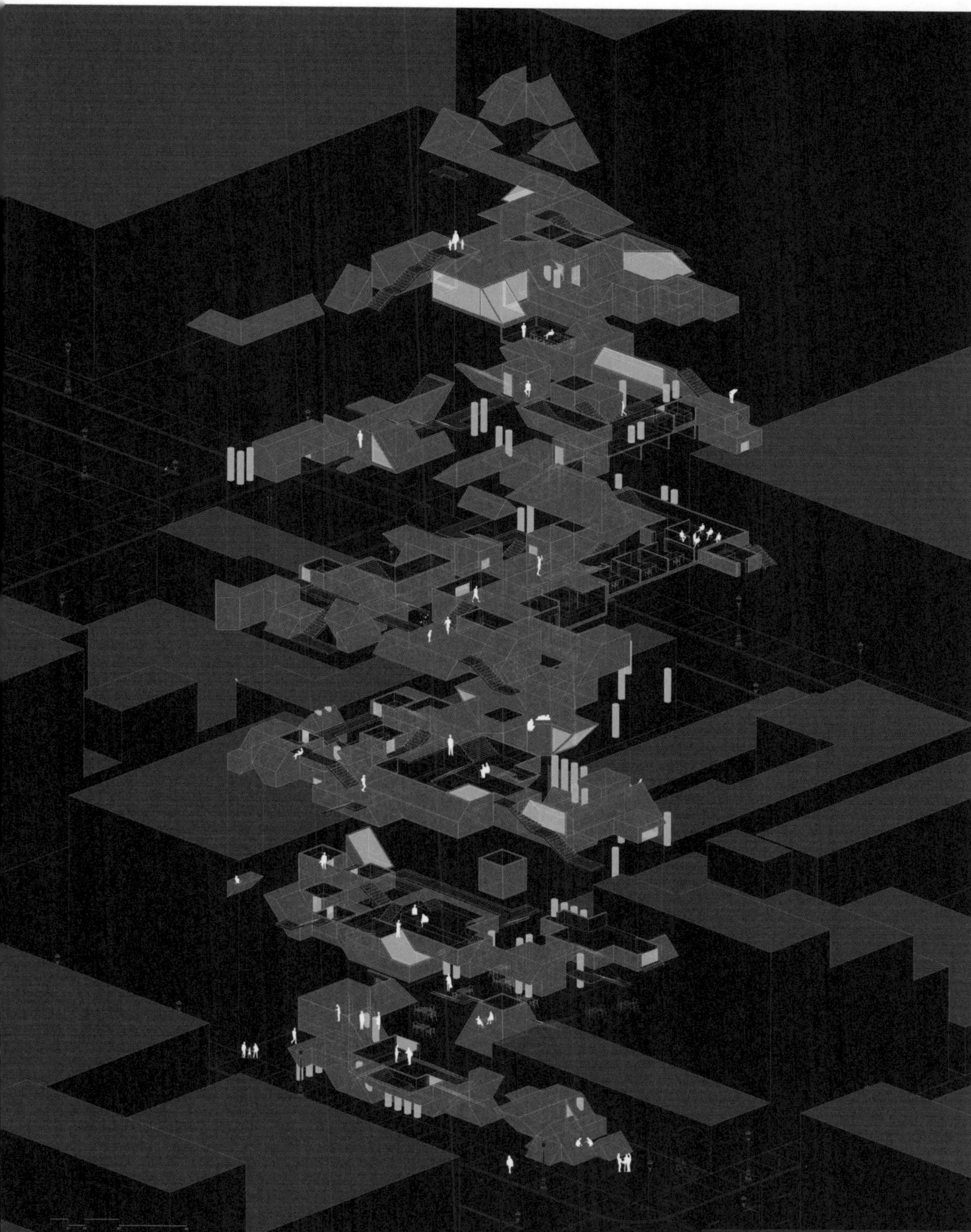
EDWARD SIMPSON / exploded axon

JACOB GIANNI / exterior perspective, rendering

CHEN LUDAN / exterior perspective

top view

detail

CHEN LUDAN / 3d printed model

perspective

PROF. RYAN BALL / Intimate Modulor

RYAN BALL
ROBERT BURNHAM (coordinator)
BLAKE LANE
RENEE MARTIN (text author)
STEPHEN SLAUGHTER

NEW HOUSING FOR OTR

Undergraduate Third Year Architecture
Site Integration
Cincinnati, OH, USA

Jean-Philippe Vassal defines *luxurious* housing as "something between generosity and simplicity that we perceive in both their economy of means and their *mise en scène*." In *Plus* (Gustavo Gili, 2007), Vassal, Frédéric Druot, and Anne Lacaton insist that public housing can, and should, provide more "more light, more fluidity in the interiors, more rapport between interior and exterior, more complexity in the boundaries between each of the functions of the flat." The studio project *New Housing for OtR* advocates the position of luxury as the fabrication of something extra from conflict and constraint.

The project site at 1907 Vine Street in Cincinnati is a wedge created by a five-way intersection and a 16-foot change in topography from one street front to the other. The southeast side is decisively pedestrian and a destination; it overlooks the proposed extension of the new streetcar line, a low-density industrial district destined to become part of the regrown brewery tradition, and the local treasure Findlay Market. The northwest faces a high-traffic corridor between uptown and downtown.

Over the Rhine (OtR)—the district stretching south of 1907 Vine—has been designated the largest and most intact historic district in the United States. Due to land banking and strategic clump investment by the city development corporation, OtR has seen a steady acceleration of rehabilitation and gentrification. Redevelopment has been creeping north, particularly along Vine Street—the primary thoroughfare between the central business district to the south and the university to the north. 1907 Vine has yet to turn over, and it is unclear when it will; it is at the northernmost border of the dense urban center, beyond which is a landscape of parks, unbuildable slopes, low-density housing, and the university campus.

When luxury is defined as generous design, it becomes both more personal and more universal. Housing production can happen up close, starting and ending with human concerns. The architect can extract from iconography, topography, and regulation the most basic comforts.

BEN BLAKE / internal perspectives

physical model

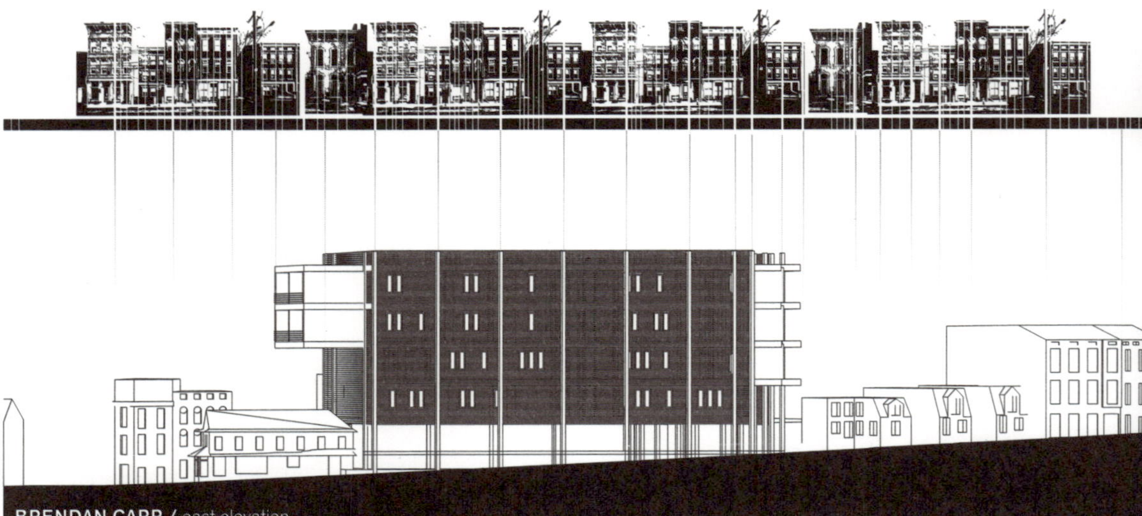

BRENDAN CARR / east elevation

DANIEL SMITH / exterior perspectives

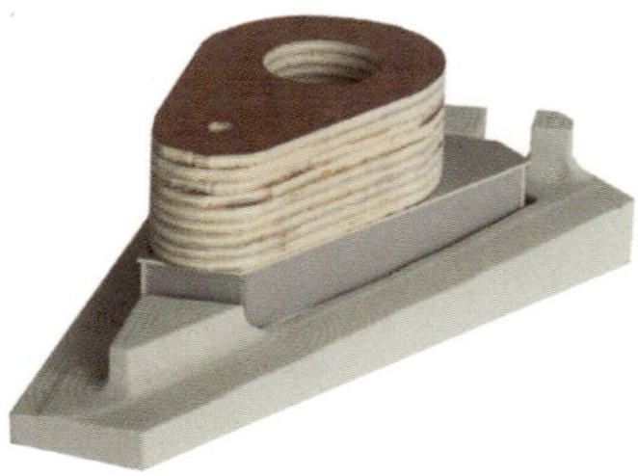

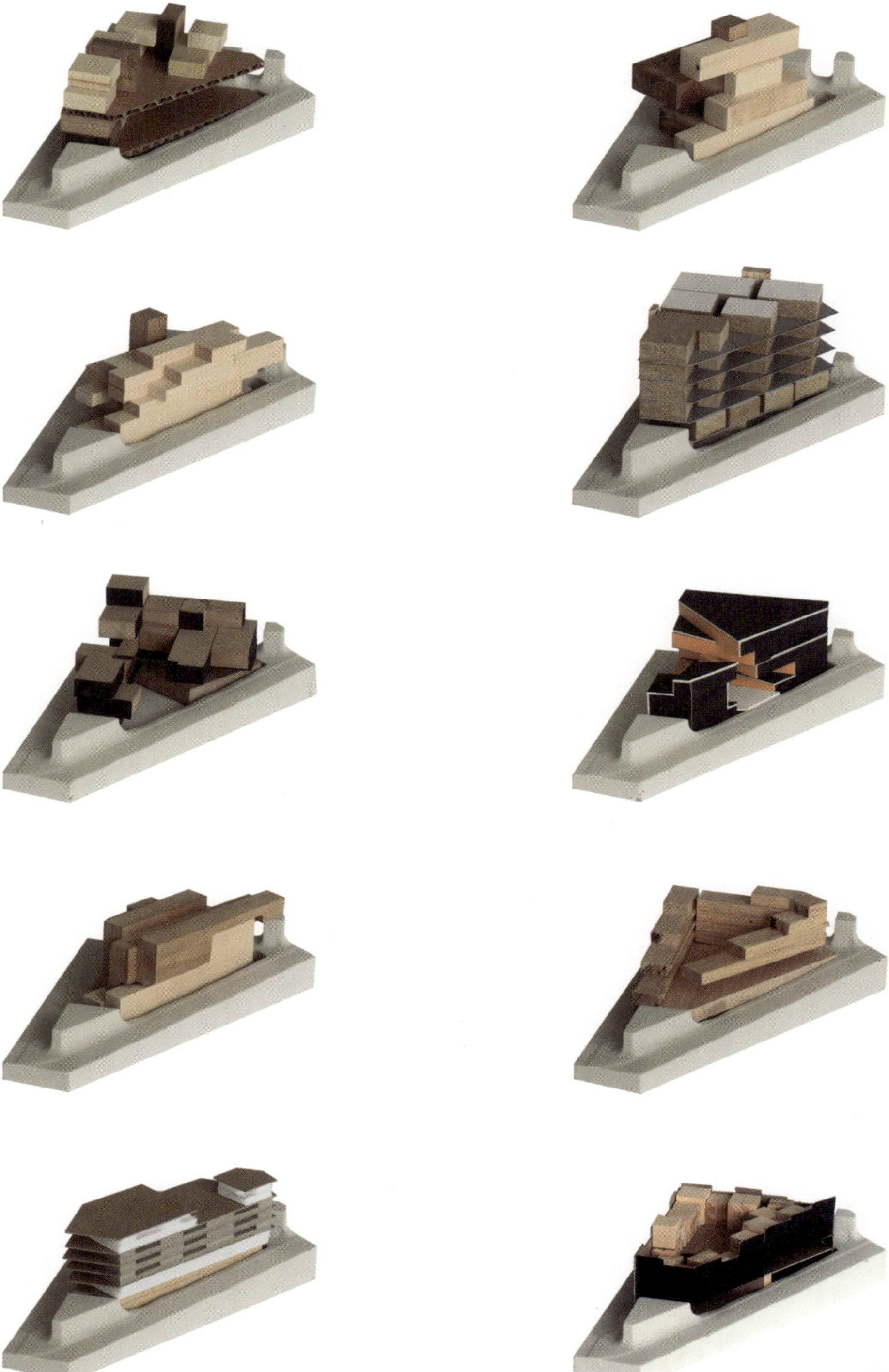

initial diagram models

OLGA KRAJEWSKA
VINCENT SANSALONE (chair)
UDO GREINACHER (member)

THEATER OF MODERN ERA: STAGE OF EQUILIBRIUM

Master of Architecture Thesis
Cincinnati, Ohio, USA

Although the United States is one of the most integrated and homogeneous countries, the majority of the American population is incredibly diverse. Generations of European immigrants are deprived of the opportunities to understand the historical implications of their heritage.

This thesis attempts to preserve and accept the conventional past as a wondrous spectacle and portrayal of architectural translation, which was embedded within the significant historical events from the time period 1914 to1945. The intention of the first stage, titled *Design in the DNA*, is to structure gathered data, generated from decoded DNA chemical compositions, in the form of an interactive analytical network or map of individual heritage streams, introducing, in this way, the second design stage of memory development. The thesis is committed to addressing the emotional representation of memory as categorized by crucial historical events. A sense of temporality, death, fear, faith, regret, and ultimately hope, shape the individual pathways of a theater museum in which the play's narrative, represented by five decisive moments in time, provide intimacy while simultaneously evoking a feeling of belonging to society as opposed to past generations. Sensorial design plays a crucial role in creating an interaction between user and architecture through memory. This renegotiates the relationship between space and time through a physical translation of historical events.

The exploration of the building is related to each user's personal history. Spaces are designed in accordance to the Ancestry.com database. As such, the journey begins with mapping the personal ancestry history, going as far back, and possibly beyond, to the two world wars. The architectural solution for choreographing thousands of personal stories is a system of bridges furrowing above major public spaces that are linked to primary historical and sociological events. This exploration pattern is adjusted to the percentage of war participants, civilians, war survivors, deceased, and immigrants. The pathway represents the telling of a story and is constructed through a sequence of sensual corresponding sections.

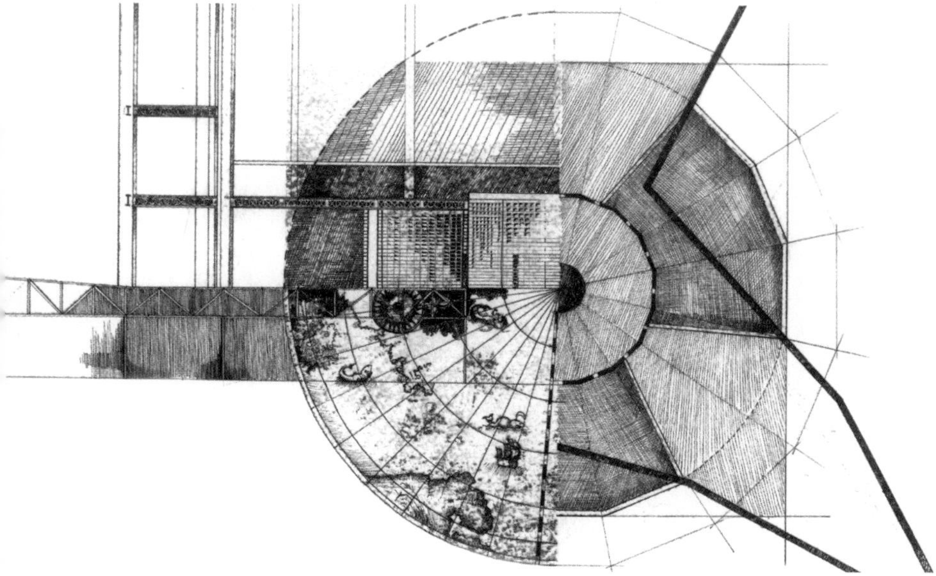

lower level floor plan

OLGA KRAJEWSKA / upper level floor plan

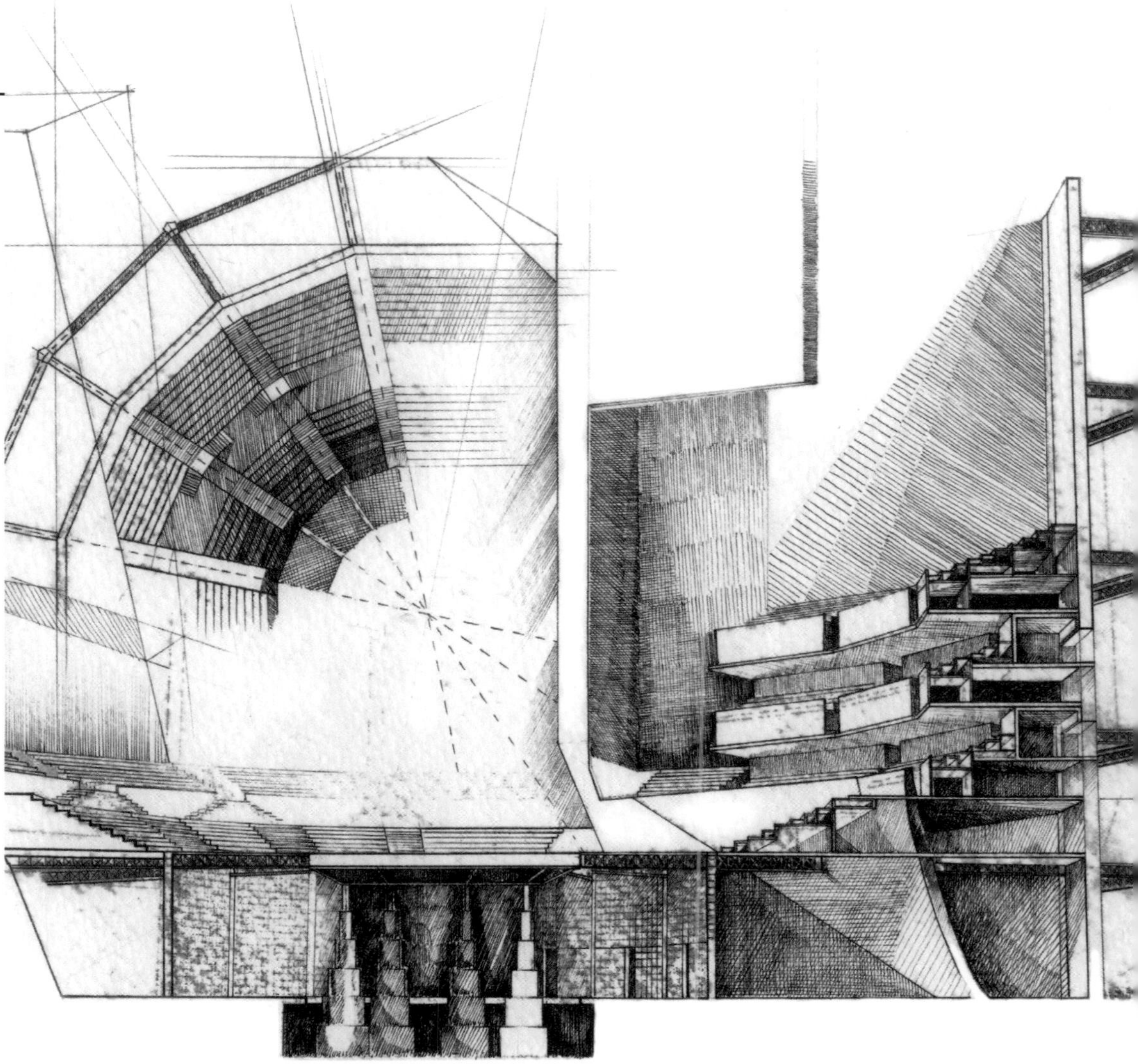

OLGA KRAJEWSKA / section perspective

section perspective

MELISSA LONG

FIRETRUCKS, ROW BOATS AND BOOMERS

For my co-op at Studio Gang, from August 2014 through January 2015, I worked on a team of four people on a fire rescue facility in Brooklyn. The office is based out of Chicago but they recently opened an office in New York, as there were many small projects coming up in the city. Studio Gang was selected for a short list of firms that were pre-certified to do public projects in the city. New York City is investing in its public service infrastructure, fire rescue facilities, police stations, etc., and there is much to be said that city officials are partnering with high end design companies to execute these projects.

My team was international. I worked with designers from Montreal, Spain, and Magda, a colleague the University of Cincinnati who is originally from Poland. The project was moving from schematic design into design development while the office was transitioning into using Revit. No one on the team knew the program, myself included. I took a Revit course at UC but had never worked with it professionally. Being the intern on the team, I had the most time to explore, so I took on the role of Revit lead. Everyone was learning together how to translate the project from AutoCAD into Revit.

During the design development phase, we designed many details and joints and chose materials. The structure was prefabricated structural concrete panels that helped with construction time and costs. The concept behind the building was the training apparatus: to become a member of the fire rescue squad, the most elite firemen must be trained at the facility we designed.

For the project, we designed what we commonly referred to as portals—terracotta openings in the prefabricated concrete—based on openings in training towers that trainees were currently using. We designed a structure within the building that they could train on. I learned great deal about truck types and the type of training equipment needed for fire rescue. The entire program required very specific technology not commonly known.

It was great being able to see some of Studio Gang's other projects. The firm had just finished the Kalamazoo Center for Social Justice in Michigan. The whole office went out for the opening. The building was very small and highly diagrammatic. They used a local vernacular facade technique of stacked wood logs. With the building being about

social justice, the program helped promote awareness and brought community together.

While I spent a lot of time in the office, we went rowing regularly. Studio Gang designed a publicly funded boat house for students in the Chicago Public Schools system. Whereas other boat houses were for rowing teams, this project was intended to engage kids in middle and high school. The kids took us out rowing. Four of us went out, and a group of high school and middle school kids showed us how to lift up long boats and put them out in Bubbly Creek. It was really cool to see the level of engagement these kids had. They were way more together and professional and outgoing than I was at that age.

We also worked on a competition designing for the retiring baby boomer population. We were challenged to address aging icons and our aging population, considering an adaptive reuse concept of the Empire State Building and, incorporating human, social and cultural aspects. It was good to start thinking about human interaction within these constraints.

Studio Gang taught me how to let go of ideas. We would have four hour meetings where we would sit and talk through ideas, and you could never be married to something. Working as a team you had to let go of ideas and concepts pretty easily and build on and off of the next person's idea. Studio Gang also has a strong emphasis on human interaction and the human experience in space. There was a huge push to think about how materials relate to the human experience.

It is great being surrounded by people who have different backgrounds and education than you. You learn from them and then try to apply those lessons in different ways. When I left Studio Gang at the end of my co-op, I said "Guys, I can't wait to go back to school after being through all this!" They laughed at me and replied, "Yeah she meant it just like that!"

RYAN BALL
SEAN CUNNINGHAM
WHITNEY HAMAKER
MARA MARCU (coordinator)
RENEE MARTIN
STEPHEN SLAUGHTER

ZOOMABLE WORLD / MISBEHAVED TECTONICS

Undergraduate Second Year Architecture
Tectonic Systems
Cincinnati, OH, USA

One of the most widespread theoretical techniques, thirding, follows the dialectical formula of thesis-anti-thesis – synthesis [1]. While combining advantages and disadvantages of seeming opposites, *Zoomable World / Misbehaved Tectonics* proposes through a highly iterative fabrication process, a reinvention of classical tectonic systems.

Departing from the tectonic categorization set forth by Farshid Moussavi in *The Function of Form*, students were tasked with rebuilding and digitally remodeling each system while engaging of six different media with their implicit ways of making [2]. They included: textile architecture, casting/hybrid analogues, 3d printing, vacuum forming, paper folding, and CNC routing. Students were asked to speculate on how constructing methodologies mutate the chosen precedent function of a sequential process. Through misuse and appropriation inherent to each of the fabrication processes new structural hybrids have emerged. In addition, each student arrived at a personal catalog of tectonic possibilities.

Exploring plastic dynamism as "a significant evolution of the rectilinear formal language of MAT into a more open-ended universe of form making", students considered intrinsic (site related) and extrinsic (program related) parameters [3]. This led to concepts such as misbehaved world and zoomable tectonics that emphasized cross-programming strategies and alluded to unique quasi-functional arrangements.

The resulting grid of artifacts, exhibited with 3CDC – a leading real estate developer in the area, is a commentary to the current state and future possibilities of tectonic manifestations. The process as product questions the use of the computer as tool and proposed a re-crafting of architecture as a starting point for the post-digital practice.

Notes:

[1] Schumacher, P. (2011). *The Autopoiesis of Architecture: A New Framework for Architecture.* Vol. I. Wiley, United Kingdom.
[2] Moussavi, F. (2009). *The Function of Form.* Actar, Barcelona, Spain.
[3] MacDonald, J. (2009). "Reticulated Form: United States Air Force Academy". *GSD Platform 2*, edited by Felipe Correa. Actar, Barcelona, Spain.

SAM KISSING / precedent: parallel tensile membrane

TOM SAVOCA / precedent: hyper-curved shell

hybrid 3d printed section models

SHINJI MIYAJIMA / sections

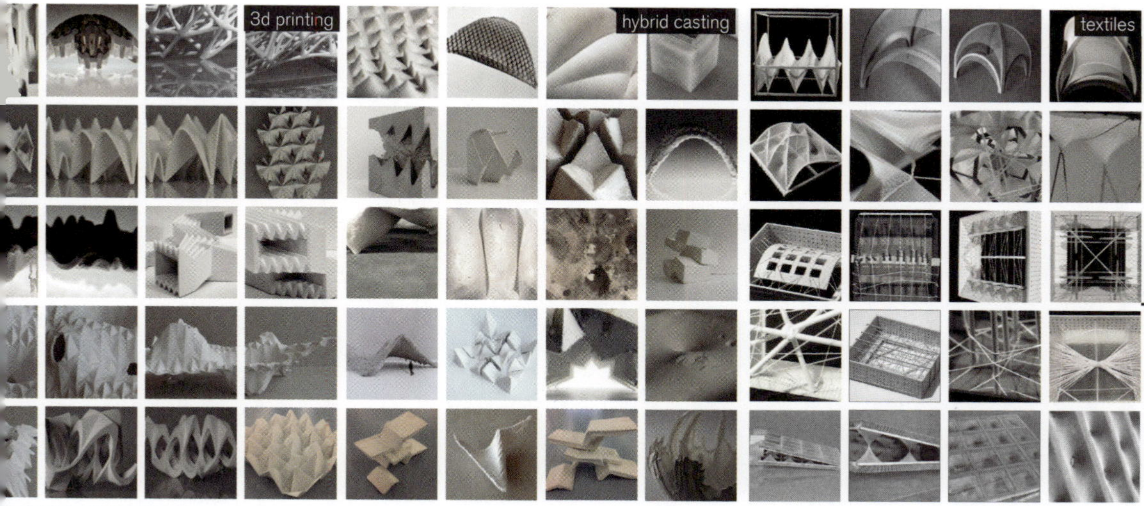
3d printing
hybrid casting
textiles

SHINJI MIYAJIMA / precedent: high-low tensile membrane

STEPHEN SLAUGHTER
HANNA HALL
INJOO KIM
ZACHARY HOH
ASHLEY NEWSOME KUBLEY

FASHION & ARCHITECTURE

Graduate Independent Study
Cincinnati, OH, USA

Anna Pettinga and Rebecca Wood, two enterprising M.Arch thesis students interested in exploring the dialogue between architecture and fashion, initiated the idea for a cross disciplinary partnership that evolved into a seminar where students from graphic and fashion, as well as architecture and interior design, work together to conceive and produce a collection of garments representative of the disciplinary synthesis. The idea was to establish a forum where the methodology, theory, and technique of fashion and architecture could be examined, debated, and through the process of design and fabrication, realized through a body of work informed by the discussion. Over the term, the students were given instruction in sewing and pattern making from Zachary Hoh, who shepherded the process from the standpoint of fashion design and fabrication. As a means of managing scope and expectations, he limited the students to designing a dress, blouse, skirt, or accessory. And to initiate the process, terms shared between the two disciplines (i.e.: layer, striation, pattern, and opacity) were used as prompts.

The students began the design process by assembling a mood board, or collection of images that engaged and expanded on the definition of shared terms within fashion and architecture. The images gave material, formal and conceptual inspiration from which the students were then to sketch no less the twenty "looks" that responded to the edited images. In correlation to designing, the seminar used two seminal contemporary texts on the subject: *Architecture: In Fashion*, a collection of essays edited by Paulette Singley; and the publication *(Parallel Practices in Fashion and Architecture)* for the *SKIN + BONES* exhibition at the Museum of Contemporary Art, Los Angeles to help synthesize the relationship between contemporary architectural theory and prevailing fashion trends.

Discussions propagating from the readings and sketches commenced, and once the group settled on what forms, details, and concepts the collection would observe, each student went about finalizing their design by making patterns for muslin mockups, and eventually fashioning their final garment. The aim of the endeavor was to review the final collection in a context that would allow the work to be evaluated relative to prevailing fashion and market trends. The initial ambition was to either have a private showing, runway review, or photo shoot, but given the consistency and quality of the work, both 2015 and 2016 collections were given a slot in the marquee event co-hosted by Macy's and the University of Cincinnati, the DAAP Fashion Show.

MADELINE TOTH

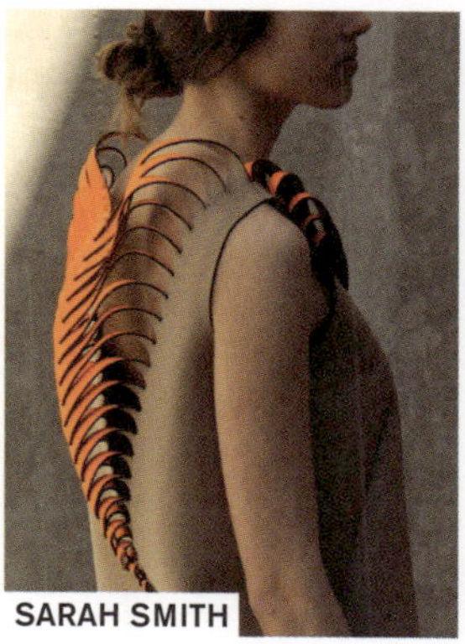

SARAH SMITH

BRIAN KIM

REBECCA WOOD

ANJALI PATEL

ANNA PIETRZAK
AARATI KANEKAR, PH.D. (chair)
MICHAEL MCINTURF (member)

WEIGHT: AN INVESTIGATION

Master of Architecture Thesis
Cincinnati, OH, USA

The thesis examines how the weight of architectural form might be used to convey the perception of lightness. It argues that weight is an integral component to all compositions and an essential subject within the discourse of architecture (for which it currently has little presence). It may even convince the reader that weight and architecture are inseparable, but argues that architecture aspires towards lightness. Examples from other disciplines such as art and literary sources compliment this basic research.

The project examines the tensions and paradoxes that can be created to achieve lightness. Though weight, or heaviness, is an intrinsic property of material and influences tectonic expression, its dynamic expression produces its opposite–lightness in architecture. Lightness should not be used interchangeably with weightlessness (the annihilation of weight). Two simple structural systems– the post and lintel and the arch–have historically been used in buildings to express lightness. These common static and other more dynamic systems share common themes.

A building dissipates its heaviness not unlike the way a dancer or gymnast negotiates their own body in order to appear light. Observations on the body shift the focus of the document to more specific precedents. Conjectures are made on how dance, specifically in the act of balancing, might also inform the design of built space. The study of the human form in balancing acts is essential to this thesis and informs the design of a Cirque du Soleil performance and training facility at the former Pruitt-Igoe site in St. Louis.

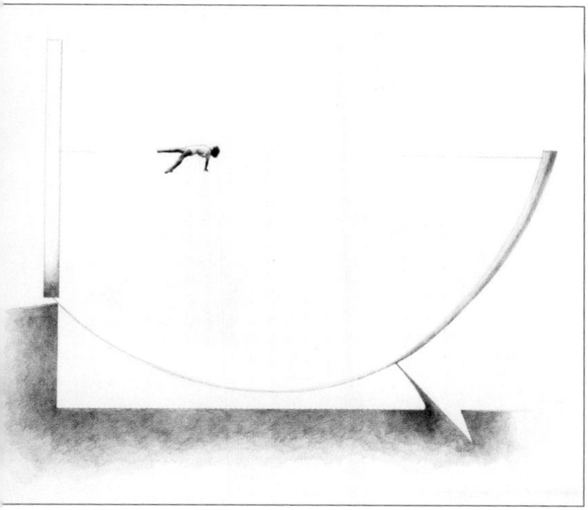

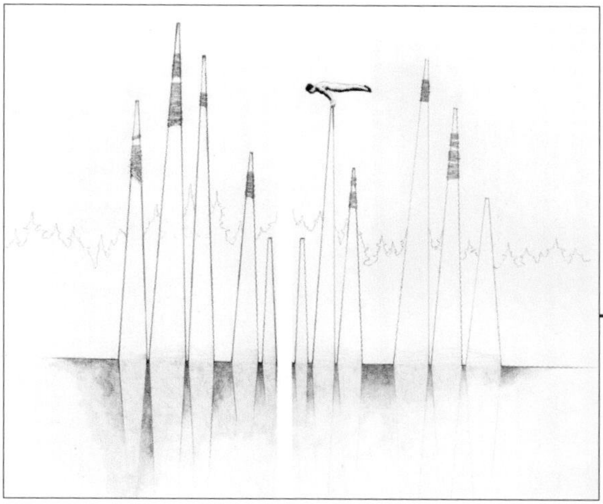

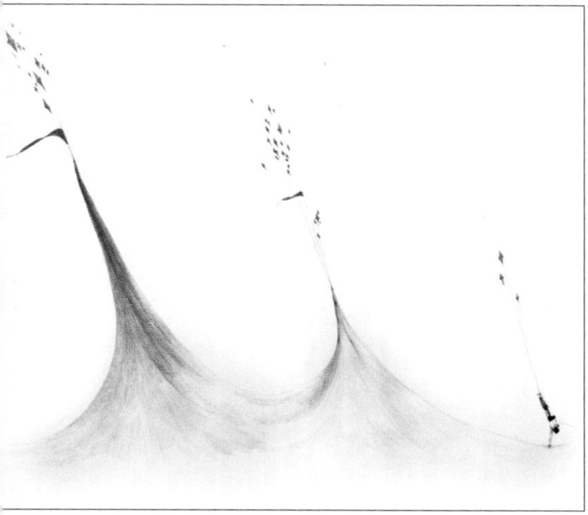

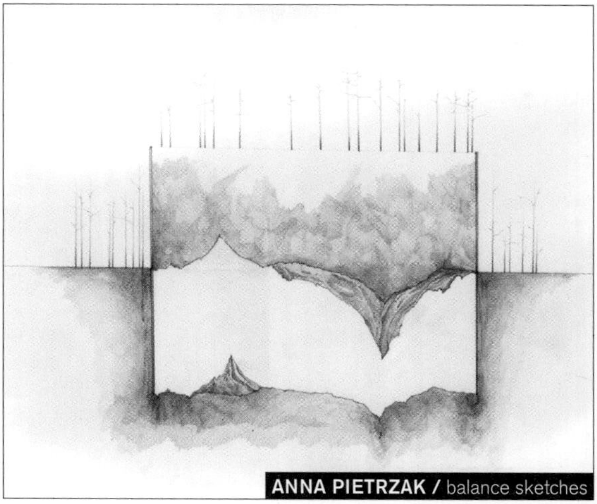

ANNA PIETRZAK / balance sketches

frames

ANNA PIETRZAK / exterior rendering

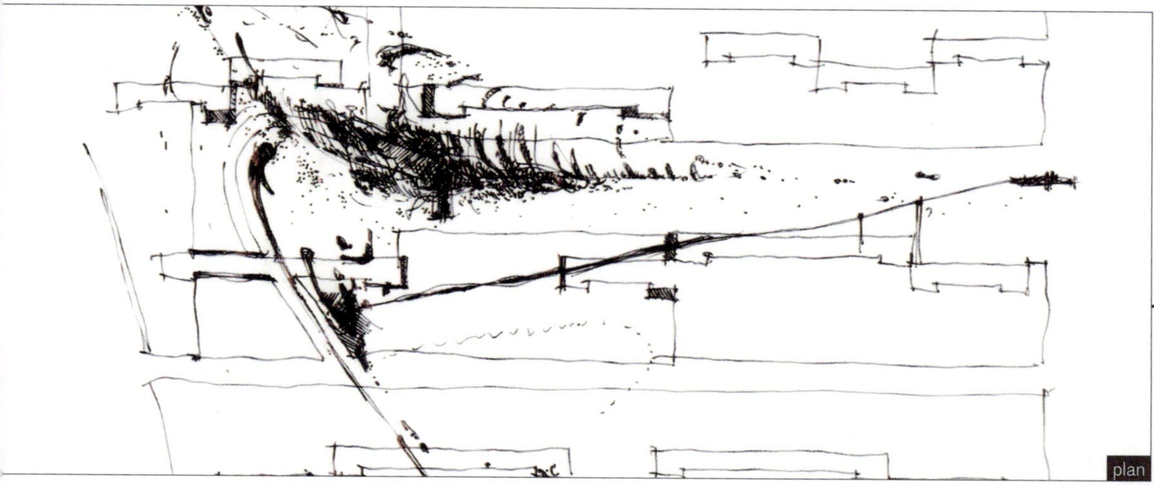

plan

exterior rendering

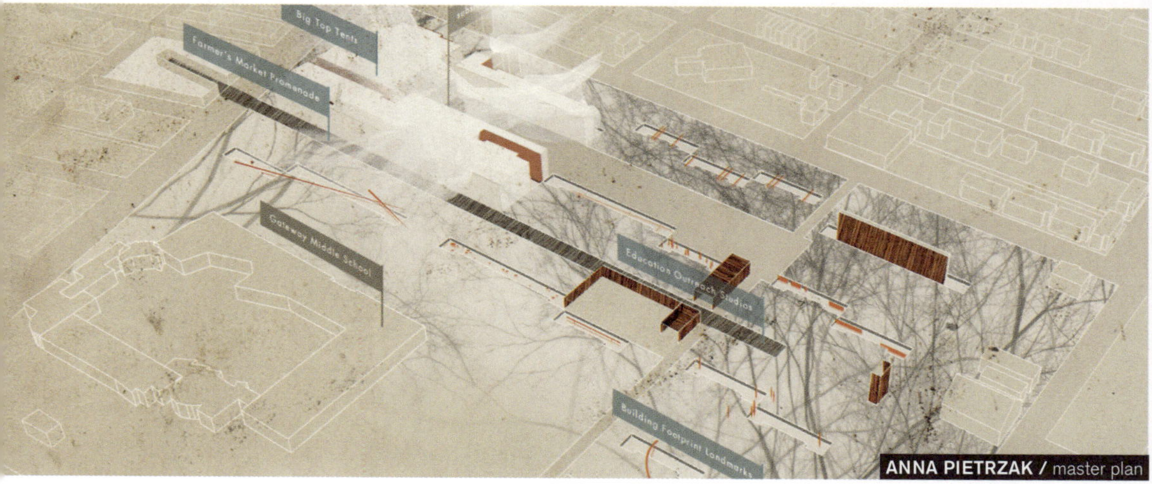

ANNA PIETRZAK / master plan

TOM BIBLE
TERRY BOLING (coordinator)
JIM POSTELL
MICHAEL ZARETSKY

DESIGN = CONSTRAINTS

Master of Architecture Comprehensive Design Studio
Columbus, IN, USA

In a period of architectural production giddy with the euphoria of computer generated form, the messy facts of construction—weight, material, weather, touch, and smell—have been supplanted by clean virtuality. Especially true in American architectural education, details are simply a means to an end, and in most cases, are simply technical solutions to problems of form. The studio took aim at this dilemma with techniques that turn constraints into opportunities. As Charles Eames so clearly articulated in his interview with Madame L'Amic for the 1972 exhibition *What is Design?*:

"Here is one of the few effective keys to the Design problem: the ability of the Designer to recognize as many of the constraints as possible; his willingness and enthusiasm for working within these constraints. Constraints of price, of size, of strength, of balance, of surface, of time, and so forth."

The intent of the studio was to join the practical with the poetic through the development of engaged architectural research, an understanding of the practical forces at work on and within architecture, and an awareness and comprehension of multiple-scale design strategies. The ethos of the studio was rooted in the development of a "construction ethic," an attitude about instrumentalizing the materials, techniques, and processes of construction. Deep investigations into specific moments of the project were encouraged in contrast to a broad, superficial comprehension of all parts.Initial exercises were paired with focused lectures addressing the categories of environment, structure and space, building envelope, and detail and material, corresponding to scales of the landscape, the body, and the hand. These exercises were intended to facilitate a generative, constructive thinking rooted in the instrumental use of design research, and intended to engage strategies at multiple scales of design inquiry, equipping students with a series of drawn and constructed design fragments—fragments with potential for siting, inhabitation, and construction.

The remaining half of the semester was spent developing—in great detail—a project that demonstrated a facility with the constituent components that make up an architectural project: the integration of structure, environment, and construction. The students were responsible not for simply demonstrating solutions to problems of form, but rather, for designing the experience of the building through the careful selection and deployment of space and structure, environmental and technical infrastructure, and material assemblies and components.

LUIS SABATER/ section perspective

models

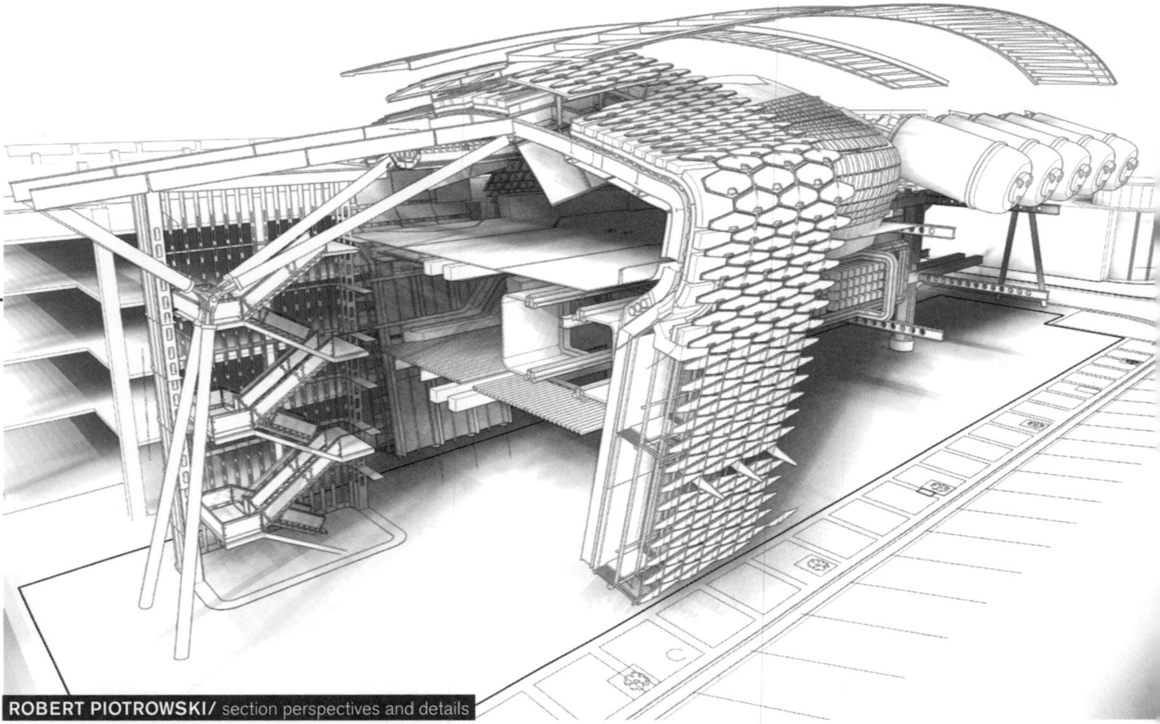

ROBERT PIOTROWSKI/ section perspectives and details

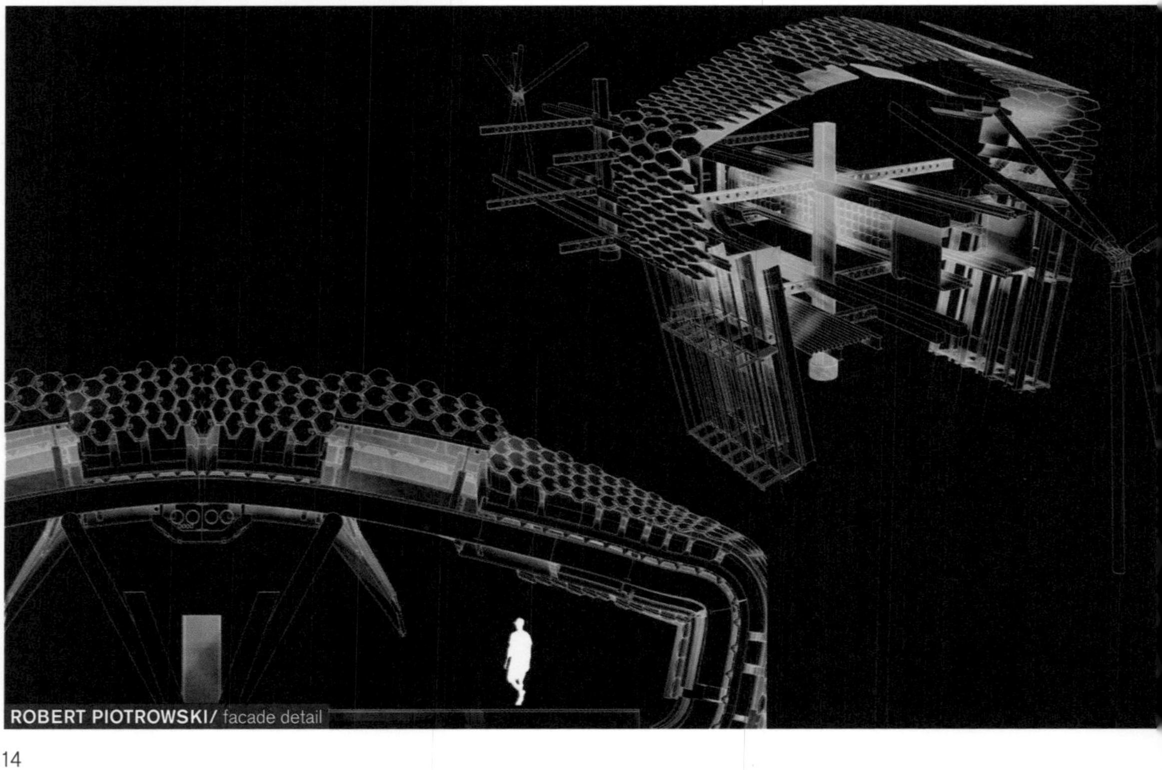

ROBERT PIOTROWSKI/ facade detail

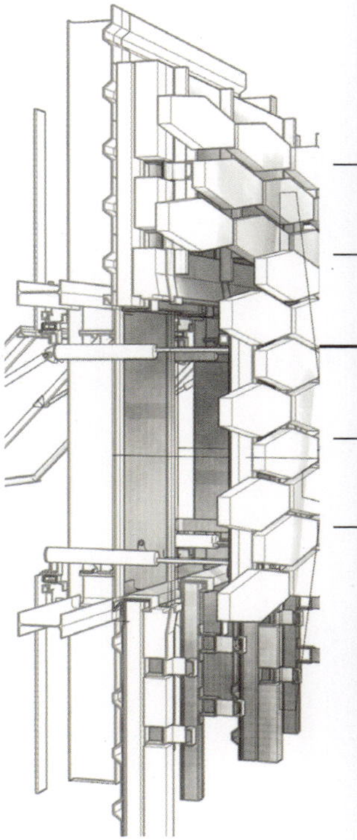

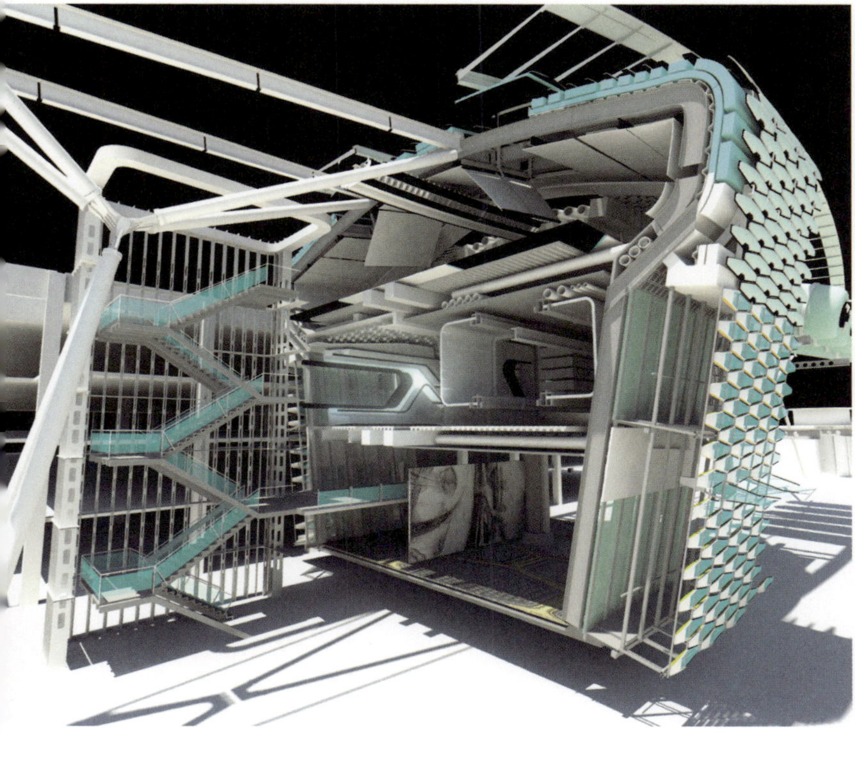

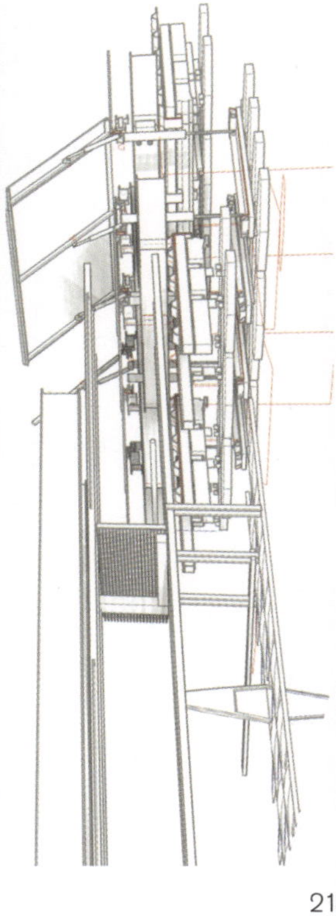

[FUTURE] +MOVE

Graduate Elective Architectural Theory Seminar
Collage Competitions: International Competition

Could we imagine an alternative society in which the free movement of people takes away part of their human rights? If people could follow the path of the internet and the migration of information, what would happen to our society? Would our ability to move depend on money, and how would it influence tourism? How can we deal with the freedom of movement and borders?

How could we overcome the dilemmas of urban mobility? Would there be a changing urban aesthetic relating to urban space and technologies of transport and communication? What could be the future of the pedestrian? And how could our movements shape the urban landscapes and our daily lives in the cities?

Kinetic Architecture is the driver behind a future nomadic lifestyle. Due to energy concerns, people have developed the technology to harness natural energy extremely efficiently and utilize it to stay on the move and simultaneously collect more energy. The form serves as in habitation and vehicle simultaneously. Thus the population is always spread out and always on the move. This re-imagination of urban density allows for a more efficient use and harnessing of the Earth's natural resources and energy. Congregation between nomadic groups happens by using the framework of the old cities to temporarily settle together.

PETAR MITEV / rendered site plan

PETAR MITEV / exterior rendering

rendered diagram

exterior rendering

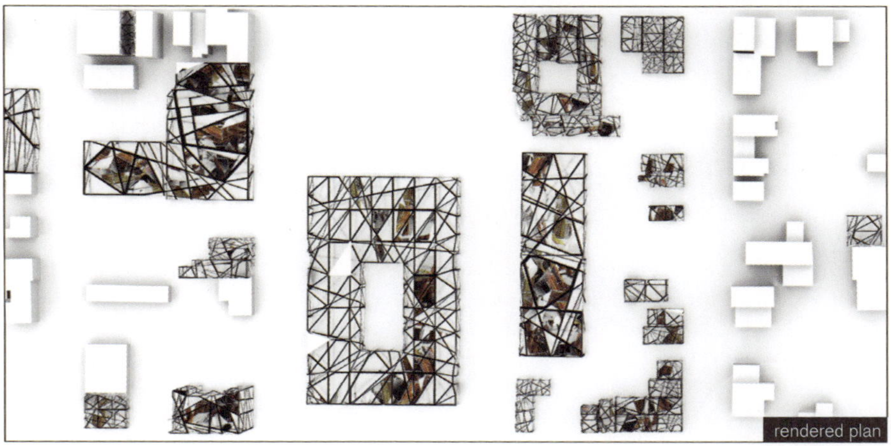
rendered plan

PETER ZELLNER

The Object City

Peter Zellner
Principal, Zellner Naecker Architects
Faculty, SCI-Arc
SAID Guest Instructor

This workshop set out five conditions or objectives for what was defined as a *differential urbanism*: an up-to-date approach to city design that produces a traversal relationality between urban figure, field, ground and network. Experiments conducted abstractedly in the studio were applied to a hypothetical 100 block urban site in Over the Rhine neighborhood of Cincinnati.

Differential Urbanism **initially set out some provisional definitions for re-modeling several historical understandings of the urban** ***topos*****, in Greek a "common place" or in Latin** ***locus*****, a place. From there the studio attempted to set out a parallel, revised and annotated history for a theory of a contemporary topological urbanism, drawn from the perspective of new works produced by avant-garde architects and architectural theorists at the scale of the city.**

As a workshop, *The Object City* quickly examined several lineages in recent urban thinking in the contemporary context: object oriented urbanism via Aldo Rossi, John Hejduk and OM Ungers; *field oriented urbanism*, via Stan Allen's Field Conditions and Fumihiko Maki's *Collective Form*; and *composite form urbanism* via Colin Rowe's *Collage City. Differential Urbanism* charted and found novel uses for Rowe's ambiguous composite figure while developing new interpretations of Rob Krier's morphological indices of urban spaces and types as spatial bridging devices between object and field.

The workshop was conducted via applied analysis and re-purposing of three sets of object types:

1. **Domestic Objects**:
Human scaled industrially designed household objects

2. **Urban Objects**:
Buildings and Urban Infrastructure
(Bridges, Overpasses) and;

3. **Functional Objects**:
Industrially designed large scale objects
(Planes, Trains and Automobiles)

The workshop scrutinized several new and topical urban design approaches that blurred figure-field relations via object oriented manipulations, kit-bashing, collaging, folding, topological stranding and landform based approaches to urbanism. Students assembleda digital library of 93 objects prior to the workshop, downloaded off the internet, and then repurposed these models as new urban objects, fields and assemblies.

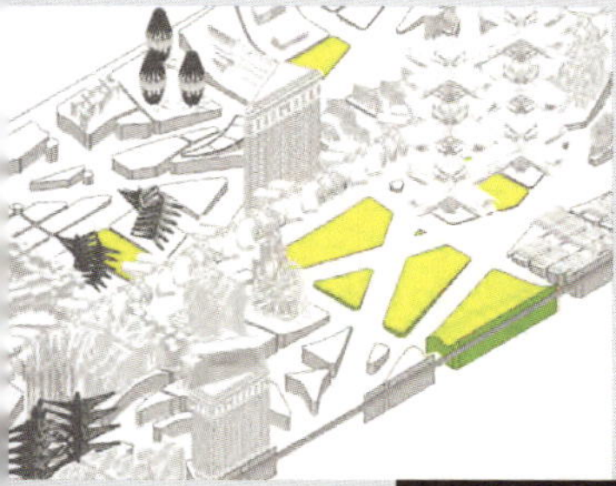

ALAN ALANIZ, MICHAEL FERGUSON, UDO GREINACHER, SERGEY KAHN, JAMIE KRUER, SARA KUSUMA, JIAZHEN LIN, MANNY MANOLUKAS, ADAM MARAGANORE, DAHAM MARAPANE, SHINJI MIYAJIMA, ROBERT PIOTROWSKI, MICHAEL ROGOVIN, EVAN SALE, LAURA SORIA

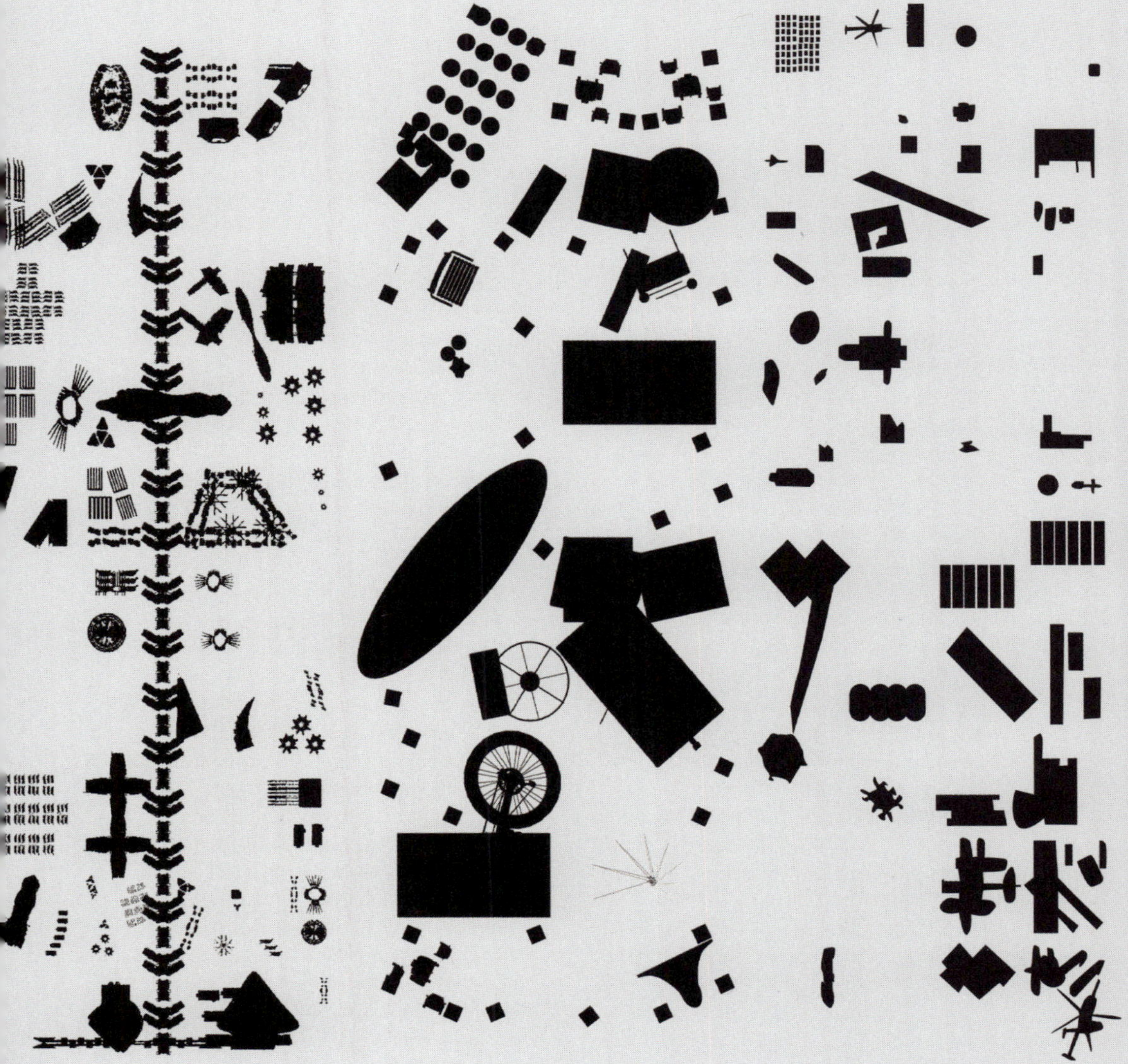

WHITNEY HAMAKER

KAMAMA PRAIRIE DWELLING

Graduate Option Design Build Studio
Appalachia, OH, USA

The Kamama Prairie Dwelling project is a tiny house that acts as many things: a vital shelter and haven for the client, Adrienne Cassel; a permanent presence on the nature preserve; and a model in tiny house design—simple, sustainable, and beautiful.

The Kamama Prairie is a 92-acre nature preserve owned by the Arc of Appalachia, located in rural Adams County, Ohio. The prairie is notable and renowned amongst experts as a particularly unique ecosystem—consisting of unique soil conditions and plant species—that houses a multitude of rare and endangered species. In particular, Kamama means 'butterfly' in Cherokee—an apt name reflecting the more than seventy species of butterflies inhabiting the prairie.

Though the prairie and the house are property of the Arc of Appalachia, the dwelling was uniquely designed for the prairie's land steward, Adrienne Cassel. A writing professor at Sinclair Community College, Adrienne began her work as the prairie's lifelong land steward in 2012. Now, with an established presence on the site in a thoughtful, sustainable dwelling, her work and the prairie itself can grow in recognition and thrive as both an educational resource and haven for all communities. The 160-square-foot house was designed around and within a new shipping container, which provided both a clear framework to build off of and unique constraints and conditions to build around. The key aims for the project's design intent were to make it beautiful and buildable, to have ample indoor / outdoor flexibility, and to be thoughtful and resourceful. A clean, minimal aesthetic was strived for, in order to not distract from the prairie, and a semi-shaded deck was essential as an occupiable outdoor space for the client.

The design challenges that were faced involved the shipping container constraints and the dwelling's potentially obtrusive site presence. The shipping container is naturally very small, and with the inclusion of furring, insulation, and finishes, there was a great potential for discomfort and confinement.

Responding to the aims and challenges, the house developed as a monolithic container with the deck and roof as a separate spatial volume. As the "monolith", the container is entirely clad in site-present materials, transforming it into a sculptural element on the site. As the separate, negative volume, the deck and roof share the same scale, structural system, and alignments, and thus perceptually linked. The roof acts to extend the sides of the home, and the deck reads as a minimal "floating" element, creating a sense of lightness on the site.

ALEX BUCHER
TOM COVERT
ALEX GORMLEY
DYLAN HOLTE
JON LUND
NAREK MIRZAEI
LUIS SABATER MUSA
JASON WU
MARISSA ZANE

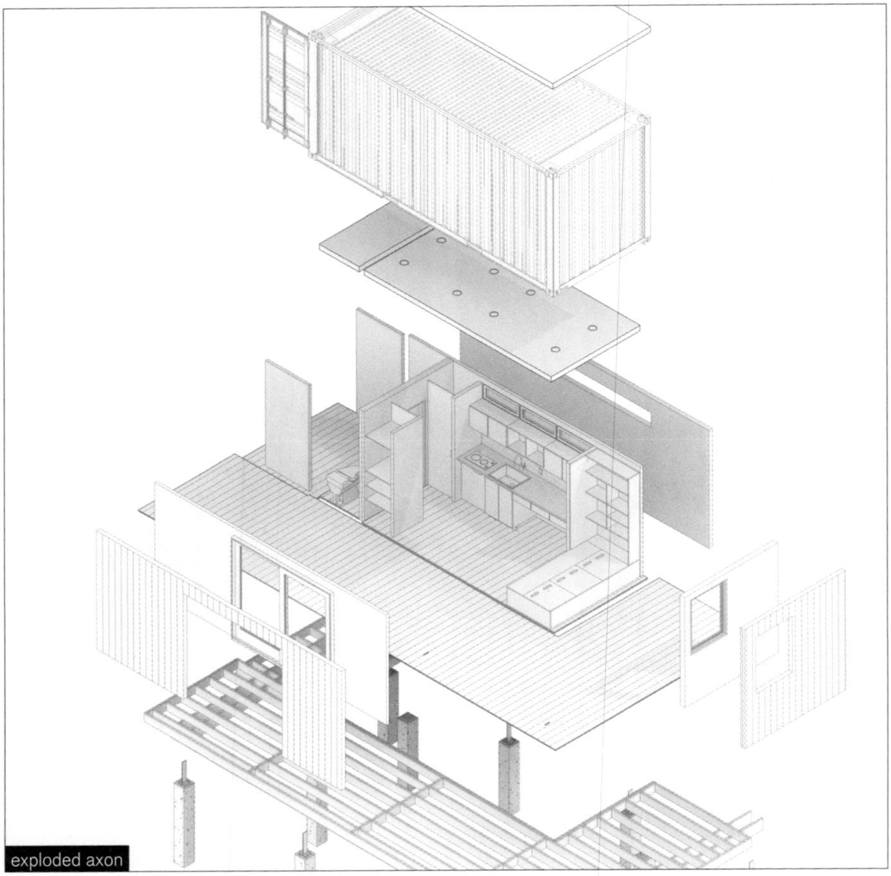

exploded axon

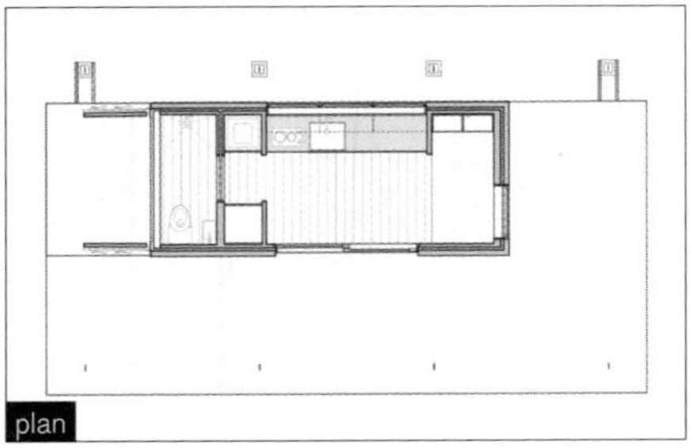

plan

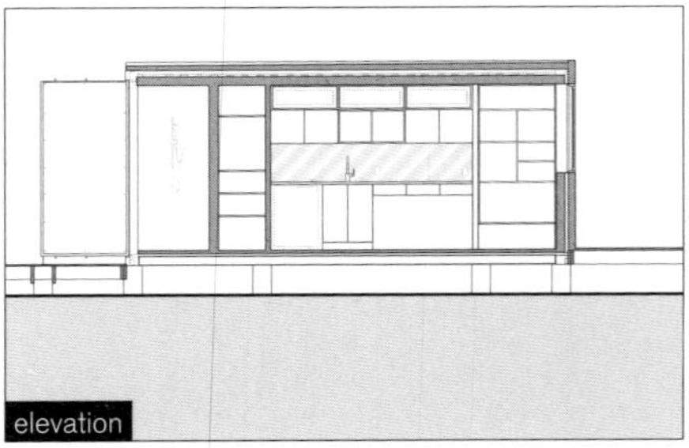

elevation

process

north elevation

students, faculty, and client

south elevation

interior

ALEX GORMLEY
AARATI KANEKAR, PH.D. (chair)
KRISTOPHER HOLLAND (member)

THE SEVEN OF U.S.

Simulation and the American Suburb
Suburbia, USA

Suburbia is dead. This death is at the hands of its own simulation. The creation of a hyperreal version of what is thought to be the authentic suburban condition has occurred and has masked the reality that this version of suburbia no longer conforms to its origin. The detached, single-family suburban home has come to signify the national residential identity of the American people for the past eighty plus years and has repeatedly come under the scrutiny of critique. Through misinterpretation, this realm of pseudo-architectural endeavor has developed a neo-vernacular architecture embodying a distilled reflection of the typical American consumer mindset and the developer's economic policy. The code of suburbia works to define an exchange value of a system of objects which has moved past simple use-exchange value in postmodern society and into a value system based on the role of symbolic values and a sign value.

Suburban America has generated an immediate, unchecked, and untapped ecosystem which has continually defined and will continue to impact the appearance and discourse of housing in the United States. This thesis seeks to analyze the suburban house as commodity, as image, and as propaganda, through the investigation of seven tropes centered around the idealistic representation of the postwar American suburb and its physical actuality. Through appropriation and recontextualization of these seven tropes, a series of seven canonical houses are explored as critique of the current suburban architectural culture. "The Seven" become a fatal strategy with the aim to implode the pervasiveness of the contemporary simulated suburb. This is an exploration towards the absurd.

This thesis does not wish to provide criticism or judgement on the decision to create the suburbs or their success/failure; it is merely interested in positing reasonings behind the rise of the suburban single-family dwelling and its future. Intended to reveal the underlying systematic elements at play in the visual and spatial construction of the suburban home, the study of "The Seven" aims to illustrate the absurdity of the contemporary suburban condition in comparison. Each of the seven houses are designed with a focus on aspects of place/no-place, image, erasure, and sequential qualities of the "home". The resultant series and analysis establish a new precedent in the ongoing discourse and raise questions for the prospective homeowner of the coming decades.

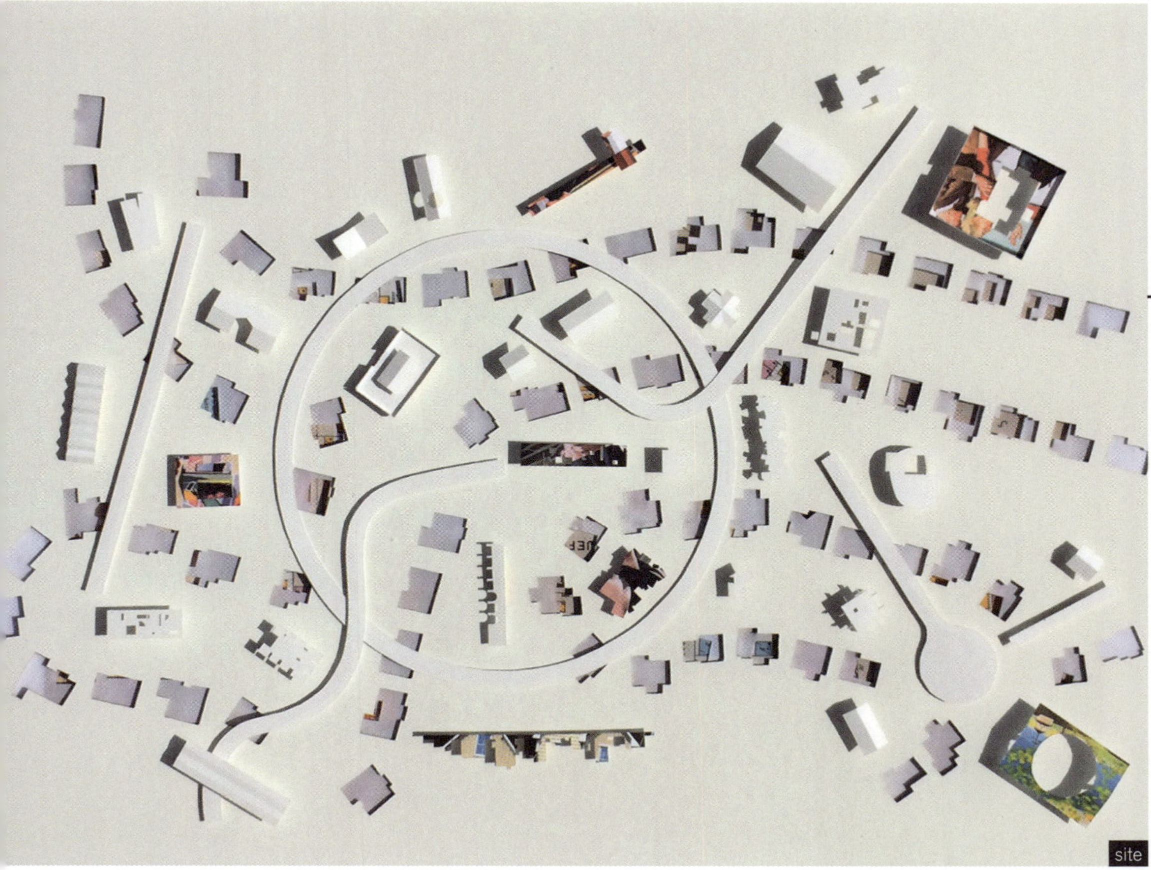

site

ALEX GORMLEY/ exhibition

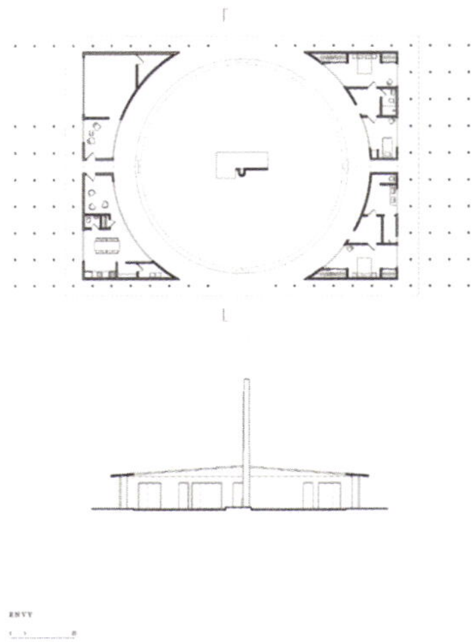

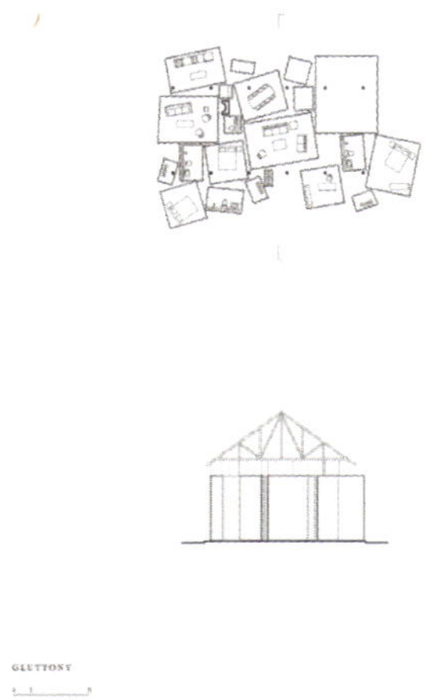

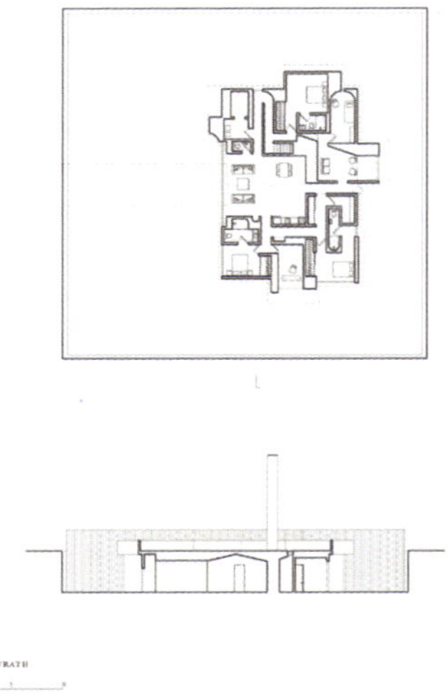

Envy

Gluttony

Wrath

Wrath

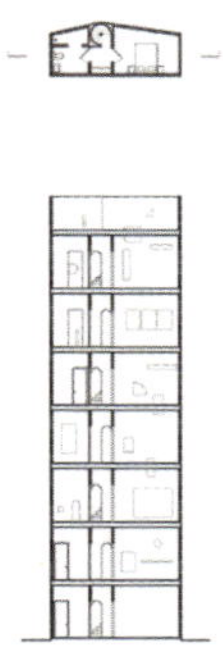

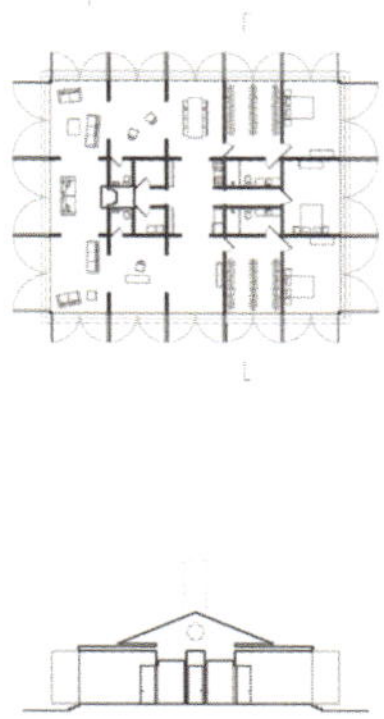

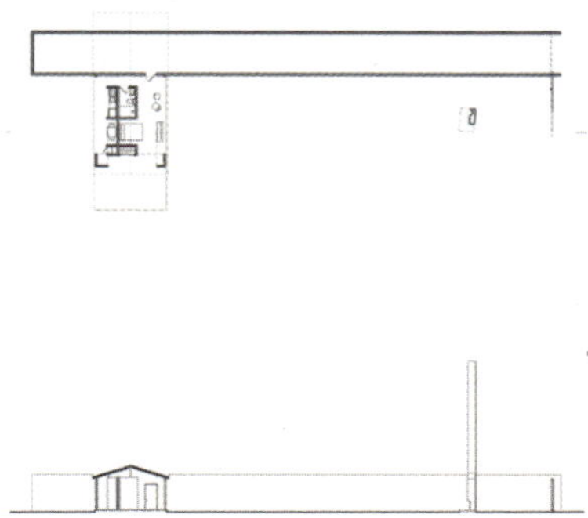

LUST

PRIDE

SLOTH

Lust

Pride

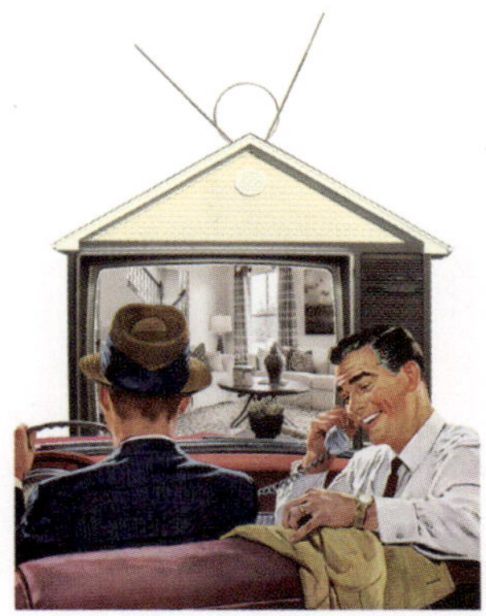

Sloth

Gluttony

The thesis employs three lenses of investigation that are representative of the three stages of development of the suburban condition in the post-war United States.

Lens 1: House as an image.
The replication over time of the image of the suburban house and its utopian image quality has been used to promote the ideal of suburban living to the masses. This replication and later appropriation of the traditional American (suburban) homestead came to a peak in the later years of WWII and the post war years with the marriage of advertisement agencies, architects, and government. Through juxtaposition and erasure, the method of collage seeks to reengage this utopian subject matter in a way which create absurdist versions of the originals as well as providing a diagrammatic understanding of each trope.

Lens 2: House as a commodity.
The image of the suburban house in turn makes it into an object of desire thereby leading to its commoditization. Up until the 2008 market collapse, the house constantly evolved from being just a mere residence to a status icon, which was necessary to secure a financial future to a near necessity in order to attain the American dream. By turning the house into a commodity that is easily bought and sold depending on current life demands or stylistic concerns, the system took the home out of the house.

Lens 3: House as propaganda;
House as simulacra.
The American suburban house has now become the most 'real' version of itself; a hyperreal construction for image and commodity value. The pervasive feelings of nostalgia centered on the ideals of the American dream and the prosperity of the post-war years have led to an increased replication of various tropes resulting in the simulation of what was once the authentic suburban home. The manipulation of the image and commodity of the house by image creators (home builders, advertising agencies, U.S. Government) is done in a way to align its procreation with the message which these entities propagate, be it the strength of capitalism or the value of a brand. In this model, the house has become a tool for propaganda and as a result has become a simulacrum of its origin self.

Lust

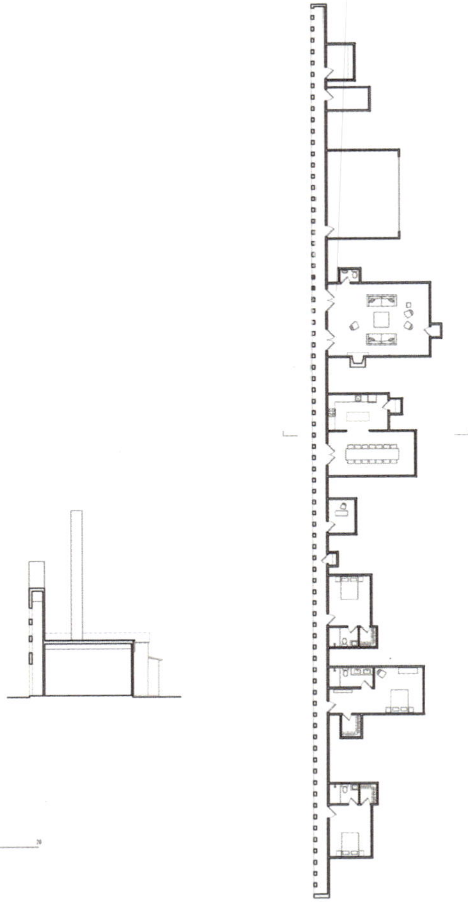

Greed

Greed

Sloth

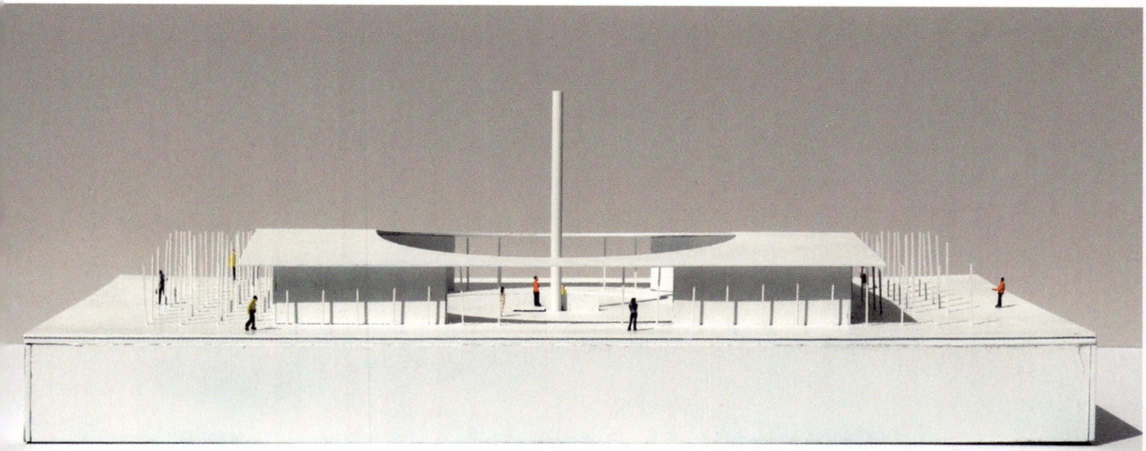

Envy

TJ DUNN / Photography Credits

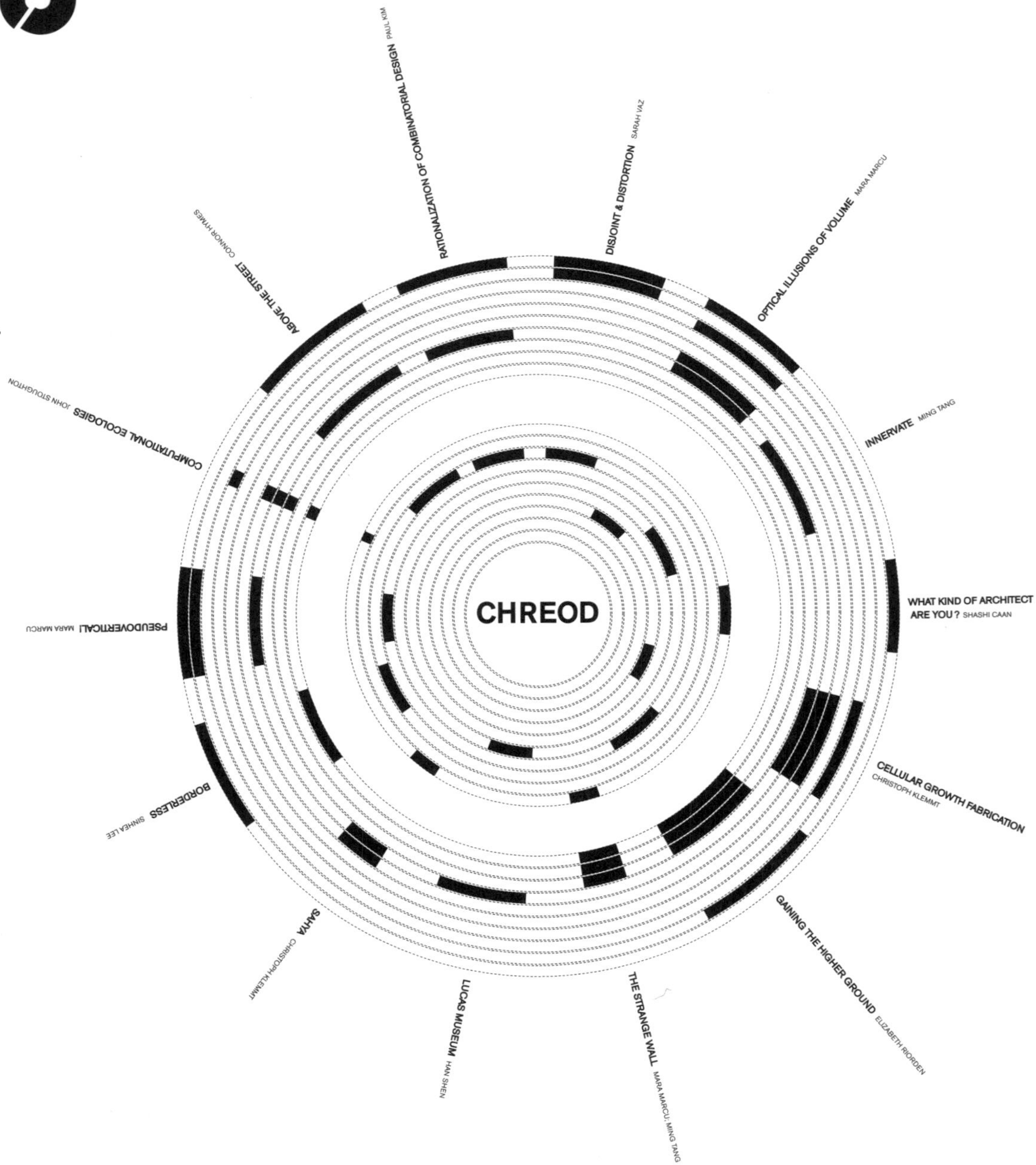

LEGEND:

1. OUTER SECTOR = ID
2. INNER SECTOR = LEVEL
3. WIDTH = SCALE

1. *From Outer Ring to Inner Ring:*
Design Thinking
History/Theory
Material Investigation
Branding
Design Build
Digital Craft
Computational Design
Fabrication
Sustainability
Public Interes

2. *From Outer Ring to Inner Ring:*
Professional
PhD
Graduate 3rd Year
Graduate 2nd Year
Graduate 1st Year
Undergraduate 5th Year
Undergraduate 4th Year
Undergraduate 3rd Year
Undergraduate 2nd Year
Undergraduate 1st Year

3. *Width of Black Poché:*
Scaleless
Object
Furniture
Body
Room
Building
Cluster/Complex
City/Region

CHREOD

In a lecture entitled "What is Life?" Sanford Kwinter called *chreod* the most important concept of the twentieth century. The term, taken from C.H. Waddington is a neologism whose Greek roots derive from *necessary* and *path*. Waddington's term referred to disturbances by external forces on a cell, such that small changes early in development would lead to later greater changes. As opposed to homeostasis, *chreod* promises more dynamic models. Borrowing from epigenetic feedback loops in cellular biology, architects have used computational tools towards the generation of form. This current interest can be seen as an indirect influence on academic approaches to urban design and architecture.

Architecture's complex historic relationship to the Natural Sciences is too long to cover in this essay. Shared notions of type, character, method of differentiation and description, classification, and the writing of histories are common to both disciplines. But *chreod* is posed as a challenge to these classical modes of discourse. Kwinter's challenge has been to think form in the broader ecology of systems. He credits the term *ecology* to an 1802 essay the *Geography of Plants* by Alexander Von Humboldt. Humboldt's thesis demonstrated how plant size shape and behaviors were conditioned by external factors - altitude, latitude, soil, and climate. One and the same genotype expressed itself differently along a geographic spectrum. The same seed produced essentially different plants depending on variables with which it came in contact. Von Humbodlt is often paraphrased "everything is connected' or more accurately "all is interaction." His thesis, which differs from and anticipates the late nineteenth century concept of evolution, was a logic to explain how species were spatially mixed and differentiated. Biologic determinism is not new to Cincinnati. In the early to mid-nineteenth century civic boosters from Cincinnati, Toledo and Kansas City among others, were influenced by von Humboldt's projection, forecasting their respective cities as the next great metropolis that would emerge along a climactic belt common to all great civilizations [1]. This early ecological thesis, a form of biological determinism, when combined with liberal economic philosophy, became a convenient excuse to justify genocide, Manifest Destiny, and other forms of colonial exploitation. More constructively, Von Humboldt's followers posited a flexible notion of type that depicted life forms as active processes of generation, improvisation and expression. For Kwinter, however, Von Humboldt's thesis can be summarized: "Form is an expression of imbedded forces."

One might rightly hesitate to attribute such deterministic and, therefore, historically suspect ideology to the more recent infatuation with algorithmic driven formal logics. But just as von Humboldt's theories were misused, reliance on mathematical formulas as simulation tools for allegedly dynamic and evolutionary urbanisms cannot be assumed innocently. That being said, interest in *creode* might challenge the more banal, static notions of sustainability as a driver in urban planning and design in general. Sustainability seems arrested in zero-energy equilibrium. Earlier biological analogies like Chris Alexander's evolving thesis of architectural and urban form mimed the emerging discipline of computational science. Alexander's pattern language of fifteen geometric properties that determine life could be reduced to algorithms, constituting a quasi-genetic system – one that could be found in more traditional urban form and which he felt contradicted the more hierarchical and tree-like logic of modernist modes of thinking. Alexander first in *Pattern Language* and later in the *Nature of Order* sought to script the process of creating *life*, which he also deemed an evolutionary process through incremental changes. Despite the mathematical underpinnings of Alexander's thesis, he sees himself as a scientific humanist, demonstrating that pre-Enlightenment, traditional cultures were not irrational, only that their complexity exceeded the limited capacity and reductive analysis of modern science. The New Urbanists would also proclaim a humanist agenda despite their neat synchronicity with most current real estate formulas. Conventional low impact carbon development and the form-'based typology adopted from New Urbanism openly declares its desire for stability, achieving ecological and cultural "balance" from "green" standards for LEED certification. While Alexander claimed to be *evolutionary* and the New Urbanist's *typological* formalism claimed tradition, both essentially arrived in similar places, advocating for familiar forms and the ethics of sustainability as an essential driver of a *critical* pre-modern culture which drained modernism of its academic futurism. Both appeared relatively conservative compared to the linguistically driven formal experimentations of architects of the late twentieth century neo-avant-garde.

Contemporary boosters of computational methods for urban design and forecasting, like Patrick Schumacher, have advocated against any regulatory controls on urban development, going so far as to call for the end of social housing and public space in favor of a self-regulating, market driven solutions for the housing crisis. While his position has seemed politically conservative and unnecessarily provocative, one can also see the slippery connections between his supply-side economic theories, neo-liberalism, and the biologic pro-life arguments. Kwinter's differential morphogeneticism freely references Gregory Bateson's "ecologies of mind" which in turn drew on anthropological patterns in its formational thesis. In these cases, one can surmise a skepticism of the limitations of the Enlightenment project of rationality. In Schumacher's case laws are restrictive of something like *progress* and never quite rational enough; in Kwinter's case, *evolution* replaces progress, but his biologic conflicts with the political aspects of city-making. One wonders if the flaw in either the turbo-capitalist or biological life-force formulas is the human element and its tendency to be contradictory and irrational. Schumacher and Kwinter, though decidedly different, are both post-humanists.

To add further complication, the intricate and complicated schism between the humanists *Homo sociologicus* and Schumacher's *Homo economicus* has been critiqued before. Colin Rowe, following Karl Popper, famously leveled a critique against "science" and "morals" in favor of the liberal free-play of form detached from its rational or ethical imperatives. Distinctly, anti-utopian as well as anti-scientific, Rowe sounded the charge for a whole brigade of critical theorists and urbanists who saw the city as the outcome of diverse, eclectic and, more often than not, contradictory propositions–one's irreducible to pure mathematics or natural orders. Rowe declared that neither the people nor the scientist should build the city–certainly he would have rejected the idea that a generative cell or an algorithm would be up to the job. Manfredo Tafuri, too, argued that Nature itself was problematic. Nature was simply bad consciousness; it sublimated the destructive conditions of capitalism in the Metropolis, simultaneously making nature into a salve for urban crisis while naturalizing the city. To Kwinter's point, however, the return to linguistic and typological arguments in the 1960s that Rowe sponsored, became a well-argued debate among the contributors of *Oppositions* and the Institute of Architecture and Urban Studies. But it confined discussions of form to the straightjacket of structuralist thought, and made formal discussions immune to the evolutionary potential of radical *ecological* thinking and the more progressive strains of modernism.

One can advocate for Nature versus nurture; the political thesis versus the scientific thesis in discussing urban transformations and morphologies. One might even say that the difference between post-humanists like a Kwinter and a Schumacher are determined by fine differences between the formal generative potentials in the genus versus the generic; but if we were to say that the former is differentiated by site, and the vectors of environment, and material; the latter is supposedly economically determined, but more likely it is willed by an author and for the most part, characteristic of the linguistic heritage of architectural composition. Despite flaws in both positions they are still relevant. A genus evolves by way of outside forces into an articulation;

CHREOD

Edward Mitchell

Director,
School of Architecture and Interior Design
University of Cincinnati

whereas the articulation of the generic through typology in architecture produces environmental reaction and response. Architecture and City making retain power as both bio-political entities and constructive speech acts.

In the end Architecture may be more economic than biological, an object determined by the market and still wedded to the politics of property. One might then argue whether our current economic system is *life* supporting. Even the disciplinary drive to sustainability is decidedly more an economically than a biologically or even an ethically-driven argument. So while Kwinter may find *chreod* an important concept of morphological generation, its applicability to architecture may remain a laboratory experiment. The milieu of urban form making is irreducible to biology and, in that regard the idea that architecture supports life forms is a notion that is utopian at best.

Notes:

[1] Other treatises of the great central city include J. W. Scott, *Toledo, "future great city of the world": as envisaged almost a century ago*, Blade Printing and Paper Co.; J.W. Scott, *A presentation of causes tending to fix the position of the future great city of the world in the central plain of North America: ... On the great lakes*, 1876; Reavis, L.U., *St. Louis, Future Great City of the World*, Gray and Baker Company, St. Louis, 1875; Goodin, S.H., "Cincinnati – It's Destiny", in *Sketches and Statistics of Cincinnati*, 1851; Drake, Daniel, *Natural and Statistical View of Cincinnati and Miami County*, 1815.

SARAH VAZ
AARATI KANEKAR, PH.D. (chair)
MICHAEL MCINTURF

DISJOINT & DISTORTION

An essay in manifesting contradiction
Master of Architecture Thesis

A contradiction exists: the systems that make our social structure possible are invisible. The CSX Queensgate train yard just west of downtown Cincinnati is one of the largest rail classification facilities in North America, and yet the public is at best only marginally conscious of its presence within the city. We accept this discrepancy as so many others. We live in an era in which paradox is paradigm. It is the incongruity of the paradoxical, Robert Venturi theorizes, that suggests a kind of truth.

This thesis investigates incongruity by looking, thematically as well as formally, at three art movements of the twentieth century that embrace **(incongruent)** processes and conclusions: surrealism, expressionism, and relational art. This investigation focuses on two methods by which the **(incongruities)** are manifested, calls them **disjoint and distortion**, and applies them towards the programming and design of an amusement park to function above the operating train yard.

I. absurd realism
instances of idiosyncrasy
aberration as absorption

II. movements + methods
surrealism, gutai, and relational art
disjoint and distortion

III. disjoint: site + program
rail yard as contradiction
amusement park as counterpoint

IV. distortion: design
mapping warped space
misinterpretation through motion

V. ad absurdum
The New Arrangement

disjoint: site + program

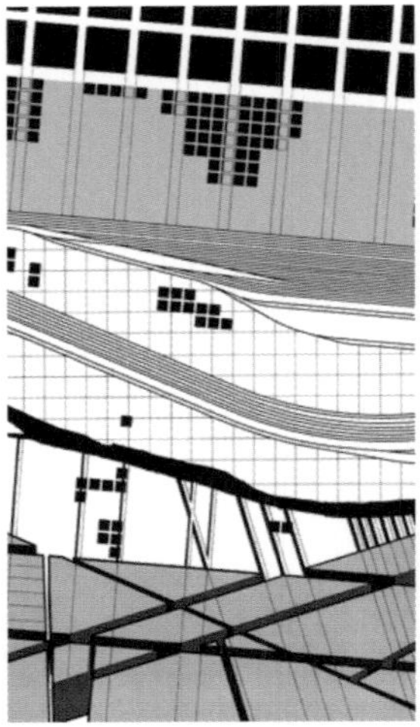
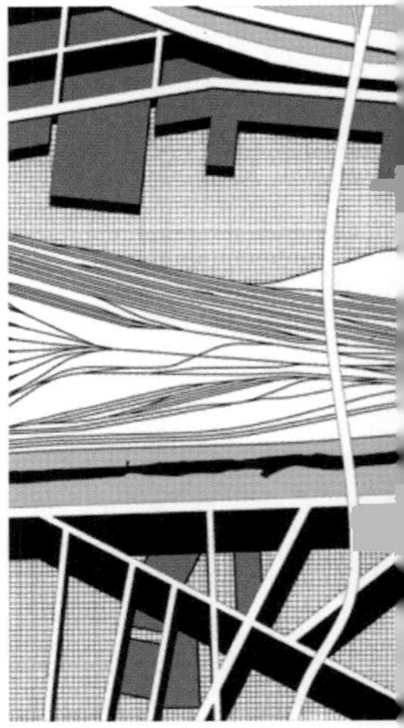

absurd realism

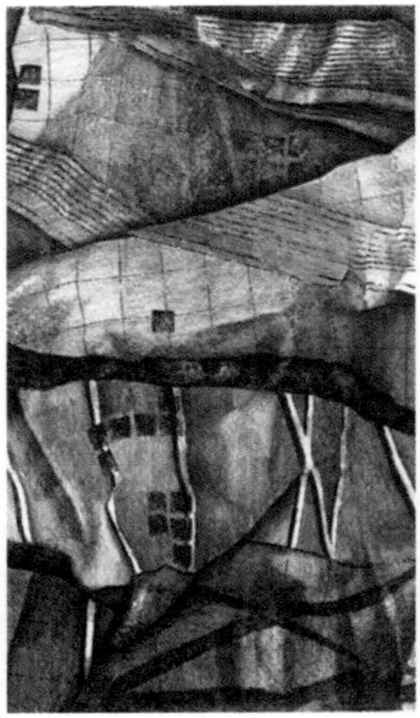

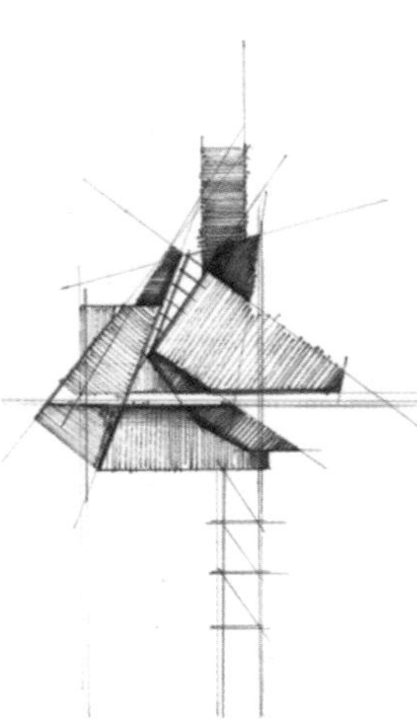
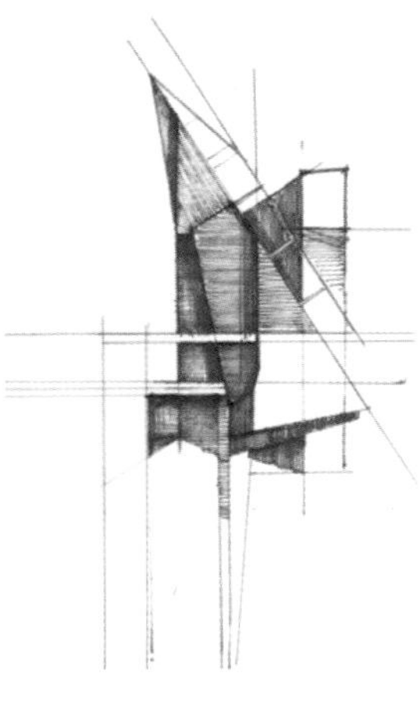
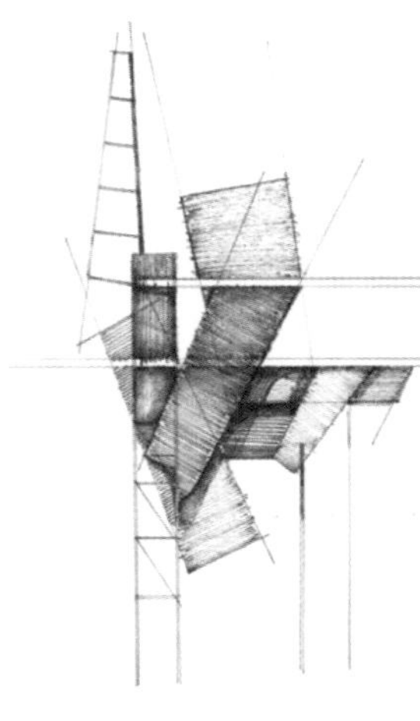
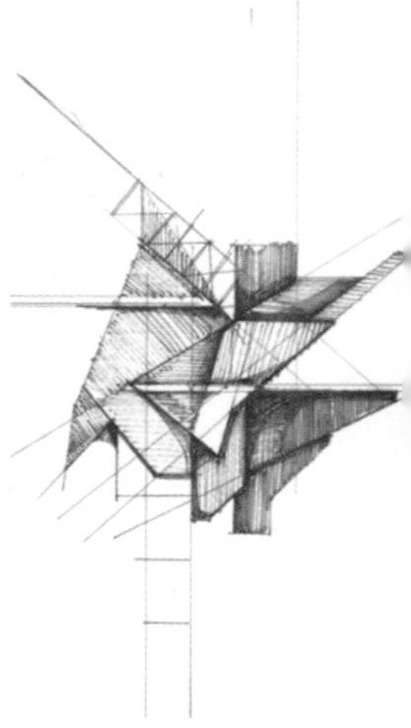

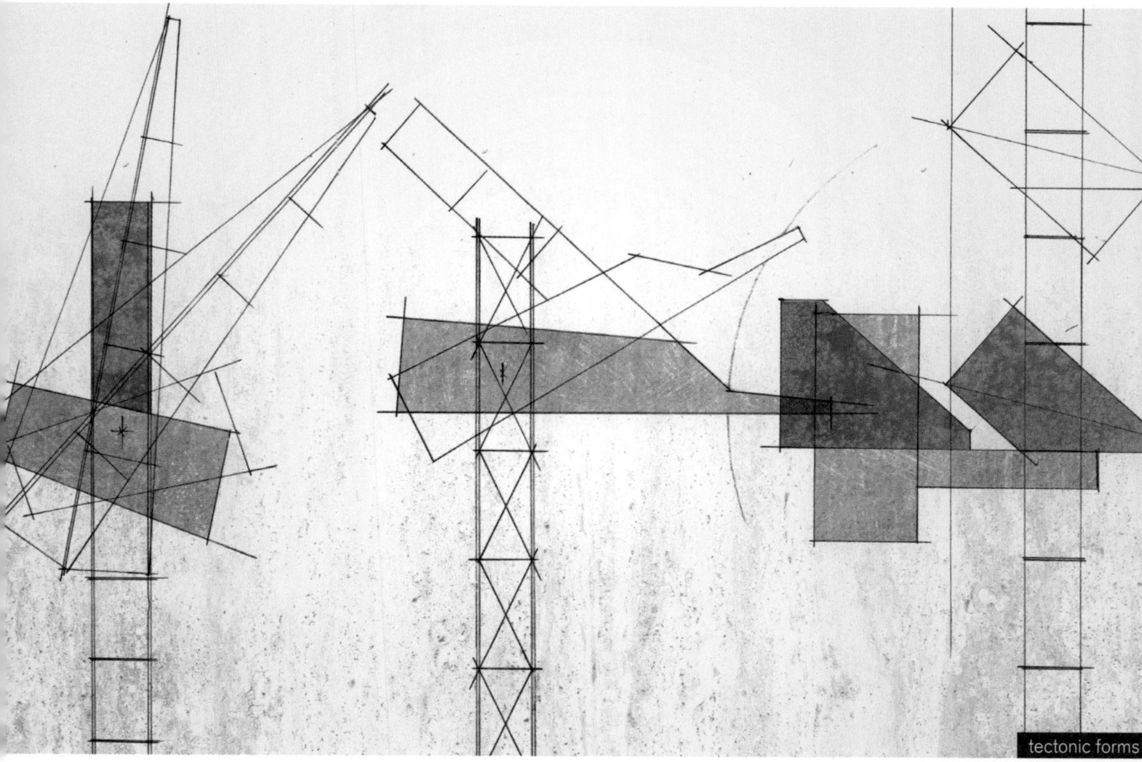

IV. distortion: design

an unnatural derivation from mapping and motion

The design seeks two types of distortion. The first is the distortion of the site experienced through the movement of the rides. The second is the distortion of the rides themselves and the development of a hybrid language that compromises both the amusement park typology as well as the rail yard typology. Two exercises in distortion are developed, one in mapping, and one in movement. The first begins with mapping and ends with a tectonic language.

The first set of maps is designed after Mario Gandelsonas' *Analytic Drawings of Boston* and explores the existing distortion of the grid by the train yards. The first maps are crumpled and form the second set. These are then distilled to tectonic forms that eventually morph into the design of the amusement park.

8252
8252
ad absurdum

The second exercise begins with analyzing the movement of the rides themselves and explores the manner in which their motion distorts perception. Four spaces encountered on the site are aligned with each movement and deformed through the collage of three views that result from the movement analysis.

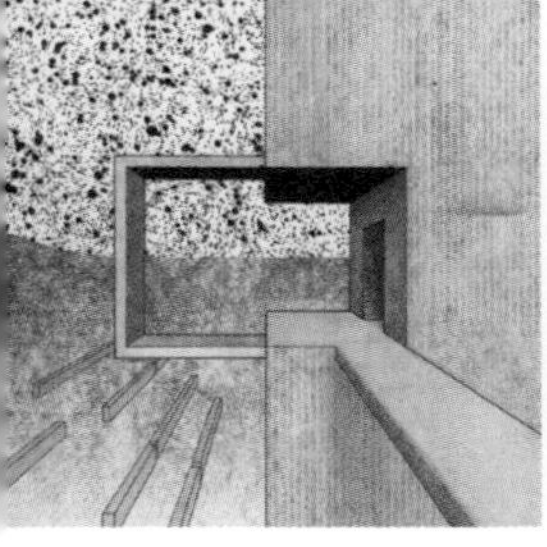

an addendum

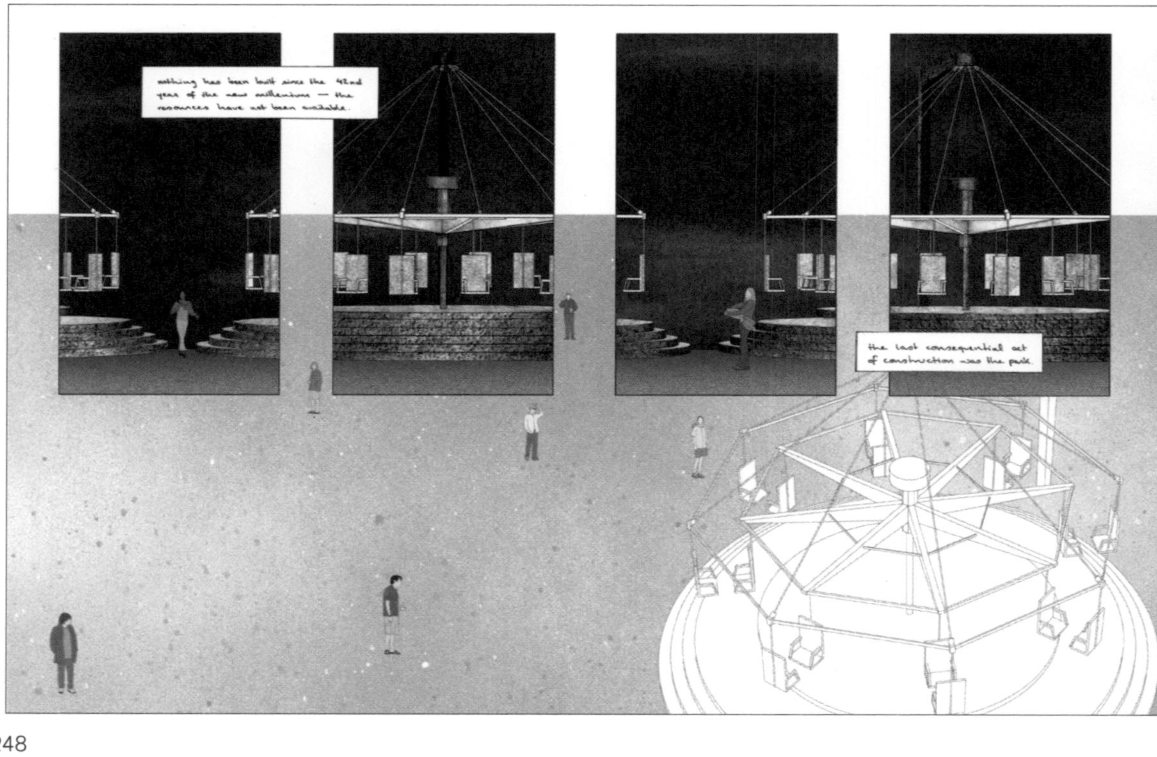
nothing has been built since the 42nd year of the new millennium — the resources have not been available.
the last consequential act of construction was the park.

the park was quickly appropriated by storytellers,
starved for novelty that could no longer be built,
operating in the last medium left to the mind.

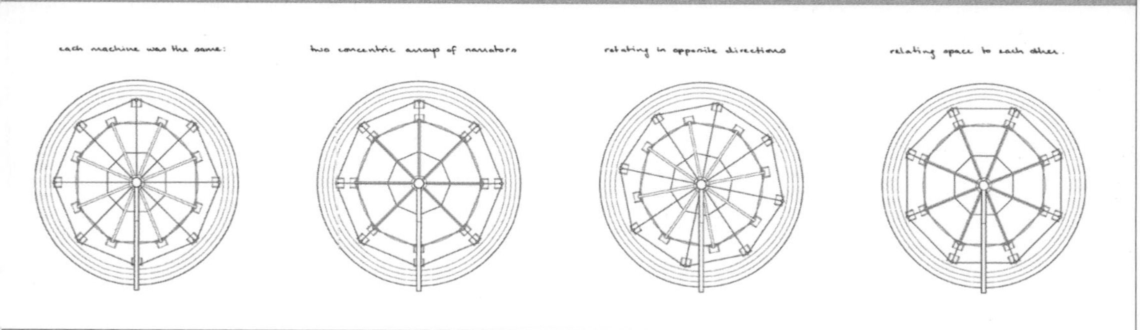
each machine was the same:
two concentric arrays of narrators
rotating in opposite directions
relating space to each other.

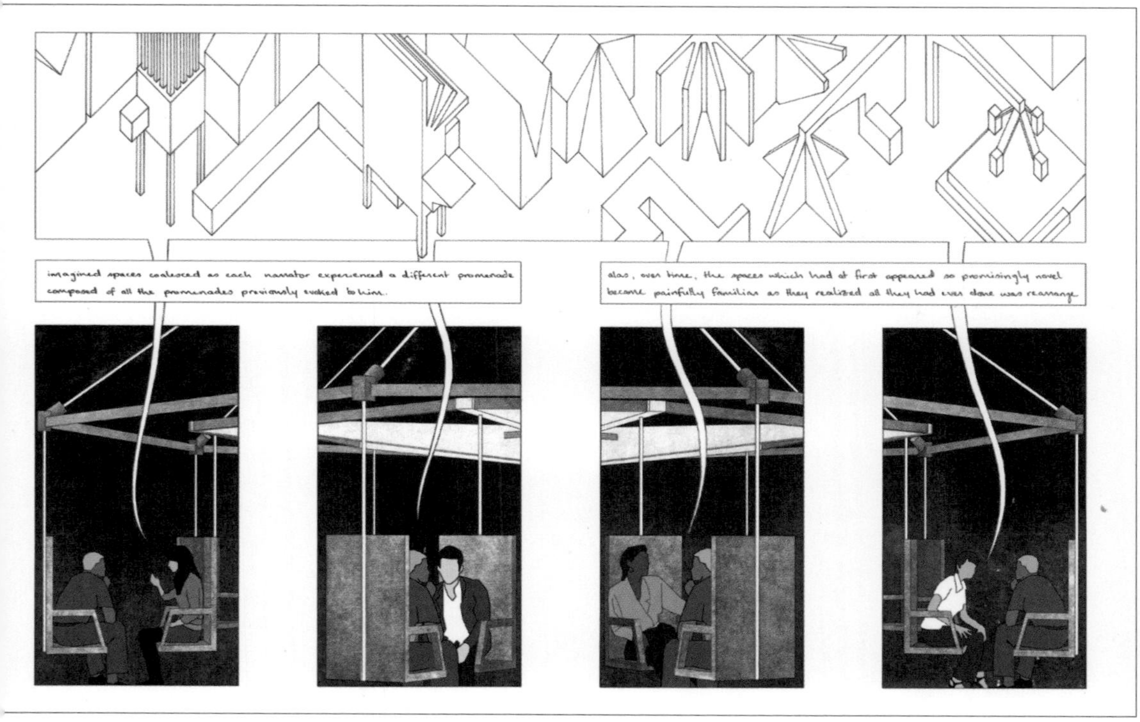
imagined spaces coalesced as each narrator experienced a different promenade composed of all the promenades previously evoked to him.
alas, over time, the spaces which had at first appeared so promisingly novel became painfully familiar as they realized all they had ever done was rearrange

MARA MARCU

OPTICAL ILLUSIONS OF VOLUME

Fourth Year Architecture Capstone Studio, Director's Choice Award
Computation and Digital Fabrication
Cincinnati, OH, USA

Traditionally *haute couture* designates high-end clothing specifically designed for a unique person's body and carefully hand-made with the utmost craft and dexterity. Contrarily, *prêt-à-porter* collections are mass produced, machine-made and replicated to reach a wide pool of consumers. In the recent "Manus X Machina" exhibition at the Metropolitan Museum of Art, New York, the hand and the machine reconcile conflicting attitudes towards technology. Instead of exploiting their antagonism, the exhibition "suggests a spectrum of practice, whereby the hand and the machine are equal and mutual protagonists in solving design problems, enhancing design practices, and, ultimately, advancing the future of fashion" [1].

Interdisciplinary in nature, the work illustrated on these next pages distills these attitudes by asking the following questions: What is structure? How can skin and frame become a fluid continuum? What are the techniques that can describe the metamorphosis of two-dimensional, flat, sheet material to three-dimensional form? Can we develop a taxonomy of folds, bends, and joints? Can we bypass any in the process of assembly? Can the analog post-digital processes be reinvigorated, and exploited as latent design opportunities in the digital era? What are the primitives of digital design? How can emergent technologies, on their immediate downfall to obsolesce, mitigate the stringent need for securing real estate with contemporary aspirations?

Optical Illusions of Volume, therefore, critiques the ubiquitous obsession with optimization in computational design and fabrication. As an alternative, several projects are presented which begin to exploit and exaggerate misbehaving behaviors in an ideal file-to-factory methodology. The work conducted together with students at the School of Architecture and Interior Design (SAID) reconciles conflicting attitudes between traditional CAD/CAM strategies, interactive architecture, virtual reality, and analog post-processing techniques. The projects mainly employ the use of a lightweight sheet material, parametric design in CATIA/Digital Project, simulation/responsive architecture via Arduino-controlled [2] sound sampling, and investigate accidental and more intuitive assembly strategies.

In this way, we aim to develop techniques within the digital process that exploit a non-linear design and fabrication approach in which the hand and the machine become increasingly disrespectful of each other's artificially delineated boundary. By contaminating and continually disrupting each other, we believe that what are considered, by norm, flaws or faulty formations within the fabrication process can open up otherwise neglected intriguing opportunities in architecture and design.

Notes:

[1] Metropolitan Museum of Art, New York. (2016). *Manux x Machina: Fashion in the Age of Technology*. Accessed Dec. 7, 2017. https://www.metmuseum.org/exhibitions/listings/2016/manus-x-machina/exhibition-galleries.

[2] Wikipedia. (n.d.). *Arduino*. Accessed Nov. 28 2017. https://en.wikipedia.org/wiki/Arduino. Arduino is an open source computer hardware and software company, project, and user community that designs and manufactures single-board microcontrollers and microcontroller kits for building digital devices and interactive objects that can sense and control objects in the physical world.

aquarium

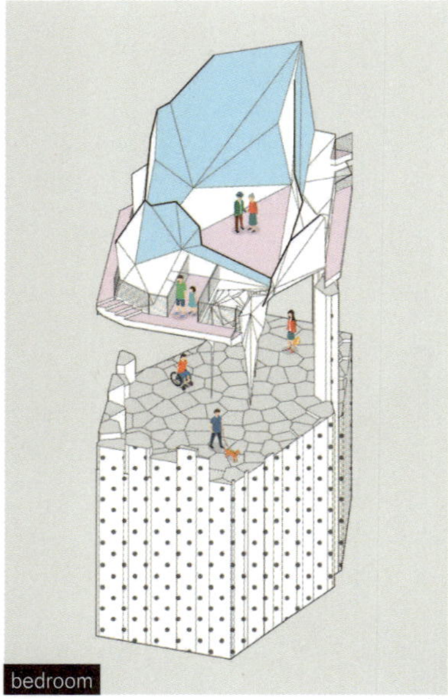

bedroom

observatory

ADAM SCHUELER, PETER FOSTER / floor plans

Cloud 9, interior perspective

Cloud 9, aerial

Cloud 9, close-up

APRIL GAO / Cloud 9, loggia

Bubbles, details

Bubbles, elevation

PETER FOSTER, ADAM SCHEULER, ANUSHA ALAMGIR, CONNOR TUTHILL / Bubbles

MING TANG

INNERVATE

Graduate First Year Architecture
Introduction to Computation
Cincinnati, OH, USA

Innervate demonstrates several operational connections among different techniques for inquiry and visualization as a critical methodology in the design process, examining the potential for transitioning from one method to another as well as the possibilities of overlapping and combining various techniques.

The process includes both a seminar and project development format, and develops techniques for manual and digital drawing and solid modeling, as through which the studio influences the process of viewing, visualizing, and forming spatial and formal relationships. Skills acquired in Architectural Drawing are further utilized in the development of more advanced compositions. The goal is to increase students' understanding of the basic ordering principles of design and develop an understanding of the interrelationship of form, space, human function, and environmental context. They develop an ability to make simple design judgments and synthesize the process of conceptualization, turning the results of analyses and spatial/formal considerations into architectural designs.

One project focuses mainly on the idea of reconnecting Pendelton district not only to its adjacent neighborhoods, but also to the rest of Cincinnati and the world through exploration and application of design strategies, education, and jobs. Coupled with an evolving housing solution, community, and fabrication process, this design strives to lead investigations centered around ever-changing stimuli and analysis.

By focusing on the ideas of connecting, designers are able to push their ideas past the walls of the classroom and reach toward the community.

ROBERT PETROWSKI / tilt

MINH DUNG LE / exterior rendering

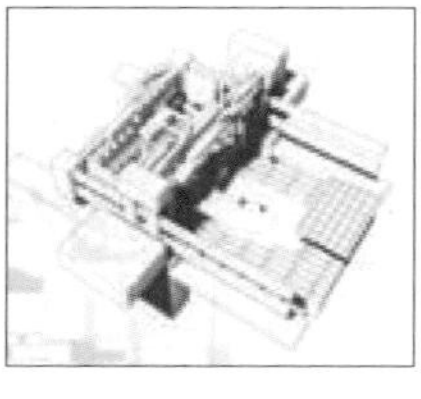

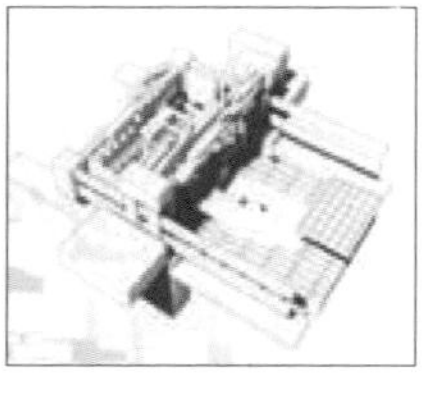

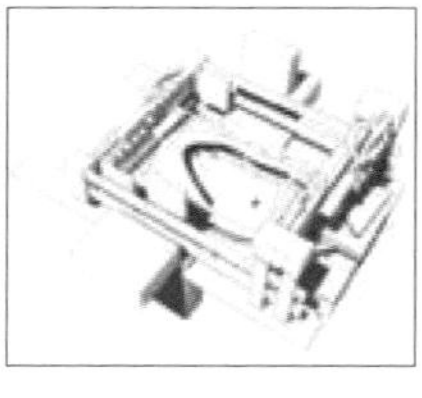

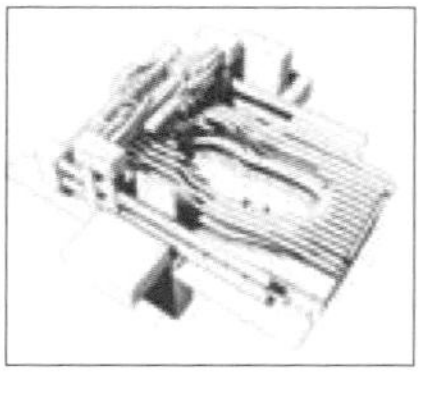

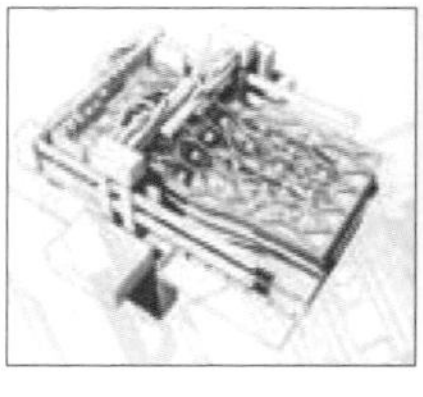

ROBERT PETROWSKI / tower shadows

SHASHI CAAN, FOIFI, FRSA, FCIDI, HON FASID, HON FBID, HON FDIA

What Kind of Architect Are You?

Shashi Caan was interviewed by Prof. Udo Greinacher at SAID on February 8, 2012. The following is an excerpt from What Kind of Architect Are You? *an upcoming collection of interviews by Professor Greinacher [www.whatkindofarchitect.com].*

An internationally recognized thought leader for progressive design, Shashi Caan has spent her life immersed in the considerations of design and its impact on humanity, our society and culture worldwide. With almost thirty years of design experience and leadership, Shashi Caan has simultaneously cultivated the three related aspects of design–practice, education, and the unification of the global design community. Constantly seeking to integrate her work and thinking within the realms of theory, application, and the resultant impacts of design, she continues to research and practice in her innovatively structured, international design firm, The SC COLLECTIVE.

I don't design all the time, none of us does.

I come from a family of architects. As a young girl in India, I was precocious, very much a tomboy, and I would always accompany my dad to his construction sites. I particularly liked the projects where he would renovate. He would walk into projects looking at his iterations, and I would walk into projects thinking about spaces: gosh, if only walls could talk. What are the stories they would tell? I loved that. I loved that there was something extraordinary about what we did within the built environment that shaped us, that changed our attitudes to all of life in general. That was my first introduction to design.

My father wanted us—my two sisters and me—to go to universities, study sciences and become doctors. He was very certain that we shouldn't be in the creative arts, that if we wanted professions, it should be something serious. I did not want to do that. I wanted to go to art college. It meant offending him, upsetting his ideas of what was the better education to have. I got accepted into art college but didn't know what to expect. I didn't necessarily think I was an artist, but I didn't know what I was. So my undergraduate education was, in hindsight, an extraordinary journey of self-discovery. I was privileged because I really didn't need to come out of that study with qualifications for a profession. I essentially spent four years exploring. I did sculpture, painting, glass blowing, made stained glass windows, made furniture, tapestries, printed textiles, woven textiles, interiors. I did everything and loved it all but particularly enjoyed the three dimensional spatial aspects of the disciplines. And then after graduating with a BFA, I knew I had a strong interest in interiors but needed more specific knowledge for that. I went on to study industrial design at the master's level, worked in an architecture practice, went back to school for architecture, got a second master's degree, and went back into the workforce specializing in interiors because that was still the one area that was of passion to me. It's been a long journey of exploring different aspects of design at different scales, at different levels.

After graduating from architecture school, there were two firms I wanted to work for. One was SOM. I always wanted to work for very big firms. I enjoy lots of people. And the other firm I wanted to work for was Gensler. And at the time, the reason I wanted to work for Gensler was because Margo Grant headed that practice. And I was very intrigued that of all the New York firms, it was the only one lead by a woman, and I wondered what that would be like. I didn't get to work directly with Margo Grant but worked at Gensler when she was still there. She was extraordinary, and I admired her. I don't think it makes a big difference, though, working in a firm with a female principal.

If I had to choose role models today, there are two women in history that I really strongly admire. One is Coco Chanel because of her extraordinary business acumen and her great aesthetic sense, but also because her contribution to the liberation of women in terms of clothing, that allowed women to be accepting of their natural bodies. I think that kind of design impact is huge, and I really admire her. Another woman that I admire in history is Anaïs Nin. She is an extraordinary writer, but I also admire her subject matter. She had the courage to express self at a time when expressing sensuality and sexuality was not really acceptable. Even today, that takes a lot of courage.

My entire work experience has been in three major New York firms. Starting my own practice was not something that was rationalized. It was something that came about after the Trade Center fell because of the bombings. I had designed a lot of space in the Trade Center. I had designed some fifteen floors of space. That was the largest footprint of a building in America at the time. Each floor plate was an acre in size. And we lost 600 individuals of that client, and I was pained by that, and equally pained by the loss of the space because I knew every single closet. I knew every single space on those floors that we had designed. SOM was in the neighborhood two blocks away. I didn't really want to be in the neighborhood after that. It was traumatic. So it was more mental and emotional than it was physical or rational.

I loved my job at SOM. It was such an amazing opportunity, such a great position, and I had such a good time working in large teams, exploring lofty ideas and doing things with the rigor that is an SOM ethos. But after 9/11, there was a period of soul searching that I think the whole nation went into. And I don't really know quite how it came about. I just know that by April of the following year, I left SOM. I took a month to figure out what I was going to do and decided that to start my own practice. The practice needed to be called The Collective. A lot of the ideas and issues that we were exploring at the time were about collaboration, life balance, working in practices in ways to be most creative while managing all other aspects of life. I had done a lot of thinking about how to improve the quality of life for all designers while at SOM.

I called it The Collective because I believe that it is the ultimate of collaborations. Our tagline is "minds multiplied" so two people come together and have the capacity of four. But that's not enough. It's really important that in the collaboration we are relaxed, we are at peace, we are dignified and respectful. This requires a different set of conditions. And so The Collective is structured to be modeled after the film industry where individuals come together to work on one project at a time. I suppose I've never been one for planning life. I've never thought five years [ahead].

Many people do that, and I've never done that. But I felt that we needed—we meaning society and culture, my generation—at this moment in time, we all need to be doing things a bit differently, thinking more profoundly about what we're doing and why we're doing it and how we might improve it. So The Collective was an idea that was about that improvement, and it came to be born in 2002.

I have three male partners. And we had the choice of setting it up as a woman-owned practice, and we didn't do it like that. I don't think it matters. But it is still very much a man led world in the twenty-first century, hugely problematic in our education institutions. In our educational [system], sixty percent of enrollment is women. So there's a big shift, and I don't think that in terms of experience at senior levels we are preparing for that well enough. I don't think gender matters if you're good at what you do.

Just starting the office has been extraordinary. We are now ten years in practice. The administration is still challenging, and we haven't mastered it yet. We expanded into the UK, so now we have a separate studio there, another office, which is very gratifying, but again, something that was not planned per se. It's fantastic to be working across the Atlantic, which I think is the way of the future. I do think that when we do things from the heart, driven by passion, they have their own path, and the path finds us or keeps us on the right track. I've made more time to focus on aspects of the projects that are more important. I love the conceptualization of our work. I love in particular working closely with the client, understanding his needs, his aspirations, less so the functional aspects which are easier to deal with, but much more the dreams, the desires. And I love working to take that client to the edge of his comfort zone, but not beyond because it is important that he feels really comfortable where he is, but also progressive. That's a gauge that is unique to every single client. And so I'm very proud of the work we do. We're not trend-focused nor do we have an ideology that espouses a particular kind of work, but we're very timely, topical, focused on issues, and focused on research. In that sense, our work has supported the people we've designed for. To me, that is the ultimate success in a project.

With every project we experiment with color, but it's always a very rational, careful insertion of color. It has nothing at all to do with my Indian background; I, of course always wear black. Still, color is one of the fundamental tools in architecture, but we don't know enough about it. In architecture, we probably understand more about light than we do about color. But we certainly place form-making on a higher pedestal than we do color and light. And I think that's backwards. I think that without light, we don't have life, we have nothing. The moment we switch that light switch or the sun comes up, we have space, and shade and shadow begin to define the scale and shape of those volumes, and color gives us an awful lot of information. I consider color to be one of those very essential design criteria that we as a discipline must really understand.

I've learned in a more theoretical exploration of color that in any volumetric space, it's important to have at least three tonalities—a light, a medium, and a dark—and different proportions. Do you remember the eighties when we were doing a lot of beige interiors? They're deathly. You walk in and you're not really sure what's going on. Well that was one kind of stylistic quality that we pursued that ultimately wasn't satisfying. Neither was the all-white interior or the all-concrete. Ultimately, it's not satisfying, anything singular is not satisfying. The human brain needs change, it needs contrast, and it understands more when there is a careful balance. And that balance includes texture, color, light and dark. Experimenting with and exploring light and color in architecture is essential.

How do we draw a client out of his or her comfort zone? I can cite several examples. We're working with the Scottish government where there is a very large approval system in place. The system is entirely based on function and in the last three or four years during the downturn of the economy, all of the requirements have become tougher and tighter. In Scotland the project is driven by function but still involves having conversations, having drinks with a client or tea with or lunch, or anything that's not so formalized, where it's possible to listen to them from a different place, and still understand or get behind why they are doing what they are doing, what they would like to see accomplished, other than "we need to save space to be more efficient, and somehow make people feel happier," which are the usual common criteria. We just finished designing a headquarters space for a brewery, for a distillery, a very different kind of client. It is owned by folks in Thailand but the [space is] in Scotland and that's an interesting international mix. They know what they do best—build breweries—but they are very much in Scotland. Blending these distinct perceptions and perspectives necessitates talking to everyone, talking a lot. This is one of the mantras that I use in the office: you can't communicate enough. As human beings, all we really have is the ability to communicate, and if we can understand each other, truly listen, and do it with respect and dignity and friendship, good happens.

I've had a foot in both worlds, academia and practice, all of my life. I went straight from undergraduate school and worked for nine months in London, and went to New York to do my Master's [degree]. Right after graduating, I started to teach. I graduated from Pratt and started to teach at Pratt. So I've never known another world. I've always known that there's a possibility of playing in this wonderful place we call school. Whether you teach or you're a student—in fact, if you're a teacher, you need to learn more to be able to do it—you're studying and you're exploring, researching and you're learning. The Academy was always very important for me to challenge some of the conventional pedagogies and processes that exist. It's not good enough to continually propagate what we already know. I challenge ideas of representation, of how to incorporate sensory knowledge within our applied works. Theory's great but only if it actually enhances our quality of life. If it doesn't then what's the point? But "practice" was always very important to me because it's not enough to have a theoretical understanding. It's equally important to test it in the practice. So I've always done both. Later a third component became very important. About ten years after doing both I became involved in developing volunteer work, pro bono work within an extended community. Cultivating a sense of excellence and an awareness among the general public is an equally important component. So the three, that triangle or sort of three-way relationship is really essential.

In our practice, we are very much an academic studio. We do a lot of research. We do research for every single project, and we research clients. And we have sixteen-foot ceiling heights—it's a small space but—in our main space, and two sides of it are full of books, bookshelves. Books are our primary resource along with materials because we think that's very important. We support this madness that we all have, being really driven to explore life. We all have our egos, but I don't think we are an ego-driven office. Our sight for our work isn't in the next five, ten, twenty years. We don't care whether we're published or not, that's really not what it's about. In fact, we don't enter competitions because the success of the project is less about what peers think of it. For us it is a testament of what clients come back and continue to want to work with us. And we go to the projects that we've built and we see the pride that the client takes in maintaining what we've done. When they don't change it in a hurry, we know we were successful. We love exploring and we love thinking and we have great conversations in the office. And there are times one of the partners will say: "okay, we should really be little more serious about billing." But on the other hand, we can deliberate, discuss, debate, talk an issue through, and bring everyone along. We love that. We have sort of like the United Nations in our small team where people are from different cultures. So we have fun with that. We push each other's buttons about the stereotypes that we all play with. To me, ultimately, that's what life is all about because if you can't make time to have a conversation with a colleague, then what is it that we are rushing to get done to do. And most people will say: "well, I want to go have time for family." And to me, this is an extension of that.

CHRISTOPH KLEMMT

CELLULAR GROWTH FABRICATION

Undergraduate Architecture, Director's Choice Award
Computational Design and Fabrication
Cincinnati, OH, USA

Organic growth processes occur through an incremental development of an entity, which allows for continuous adjustment and alterations according to external and internal requirements during its formation—a truly emergent development. Growth processes of this kind lead to the formation of fauna and flora, of mineral agglomerations or of organically grown human settlements. The processes are based on small units of material, such as the biologic cells that make up organisms, and on rules and behaviors for their accumulation, proliferation and differentiation [1].

Cellular growth processes of this kind can be simulated computationally [2-3], and the simulations can be appropriated as a design tool by assigning behaviors, functions and constraints to the cells that guide their development toward desirable formations, and especially toward a desired internal organization that fulfills the given requirements. This system allows for a truly bottom-up design, as has been desired by the parametric design community for many years [4], by going beyond merely setting up a geometric relational model in which the underlying graph remains fully static and only isolated parameters can be varied [5].

The difficulty of using a truly emergent system for design, however, lies in controlling the physical outcome. Without a top-down design and without the set-up of a relational model, all requirements of the entity to be designed must be translated into rules that are executed on the cellular level [6]. This includes very basic behaviors, such as cells recognizing their immediate neighbors and their geometric relationship towards them, larger organizational principles such as the enclosing of volume and programmatic distributions, as well as overall constraints on the growth system, like site influences and growth terminating conditions. The understanding, translation, and control of those behaviors is an evolutionary process of trial and error.

Amongst the many requirements any building faces, the issues of fabrication and structural stability may be the most basic. Any successful formation that has been generated through a cellular growth system must, therefore, be buildable as well as structurally stable. In our projects, this behavior was tested through the design and physical construction of a series of 1:1 prototypes. During the design phase, the cells of the simulations were set up to follow various internal behaviors as well as

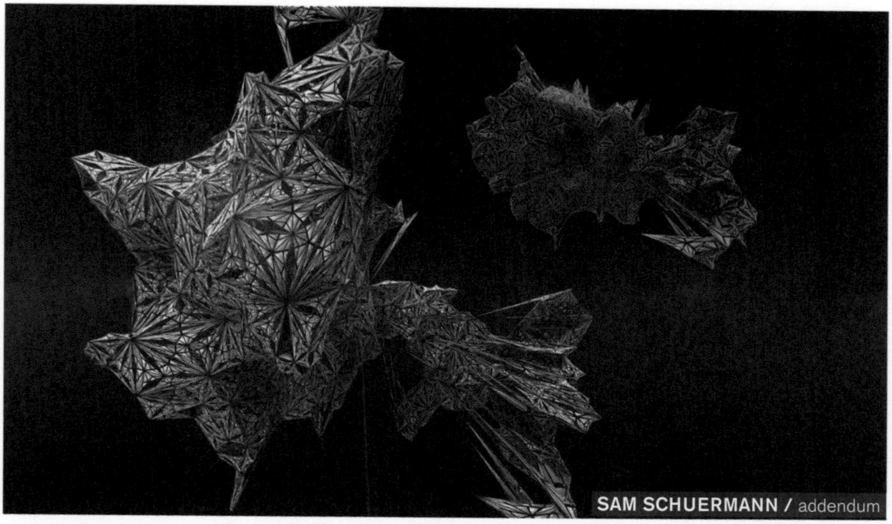

external influences. The internal behaviors related especially to local geometric relationships that corresponded to material constraints and corresponded to material constraints and construction details. On the contrary, the external influences on the contrary were derived from site conditions and large scale structural requirements.

De-Form

De-Form describes a system with a static cell neighborhood. The intercellular forces remained constant while the influence of various external forces were explored. The successfully applied forces related to different directional vector attributes and vector fields that shaped the final geometry. The resulting surface was patterned into an aluminum strip texture [7].

Tension

The installation was constructed as a double layer system from an elastic fabric material. The local behavior of adjacent cells was, therefore, based on spring forces that simulated the behavior of the fabric. In order to generate a functional tensile overall geometry, the growth of the cellular system was directed towards suitable anchor points that had been identified on the site. Further site conditions, such as requirements for human circulation and light conditions, were translated into forces that acted on the cells during the growth process.

Fission

All cells were arranged in a planar organization. Different rules were explored for the insertion of new cells into the system, for forces acting between adjacent cells, and for external influences that were controlled by static attractors. In order to create a stiff skin that can carry its own weight, the cellular arrangement was guided to create a folding triangulation. Together with a stiffening sublayer, the formation yielded a stable central dome with a cantilevering marginal corona.

Conclusions

If attempted as a functional rather than a purely aesthetic design tool, the use of a truly emergent system such as a cellular growth simulation has proven successful, although the designer executed guidance can be difficult to control. In all of the prototypes, it was possible to translate material constraints into intercellular behaviors that resulted in efficiently constructed formations. Basic programmatic requirements and site conditions could be accommodated, and further research will be directed towards refining the control over those.

De-Form, details

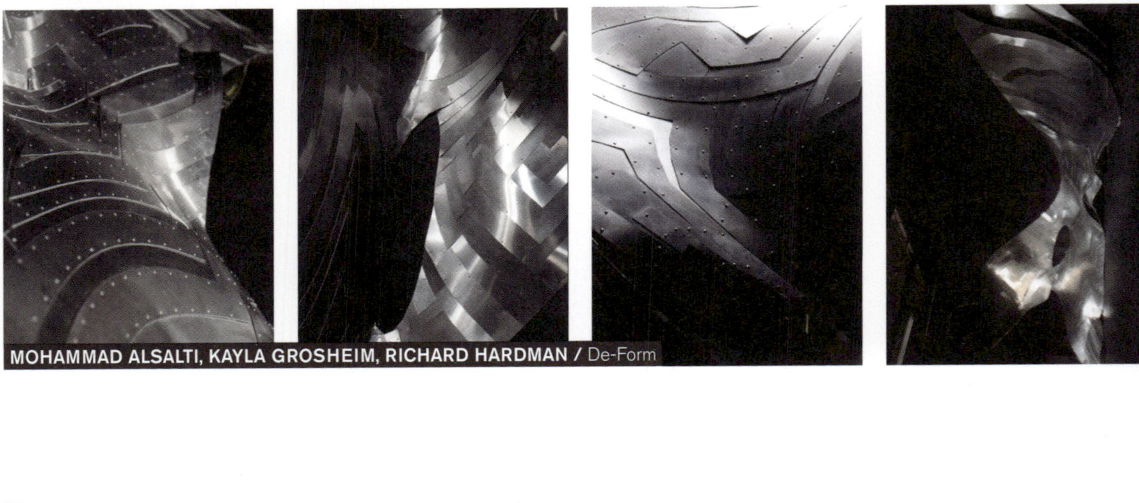

MOHAMMAD ALSALTI, KAYLA GROSHEIM, RICHARD HARDMAN / De-Form

Fission, details

JAMIE KRUER, AMANDA STEPHENS, SAMANTHA SCHUERMANN, JEROD TURNER / Fission

BRENDAR CARR, SHINJI MIYAJIMA, TYLER STOECKEL, TSUI-LUN WANG / Tension

Notes:

[1] Wolpert, L., Beddington, R., Jessell, T., Lawrence, P., Meyerowitz, E., Smith, J. (1998). *Principles of Development.* Oxford: Current Biology Ltd, Oxford University Press. p. 437.

[2] Merks, R. M. H., Guravage, M., Inzé D., Beemster G. T. S. (2010). "VirtualLeaf: An Open-Source Framework for Cell-Based Modeling of Plant Tissue Growth and Development." In *Plant Physiology 155: 656-666.* doi:10.1104/pp.110.167619.

[3] Milde, J. F. (2013). *Computational modeling and simulation of cellular growth and migration in angiogenesis* (Doctoral dissertation). Zurich: ETH. doi:10.3929/ethz-a-009756864.

[4] Leach, N. (1999). "Digital Morphogenesis: A New Paradigmatic Shift in Architecture." In *Architectural Design 79.* London: Wiley.

[5] Liaropoulos-Legendre, G. (2003). IJP *The Book of Surfaces.* London: The Architectural Association.

[6] Kwinter, S. (2008). *Far From Equilibrium: Essays on Technology and Design Culture.* Barcelona: Actar.

[7] Fornes, M. (2014). "Nonlin/Lin Pavilion." In *Paradigms in Computing*, edited by Gerber, D., Ibanez, M. Los Angeles: eVolo Press. 184-189.

KAYLA GROSHEIM / addendum

JEROD TURNER / addendum

ELIZABETH RIORDEN

GAINING THE HIGHER GROUND: MAKING CEMETERY REMOVAL ACCEPTABLE

Graduate Option Studio
Planned Retreat After Hurricane Sandy
Brooklyn, NY, USA

All cities will confront climate change in the near future, but the plight of coastal cities is especially challenging. Populations and activities may be forced to seek refuge in contested higher ground, leading to disorder and conflict. Planning for such needs (called "planned retreat" or "adaptation") could be a mechanism for a healthier transition, but as humans our tendency is to deal with short-term priorities and ignore the rest, despite having reliable data. A public discourse on these clear and potential dangers, and possible planning and design solutions, is a first step towards a relationship with the future which is proactive rather than reactive.

Superstorm Sandy was the "canary in the mine" for New York City. Following the catastrophe, many scientists had an audience for reiterations of their previous warnings (see Paul Hond, *Columbia Magazine*, Winter 2012-13). Some noted that substantial high ground within the NYC urban area, the area needed for planned retreat driven by climate change, is occupied by large, historic cemeteries. In the New World, unlike in Europe, for example, citizens are neither acquainted nor comfortable with cemetery reuse. The urban design problem is a question of societal values and finding a way to commemorate the deceased, through attentive design, while occupying less footprint. Once free of the burials, this land becomes prime resettlement areas, allowing the resiliency of the city. In the early months of 2016, an advanced urban design and architecture studio grappled with the problem of planned retreat and re-use of burial grounds.

PRIYANKA SEN / site diagram and perspectives

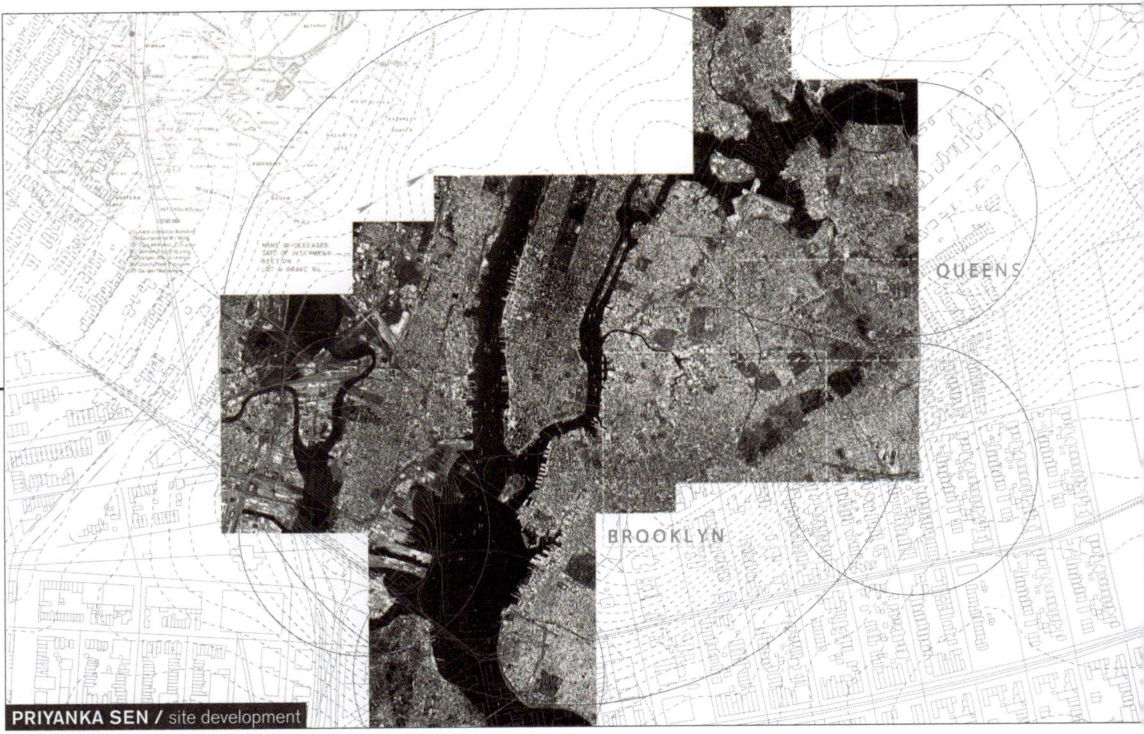

PRIYANKA SEN / site development

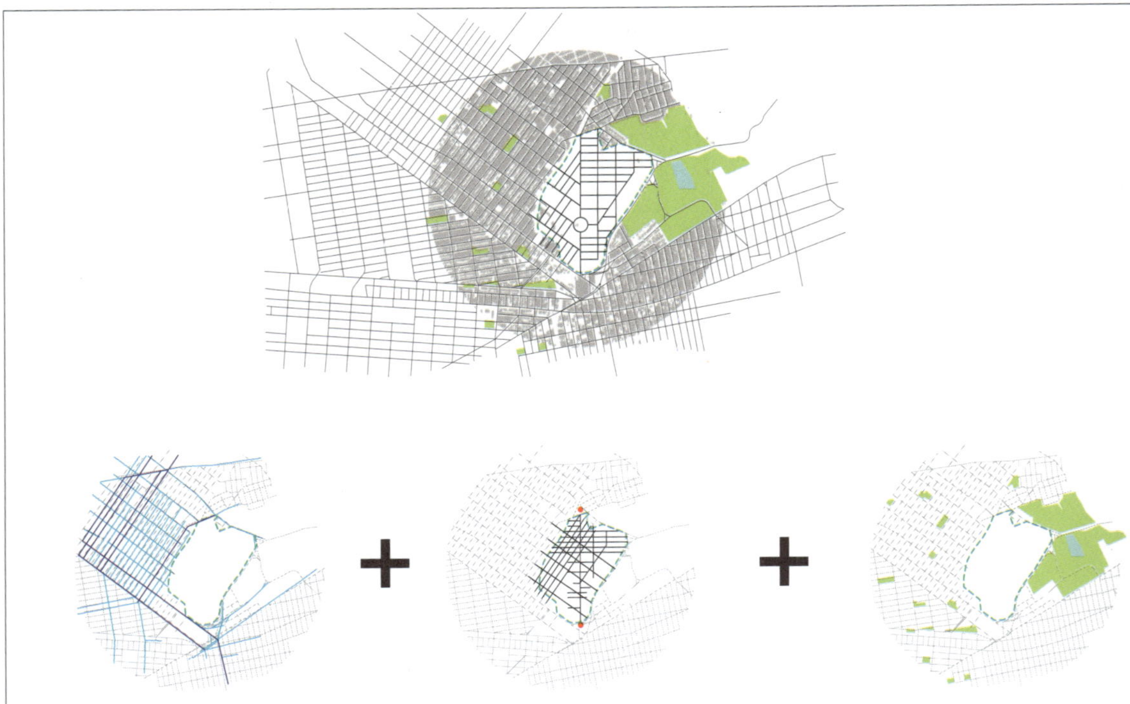

EXISTING CONTEXT + SITE

EXISTING LANDSCAPE

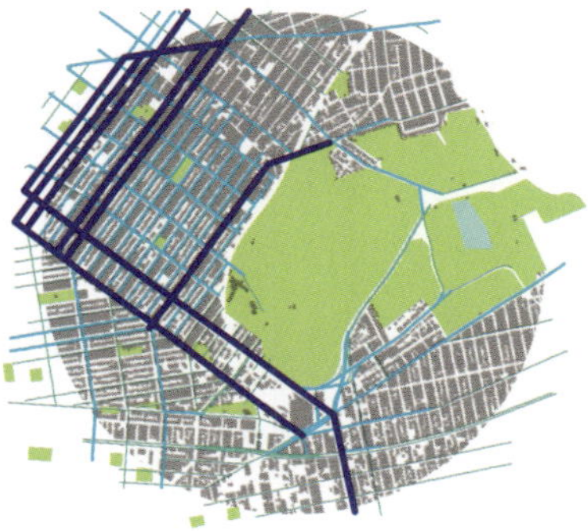

EXISTING MOST INTEGRATED ROADS

EXISTING SUBWAY TRANSIT AND BIKE PATHS

EXISTING CONTEXT WITH NEW SITE

NEW SITE LANDSCAPE

MOST INTEGRATED STREETS

NEW TRANSIT AND BIKE PATHS

MARA MARCU
MING TANG

THE *STRANGE* WALL

Sculptural Objects Functional Art and Design International Fair
Chicago, IL, USA

In music, the strange loop, refers to the phenomenon in which a pattern set by a composer is then broken only to return whole again, as in Bach's canons. As Hofstadter remarks, implicit to the concept of the strange loop is the concept of infinity, since "what else is a loop but a way of representing an endless process in a finite way?" [1]. As seen in Escher's "Metamorphosis," infinity plays a large role. Copies of one single theme often fit into each other, forming visual analogues to the cannons of Bach. Through a process of incremental mutation, various taxonomies were developed. The following of a 'paste special' methodology led to the breeding of multiple offshoots. The outcome became in itself, an abstracted strange loop of tectonic permutations.

Using CATIA, a total of 66 cells with variable inputs were instantiated within an armature via a knowledge pattern that automated the insertion of each user-defined-feature (UDF). Eight sheets of high-density foam were flip-milled and joined with a two-part epoxy adhesive. Following assemblage, the installation was coated with thin layers of latex primer and gold metallic paint.

The tool path pattern—conducted in relation to digitally assisted analytic methods—is a study in the creation of ornament that learns from the geometric mass. Surface curvatures, sizes, and normal forces became the focus of our computation method. Various scripts were developed to induce the visualization of this surface data. The 2D pattern was then mapped to the correct UV points on each surface while taking into consideration accessibility for the CNC tool head. The tessellation process was then applied based on the thickness and step-over values mapped to each tool. The resulting pattern was programmed as a customized tool path in the Power Mill software, embedding memory of data mapping and fabrication processes into the final product.

The moiré effect created by the friction of the striped patterning amplifying shadows accentuate the perception of the wall as landscape, or territory, with juxtaposed rhythms and logics, and minimize the otherwise modular or composite reading of an additive assembly process. The specific joining of the various cells becomes insignificant as the eye becomes preoccupied with the reading of the nomadic invasiveness of the various ordering systems that cut across arbolic-like divisions. The inherent interpretation of ornament as having both function and affect calls for an open-ended dialogue on the untrivialization of the concept and anticipates accentuated forms of interaction between the inhabited and the uninhabitable.

The Strange Wall, detail

base unit taxonomy

Notes:

[1] Hofstadter, D.R. (1999). *Gödel, Escher, Bach: An Eternal Golden Braid.* New York: Basic Books; Anniversary edition.

Credits:

Abed Breir, Adam Rayne, Maggie Ming, and Garcia Ghislaine–for help with assembling, set up and painting.

Special thanks to William Williams, former Director of the University of Cincinnati School of Architecture and Interior Design (UC SAID) for his support and to Nick Germann, UC SAID Rapid Prototyping Center Manager for his invaluable and incredibly generous consulting on fabrication and CNC routing.

HAN SHEN
LUCAS MUSEUM

During my first semester while I was applying for my first Co-op internship, I got a call from my friend in Chicago asking if I am interested in working on the Lucas Museum. And just like that, I am off to Chicago to work for VOA Associates on the Lucas Museum of Narrative Arts for four months.

On my first day at VOA Associates, I was introduced to the design team of twelve people (which is surprisingly small considering the scope of the project), and the project model on the cloud (a whopping 16 GB Revit model with structure, MEP system and interior details). Once I familiarized myself with the project, I was given my first assignment: remodeling a spiral ramp in the plaza to be code compliant and researching a better way to import Rhino geometry into Revit. I then spent the next two weeks exploring all the possible ways of interoperability between Rhino and Revit and finally delivered my first model. It was one of my proudest moment when the structural engineer called my newly improved model a masterpiece during a meeting.

My next assignment was to redesign an interior ramp revolving around a dome. As the dome are designed as the focal point of the museum lobby and the ramp is the major circulation path around the museum galleries, the design of the ramp and all the architectural elements around it was a complicated problem. In order to make the design code compliant while keeping it true to the design intent, I decided to write a Grasshopper script to solve the problem.

When I first started, the project managers are skeptical about using Grasshopper as it is often perceived as a tool to create cool-looking but impractical designs. So I wrote a proof-of-concept script during my off-time to show how I can use Grasshopper's computing capability to generate rationalized, code-compliant geometries. After show the proof-of-concept to my teammates, I was tasked to create a set of Grasshopper scripts that calculates all the architectural elements on the ramp. The end result is a massive Grasshopper script with 2,300 components that generates everything around the ramp, from the ramp itself and the balustrade walls to the floor pattern. Near the end of my co-op internship, I was asked to demonstrate my work in Grasshopper to the rest of the company. During the demonstration, my project manager said that this new technology has changed the team dynamic completely. He said that while I have no idea how to build the project (I really don't), he has no idea how to draw it. So instead of handing me redlined drawings to correct, we'd have to work as a team to solve problems and share information.

Looking back on my first Co-op experience, it is amazing how the new technologies have enabled our generation of students to take on more responsibilities in the professional environment. The Co-op experience has provided a perfect opportunity to test the skill we gained in the academic world in the real world.

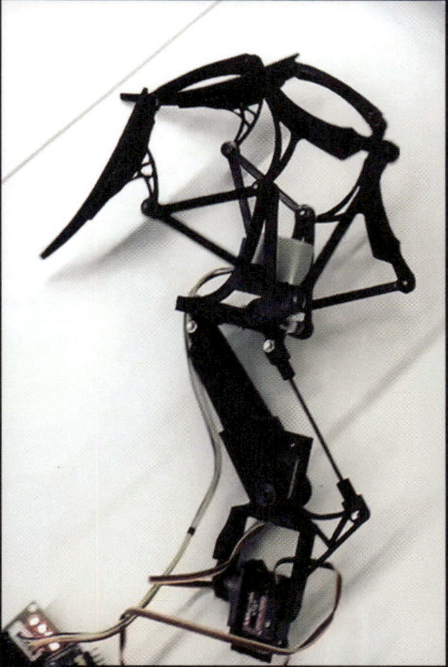

HAN SHEN / A Retreat to Autonomy, thesis

SAHYA

Venice, Italy, EU

Economic Construction
Orproject is interested in the feasible and economic construction of complex and double-curved geometries. The prohibitive cost of molds, however, often renders the use of double curved elements unsustainable for projects which need to remain commercially viable. With Sahya, Orproject explored the possibilities and variation which can be achieved by only utilizing one single mold.

Facade System
All 200 panels of Sahya are double curved and have been formed from the same mold, and more than 50% of the panels are identical. The remaining panels are smaller segments that have been cut from the full panels. By arranging the panels in several parallel layers, the system allows for a large amount of variation in the resulting overlay as an aluminum facade system. The possibilities to create varying openings and shadow patterns can be used to generate a perforated lattice screen.

Structural System
Sahya is the further development in three dimensions of Orproject's previous installation Anisotropia, which was built for the National Museum of China. In their three-dimensional implementation, however, the panels now also start to form a load-bearing structural system that enables free standing applications without additional support systems.

Shading Pavilions
Employing structural as well as shading properties, Orproject is working on a pavilion for a hot climate, for which Sahya has been constructed as the initial prototype. The pavilion will protect from the sun and provide a comfortable outdoor environment. The variations in the wall translucencies are used to control the views and to generate continuously evolving shadow patterns, while the curved elements evoke associations of waves and cooling water.

Sahya was constructed for the exhibition *Time - Space - Existence* at Palazzo Mora that took place with the occasion of the 2016 Venice Biennale.

Credits
Project Architects: Christoph Klemmt, Rajat Sodhi, Haseb Zada
Photography: Valerie Bennett, Orproject
Images by Orproject (www.orproject.com)

Sahya, details

Sahya, Venice Biennale

Sahya, Venice Biennale

SINHEA LEE
HANK HILDEBRANDT (chiar)
GULEN CEVIK (member)
EDSON CABALFIN, PH.D. (member)

BORDERLESS

Masters of Interior Design Thesis
Cincinnati, OH, USA

Reconciliation between North and South Korea

Since the ceasefire between the two Koreas in 1953, there have been various provocative actions in North Korea and South Korea. After North and South Korea were separated, their social systems were developed based on how the two countries have been constructed, North Korea with a socialist ideology, and South Korea with a national capitalist ideology.

Currently there is a village, Daesong-dong 'Freedom' Village, in the southern part of the Demilitarized Zone (DMZ), which is located along the Border line and was first established on August 1953 based on the "Agreement About Civilian's Entrance Into DMZ." Daesong-dong Village is the one of two villages that exist in each side of the DMZ. The other village is Kijong-Dong, a village of 'Peace' in North Korea, which is located only 1.11 miles from Daesong-dong Village. They were once neighboring villages with significant interaction; however, sixty years of extreme isolation have resulted in disconnection and extreme limitations on cooperation.

The goal of this project is to create a place for reunification without any consideration of the border line or military force in the location of the Joint Security Area, the only place in the middle of the border that can facilitate coexistence between the two Koreas. It will be a new identity and a new geography – creation of one organization of a united mindset and dissolution of the border – that will dissolve the contrasting powers and ideologies. By providing a place on the border line, there will be an opportunity to create –in the present – moments that were possible in past. This is best exemplified by the room for the tea ceremony, a traditional ceremony from Korea's past, present in the building of Borderless.

Journey to release the resentment

"Han" is a concept in Korean culture and language attributed as a unique Korean cultural trait which has resulted from Korea's frequent exposure to invasions by overwhelming foreign powers.
Han denotes a collective feeling of oppression and isolation in the face of insurmountable odds. It connotes aspects of lament and unresolved injustice [1].

Han as a "feeling of unresolved resentment against injustices suffered, a sense of helplessness, a feeling of acute pain in one's guts, making the whole body writhe and squirm, and an obstinate urge to take revenge and to right the wrong—all these combined" [2]. Han can be nearly translated

trajectory of dance

SINHEA LEE / Tea Pavilion of Meditation

trajectory of dance

Tea Pavilion, entrance

as sorrow, spite, rancor, regret, resentment or grief, among many other attempts to explain the concept. Han is an inherent characteristic of the Korean character and, as such, finds expression, implied or explicit, in nearly every aspect of Korean life and culture. As expressions of Han, Koreans have elevated the Han into many art forms such as paintings, comedy, or dance. For example, there is a Korean poem by Ji-hoon Cho, describing a dance of a young female monk's Han by "kleshas." Kleshas, in Buddhism, are mental states that cloud the mind and manifest in unwholesome actions and include states of mind such as anxiety, fear, anger, jealousy, desire, and depression that, in turn, can be translated into afflictions, defilements, destructive emotions, disturbing emotions, negative emotions, mind poisons, etc. [3]. Cho described the 'Han', narrating the movement of a young Buddhist Nun expressing her sorrow without any word.

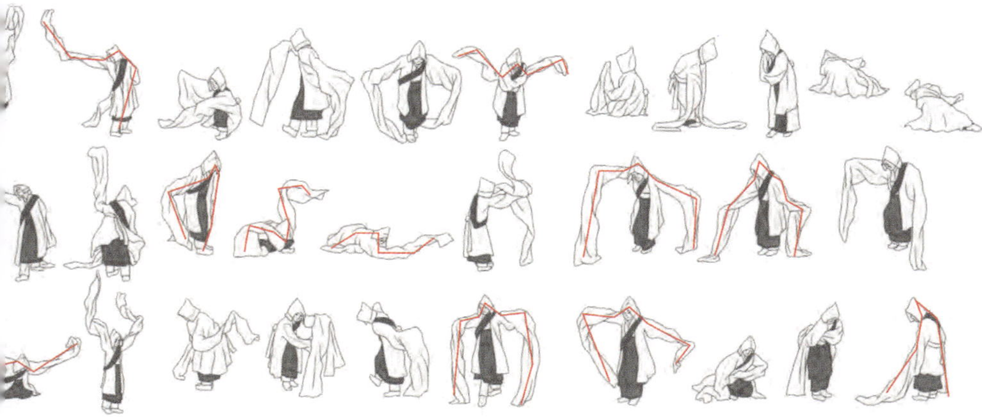

Tea Pavilion of Meditation

The seven cottage-like Joint Security Area committee buildings in the DMZ are the place where the whole separated Korean 'Han' originated. Since the poet described the moments of dance moves releasing the Han, a mass will be floated up, faces will be actively curved and bent to show the struggle, the very even energy of powers from two organizations and two mindsets confronting each other. As a stillness of overwhelmed moment whereby all the Han is purified as a highlight of the journey in the building, a tea pavilion of meditation will complete the organization of one mindset.

Notes:

[1] Kim, Luke I.C. (2012). *Beyond the Battle Line: The Korean War and My Life*. Xlibris Corporation.
[2] Yoo, Boo Wong (1988). *Korean Pentecostalism: Its History and Theology*. Publications Universitaires Europeennes.
[3] Kim, Jaihun. (1994). *Modern Korean Poetry*. Freemont, CA: Asian Humanities Press.

MARA MARCU

PSEUDOVERTICAL!

Graduate Option Studio
High Line, New York City, NY, USA

***PseudoVertical* proposes to understand the vertical-scape as a self-generating, autopoietic entity [see Humberto Maturana and Francisco Varela definition of the terms as "the self-maintaining chemistry of living cells"], in which systems and typologies are in a continuous flux. Situated along the High Line, *PseudoVertical* seeks potential resolution in the very surreal culture of congestion itself: New York. The epitome of super imposed artificial order anticipating unforeseen social structures and human interactions, New York offers a multiplicity of tentacular opportunistic synapses between unpredicted amounts of strata. The High Line is seen as a prototypical example of connections and cross-pollination possibilities that, when reiterated vertically, define a pseudo-vertical environment.**

This studio builds on the assumption that the traditional skyscraper has surpassed the mainstream and—like any totalitarian system—has collapsed in terms of social relevance, lost credibility and bored the public eye for the past decades [see "Verticalism (The Future of the Skyscraper)" by Inaki Abalos in *GSD Platform*, 2008]. A product of the industrialized age, the skyscraper represented, as its very name suggests, the axis mundi, the connection to the above, and–consequently–a tangible utopia. If utopical ambitions were the agenda of the first third of the 20th century, today, however, such speculations are regarded as rather suspect and definitely naive [see "The Autopoiesis of Architecture" by P. Scumacher]. For this reason the studio aimed at producing mutations, understood as opportunities, rather than solutions.

Quantitative and qualitative programmatic analysis, as well as social and cultural attitudes elicited the speculation of various typologies generated by the New York's Greatest Vertical Hits. While employing spatial grammar, disruptive vertical arrangements began to populate the urban habitat. Special attention is placed on representation, seen here not as a visualization tool but as a design generator. As such, each misalignment in the digital output has been exploited and re-calibrated back in the conceptual feed. Students oscillated between the ludic and the investigative, while aiming at the elaboration of novel form-function relations. Through post-rationalization and programmatic adaptability a new form of urbanism has emerged.

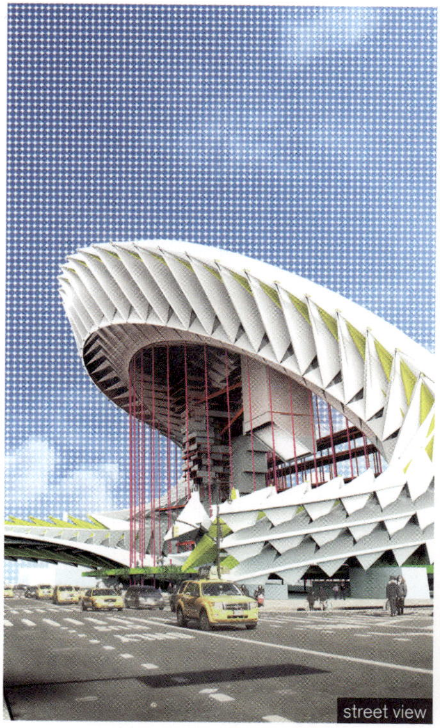
street view

runway from the High Line

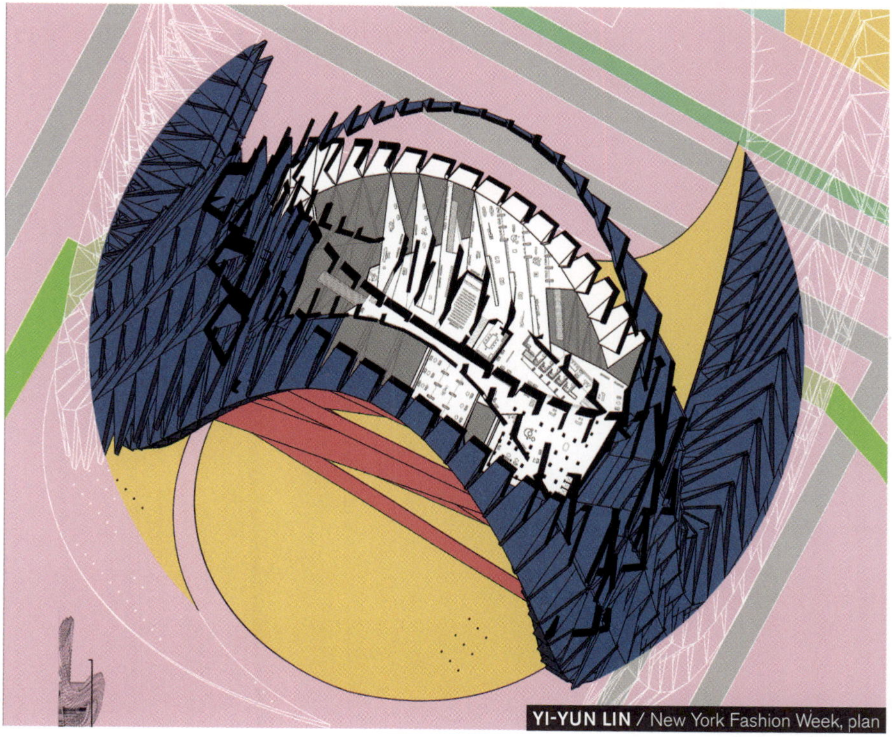
YI-YUN LIN / New York Fashion Week, plan

DUNG LE / Heaven, section

Distraction

Entrance

Revelation

At the Top

Venus, base unit aggregation

Infinity Cloud

Bird's eye

The Cloud Atlas

JOHN STOUGHTON (article and image credits)

COMPUTATIONAL ECOLOGIES

Design in the Anthropocene

Organizers included:
Lonn Combs, Technical Chair
Chris Perry, Technical Chair
William Williams, Site Chair
Mara Marcu, Exhibitions Chair
Brian Ringley, Workshops Chair
Stephen Slaughter, Site Co-Chair
Ming Tang, Media Chair

The Association for Computer Aided Design in Architecture (ACADIA) [http://acadia.org/] is an international network of digital design researchers and professionals. ACADIA was formed for the purpose of facilitating communication and critical thinking regarding the use of computers in architecture, planning, and building science. The organization is committed to the research and development of computational methods that enhance design creativity and that aim to contributing to the construction of humane physical environments. A particular focus is placed on education and the software, hardware and pedagogy involved in academia.

The 35th annual conference of the Association for Computer-Aided Design in Architecture (ACADIA) took place in Cincinnati. The international conference, a three-day long academic event, presented peer-reviewed research and experimental work of fifty computational designers, students, and architects.

The conference topics ranged from material science, biomimesis, geomimesis, robotics, environmental parametrics, ecological urbanism. Advanced computational design methods, building information modeling, and digital fabrication workshops preceded the conference event. Full research papers, short work-in-progress papers, and juried design and research posters were presented. Work-in-progress presentations were enriched by mentoring and structured feedback.

The event was enriched by curated projects including publications on emerging teaching models for complex systems and adaptive architecture, exhibition of architectural prototypes, and installations by visiting student teams.

The conference was bookended by a series of three-day workshops at the beginning of the week, and a one-day post-conference hackathon, orwganized by Site Coordinator Brian Ringley of Woods Bagot and Pratt Institute.

The workshops provided a range of projects catering to both students, industry leaders, and design professionals. Topics covered ranged from CNC machining to Interaction Design (IxD) to BIM analysis and optimization. Tools featured in the workshops included Processing (Java), Dynamo (Autodesk), and Rhino/Grasshopper.

The conference presentations and discussions were distributed between downtown Cincinnati (Deborah Berke's 21c Museum and Zaha Hadid's

Contemporary Arts Center) and the University of Cincinnati two miles north of downtown, where a large portfolio of signature contemporary architecture has been built largely within the past decade.

Keynote lectures by Stefan Behnisch, amid.cero9, Francois Roche, and Nader Tehrani were spread throughout the daily sessions. A curated exhibition of installations debuted during the conference, expanding on the 'computational ecologies' theme.

Brian Ringley saw the conference as a "unique way to showcase innovation embedded within the historical richness of a post-industrial Midwestern context." Local flavor from this year's conference included an evening coordinated by Matt Anthony's Cincinnati Made initiative at a 25,000-square-foot renovated 1850s brewery in the heart of Over-the-Rhine's brewery district—a neighborhood which contains the country's largest historic district. Outside the brewery, Giacomo Ciminello showcased his People's Liberty, a funded "Spaced Invaders" projection-mapped video game and an ongoing art project calling attention to underutilized urban spaces in the city.

A full list of organizers, sponsors, and participants can be found on the conference website (2015.acadia.org). Papers may be found on CUMINCAD, an open access digital library of 8,300 PDF full papers from this and other related events.

CONNOR HYMES
CHRISTOPH KLEMMT (chiar)

ABOVE THE STREET

Master of Architecture Thesis
New York City, NY, USA

This thesis responds to the future needs of Manhattan as an increasingly interconnected and diverse network of people and their relationship to the city; it reimagines how humans interact with the city, creating connections above the street as shared public spaces in between buildings. The methodology applied to this research designs agent-based interactions at multiple scales of the city, and allows for the ability to refine agent to agent development inbetween varying scales, and is implemented as a way of programming agents and investigating how they can be used as design generators through their interaction with other agents and their environment. As a recursive method of design, the thesis attempts to create relationships of agents at the local scale that form complex emergent systems with contextual relationships to the city, setting up a newly proposed urban framework of connective spaces to re-activate Manhattan. Through the connection of the city's upper areas, this project engages numerous buildings and forges new relationships with Manhattan's verticality.

Agent-based swarms are the result of the basic principles of flocking outlined by Craig Reynolds in the project *Boids*. Agents within a swarm use the steering behaviors of separation, alignment, and cohesion in order to control agent-to-agent interaction of a swarm within a given three dimensional simulated environment. Swarms use a variety of coded variables that are designed before the simulation begins and allow the agents in the swarm to self-organize through design intent. The origin of swarms simulated flocks of birds, but that is not the principal intent of this research; the understanding a bird and its relationship to the flock led to a better understanding of the movement of an agent within a swarm. Within agent-based swarm models, the agents react to other agents at a nearby distance allowing for localized customization of agents that are not aware of the entire form of the flock. This has been described as bottom-up design methodology that can create complex systems from designing interactions at the smaller scale create emergent self-organizing systems.

Within Manhattan research was conducted on multiple scales in order to create more intensified connections to the city through agent-based design. The scales of design include the city, the city block, building, and details.

section detail

CONNOR HYMES / section

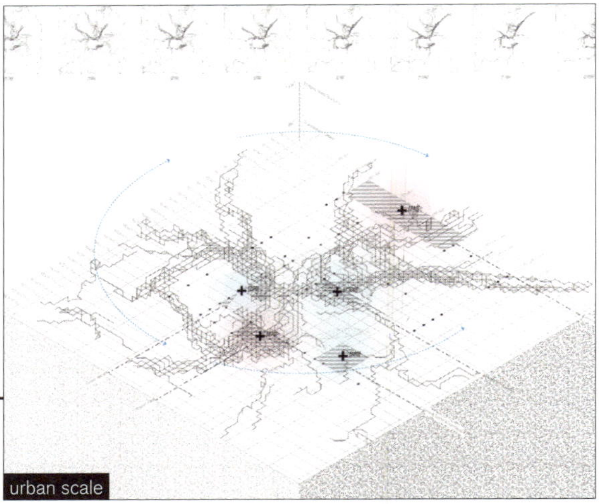
urban scale

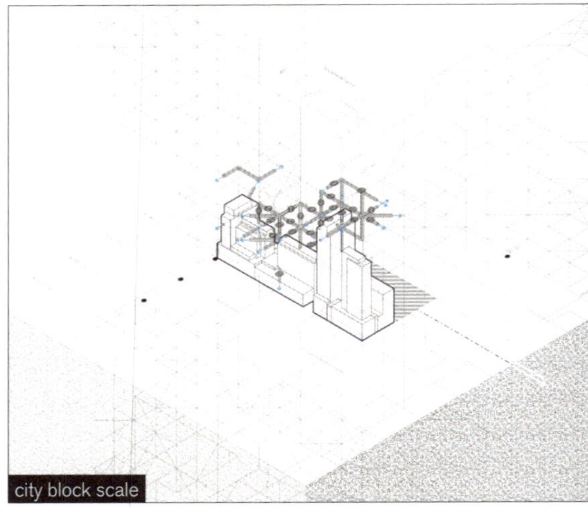
city block scale

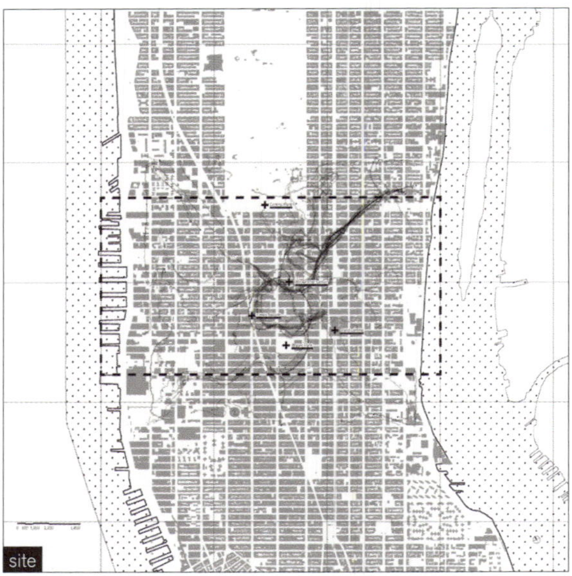
site

city agents

site, circulation, structure, skin

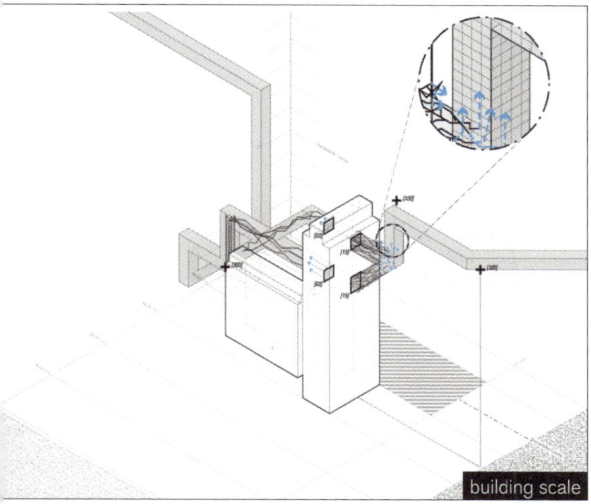
building scale

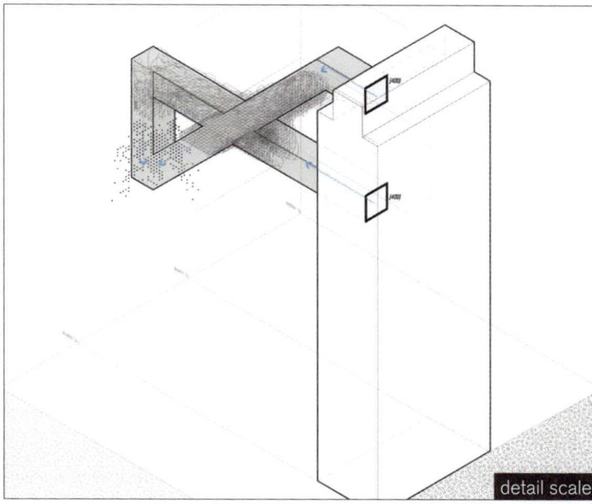
detail scale

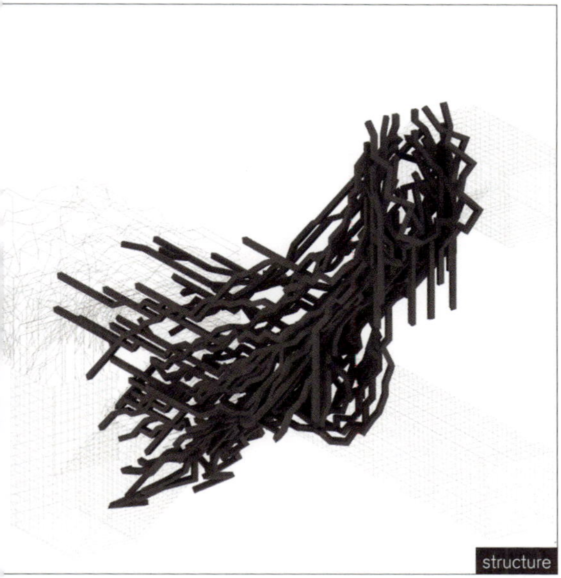
structure

window detail

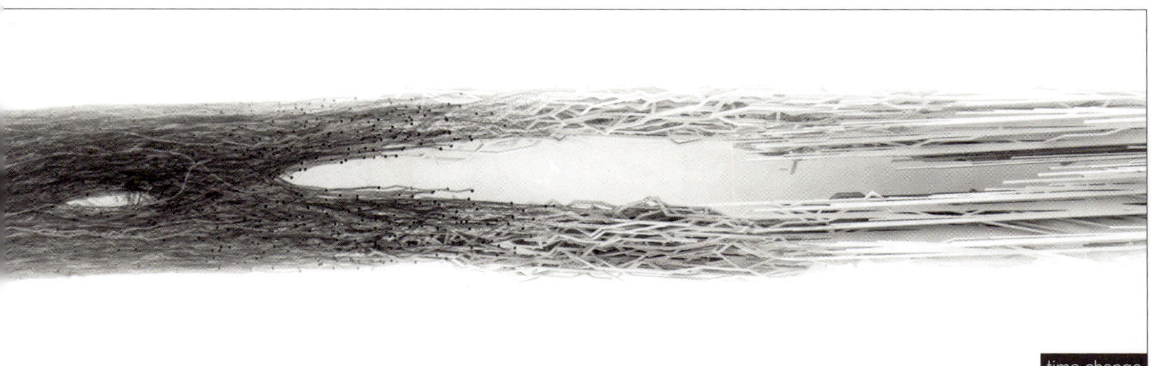
time change

agent design sequence

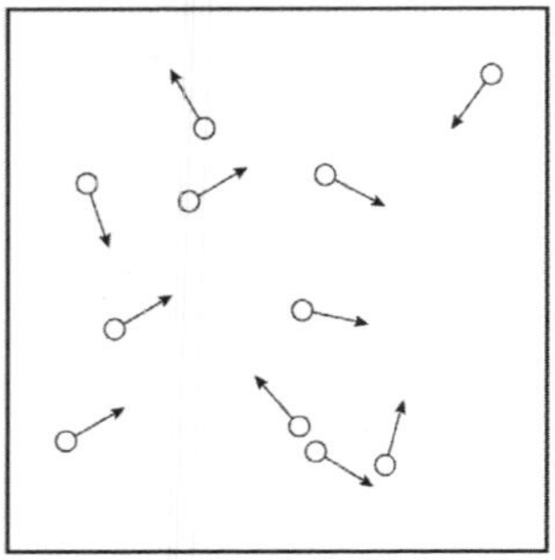

Agents Moving in Space
agents begin to accelerate in the given environment in random directions.

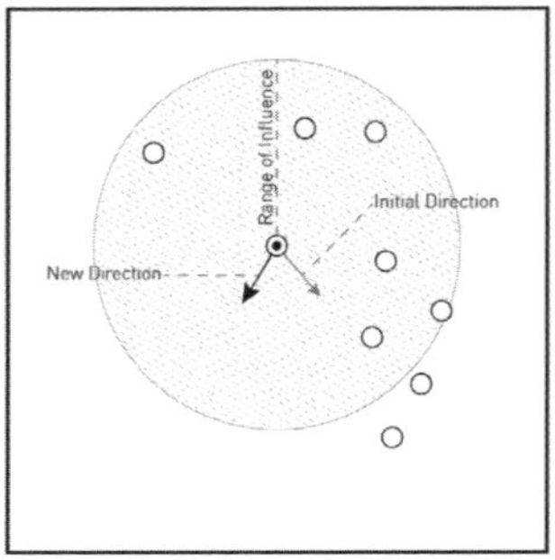

Separation
agents move to avoid other nearby agents.

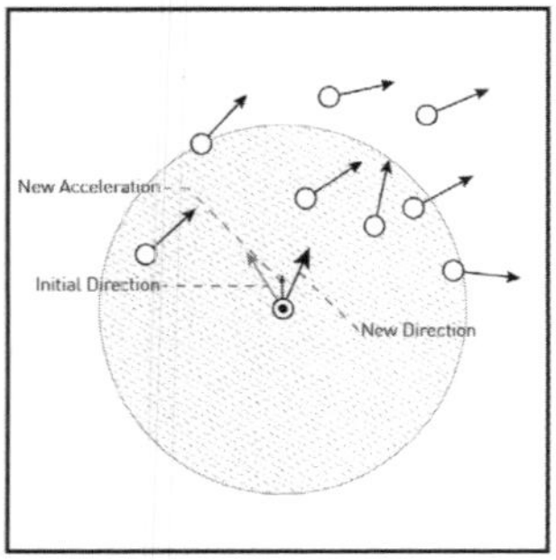

Alignment
an agent will move towards the average direction of other local agents and trails drawn.

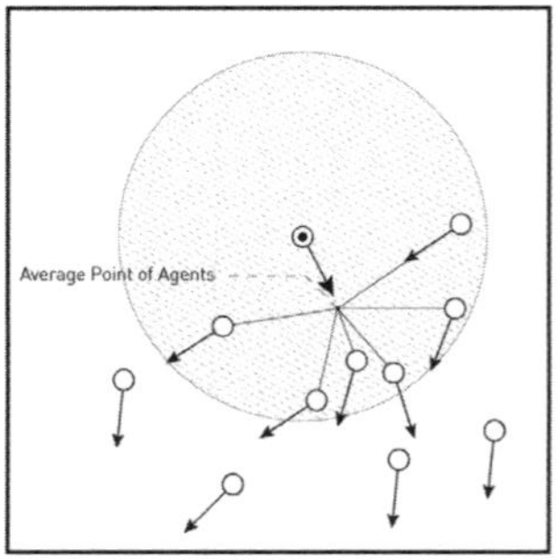

Cohesion
agents move toward the current position of other agents.

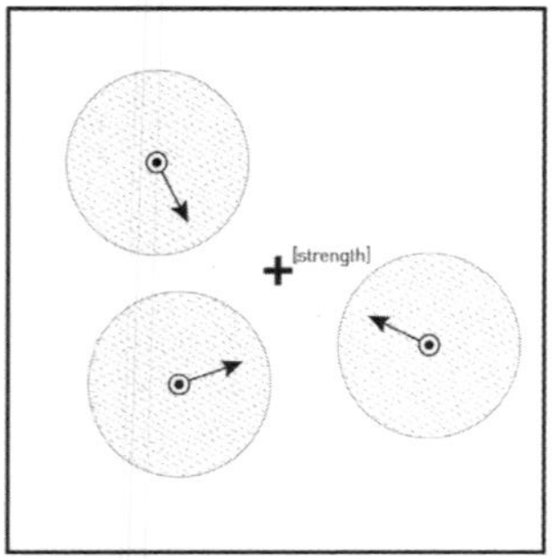

Point Attractors
points attractors in the given environment can attract or repel agents and swarms influencing the overall design.

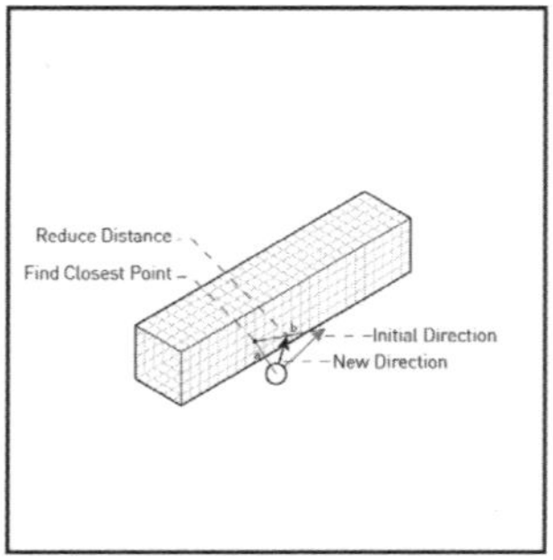

Mesh Attraction
agent mesh interaction is used at the local scale allowing the agents to be influenced by a given form.

detail renderings

PAUL KIM
CHRISTOPH KLEMMT (chair)

RATIONALIZATION OF COMBINATORIAL DESIGN FOR MICROHOUSING

Master of Architecture Thesis
Cincinnati, OH, USA

By taking a combinatorial design approach, this thesis explores spatial and programmatic arrangements of residential units to design microhousing for temporary residents living in urban settings. In order to explore spaces, it was critical to itemize a building's spatial components. By distinguishing the essential and non-essential components of each space, necessary spaces are defined by the activities of daily living. Then boundaries were created around the essential components considering anthropometry and circulation suitable for microhousing. These essential action spaces became templates throughout the thesis.

A growth of architectural form is one of the most critical factors in this exploration. Spatial combinations from the smallest to largest scale have facilitated this study in generating an ideal microhousing community. Rules and constraints are implemented to keep layouts organized and forms intact. The initial goal to preserve spatial efficiency was carried throughout the exploration. As scales grew, the primary focus was shifted from maintaining spatial efficiency to preserving modularity of combinatorics.

The premise was to analyze necessary spaces and to generate an architectural form by combining modular components through spatial combinations and analysis of their spatial efficiency followed by the analysis of generated forms. The design proposal hopes to benefit public and private interests, including single residents, students, young professionals, rehabilitating patients, senior citizens, and visitors. This research can persuade future real-estate developers, architects, and contractors to engage in the combinatorial design of microhousing to advance its construction techniques, to meet the housing demand, to sustain housing affordability, and to encourage innovative design strategies. More importantly, this work encourages the combinatorial design method to architectural students to expand their knowledge in generating innovative systems of modular combinations.

interior unit perspective

interior unit perspective

interior courtyard perspective

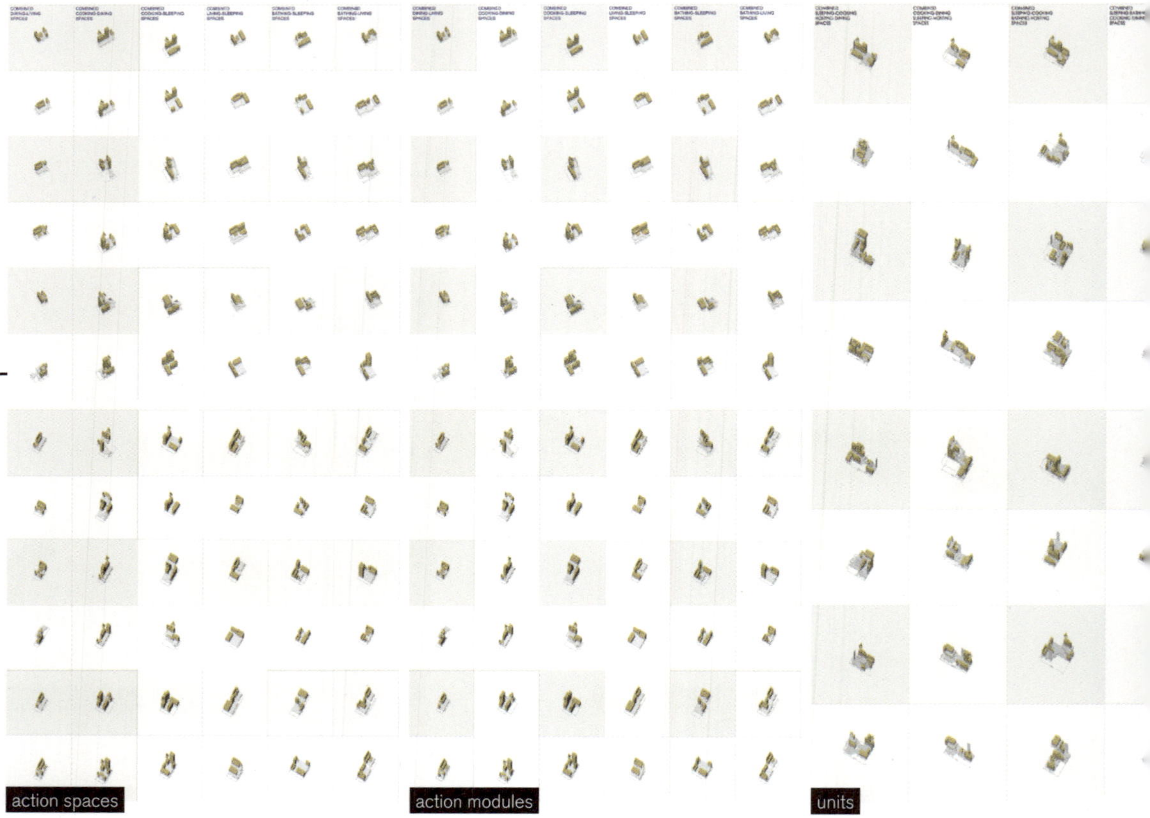

overall bird's eye view

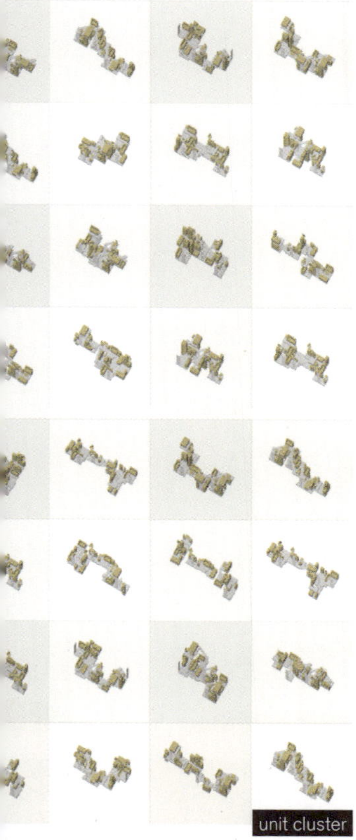
unit cluster

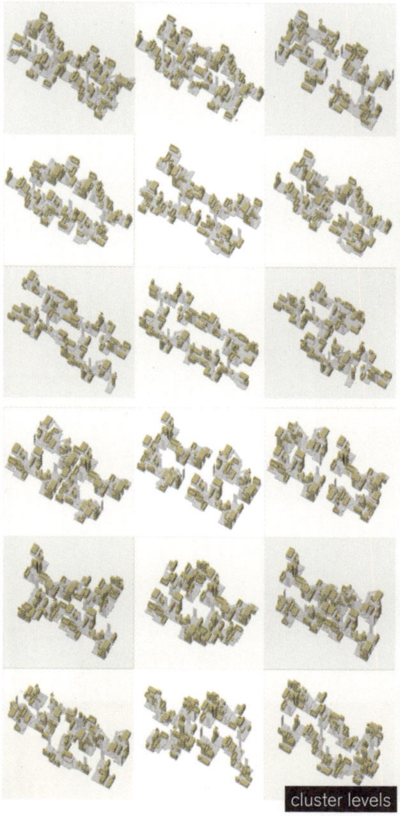
cluster levels

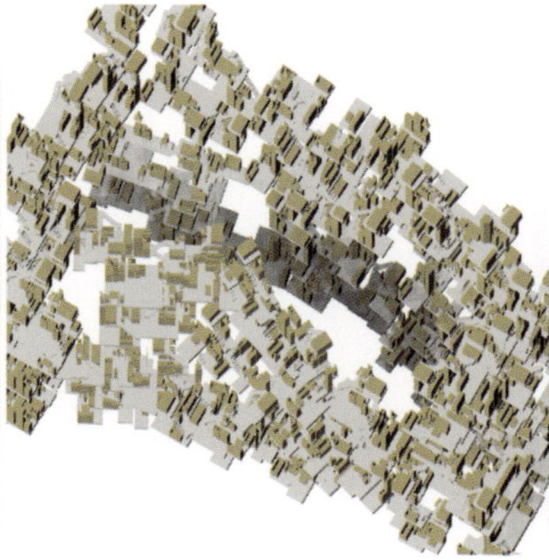

buildings

row bird's eye view

amoeba bird's eye view

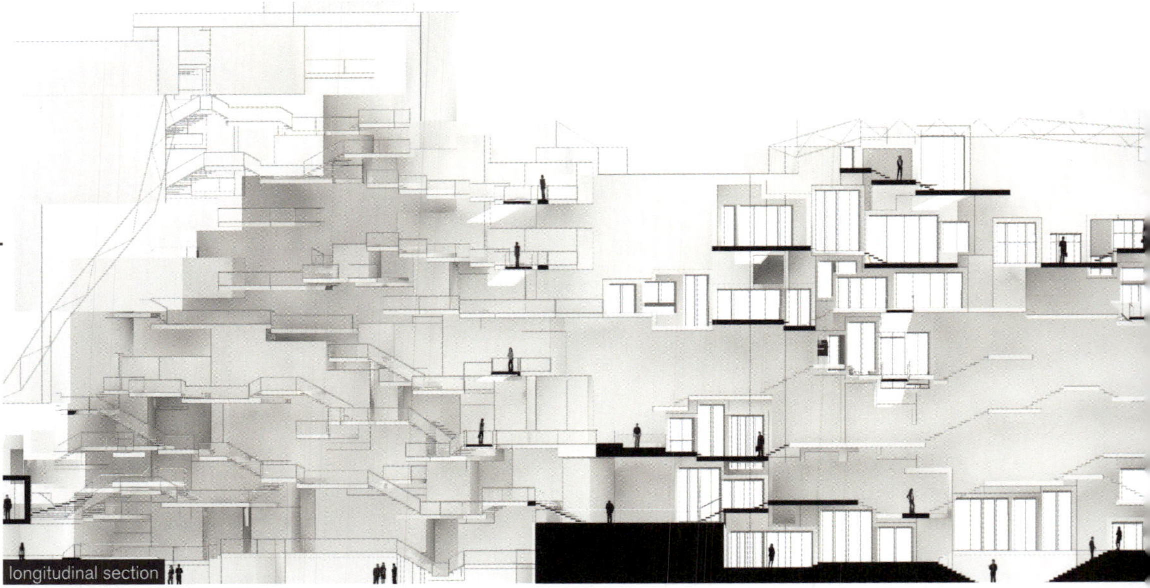
longitudinal section

cluster armature

cross section

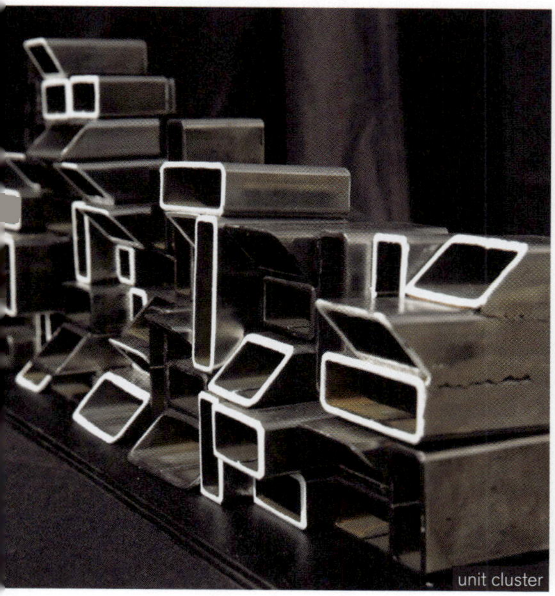

unit cluster

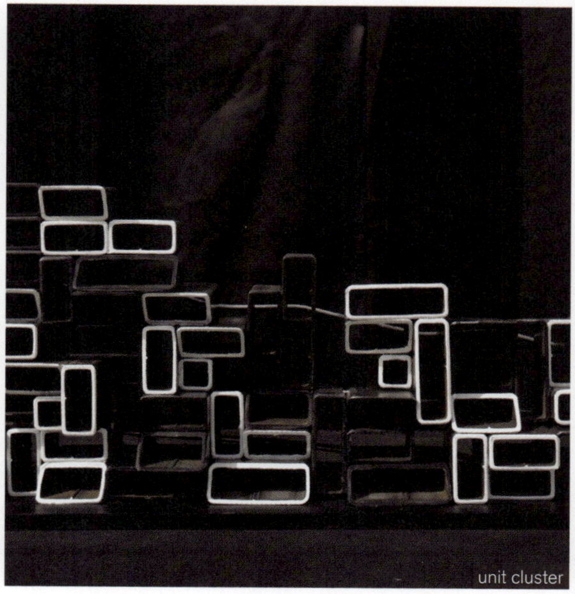

unit cluster

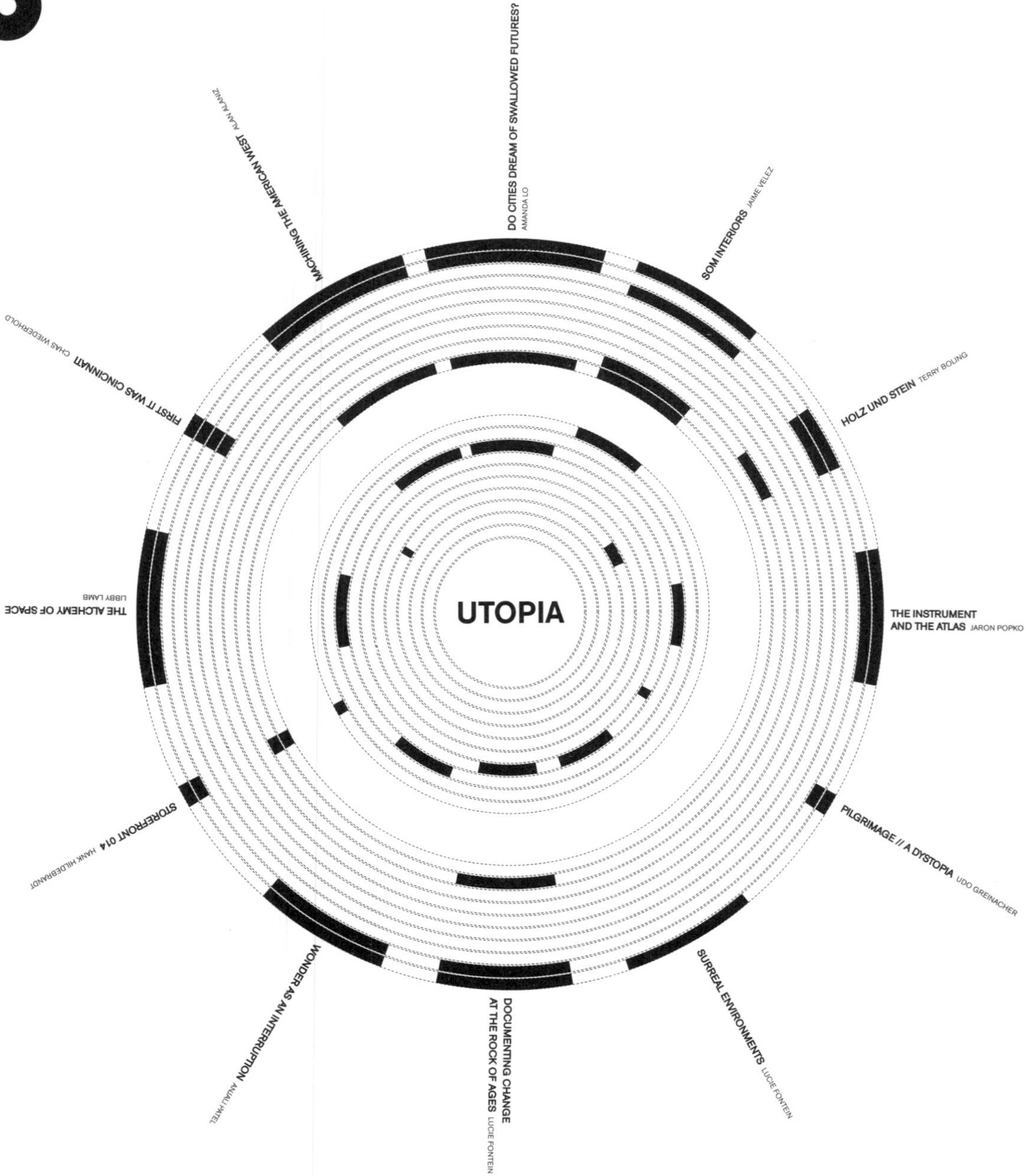

LEGEND:

1. OUTER SECTOR = ID
2. INNER SECTOR = LEVEL
3. WIDTH = SCALE

1. *From Outer Ring to Inner Ring:*
Design Thinking
History/Theory
Material Investigation
Branding
Design Build
Digital Craft
Computational Design
Fabrication
Sustainability
Public Interest

2. *From Outer Ring to Inner Ring:*
Professional
PhD
Graduate 3rd Year
Graduate 2nd Year
Graduate 1st Year
Undergraduate 5th Year
Undergraduate 4th Year
Undergraduate 3rd Year
Undergraduate 2nc Year
Undergraduate 1st Year

3. *Width of Black Poché:*
Scaleless
Object
Furniture
Body
Room
Building
Cluster/Complex
City/Region

UTOPIA

u·to·pi·a
yoo'tōpēə/

noun
Utopia; *plural noun*: Utopias;

1. an imagined place or state of things in which everything is perfect. The word was first used in the book Utopia (1516) by Sir Thomas More.

2. synonyms: paradise, heaven (on earth), Eden, Garden of Eden, Shangri-La, Elysium; idyll, nirvana, God's country; literary Arcadia "it may be your idea of Utopia, but it's not mine"

origin
Based on Greek ou 'not' + topos 'place'

I paused in Cincinnati for 11 months, some place between the coordinates of Princeton and Peru. There John Meunier inspired me, with student Tom Lannahan, to produce the Parasol House as a pivotal parting project envisioned to serve as a campsite in Houston for Surveyors, Nomads, and Lunatics. This project was realized in Parcel X; both are visions of Utopia, as not-place, for the American Nomadic Condition. Eden was a short-term 6-day project; Noah's Ark lasted for no more than 40 days, time enough to build the World as New with 1+1 of each kind.

I have been fascinated with the idea of the number 11 for sometime now. After learning early on to count my fingers and then my toes from 1 to 10, twice over, I found it necessary to pause before making the synthetic leap to 11, then 12, etc., until conceptualizing 20. At the time of his father's death, Thomas Jefferson, as a pre-adolescent 11-year-old, sat under a giant shade tree on top of Mt. Alto and mused on how he would build his own Monticello upon his father's legacy as the King's Surveyor, with the inheritance of five thousand acres, the help of five hundred slaves, and 256 books including an English translation of Palladio's treatise on the *Utilitarian Classification of Then and Now.* Utopia is useful for me as an eschatological covenant with the world, again as we imagine renewing the world in the face of disaster currently termed the Wicked World of Dystopia. Sanford Kwinter challenges us all with the question 'what can be more Modern than the Archaic?' For me Utopia is an Approximation with Building understood as a Verb, a gerund, an on-going construction site.

After 11 years teaching at Princeton, as an extension of my own adolescent education after two years away in Peace Corps Peru, I accepted in 1980 a tenure track offer from the Utopian Retreat/ or Enlightenment Experiment of the University of Virginia. Months after my acceptance to join the Virginia countryside, John Meunier, then Director of Cincinnati's Architecture Program, called me regarding a faculty recommendation of two former Princeton students. In my enthusiasm I told him to hire them both. He asked me how about one of me instead of the two of them; and then immediately asked: *What was your post-Princeton plan? I'm off to Virginia*, I said confidently, knowing well what was well known to be the destination of recent Princetonians Dripps/Abbey/ Schumacher. He asked what I knew about Cincinnati, and I told him very little, but that I had the greatest respect for two notable alumni: Michael Graves, my mentor, and John Hejduk *my soul mate in fiction*, so there must be something amazing in the water there. He casually then asked me to come for Thesis Reviews and to sample Grater's Ice Cream. Expecting to arrive at the Cincinnati Municipal Airport, I lost my cool when I arrived at the Daniel Boone Regional Airport in Kentucky, but was forensically reoriented immediately by Dennis Mann: *Cincinnati is at the thickened edge between here and there, north and south, east and west.* Crossing the Roebling Bridge, I suddenly saw a vision of a booming Working Metropolis, with an aerial perspective of a Frank Furness Skyline. Between Agrest's *Memory and Amnesia* this Utopia approximated my early memories of the 1940's NYC, and *not place* of towering Mirrors for the Moon which began to dominate a vision of the new American Utopian Skyline, and which might suffer from the excesses of the Emperor's new clothes.

UTOPIA

Peter Waldman

William R. Kenan, Jr.
Professor of Architecture
University of Virginia
School of Architecture

I thought I was going for a quick one day turn around: thesis reviews and an expansive *5 way Chili*, washed down with pop, rather than Virginia's Iced Tea. But on my way back to the airport, that very day at the 11th hour of the 11th day of June, John Meunier asked me to join the faculty at the University of Cincinnati and knew enough to offer me tenure. The City amazed me, a free Zoo in the heart of the City where *Aida* was performed regularly with a resident cast of 11 pachyderms on hand. To be sure there were grand equestrian events and hunting with the hounds to anticipate in Jefferson's country, but with two little girls I could not imagine a more Utopian setting than Cincinnati's Zoo to start life again somewhere beyond Over the Rhine and the Ohio River Banks. I was doubly impressed when I remembered that my father spoke highly of Pittsburgh, his River City where the Alleghany and the Monongahela formed the Ohio. He grew up in an orphanage and at the age of 11 won a citywide Art Contest at Carnegie Tech, which gave him admittance and a full scholarship. I guess 11 had Utopian significance for him as well. I felt I was at the headwaters of an eschatological covenant across generations. Pre-adolescence permits a head start on David Leatherbarrow's anticipation of *Weathering*.

My then, not so old, but eternally wise pal Emilio Ambasz heard the news and said at the time that it was a good signal to follow in the footsteps of General Cincinnatus, who was banished from the prestige of still tribal Latin Rome, only to transplant himself at the frontier as a farmer attendant now to the forces of Nature rather than the canons of humankind, awaiting his turn to be called back in favor as the leader of the newly conceived Roman Republic. The Society of the Cincinnati, a major contributing force of the American Revolution, served a similar role in the newly institutionalized American Republic as the Cabalist Circle did in Vicenza, which inspired adolescent Palladio to make his own imagined voyage to Rome seminal to his work in the cities and institutions of the Veneto. To be instrumental again and again at the scale of our digits, beyond the concept of decades, and particularly refusing to start always anew in the Vortex of

Crisis is the lesson of Thomas Cole's painting series *The Course of the Empire.*

From the *Savage State*, to the *Pastoral Setting*, we trace the *Construction of the City*, its *Self-Destruction*, yet ending in the slowly generative calm of *Desolation*. In this final yet regenerative painting, an energetic vine begins to be nourished off the remains of a marble column as the Moon replaces the Sun. This is another *Not Place*, a shot-term Utopian moment. The topographical and archeological imaginations are combined to reimagine Utopia as a sign of resilience, a new beginning based on the resources of the past.

I value my teaching with John Hancock and David Niland and the concept of the syncopated Work/Study Quarter system. There was an intensity to that specifically *city university*, a threshold to higher education for immigrant populations that made Cincinnati the Queen City of the American Industrial Revolution. This topographically wild city had no Utopian singular plan, but was indeed peppered with hilltop and valley neighborhoods. Tod Williams, my long-term Princeton classmate and friend, writes on the coincidence of Life as Work. In my intense four academic quarters traveling from Wyoming to Clifton on public transportation, before sunrise and after sunset, I retain the transformative memories of witnessing a new sense of citizenship as we workers and workplaces came alive as trains and trucks and bridges framed an industrial powerhouse of optimistic first generation students who had eschatological genes.

11 months later in 1981, after envisioning the Parasol House inspired by John Meunier's *Orchard House* in Cambridge as parting project, I left Cincinnati to join the faculty at Rice University where I remained for another 11 years. I returned in 1992, now finally settled into Virginia's Piedmont, 11 years later to give a talk at an ACSA Regional conference there on *Specifications for Construction* in conversation with Daniel Friedman & Ann Marie Borys. Finally, seven years later in 1999 I broke my 11 obsessed pattern and returned at the invitation of David Niland for thesis reviews and specifically encountered yet another one of Cincinnati's finest students. Kiel Moe's thesis directed by David was the epitome of Specifications for Construction as a Spatial Tale of Origin. This thesis had nothing to do with a tiresome search for an Utopia of originality, currency or the innovative, but was entrenched in the richness of double mirror of Gravity and Orientation; 1 & 1, the *beginning* and the *beginning again*, framing *Genesis & Exodus*, as well as *Acts & Numbers*. It was a good omen, no inaugural event, at the beginning of the new Millennium in the year 2001 that Kiel Moe, informed by Hancock and inspired by Niland, came to study, to work and to live with us at the University of Virginia.

Once a millennium one might have a chance to rediscover an oasis where Narcissus and Echo coincide at the banks of the Ohio, where the Utopia of Resilience if not the tonic of Eschatology make connective tissues possible. Raphael's *School of Athens*, an Utopian frame of rod & compass, envisions coincidentally a setting where Socrates and Aristotle in the 5th Century BC are sharing space with Michelangelo and Pope Julius II in the 16th Century AD in a topographic and archeological setting some might recall in the mighty portal of Union Station pausing now in the City of Cincinnatus.

Image Credits / PETER WALDMAN

AMANDA LO
AARATI KANEKAR, PH.D. (chair)
EDSON CABALFIN, PH.D. (member)

DO CITIES DREAM OF SWALLOWED FUTURES?

Master of Architecture Thesis
Cincinnati, OH, USA

With the world shifting as quickly as it does today, people seem to be striving towards identities that no longer exist. We are swept along by the tides of change, with only a tenuous grasp on our place in a world where nothing remains fixed for long. Identity is a device we use to validate our being and establish place, formed as much from our environs as it is from our inner selves. We represent our own self-concept through image; yet, society is filled with hollow signs that conceal their own lack of meaning.

Shanghai is one such place; it exists as much in its own invented mythology as it does in its physical location. The city is more than the sum of its parts: people, buildings, history, culture. It is most valuable to the Chinese government as a symbol. The Pudong New Development Area began as a collection of empty signs, meant to project the image of a successful, global city, and Shanghai has increasingly come to resemble the simulation of a city, masking what might be the absence of any reality. In trying to assert a homogeneous image to the world, the city fails to recognize the multiple identities that define it. It is impossible to pin down a collective identity for anything longer than a brief moment. The city acts as an ever-changing, fluid network that brings in outside influences as it sends its own out into the world.

These themes are specifically addressed in this thesis through Shanghai's land subsidence problem. The city sits on five aquifers, separated by layers of soft clay and silt. As a result of excessive groundwater withdrawal and the weight of new construction, the entire city is gradually sinking. Surgical processes are performed upon existing buildings with the ultimate goal of new tissue formation to create a habitable landscape. A momentary, heterogeneous collective identity is pieced together through the shared experience of survival.

AMANDA LO / model

The city began as a small fishing village at the confluence of two rivers.

As the city became wealthier, walls were constructed to protect the city against pirate raids.

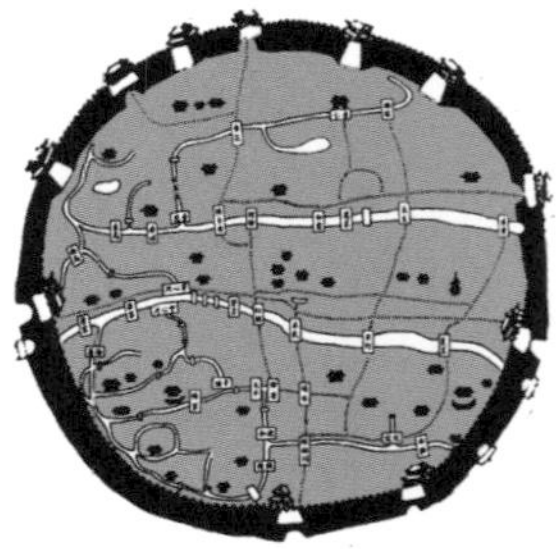

The city belonged to an empire that was in self-imposed isolation from the rest of the world, always guarding its ancient secrets. However, foreign lands eyed the kingdom jealously, hoping to extract some of its great wealth in tea and silk. Their diplomatic appeals to the empire were to no avail.

War erupted once peaceful attempts to open the city to trade broke down.

A treaty was signed forcing the kingdom to open itself up to international trade.

Foreigners from many different lands came from far and wide to begin to settle outside the original walled city.

The city grew into a sparkling den of inequity, rich and vibrant, a place where a man could make his fortune.
Then, a great war tore through many kingdoms and the city was no exception. The foreigners were driven from the city.
Soon after, the empire fell and was replaced by a republic. The city was closed off from outside lands, and without trade, it soon began to fade.
Eventually, the republic decided to open up the city once again to trade.
The republic sanctioned construction of a new financial district across the river from the old city.
Built from nothing, this new district began as merely an empty symbol of the city's aspirations; however, the city eventually fulfilled the image it had been merely projecting.
This glittering district emerged as a symbol of the city as a truly modern, global city, as well as the success of the republic.

The city sat upon five aquifers. Bedrock was on average at least 300 meters below the surface.

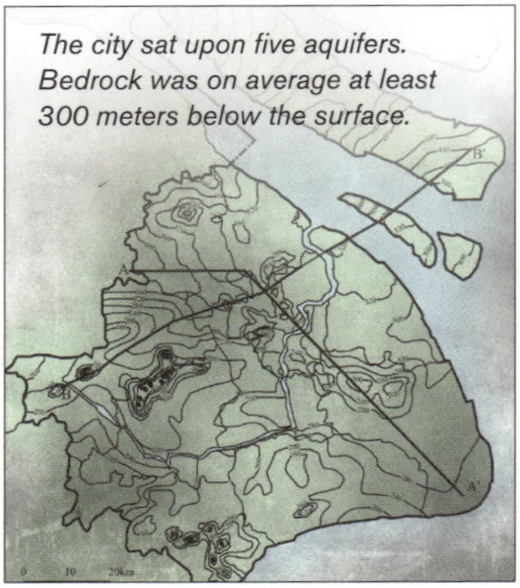

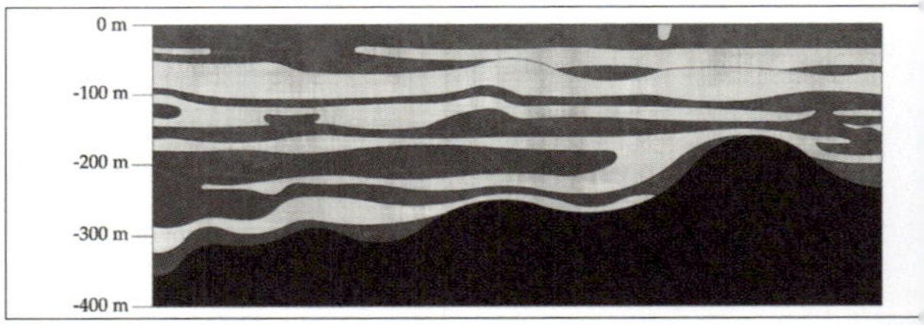

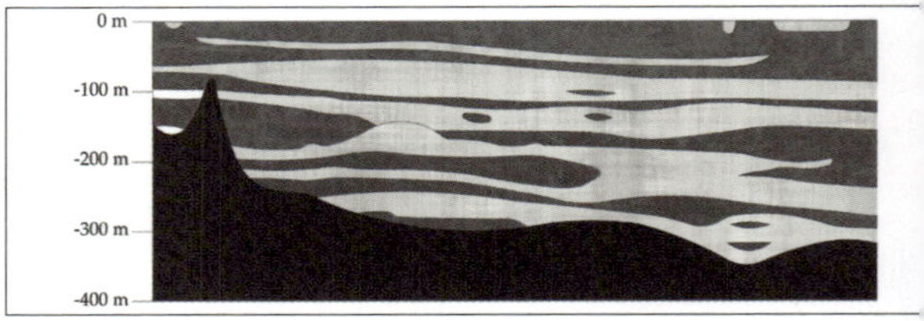

The city was sinking 2.64 meters every 100 years due to excessive groundwater withdrawal. To reverse the land subsidence, the city began to pump water back into the aquifers. This happened in the winter when the factories were not operating. However, 30% of the city's land subsidence was construction-induced; thus, aquifer recharge alone was not enough to stop the sinking.

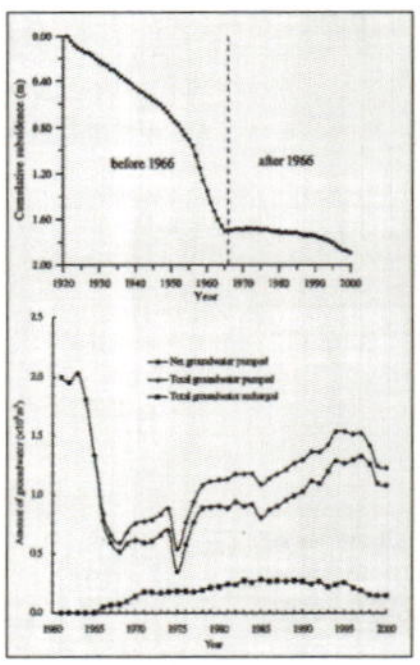

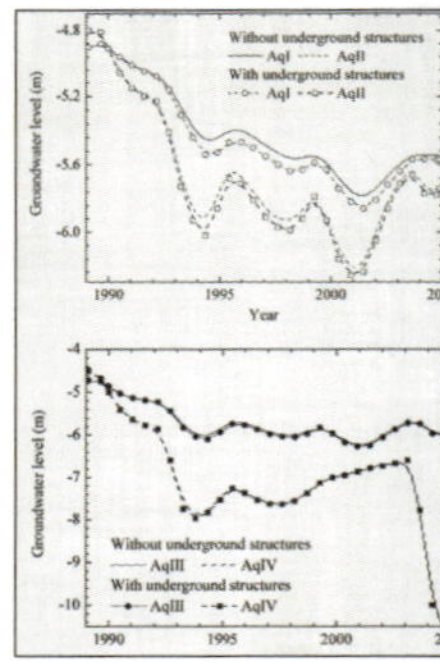

The city continued to expand, so attempts to recharge the aquifers could not stop the sinking of the city.

Collapsing aquifers began to cause massive problems at the surface in the form of huge rifts in the ground and unpredictable sinking.

On the surface, the buildings were stripped until only skeletal forms remained in the image of a city that could no longer be inhabited. The city was preserved in a glorious moment of its past, frozen in time.

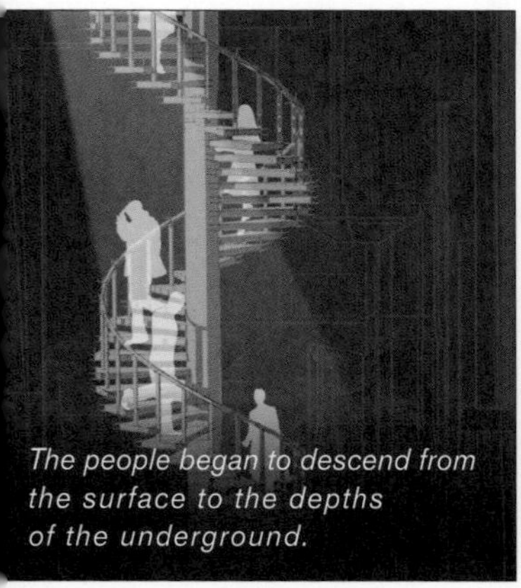

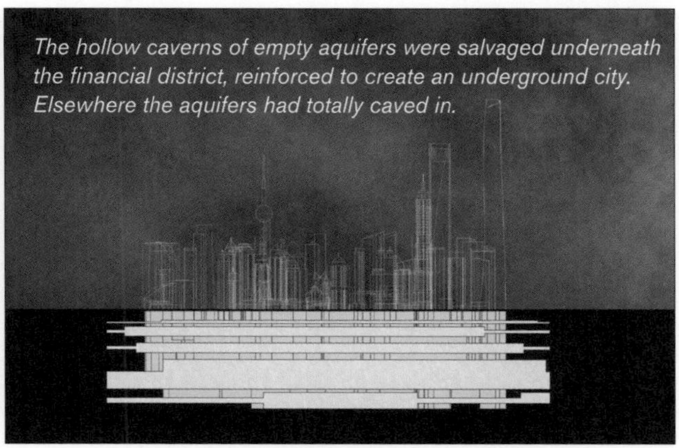

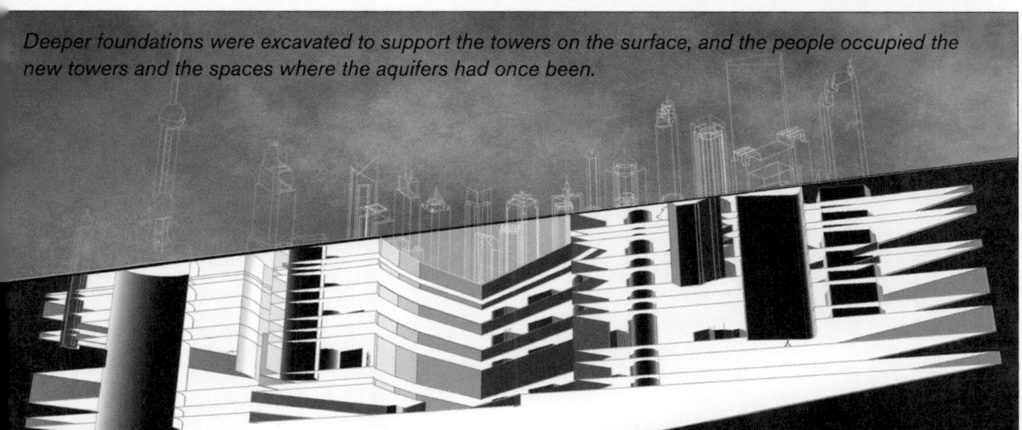

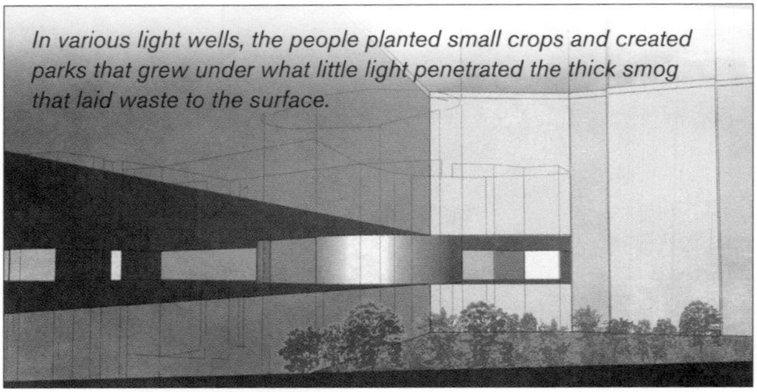

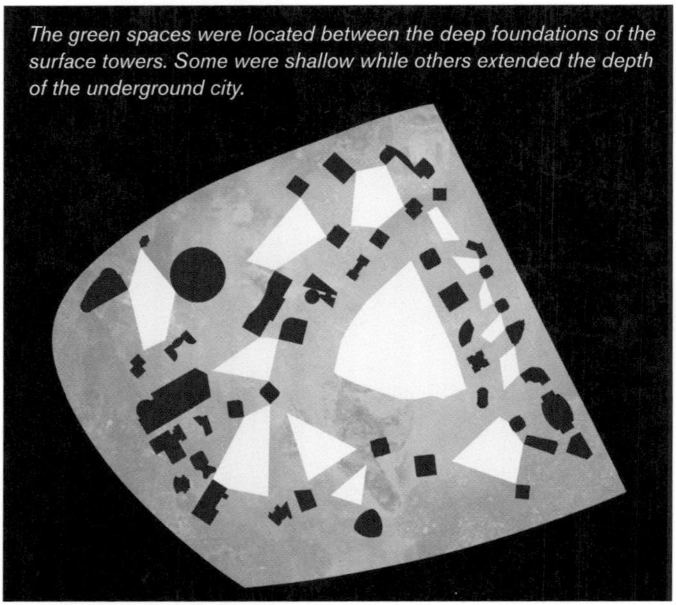

Meanwhile, the buildings deemed unimportant to the city's skyline, the swathes of mid-rise housing outside the Financial District, were left to sink.

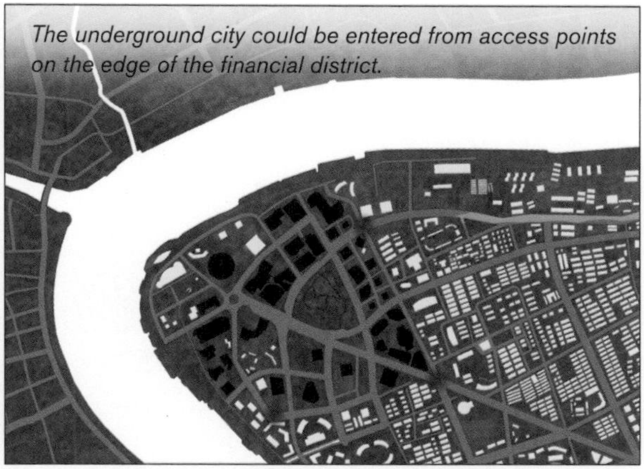

The sinking buildings came to be occupied by the migrant workers who had no place in the formal city. Machines roamed the surface, trying to stabilize the surface buildings.

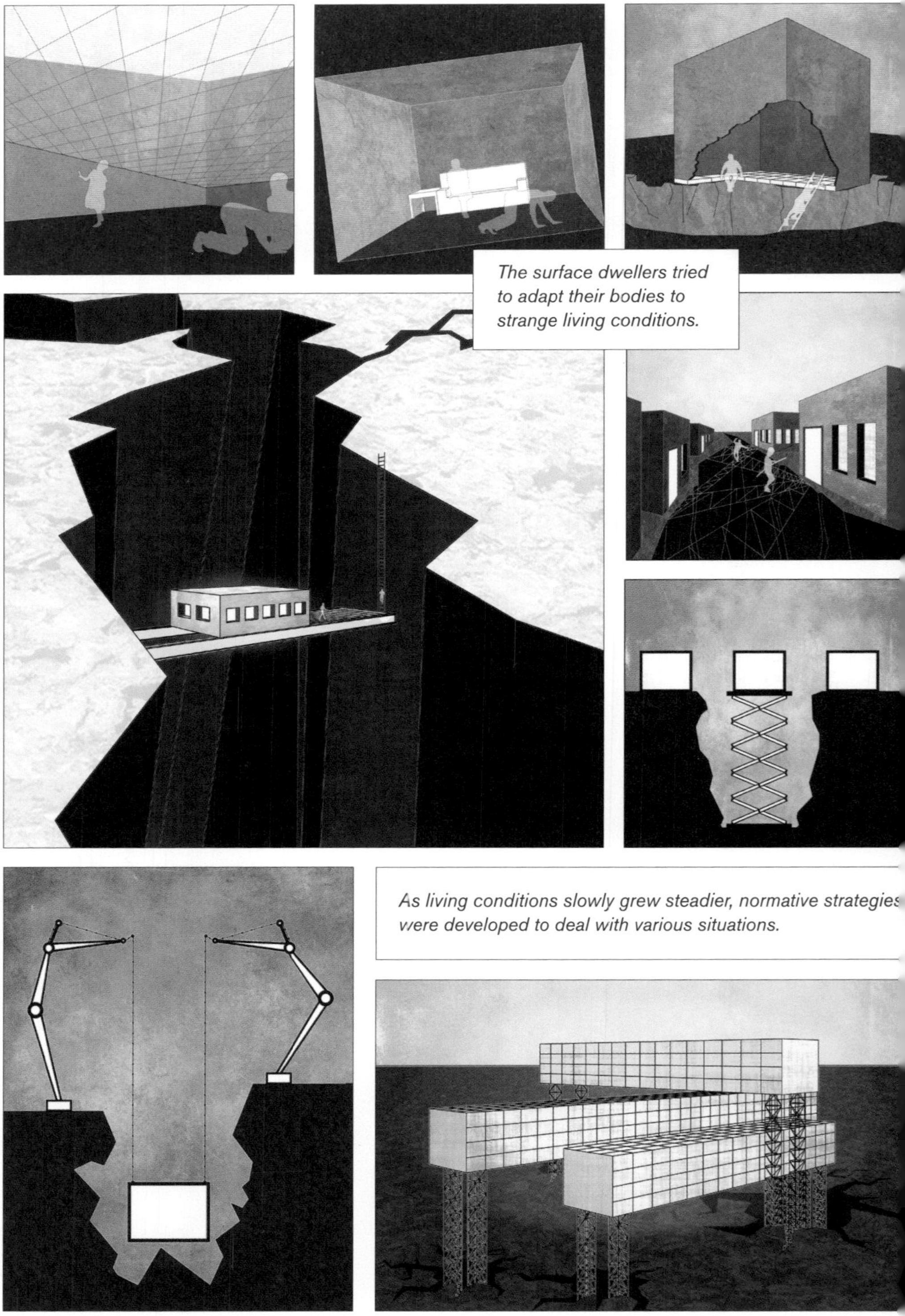
The surface dwellers tried to adapt their bodies to strange living conditions.
As living conditions slowly grew steadier, normative strategies were developed to deal with various situations.

Suturing
Grafting
Cauterizing
Filling
The people developed strategies to deal with the sinking as it affected individual buildings.
With these interventions they sought to maintain the existing buildings in their former positions.
Using scrap from the stripping of the city skyline, they propped and patched the crumbling buildings.
The people soon discovered they would have to create their own landscape as the ground shifted beneath them ceaselessly.
The interventions the people constructed were rough, put together with whatever they could find.
Sometimes they used scrap from the stripping of the skyline: glass and metal panels and steel beams.
Other times, they simply filled in holes with masonry and brick rubble.

In the beginning, the people sought to normalize the interiors of the crumbling buildings by creating new floors and walls at level planes.

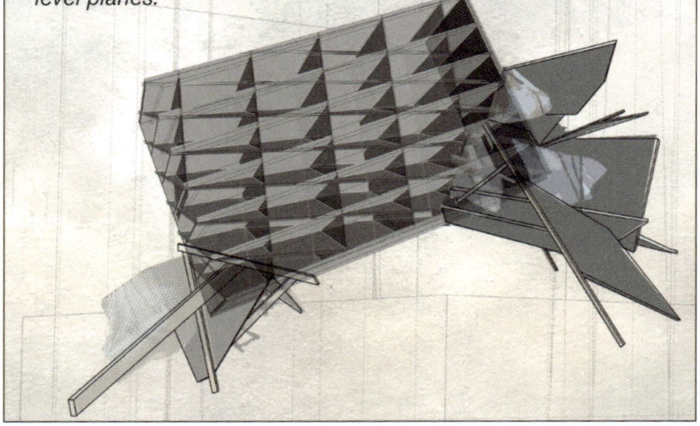

As the building envelopes began to lose structural integrity, the strategy gradually shifted from normalizing the existing buildings to creating an infrastructure that could adapt to the changing landscape.

The supporting infrastructure ceased to become mere propping devices and became the spaces where people lived.

Eventually the surgical processes being applied on the buildings changed in scale from individual buildings to processes that covered multiple buildings at a time.
Connection
Excision
Fusion
Ossification

It soon became evident that simply creating level floor planes in building shells was not enough to reconcile the buildings with the shifting ground.
And thus, completely new spaces were created that were no longer constrained by the crumbling shells of the existing buildings.

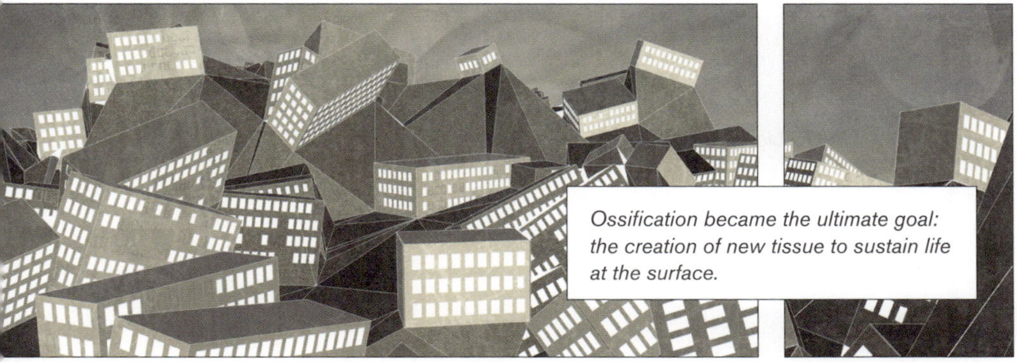

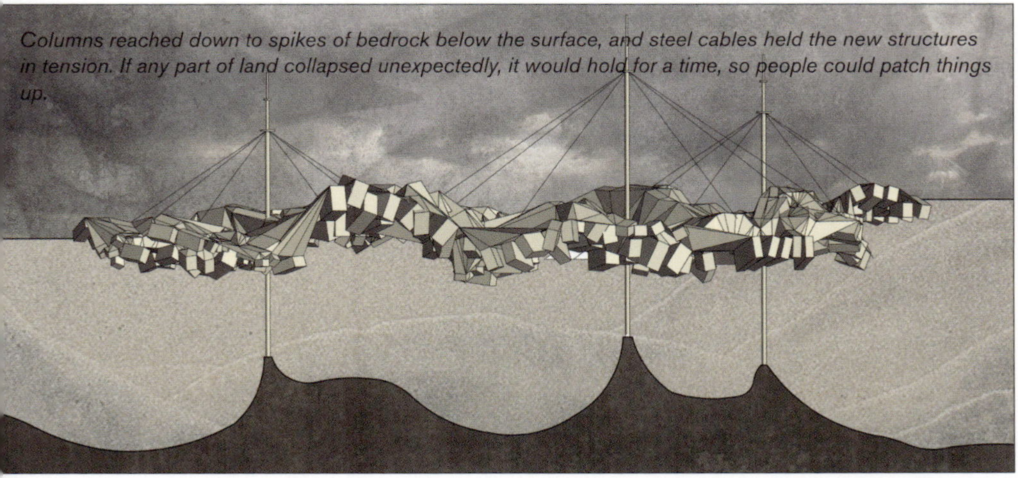

The migrant workers dwelling on the surface had all come from different places and lived different lives, but they pieced together a momentary, collective identity from the shared pain and experience of survival.

AMANDA LO / comic

JAIME VELEZ, FIIDA, ASID

SOM Interiors

Excerpt from an interview at SAID
Conducted by Mara Marcu
Edited by Chas Wiederhold

Jaime Velez is the Director of Interior Design at SOM. He has led interior design for various architecture projects located around United States, Europe, and Asia. He believes that a space should reflect the unique characteristics of the culture of its users. Building on the strong interiors tradition at SOM, his projects possess a timeless quality and a strong sense of order and clarity.

Mara Marcu: Your education is in architecture. How did you begin working in interior design and leading the interior design office for SOM Chicago?

Jaime Velez: It's a story I wish were a little more deliberate. Life drives you in a variety of different ways. Like you mentioned I have a Bachelors of Architecture and a Masters of Architecture. I graduated from school, and I got a job at SOM and I started on the architecture team. The life of a large firm is tethered to the state of the economy. A lot of peaks and valleys. In 1991 things were not looking very good at the firm, and I had become really good friends with the person who had become the director of interiors. At that time SOM went from being eight hundred people in the Chicago office to, when everything was said and done, one hundred and twentyfive.

At that time, I was working on a project in Spain for the 1996 Olympics. My boss came to me one day and he said, you have two choices: either you switch to interiors or we are going to have to lay you off. I was going through some personal issues at that time and becoming laid off was definitely not an option. I took the job in interiors not knowing anything about it. They dumped this enormous project on my lap: a 400,000 square foot project in Detroit, and I really got into it. The more engaged I became, the more I realized that the differences between architecture and interior design are so negligible. One element is water. One deals with water issues and the other one doesn't. However, the whole strategy of composition and proportion and experiencing the space is exactly the same. I realized that interiors afforded me something that architecture didn't, which is to have a greater impact on how people really use space. In fact, for you and me, the comfort of this chair is more relevant than the facade that Peter Eisenman gave to this building.

I have approached interiors with an extremely architectural point of view. For example, traditionally as office buildings began to develop they became more and more glass boxes, and the only times there was some sort of a gesture toward the outside was for the few who would like to smoke a cigarette. I just had lunch with some of your students, and I asked "So hands up: how many of you like to work outdoors?" and I would say that probably 90% of the students raised their hands. This new paradigm can begin in a very small way and will begin to define a new way of how buildings could be composed. To me that is very rewarding.

One of the things you're focused on is revealing the cultural identity of the place you are working in. Because you are trained as an architect, it's almost like that is the site that you are starting with: the cultural condition of a place. I was wondering if that assumption is true, and if you could elaborate on how you start an interior design project.

One of the things you're focused on is revealing the cultural identity of the place you are working in. Because you are trained as an architect, it's almost like that is the site that you are starting with: the cultural condition of a place. I was wondering if that assumption is true, and if you could elaborate on how you start an interior design project. In the early stages of a job, the interiors are fortunate to spend much more time in the programing phase. We conduct focus groups. Those focus groups are extremely revealing. I'm working on a job in Saudi [Arabia] right now—speaking of a culture we don't know or understand a lot about. We have a series of tools that we use. One of them I value tremendously. It begins to gauge how employees feel about certain aspects of the organic space. In discussing this element you can really see the level of relevance of certain things. In the Saudi [project], it was probably the most extreme case I've ever been in. The company—even though there were four thousand employees—has thirty women, and the women were not allowed to work in the same place as the men, but they came to a focus group. So just imagine a focus group where there were ten women in different stages of covering. Some were fully covered, others you could see their eyes, and some that you could see their face. The whole discussion was so intriguing. I really try to immerse myself in trying to understand what they do.

However, now I have this new project that I'm working on which is unbelievable, a project of a lifetime: we are expanding and renovating the headquarters of the UN in Geneva. It's 2.2 million square feet and speaking of the multicultural, at the UN you can't quite cookie cut it. It's been really interesting to begin to navigate these issues and talk to the different groups. You understand that there is more cultural nuance, but the culture of the place is still the overriding theme and this is what you want to be able to dissect.

What is more important: personal culture or experiences?

I don't think my culture has a lot to do with how I design, but I think my experiences throughout a long career do. Right now we are getting into some high-end residential project in my hometown. But I find if you ask a graduate here to design the presidential suite at a hotel the struggle is huge because they've never lived it. What I am trying to say? You've been to many airports so you are familiar. You've been to many banks. I've been to many cocktail receptions. I've been to private clubs. It is the experiences that make you who you are. I can begin to draw images. I can begin to draw ideas from things that I've seen that I think may be relevant and I think could be transformed.

Do you think we have begun to share a collective sense of identity that goes beyond political and geographical boundaries?

Let's say you are Jacques Herzog. You practice in Switzerland. You have twenty years plus of practice in Switzerland. I think it's going to dictate, to a degree, the way that you respond. My whole career, I never practiced anywhere else but the U.S. The process of education never ends. We continue to gain experiences, and all my experiences I gain are through the eyes of a designer in the U.S.

How did SOM overcome the economic crash in 2008. Is there anything you learn as an office, and as one of the major offices in the world, about how we should structure the way we practice, the way we function, so that you are more resilient in the future?

I would say that one thing that we have learned from the past is three words: diversify, diversify, diversify. I would say in our case what helped us navigate the recession was China. If it weren't for the work in China, things would have been much worse for us. I think we are trying to get better in our office in Chicago, to diversify not only geographically but also in terms of areas of expertise. We have begun to adapt. There are a few projects we were lucky enough to win in Chicago during the recession. At the time healthcare was what was fueling the fire here after the recovery package. We did get this enormous hospital in Denver. We got another hospital, in fact, here in Cincinnati, which we are building right now, The Christ Hospital. Diversify, but not only diversify yourself in terms of areas of expertise but also geographically. That is a bit tricky because at the end of the day we are a business. When people begin to run a business they become a little too ambitious.

Columbia and Chile are going through a really interesting time right now. Currently they are interested in looking at architects outside the country. However, their projects are not of the magnitude as the projects in China and neither are the fees. The firm needs to make sure that it still has a tolerance for projects that are not of the size or the fees the amount they are accustomed to. It takes some adjusting. You have to be constant. You have to be there through thick and thin. If you are too fair-weather, it won't be very good for you. We never left Dubai even in the bad times. I remember going to Dubai and getting on the plane and seeing the lines of immigration that you would say "Oh lord, how long is this going to take." Then four years later you could hear the echo of the airport. You maintain contact to maintain credibility.

How do you think education can help prepare students become more resilient?

I am a firm believer that the school should stay the furthest away as possible from reality. I think there is plenty of time in your professional life to learn how to detail a partition, or how to look at a foundation drawing or how to design a bathroom. But I don't think there is enough time to dream and to think. I get extremely turned off when I look at portfolios [in] which I see the results. I don't blame the students. I blame the faculty and the structure of the school that is imposing these overly realistic projects. Exercise is in universal thinking hence the term "University." However, for instance I just had lunch with some students, and they were all saying what I want to be doing, hospitality, residential, or workplace. My advice to them is was, "You are too young to decide what you really want to do." There is a craft to what we do that needs to be learned. The best place to really learn it is not in school; it's on the job. So I figure rather than saying that you want to be in hospitality or I want to be in workplace or I want to be doing senior living, how about you tell me you want to learn how to build buildings, and you want to learn how materials go together, or that you want to understand how a project is run. Just allow yourself a little bit of time and remain flexible.

Twenty years ago when you graduated from architecture school, all you could be was an architect. Now you can be many things. I have friends that are software designers that have architecture degrees. Why limit oneself? It scares me when I see the schools not focusing on universal thinking and intellectual exploration. I'm more intrigued by portfolios where I have no clue as to what I am looking at. For instance, I am very interested by the work that comes from the Art Institute in Chicago. Extremely provocative. However, there are many audiences. There are firms that say, I want to hire this guy because I was looking at his portfolio and he knows how to detail. I am unfortunately a product of the education that I disagree with. And it wasn't until I started working at SOM that I thought that. Working at SOM is like being at the largest school of architecture. When I started there, there were 600 of us in Chicago, of which 80% of us were 25 years old or less, all fresh out of school. We began to compare portfolios and remember at that time I was looking at the work of my co-workers who had gone to Virginia Tech. I was blown away. There were exercises in geometry, there were exercises in color, there were exercises in space perception, and there were none in my portfolio. My projects had bathrooms and living rooms or theaters. They were so conventional. Maybe it was my fault for not pushing it. The role of the faculty is to push.

How did your own education influence your current practice?

I went to school through a very dark period of architecture. I despised Postmodernism from the get-go. I could not deal with it. Obviously I can see the value of history and understating what was done, but I could see reinterpreting it, not copying it. I was going to work after I graduated, and I was lucky to put on a job that had nothing to do with [Postmodernism]. That was more about structure. It was more interesting in that regard. Well it's interesting. While there was disconnect between my undergraduate and my graduate school. Columbia, really the majority of the Latin American countries, never really embraced the post-modern. Frankly, I had barely heard of it when I graduated in 1980. In that school, which is five years of undergraduate school, was a lot about talking about performance. Mostly based on sense of order and clarity. Extremely functionally driven. I've always embraced that. I've never been able to be very frivolous with the things that I do. That resonates with the type of clients we have. Mostly corporate clients that are interested in fine-tuned machines, for lack of a better word, that are all about performance and they are not about fluff or architectural expression for the sake of architectural expression.

What are the things that fascinate you to work with? Do you work with light? Do you work with color? What identifies you as a designer?

My biggest strength is that I can take a bowl of spaghetti and put all the pasta in a row for you. So what really intrigues me is this whole idea of establishing order and making sense of things. At the aesthetic level I like to express myself in a very simple direct fashion. I don't like things that are adorned. I like things that are very simple and truthful.

Is it harder to work within a building you are renovating or is it easier to work within a building that SOM is designing or is there no difference at all?

I like to work in buildings where I am able to drive the strategy of how the building is composed. The projects I like the most are where I can be a part of the team in a proactive fashion. All buildings have their challenges. Probably the most difficult building that I have ever worked on is the one I am doing right now with the United Nations. It is a building that was built in Geneva in 1956. It's enormous. How do you make something relevant that was built for a completely different mentality of work or mentality of behavior or even gender occupancy? It becomes really difficult but at the same time if becomes very challenging and very exciting. Same issue in the Renaissance Center in Detroit. The building was a huge failure when it was first built. Henry Ford Jr. supposedly built the building to symbolize the renaissance of Detroit, however, the plinth at the ground level looked like a bomb shelter. Completely sealed off. You drove through the main street in Detroit, and there were these two berms that were two stories tall that house all of the mechanical equipment and you drove between those two and you saw absolutely nothing but the glistening towers from afar. I think breathing new life into an existing structure is really rewarding.

Do you find it difficult that interior design is about everything that you see and that it is also about everything that you don't see? We talk so much about having resilient buildings that sustain the test of time, yet technology is changing so fast that the custom fit needs of today may be very different than the ones of tomorrow. Do you have any guidelines to follow?

We still don't have an answer. I think there is a term that everyone loves to use, and we throw around all the time, which is "future proofing." It is, to a degree, very altruistic to believe that one may achieve it. Realistically I think "How?" Technology was in a three-year cycle. Now it's on a year and a half cycle. If you look at—this may be an odd analogy—but if you look at a warehouse building in Michigan from the end of the 1800s or the early 1900s, they continue to thrive and they continue to be alive and well and I think it is because they are simple. I think to a degree a trick may be to steer away from customization. As I begin to work with my clients to configure the space, my speech is trying to convince the groups that just because you have one hundred file cabinets, it doesn't mean you will have them three years from now. I would say looking at solutions that are a little more generic. Taking the specificity out of design. Though, on the other hand it's a fine balance. I don't think that future proofing is something that someone can say to you: "Exactly, OK, we get it. Here it is."

How important is sustainability to you? Can you elaborate on it and, implicitly, on the role of technology in interior design?

Sustainability is incredibly important. Our understanding, at this point, has been limiting in some aspects. Particularly if you look at the red list materials you begin to try to avoid any of that. We are a country of choices, which is sort of intriguing. For instance, if you look at the leather offering for an American country for chairs versus European—if you buy a chair from Vitra and you buy a chair from Knoll, the chair from Vitra would come with four choices of leather. The chair from the US will come with 300. We need a lot of retooling in that sense. We need to limit ourselves. We are trying to be as sufficient as we can in that regard; responsible. Technology is key in interiors to make spaces perform. On the other hand, technology is driving this whole mobility issue in the workplace. In the past five years, mobility has really risen to the forefront, and it is completely changing the way in which space is organized. There is no turning back. What we haven't really talked about though is the whole human aspect of interior design. The majority of my career has been in workplace. How do we begin to accommodate all of the changes in behavior and culture that are taking place? The fact that we are living longer, and that we can't quite retire because we haven't saved enough money, or there is no money to be saved. The whole multigenerational aspect of the workplace is going to be very critical in how spaces are configured. I don't know what the responses are. For a couple of projects, we have brought on board a couple of cultural anthropologists. Their output is unbelievable. What is interesting about us is that we are one of the few large firms that are still left that are completely multidisciplinary. In our Chicago office, we have architecture, interior design, urban design, structural engineering, mechanical, electrical, plumbing and fire protection, sustainability, wayfinding, and graphics. I like to emphasize to the young staff that you have an opportunity at SOM you don't have in other firms; gaining that knowledge through the ease of communications at the onset of the job as opposed to when you work with consultants and they come in one day a week. We are next door talking to our engineers. Suppose we are designing a railing system, how does it respond structurally to the amount of pressure that is required by code? Or working with our architects; letting them know that you can't do apartments when a space is 60 feet deep because light doesn't drive that far in. We are a global firm. We take advantage of that because there are different ways of looking at a problem. I think our colleagues in San Francisco, with their client base being more tech-focused have a lot to teach. Our guys in New York deal more with financial institutions. That's a completely different paradigm. We do a lot of work in the legal arena in Chicago. You begin to blend all of these things at different levels. At times as consultants—the only ones that we really use above and beyond acoustical and lighting for a couple of really key projects—the cultural anthropologists really help us out with the clients who are really interesting and are a new paradigm.

ow helpful is the LEED system o you? What rules do you follow o achieve sustainability?

Unfortunately, I think that LEED needs to catch up. I think there is too much focus on some elements that are really basic like carbon footprint and energy and water. Those things are essential, okay, we're running out of water, were running out of fuel, we are emitting too much CO2. But then again, it seems like there needs to be more emphasis on air quality. The European companies are definitely more advanced in regulation. Buildings in the Netherlands: when you do a building in Holland, the maximum distance from the core or any occupied space to the exterior wall is maximum eight meters. Same thing in Switzerland. That doesn't exist here in this country. The buildings here are big and robust. It's not unheard to have buildings which are sixty feet deep, which is eighteen meters deep, and I just told you that the maximum is eight in the Netherlands. Access to [the occupant] and daylight being key, and the second [key] being issues of indoor air quality. We have been conducting some testing of spaces that are LEED certified, and we find the air quality is not exactly up to snuff. We did some testing in our offices, Silver LEED certified, and they are not quite as good as one would expect or want to be.

n that regard, I want to go back to topia. SOM is very well known for uilding skyscrapers. Some of the nteriors you worked on are within igh-rise structures. I was looking t the Kirkland Ellis interiors, and ou have these really beautiful enderings. Everything is so horizontal, anoramic, and endless. It reminded e of [Antonio] Sant'Elia's Futurist anifesto; a conglomeration of floor abs within a vertical landscape. How o you envision the skyscraper f tomorrow?

All you need to do is take off from the Chicago airport to see how we are just eating the prairie at a speed that is just absolutely obnoxious. I am a big proponent of city living. I'm a big proponent of density. I am not a proponent of amenities that are located off of the street. I spend a lot of time in Toronto [and] Minneapolis. One with an above ground and the other with an underground system; you completely begin to kill the street. I am a big proponent of street life and of mixed-use. Maybe that is the cultural side of me. We grew up in cities. The city that I grew up in did not have a central business district, per say. I grew up in a townhouse that had a store at the ground level. I am a firm believer in cities. In fact, for a while they asked me to help out with the office in Los Angeles. I moved to L.A., and I couldn't fathom this whole idea of this car society, car culture. The lack of being in touch with what was going on around me. I currently don't own a car. If you see me behind a wheel steer clear, stay away. I believe in cities. Would I prefer to work on a project in a high rise rather than a low rise? I think it's inconsequential to me; it doesn't not matter. There are good high-rises; there are bad high-rises.

Jaime Velez in lecture at SAID

TERRY BOLING
RENEE MARTIN
JEFF TILMAN

HOLZ UND STEIN

Undergraduate Study Abroad
Bohemia (Vienna, Prague, and Budapest), Croatia (Zagreb, Split, Pucisca, and Bol), Northern Italy (Venice, Vicenza, Verona, and Milan), and Switzerland and the Vorarlburg in Austria

Wood and stone–*Holz und Stein*–are two of the most ubiquitous construction materials in the history of architecture. Both are on the brink of ground-breaking changes as a result of new manufacturing technologies.

The SAID 2017 travel studio, conducted by Professor Terry Boling, examined these materials and their manifestations in their native environments. In addition to seeing the seminal architectural works of Western Europe, we toured the offices and projects of several internationally prominent architects, visited universities researching innovative construction methods, and worked for several days in one of the few remaining stonemason schools in Europe. Twelve fourth year architecture students and six fourth year interior design students participated in the travel, and were joined by Professors Jeff Tilman and Renee Martin for two week periods at the beginning and end of the trip respectively.

Upon returning, the students were asked to produce an exhibition that chronicled their journey. While not sufficient to simply represent what was experienced (seen, heard, tasted, and felt), the students were challenged to somehow synthesize the myriad sensations that comprised the trip through drawings and fabrications. Collage and Bricolage were used as techniques to capture the experiential memories of the trip and to re-construct them as generative tools–provocations for possibilities. The collages create new worlds through the manipulation and rearrangement of existing imagery, and the constructed artifacts act as detail machines–creating the DNA for future fabrications.

The exhibition is organized around four regions; Bohemia (Vienna, Prague, and Budapest), Croatia (Zagreb, Split, Pucisca, and Bol), Northern Italy (Venice, Vicenza, Verona, and Milan), and Switzerland and the Vorarlburg in Austria. Each region is embodied in the exhibition through photography, collage, and constructed artifacts.

Split, Diocletian's Palace

Zagreb, stone wall

Brion Cementery, Scarpa detail

Croatia, quarry

Brač, stone school

Exhibition, Switzerland

Exhibition, Italy

Exhibition, reception

Exhbition, frames

Exhibition, stone mock-up

JARON POPKO
AARATI KANEKAR, PH.D. (chair)
MICHAEL MCINTURF (member)

THE INSTRUMENT AND THE ATLAS

"Metalepsis: A Lens for Reading the City"
Master of Architecture Thesis
Cincinnati, OH, USA

Architecture is an art of framing and mediating the experience and perception of the world through the activation of latent morphologies. Managing the relationship between the visible and the invisible, architecture performs a level of narrative operations that share a border with literary theory. Both architecture and literature structure experience through spatial and temporal expressions, allowing for cross-disciplinary influence. The processes of reading, re-reading, and re-writing allow for imaginative translations across media and a creative architectural experience.

The literature of the fantastic employs narrative strategies that blur the boundaries of the visible and invisible, of reality and fiction. The writings of Jorge Luis Borges exist within this complex and dissonant landscape punctuated by constantly constructing and collapsing realities. His stories leave the reader with a feeling of the bizarre uncanny, but more importantly a sense of profound discovery. Looking at Borgesian narrative techniques, this thesis proposes an intervention within the city that provides the user with a similar disjunctive reading of reality, acting as an unstable atlas of the city.

The Atlas is a machine for the collection and facilitation of knowledge about the world we live in. It seeks to uncover and analyze natural and complex phenomena. Investigating the role of architecture in shaping and enhancing perceptual experience, the program provides tools that allow the user to locate, codify, and interpret his/her findings and to visualize the complex relationships between them and provide new interpretative views. It is a place for inquiry and understanding, an instrument for looking, a position for orientation, and a site for unearthing hidden and unstructured worlds.

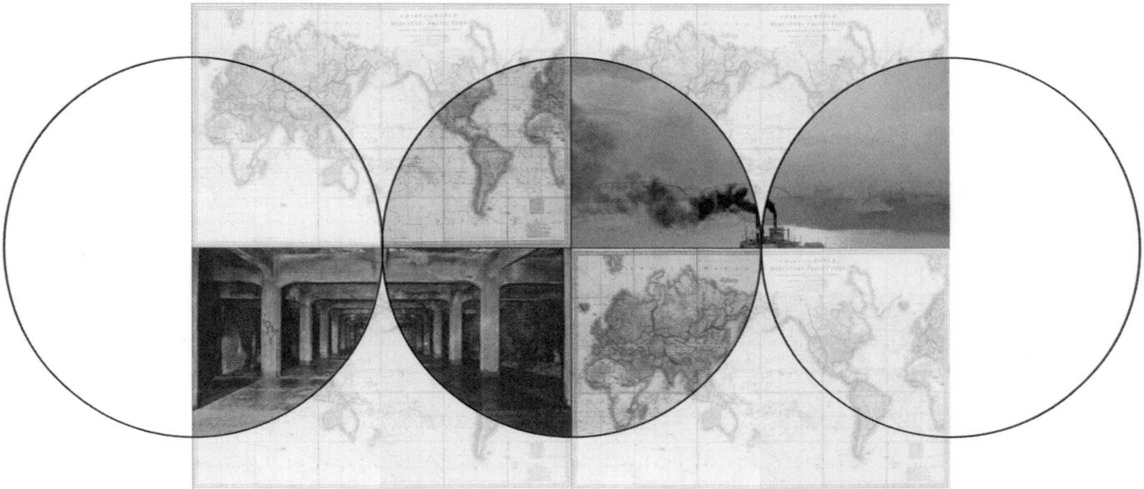

JARON POPKO / abstract collage

final composite

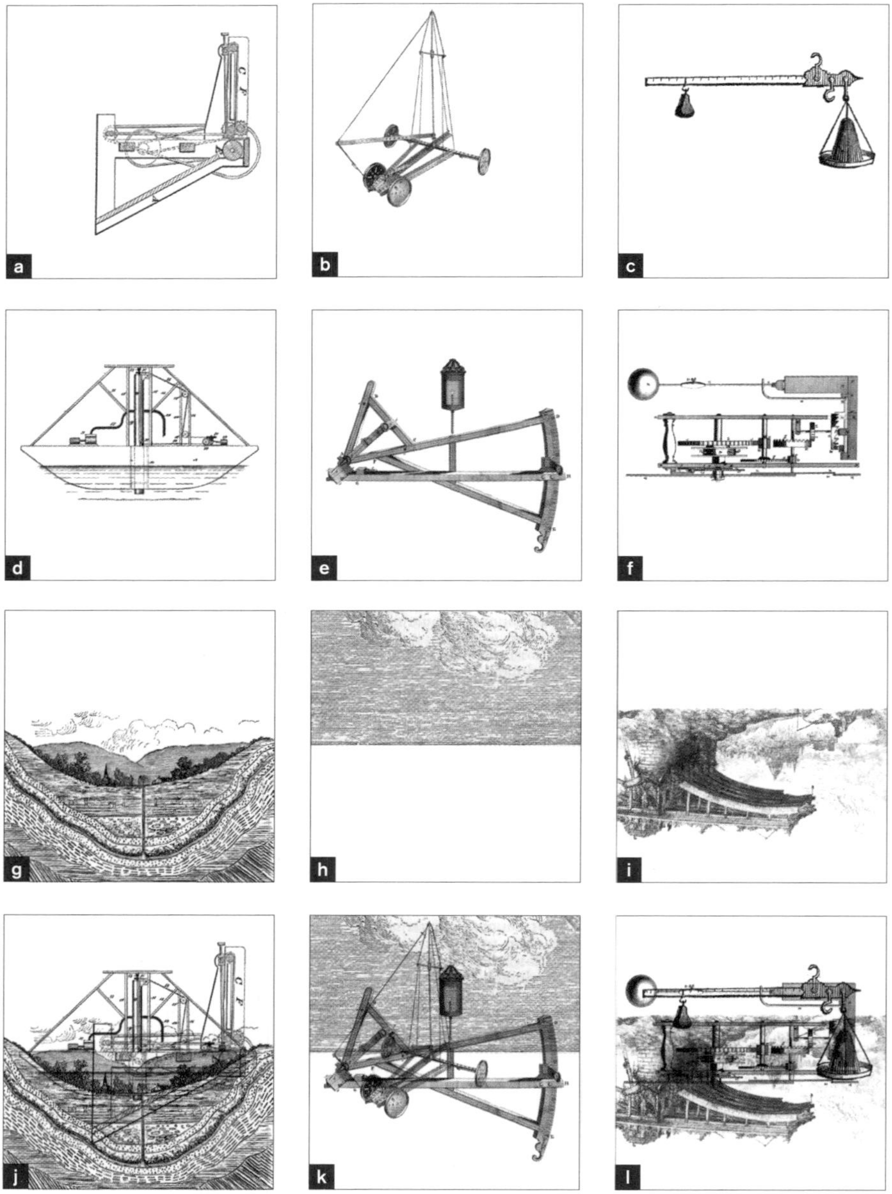

a - l // sequential diagrams of archive, observation tower, and welcome center.

JARON POPKO / site plan

Central Parkway has a long and diverse history in the city of Cincinnati. First, it was a canal. Part of the Miami and Erie Canal, it ran over 300 miles from Toledo to Cincinnati, connecting Lake Erie with the Ohio River. The canal created a clear boundary between downtown Cincinnati and the neighborhood immediately north, known as Over-the- Rhine.

Around 1920, the canal was removed and construction began on a subway tunnel system for the city with Central Parkway as the main artery. The subway was never completed. Today, Central Parkway sits above the abandoned tunnels that have been sealed off for close to a century. Including the 35-foot wide median system, the eight-lane boulevard is 125 feet wide in most parts. This project inhabits several of the medians along Central Parkway, opening up the abandoned subway tunnels below and revealing a hidden and forgotten past. In keeping with the idea of the Atlas as a machine, mechanical devices are selected that are representative of different aspects of Borges's narrative of the world of Tlön and also provide necessary functions to achieve a full reading of the city. The program is divided into three elements: a welcome center, an observation tower, and an archive. Altogether, the program elements work in conjunction with one another in order to provide the user with a full experience and understanding of the city, from past to present.

The archive and the observation tower work together to create an experience that transcends time from a series of present moments to a non-linear sequence of events. The welcome center helps to create the transition between these separate events.

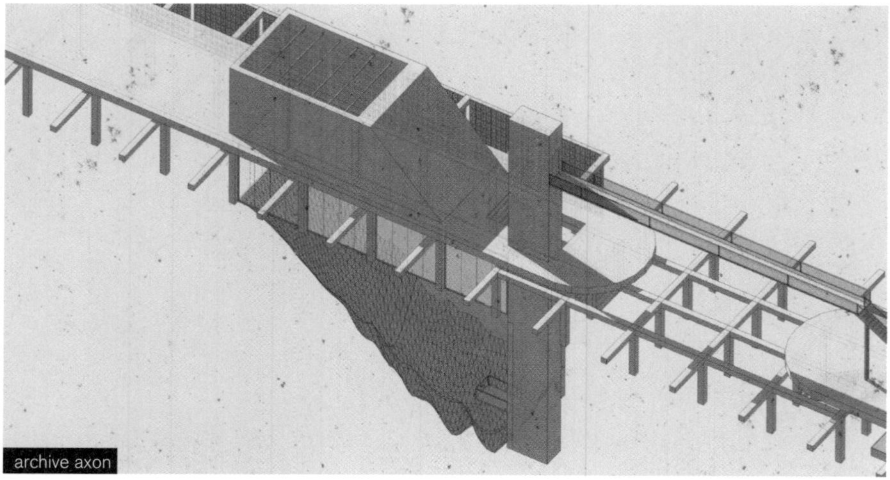
archive axon

observation tower axon

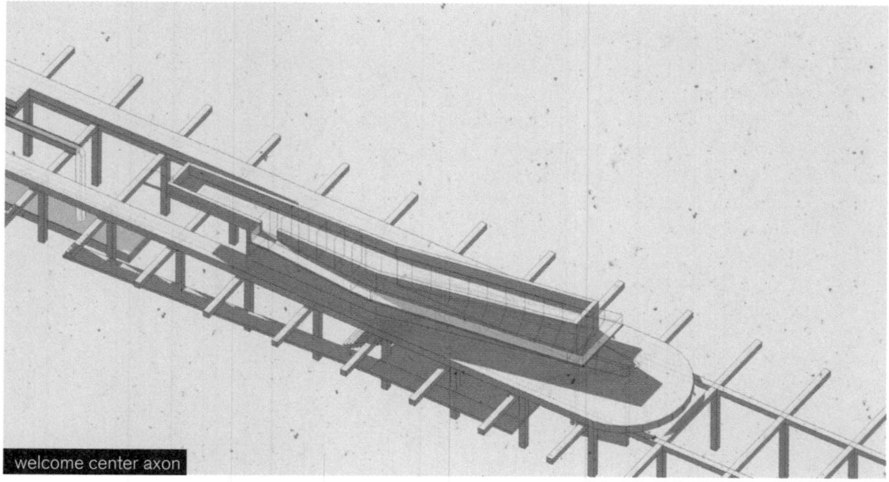
welcome center axon

Welcome Center // composed of a balance, a clock, and an unfinished bridge. It acts as the transition between layers and history of the city. The unfinished bridge represents the unfinished subway beneath the city. The clock represents time, a common theme throughout Borges' work and a depiction of how the site has changed throughout history. The balance illustrates how the pavilion facilitates the transition across these levels.

JARON POPKO / plans + elevations

Observation Tower // allows the user to notice and perceive elements of the city in a different way. It is composed of a sail, sextant, and clouds. The clouds are representative of the omniscient view of the city that the tower provides. The sextant is an instrument used in measuring distances and the sail is representative of search and discovery.

Archive // provides the user with a journey through time into the past, revealing layers of history. The archive is composed of a printing press mechanism that represents the facilitation of knowledge. A mining machine depicts the action of digging below the surface. The archaeological dig illustrates how the archive cuts away and reveals hidden layers of the past.

observation tower section perspective

welcome center section perspective

archive section perspective

PILGRIMAGE // A DYSTOPIA

Graduate Option Architectural Studio
International Collage Competition First Place Winner

Due to cultural homogenization in the 21st century, humans have evolved to respond to only one common signifier: the arrow. Around mid-century, the arrow was found to be the single universally understood and accepted symbol, and was thus adopted as the principal communication tool of the first world.

Other less universal tools, such as language or complex imagery were too culturally loaded, and consequently, were abandoned. A modern world needed signs that were not burdened with history, that were not exclusive to particular ground.

Over time and across the globe all other symbols were lost, purged or buried. At last, the world was left with one single means of expression: an indicator of the direction of movement. With nothing left but this, people began building monuments of the indicator. One cannot build an indicator with nothing to indicate, and since the people were capable only of building the indicator, they built indicators indicating indicators. And so, the building of one monument led to the building of a complex network of signifying signfields. The resulting labyrinth became so complex that it was impossible to determine for certain if it had any beginning or end. All that could be confirmed was perpetual movement.

**Sarah Vaz won the First Place in the competition.*

SARAH VAZ / graphite + collage

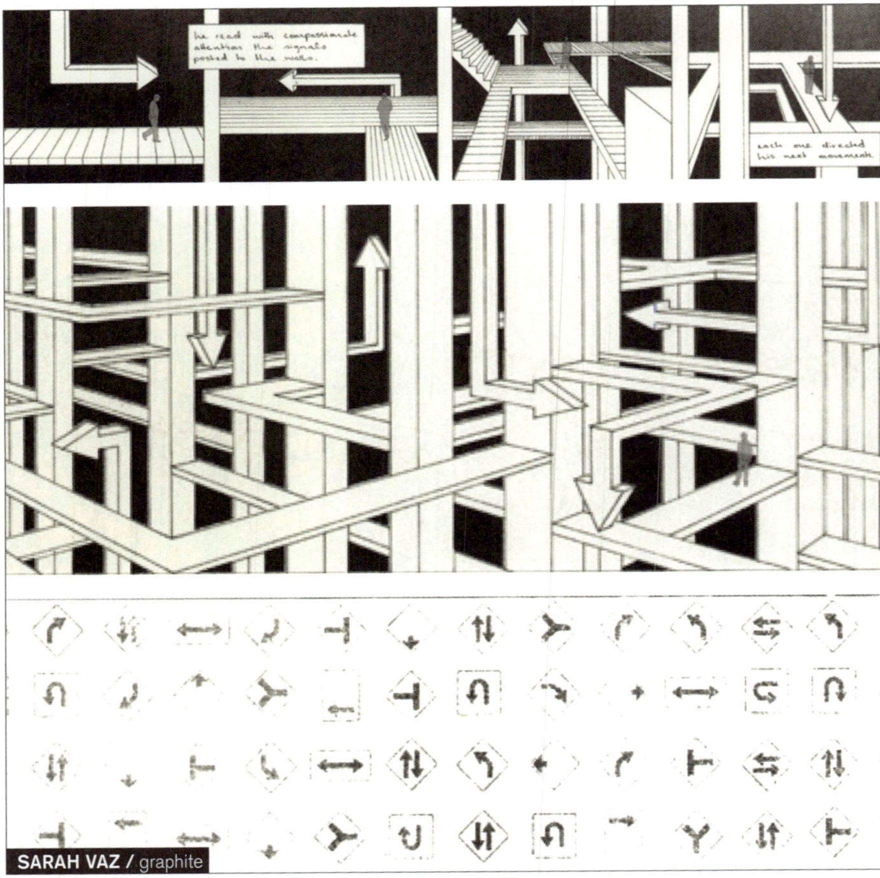

SARAH VAZ / graphite

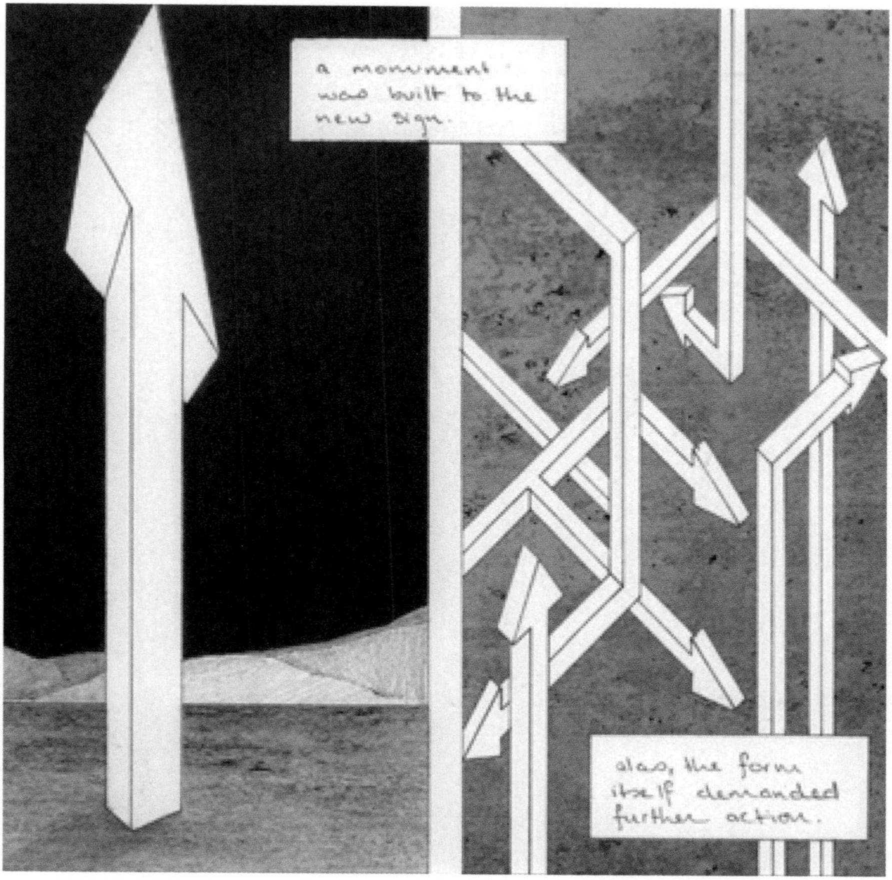
a monument was built to the new sign.
also, the form itself demanded further action.

LUCIE FONTEIN

SURREAL ENVIRONMENTS

Masters of Architecture, Competition Studio
Bonneville Salt Flats, UT, USA

The brief for the Lyceum 2009 Competition called for proposals for the design of a 20,000 SF Zero Energy Rest Area that engaged a proposed Land Art Installation entitled *Earth Curvature*. The site is at the intersection of The Great Salt Lake Desert and Interstate 80. The studio was organized around three distinct architectural questions: What role does the experience of site play in the development of a project? How can sustainable strategies inspire remarkable architecture? What do we understand by the concept of the surreal with respect to trucker/tourist culture and landscape?

We took a three day field trip to the Bonneville Salt Flats in Utah to experience this unusual landscape first hand. The effect on the designs was dramatic. First, and most striking of all, was the discovery that for many months of the year, this "desert" landscape is flooded. The experience of wading in this one foot deep mirroring expanse of water contributed to a deep appreciation of the importance of fully understanding the yearly transformations of a site before embarking on a project. Climate websites provide useful data but don't come close to capturing the experience of standing on the edge of the salt flats leaning into a wind that simply does not let up, with the salt spray off the surface waves lashing at your face. The obvious question emerged: How could this energy be harnessed in a way that would capture the imaginations of travelers in this bleak landscape?

Ryan Ball's project addressed all of these questions with his entry entitled 24 Strings. From his competition description:

Every winter the barren Bonneville salt flats are cleansed by a rising water table and through the process of evaporation, the imperfections are washed away to leave the perfectly flat surface they are known for. The salt flats are a lonely and inhospitable place, only inhabitable when we adapt to the landscape's cycles and learn to harness its energies. High above the salt flats, the wind generates enough energy to supply a simple dwelling with electricity. The use of weather balloons equipped with wind cell technologies creates a startling spectacle in the expansive sky that speaks to both the trucker and the high art enthusiast. Is it a mirage or does it really offer the opportunity to rest and dream in this surreal environment?

RYAN BALL / perspectives

CAFE

RYAN BALL / section perspectives

LUCIE FONTEIN

DOCUMENTING CHANGE AT THE ROCK OF AGES

Masters of Architecture, Competition Studio
Post Industrial Earth

What happens when industry leaves substantial marks on the earth? This was the question posed by the competition brief for the 2012 Lyceum Competition. The specific site in question was an abandoned granite quarry near Barre, Vermont. The walls of the quarry are nearly vertical, going five hundred feet down into the earth. The quarry is filled with water.

The contrast between the sharp granite edges disappearing into the dark depths of the water and the surrounding natural wooded landscape is a powerful reminder of the constantly changing nature of place. Such a striking condition can attract visitors and encourage reflection on the environmental consequences of human activity.

The prompt called for the design of a building complex for an institution devoted primarily to visual, literary, landscape and performing artists and consisting of an educational pavilion, artist's studios, residences and a memorial.

In addition to doing basic research on passive design strategies and energy and water management systems, students participated in a reading seminar that explored the role of technology in contemporary society, specifically ideas of craft, tools, phenomenology and possibilities for action in the digital age.

Todd Ebeltoft's competition entry entitled "Hello Hal, do you read me?" was captioned with quotations from *2001: A Space Odyssey*. The project is at once a celebration and a critique of the results produced by the manipulation of mechanical advantage.

The arrival tower is the gateway to a grid of cables that crisscross the site, offering a coordinate system by which objects and events on the site may be mapped. Within the tower, a conveyor belt system allows the artist/visitor to select the equipment desired for the day's outing: hammer and chisels, watercolor paint box and easel, writing pad, chair and umbrella, box lunch, etc. Users can punch in the coordinates of the area they wish to visit and the equipment that they wish to take with them, and the vessel will prepare itself and deliver them to their desired location.

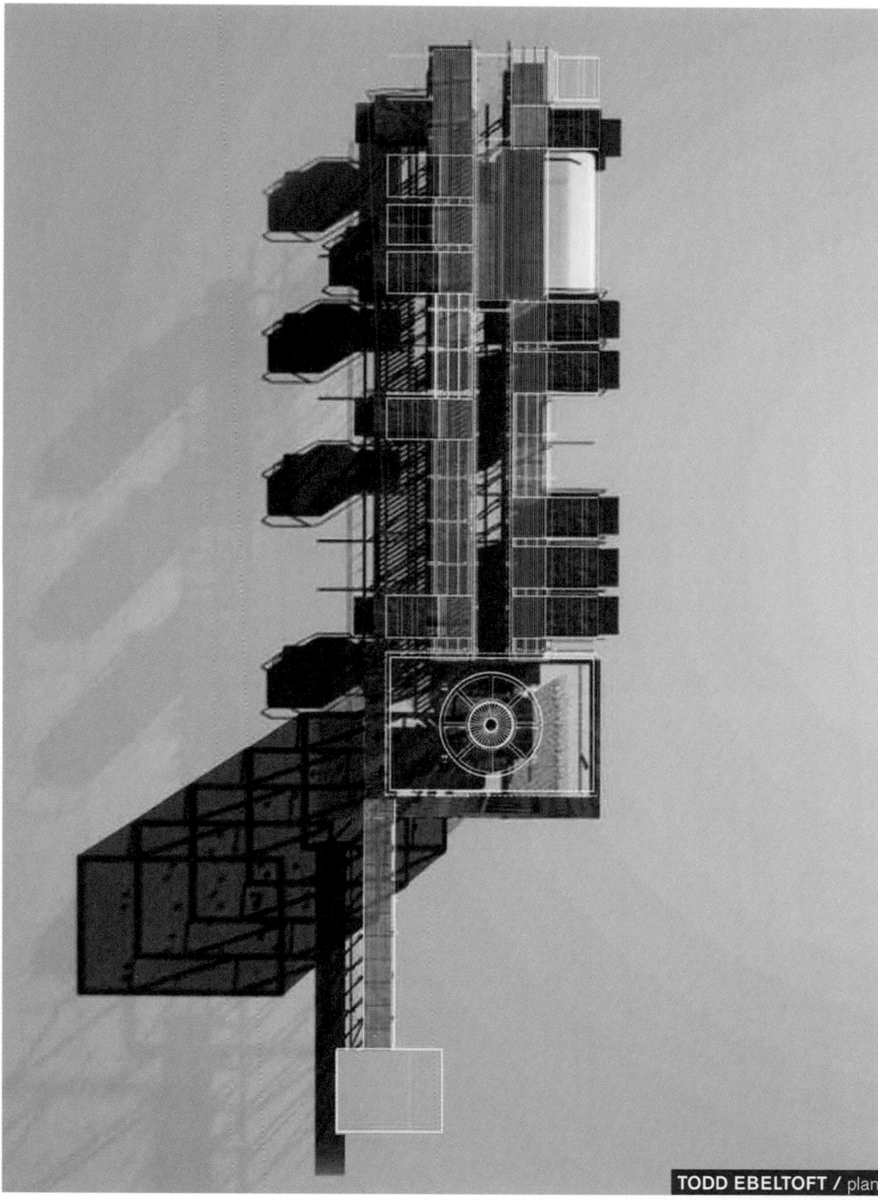

TODD EBELTOFT / plan

Vessels attach to the moving cables at the top in the x-direction and at the bottom in the y-direction, allowing for access to all parts of the quarry. Movement in the z-axis is achieved through a pulley system that allows the vessel to descend to the ground/ water as desired.

A history of all visits is collected and mapped for the information of future users.

approach

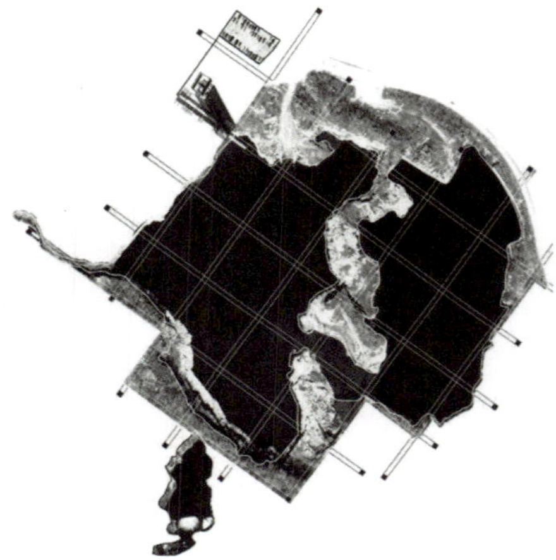

aerial

perspective

TODD EBELTOFT / aerial

ANJALY PATEL
VINCENT SANSALONE (chair)

WONDER AS INTERRUPTION

Masters of Architecture Thesis
Cincinnati, OH, USA

The investigation looks at a qualitative study of wonder in architecture as it transpires at three levels: frame, spectacle, and interruption and at the subsequent translation of these moments. Frame is understood as wonder at a distance. Spectacle is presented as that which is consumed and produced by a normative, ideal standard of wonder, the circus. And lastly, interruption, the most subtle of the three, stands for "the happened-upon", the peculiar, the strange in the familiar, the unexpected in the expected, the unspoken in the spoken, the impossible in the possible.

In order to instill the strange in the familiar, a certain unlearning of premature assumptions was in order: traditional architectural elements were dismantled to understand their potential beyond initially preconceived considerations. The downtown Pedway, an overlooked and undeveloped industrial portion of land, fostered the fertile creative siting for the quest. Primarily used by locals, the site became the perfect in-between where an interruption might transpire.

The thesis proposes an interruption in the urban scale as a future Pedway extension. Excavating space from within, while choreographing subtle circulatory details entices the pedestrian to meander. Seen as a pretext to escape from the everyday, the beauty of this wondrous interruption is that it embraces possibility while offering an alternative from quotidian numbness. It hopes to set the scene for interruptions to come.

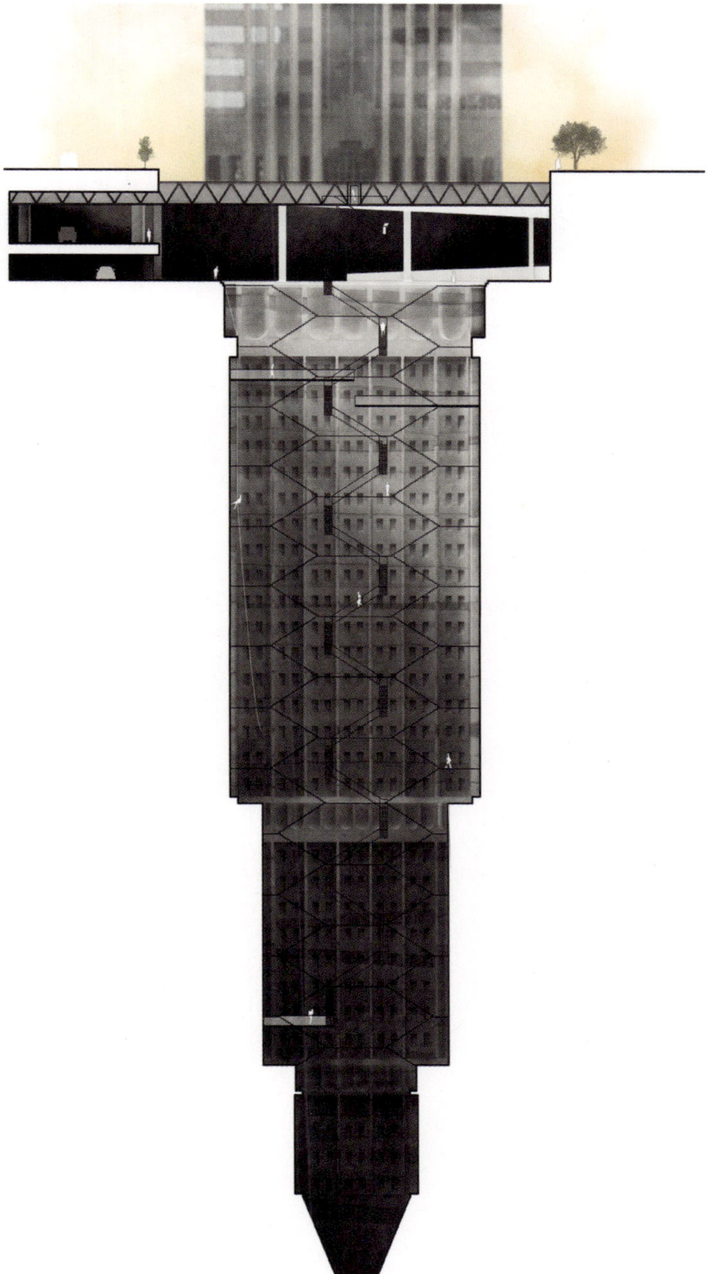

ANJALI PATEL / Section, path+rammed earth void

path from above

ground level

observation deck within tunnel flooding

ANJALI PATEL / observation deck at lowest point of Interruption

CHAS WIEDERHOLD

FIRST IT WAS CINCINNATI

First it was Cincinnati, Cincinnati, Cincinnati...

But then it was a recession and it was my first time seeking a co-op. Jobs were scarcer than my professional experience. I met an architect from Cincinnati while touring Washington D.C. soon after I was accepted to the University. He and I got along well enough for me to be awarded a business card and kept in touch frequently enough to maintain a place in each other's consciousness. It came time to redeem our connection and in applying to the firm, I wrote a glowing essay to their hiring partner complementing their firm endlessly in hopes that it would mask my woeful inexperience. In the days of old, when the University was on a quarter system, you could co-op for a double section, six months in one place, and this made me victim of my own inertial comfort. A bad economy does not make fruitful grounds for an exploratory job search. I stayed, and retrospectively, perhaps, over-stayed, at the firm more than I may have benefitted from the diversity of experience that the co-op program could, and should, and does, provide.

The first co-op is a bit of an out of body experience. Everything you are doing you are doing for the first time. Not only are the tasks you are asked to perform unfamiliar to you, the environment and professional structure you are expected to perform them in is unfamiliar as well. Swooped out of your second year of college and launched into this recognizable but foreign space, memories of this time are distorted: was I an effective intern? Did I like my job a lot? A little? Not at all? I cherish the people I worked with. I point at the building for which I drafted the landscape plan and the building where I took a first stab at designing the stairwell and proudly explain that I was involved. Did they keep any of my drawings or just have to redo them? Writing about the first co-op five years later certainly feels like writing a biography of a stranger more than my own experience.

Then it was Raleigh, Baltimore, New York, Chicago.

And I was a bit more intentional in what I sought in a professional experience. I was invited to a wedding, and I had a sick family member, so I told myself that I had to stay east of the Mississippi River. Realistically though, it was going to take a rooted person like myself a little encouragement to fly away. This said, my ambition at the time was to work for a firm serving a specific type of client. I had studied humanitarian design and flown to Tanzania to observe its practice. I helped organize a conference that brought Bryan Bell of Design Corps to my school. More and more, the age of information was exposing the ugly underbelly of the corporate world, and I completely lost interest in participating in architecture that supported that.

I found a firm in Chicago that had won several awards for their work within their community, serving those traditionally unserved by the architecture profession. I quickly convinced myself that this was the best place for me in this station of my life, and I aggressively pursued working for the small practice of two. If the co-op program is good for nothing else, then it is good for teaching young people like myself how to represent skills, exercise persistence, and interview for a job.

After countless calls, missed calls, voicemails, an over-the-phone interview, and driving to Chicago to interview in person (typically not a requirement, but I was in town and the interview was at Revolution Brewery, so I did not mind the trip), I was hired on a contract written on a scrap piece of paper. We negotiated a stipend by counting up my potential expenses plus a percentage. It was going to be a frugal term, but for the sake of learning how to serve the unserved, a passion I maintain, it was going to be worth any discomfort that may have ensued.

In Chicago I learned to enjoy myself by myself. I made friends, yes, but gained a better companion in cycling. This remains as my chief hobby outside of architecture (both a hobby and a profession). I learned that strong relationships with clients are the bedrock of good projects and that building cooperative teams can make architecture a reality for good people who deserve it. What I sought out in a business plan for public interest design resulted in learning that there are some endeavors in life that require more heart than reward.

Zaragoza, Paris, San Mateos, Cincinnati...

By the time I finished my undergraduate education, I was less sure than ever that I wanted to be an architect. It was to no fault of my education, in fact, I thrived in the academic environment. My classroom had no walls but an air-conditioned office certainly did. I applied to several architecture firms despite this. Fortunately for me, my charged attitude and insistence that I work in some type of community-building capacity, didn't make me a good fit for those corporate environments, and I was able to narrow my professional search to fields outside of architecture. I was hired by a social service agency that used my interest in social equity to work with children in immigrant families, primarily from the San Mateo region of Guatemala. This fulfilling work was followed by another opportunity to serve my community on a campaign to save a historic building. I managed volunteers, attended events, and rallied support for a $170 million sales tax campaign. In these capacities, I felt more useful than I had before. My organizational, communication, and people skills were the biggest contributors to success at these jobs. I was happy, useful, and felt ambitious and secure. One problem existed though: I missed architecture terribly. I missed the studio environment. I missed talking about development and technology and material and anthropology and behavior. I craved the ability to preserve the relationships I had built in Cincinnati over the past five years while picking up gainful experiences in other places. I wanted to live in two worlds.

Considering my options for satisfying my contradictory cravings, I found a solution in my past: the University of Cincinnati co-op program. In what other program would I be required by curricula to fully immerse myself in another place; create a life, get a library card, a gym membership, a morning routine, all in a place that is not my own and then—without the damage incurred by quitting a job—depart from that place to return to home base? Granted, I thought, in this imagining of myself in another place, I may end up falling in love. That is a risk I would take in exploring the world. Building professional and personal relationships in another life complicates this rootless utopia of everywhereness.

My hope lies in a future reality that contracts the second dimension, that makes these places I have fallen in love with draw closer to one another, to be able to preserve the functionality of my experiences around the world without having to sacrificing one for the other. And we are watching that happen. The world is shrinking. Every day the land contracts a bit around me, the continents inch closer and closer, voices from neighbors become clearer and more complete. Our awareness of the condition of others is delivered to our pockets instantly. Never before has so much information been accessible by so many across such great distances.

I miss my job in Seattle. I thrived there. I fit in. I felt useful, challenged, appreciated. In a way that wasn't clear to me in my first co-op, in my Seattle job it was very apparent to me how I could be an impactful member of the team. This, of course, comes with time. I can only imagine how I will be able to contribute in my second and third co-ops in graduate school. I can only hope that the subsequent experiences build upon the years-long project that has been my professional development. In a way, being able to love so many places on our quickly shrinking planet makes me feel like a better, more appreciative member of the human collective. The co-op program at UC has afforded me an opportunity unparalleled; travel the world, commit to a places, fall in love, experience loss, celebrate successes, embrace challenge, and come back to a place called home.

ELIZABETH LAMB
ELIZABETH RIORDEN (chair)

THE ALCHEMY OF SPACE: A TRANSLATION

Master of Architecture Thesis

Architecture is a tectonic manipulation, actively engaging the core elements to conceal and reveal vital data essential to an understanding of the whole, similar to narrative strategies active in literature. Meaning derived from a text allows expression to permeate traditional material barriers, taking away the dividing line between the disciplines of literature and the visual arts. This thesis aims to unearth the existing relationships between architecture and the text by examining translations across media.

Translation is an act of communication, presupposing the existence of two distinct reciprocal media forms.

Walter Benjamin, the German-Jewish philosopher, cultural critic and theorist, and author of *The Task of the Translator*, references the creative process of translation as a method of comprehension, followed by deformation, which allows for embedded meaning to be extracted, and lastly for the illumination of the translation [1]. For Benjamin, translation is thought of more as a "kinship" than a direct reflection of the original work, orbiting the intent. Likewise, Annie Brisset, Professor of Translation Studies and Discourse Theory, postulates in *The Search For A Native Language: Translation and Cultural Identity* that translation is a "dual act of communication" allowing for the existence of two paths, the translation giving life to the original [2].

Sophia Psarra, author and educator at the Bartlett School of Graduate Studies, writes in her book *Architecture and Narrative* that the idea of *conceptual* versus *perceptual*, regarding their convergence within the realms of architecture and literature, gives depth to meaning and understanding within the built realm. *Architecture and Narrative* calls for a paradigm shift in the known methods of conception by exploring the "morphological properties of architecture in terms of how they relate to conceptual and perceptual notions of space and embodied experience."

Narrative strategies work in unison to form the narrative of the magical realism genre. Doubling, hybridization, focalization, and the irreducible element uniquely format the structure in Paolo Coelho's magical-realist text *The Alchemist*. Of the themes and structures found in *The Alchemist*, focalization and the irreducible element are especially at play [4].

Focalization is the lens through which the narrator shares elements of the story with the reader. It is solely dependent on understandings, biases, and worldly perceptions. It can be understood as the compression and expansion of insight into the understandings of the narrator's surrounding world. It frames and focuses the comprehension of the progression through the text. Focalization is a notion of perspective, associated with matters of vision; it is a theoretical bridging of the perceptual and conceptual, and can be gainfully employed to analyze artifacts that combine the visual and the verbal.

The irreducible element is the disturbance and displacement of the logic of the understood realm. It represents a shift in perception to conceptualization of a new structured logic of the textual domain, re-associating the reader with the understood notions of the perceived reality. The unexpected exchange can occur in objects and their abilities in the new realm or through interactions within nature.

In the world of *The Alchemist* the protagonist seeks out a pilgrimage route given in a dream. Guided by an invisible force, the elements, and a universal language of the metaphysical realm, he searches for and discovers a new perspective. This thesis serves as a pilgrimage of growth, questioning perception of spatial creation and meaning through a lens of the literature using themes and narrative construction strategies from within the text.

The experience of the journey is translated into a series of transformations based on a progression through time, mediating text to a new reading of architectural reality. By referencing the narrative strategies and themes established in *The Alchemist*, the design parallels a similar technique in utilizing the architectural elements to portray an allegory of space and time.

ELIZABETH LAMB/ The Innocent in the Nest

Notes:

[1] Benjamin, W. "The Task of the Translator." In *The Translation Studies Reader*, trans. by Harry Zohn, edited by Lawrence Venuti. New York: Routledge, 2012. 15-25.

[2] Brisset, A. "The Search For A Native Language: Translation And Cultural Identity." In *The Translation Studies Reader*, trans. by R. Gill and R. Gannon. New York: Routledge, 2012. 343-375.

[3] Psarra, S. *Architecture and Narrative: The Formation of Space and Cultural Meaning*. Oxford: Routledge, 2009.

[4] Coelho, P. and A. Clarke. *The Alchemist.* San Francisco: Harper San Francisco, 1993.

The Soul Apprentice at the Wellspring

The Explorer in the Garden

object: *sword*
narrative structure: *rhythm*
element of place: *time*

object: *silence*
narrative structure: *infinite*
element of place: *ordinary vs. extraordinary*

The Wonderer in the Cocoon

object: *crystal*
narrative structure: *hill*
element of place: *known vs. unknown*

object: *snake*
narrative structure: *mirage*
element of place: *irreducible element*

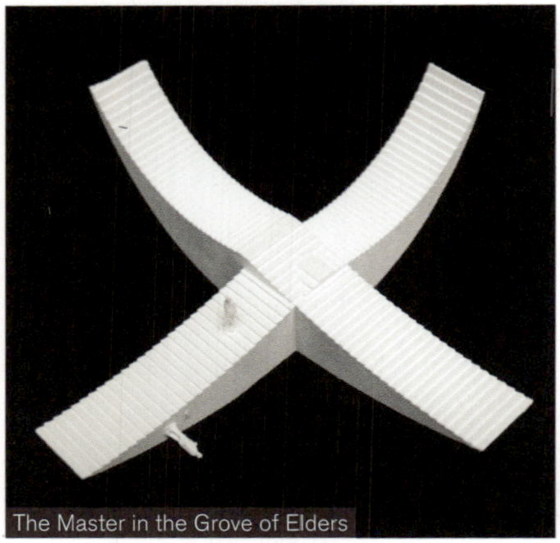

The Master in the Grove of Elders

The Thespian at the Oasis

object: *water jug*
narrative structure: *sacred vs. forbidden*
element of place: *merge*

object: *scarab*
narrative structure: *sacred scale*
element of place: *discovery & ascension*

The Sage in the Mountain Cave

HANK HILDEBRANDT

STOREFRONT STUDIO

Undergraduate Study Abroad
The Bridge of Cultures; Urban Design, Design, Architecture, Interior Design
(The Visions and The Realities)
France, Switzerland, Turkey &Their Environs

The natural extension of a nine-week Foreign Study Studio and travel experience was a six week Store Front Studio. The Store Front Studio idea followed the pattern of the foreign study experience in using the streets from Paris to Istanbul and the environs in between as ***the classroom*** for the studio. Acknowledging the nomadic nature of the travel agenda in visiting sites, drawing them, analyzing contextual settings, and being asked to synthesize the experience in pulling together an application into an architectural statement meant reproducing an experience that captured the energy of global urban street life. The studio drew from and used as the classroom the intensity of places like the Grand Bazaar and Spice Market of Istanbul; the powerful 'fairy chimneys' landscape structures in Göreme, Cappadocia; and the historic and contemporary architectural works in European cities like Paris and Basel, Switzerland. The experience of the diversity of architectural details—inside and out—the contextual relationships of building, street, site, and 'place' set the tone that the street, the sidewalk, the open space, the interior, the landscape are one big classroom, a sand box, of opportunities for learning architecture and design as an outgrowth of culture and surrounding social context. The experience set up the Store Front Studio, a required design studio for both architecture and interior design students, and utilized both analysis and design tools required to be placed in the urban context. Of each student, the studio required a focus to develop an ***insertion*** of an architectonic condition or program into a notable architectural landmark or several architectural monuments visited. Each student was expected to research a building or buildings from a significant designer/architect or firm that can be visited, and to subsequently visit the site / structure to gather and document the significant condition, and to generate design proposals. Students researched and analyzed the existing site, programmed, designed, and developed the required architectonic insertion(s)—whether interior or exterior—as additional architectural conditions around or within the existing architecture(s).

For example, Corbusier's **Notre Dame du Haut** in Ronchamp had an additional visitor center added with much protest. The architect, Renzo Piano, came under protest by many notable architects around the world, and his insertion into this significant architectural site serves as an example for a type of interiors studio project, namely a gift shop within the Blue Mosque in Istanbul.

The Store Front Studio was developed to accommodate formalizing the Foreign Studies experience upon returning to campus. The nomadic conditioning of traveling and studying within urban settings was the inspiration for using an abandoned store front space off-campus to set up a substitute design studio classroom as the alternative to campus studios. Inexpensive MDF on standard sawhorses provided tabletop surfaces, the local Knoll representatives furnished loaner furniture and seating, and within two days a complete operational off-campus design studio was up and running to accommodate the remaining six weeks of the semester. The studio ended the semester with an exhibition and opening to celebrate the foreign experience and ***Insertion*** solutions.

Storefront Studio, exhibition

Storefront Studio, signage

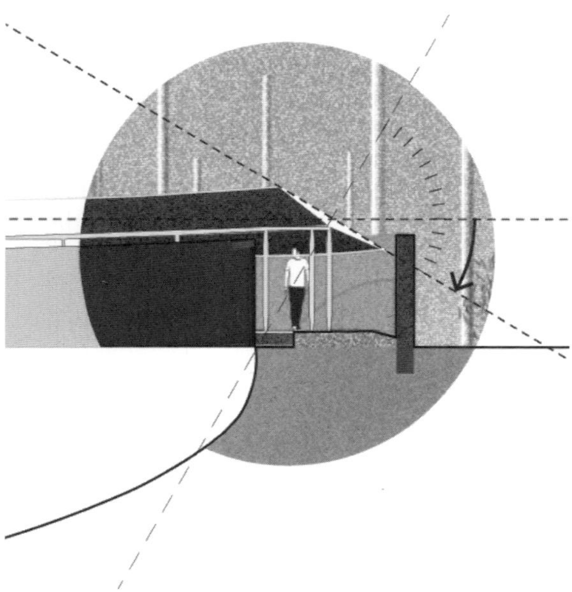

JONATHAN WILKINSON/ *The Wall* for Storefront Studio

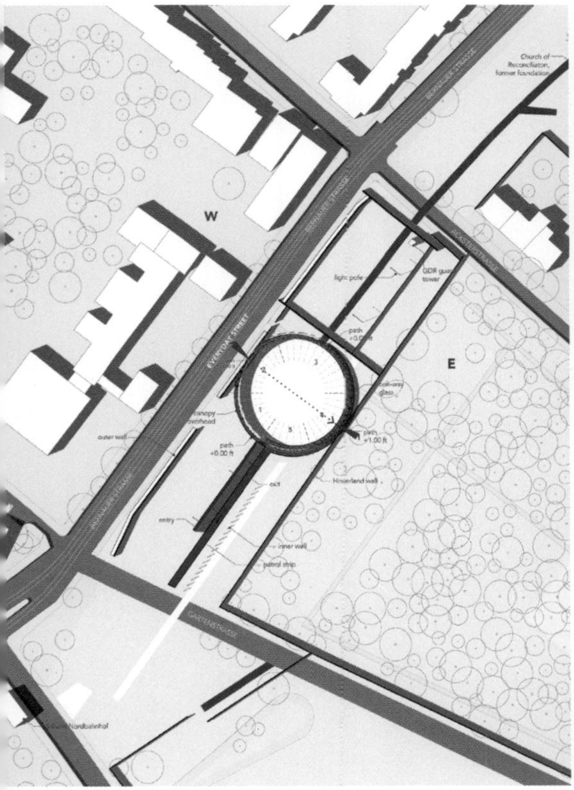
Church of Reconciliation, former foundation
W
E
light pole
GDR guard tower
EVERYDAY STREET
path +0.00 ft
path +1.00 ft
canopy overhead
outer wall
Hinterland wall
exit
entry
inner wall
patrol strip
GARTENSTRASSE
Nordbahnhof

Storefront Studio

Exhibition, reception

Exhibition, still life scene

ALAN ALANIZ
AARATI KANEKAR, PH.D. (chair)
ELIZABETH RIORDEN (member)

MACHINING THE AMERICAN WEST

Master of Architecture Thesis
The American West, USA

Interpreting architecture through a machinic lens reveals its capacity for opening new frames of reference from our existing environment—constructing conceptions of place, culture, and identity out of empty space. Within this framework, architecture ceases to simply be a product of actions and desires but instead is regarded as an active contributor to our understanding of our surroundings and ultimately ourselves. The architectural and mechanical elements presented in this project set forth new forms of engagement between disparate bodies and ideas. Through this process, entire histories are disassembled and reassembled to reveal their inner workings and construct new assemblages of thought and space. The starting point of this process is the fundamental understanding that our socio-cultural environment is the product of a network of forces and desires of individual, heterogeneous elements, human and non-human, material and immaterial. These multiple forces continually push, pull, and reshape our lived world across time, positing the potential for one space to accommodate multiple places.

This project utilizes Lévi-Strauss's *bricolage* concepts alongside Deleuze and Guattari's assemblage theory to create a unified methodological lens capable of evaluating and constructing our prior understanding of history and our relationships to it. Ultimately, these frameworks expand to create a comprehensive concept effective in the use of architectural design.

Within this project, the American West is interpreted as both site and idea. Employing a design process imbued with the methodology of *bricolage* reveals the engrained heterogeneous composition of a space steeped in national myth while continually in flux. Consequently, our understandings of the West are broken down into four distinct components: Myth/ History of the West, Griddedness of the West, Transience of the West, and West as Palimpsest. These individual components engage with one another to tell the multidimensional story of a region whose stories are the result of a constant struggle between concepts of "control" and "chaos."

In order to explicate the multidimensionality of the West, this project utilizes the design of four individual, autonomous machines and a central "hive" structure that functions as a depository for the information collected by these creations. Methodologically, these machines and architecture are designed through a process of *bricolage*, but more specifically kitbashing, a practice whereby commercial model components are altered and combined to create new formations disassociated from their original intent. This process highlights the potential for designing with "whatever is at hand," and making do with the available material or instruments. These creations will function as the archival apparatus of the "Western" experience, tasked with the continual updating, reconstruction, and redistribution of ideas and understandings of a particularly recombinant region.

The architecture presented in this project mirrors the combinatory nature of the American West through a process of enframing *bricolaged* histories through the lens of *bricolaged* machines. By interpreting architecture through this framework, this project begins to approach works based on their interrelational properties and their potential for bridging new connections between bodies, things, the spaces they inhabit, and the social organizations that order them.

ALAN ALANIZ / Transient Array

Dialogic Containment

Palimpsestic Herd

central "hive", overall

Destratifying Excavator

Transient Array

ALAN ALANIZ / detail

Dialogic Containment, detail

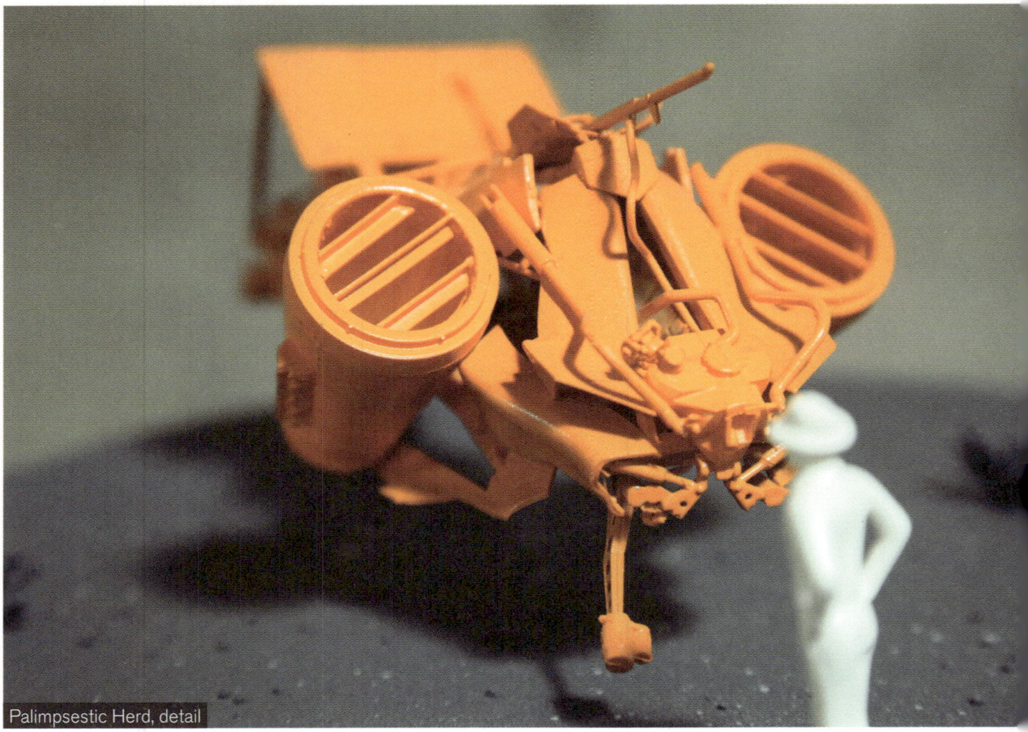

Palimpsestic Herd, detail

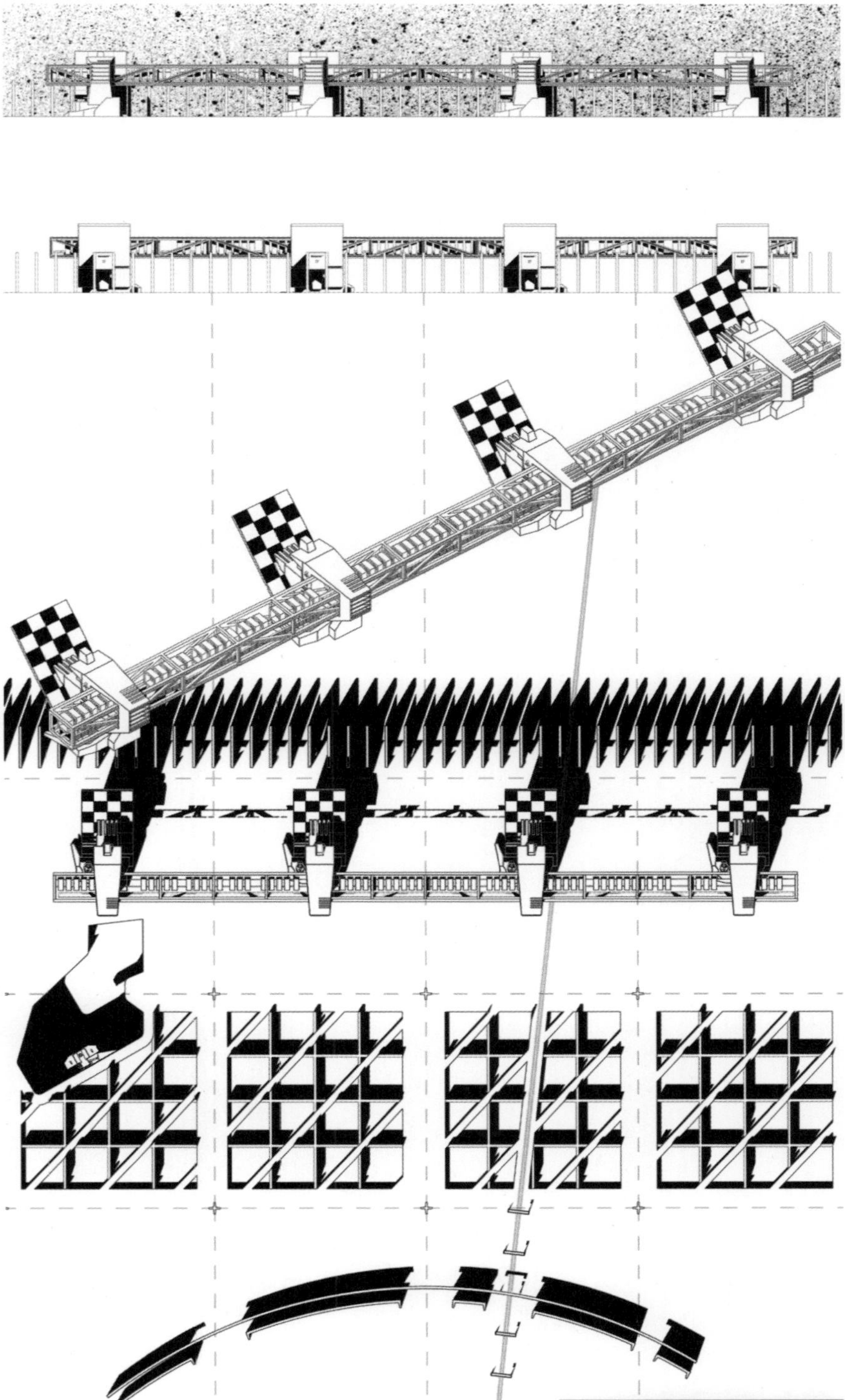

ALAN ALANIZ / central "hive", plan

Photography Credits / **JOSHUA ANDERSON**

SAID

Faculty

School of Architecture and Interior Design
University of Cincinnati

Kory Beighle | Adjunct Assistant Professor
Pravin Bhiwapurkar | Assistant Professor
Tom Bible | Associate Professor
Ann Black | Associate Professor
Terry Boling | Associate Professor Practice
Kimberly Burke | Adjunct Assistant Professor
Robert Burnham | Professor Emeritus
Edson Roy Cabalfin | Associate Professor
Jayanta Chatterjee | Dean Emeritus, Professor Emeritus of Architecture and Planning
Bradley Cooper | Adjunct Assistant Professor
Sean Cottengim | Adjunct Assistant Professor
Karolina Czeczek | Visiting Assistant Professor
Lucie Fontein | Adjunct Assistant Professor
Bruce Edgar Goetzman | Professor Emeritus
Udo Greinacher | Associate Professor
Whitney Hamaker | Adjunct Assistant Professor
John Hancock | Professor Emeritus
Anton Harfmann | Interim Coordinator of Architectural Engineering
Henry Hildebrandt | Professor
Aarati Kanekar | Associate Professor
Erin Klein | Adjunct Assistant Professor
Christoph Klemmt | Assistant Professor
Gerald Robert Larson | Professor Emeritus
Raymond Laubenthal | Professor Emeritus
Dennis Mann | Professor Emeritus
Mara Marcu | Assistant Professor, LEED AP
Renee Martin | Adjunct Assistant Professor
Michael McInturf | Associate Professor
Meghan Minton | Adjunct Assistant Professor
Edward Mitchell | Associate Professor
Adrian Parr | Professor and Director of The Charles Phelps Taft Research Center; joint with Department of Political Science, UNESCO Water Chair
James Postell | Professor
Wolfgang Preiser | Professor Emeritus
Elizabeth Riorden | Associate Professor
Michael Rogovin | Adjunct Assistant Professor
Virginia Russell | Professor of Architecture Horticulture Program Director, FASLA, PLA, LEED AP, GRP
Vincent Sansalone | Assistant Professor, Educator
Stephen Slaughter | Assistant Professor
Priyanka Sen | Adjunct Assistant Professor
David Lee Smith | Professor Emeritus
Patrick Snadon | Associate Professor
Barry Stedman | Associate Professor Emeritus
Melanie Swick | Adjunct Assistant Professor
Ming Tang | Associate Professor
Jeffrey Tilman | Associate Professor
Stephen Vamosi | Emeritus
Julian Wang | Assistant Professor
William Daryl Williams | Associate Professor
Rebecca Williamson | Associate Professor
Michael Zaretsky | Associate Professor

With guest features by:
Peter Zellner | Invited Guest Critic '17
Victoria Meyers | Visiting Assistant Professor '12-'14
Peter Waldman | Assistant Professor of Practice '80-'81
Aaron Betsky | Associate Professor '12-'14

SAID Administration:
Edson Roy Cabalfin | BSIntD Program Coordinator
MIntD Program Coordinator
Kimberly Lawson | Program Coordinator
Michael McInturf | MArch Program Coordinator
Edward Mitchell | SAID Director
Moira Morgan | Executive Staff Assistant
Melanie Swick | BSArch Program Coordinator
Jeffrey Tilman | SAID Associate Director
Rebecca Williamson | MSArch and PhD
Program Coordinator

DAAP Administration:
Robert Probst | Dean, Professor
Gail Trahan | Assistant to the Dean
Laurie L Wilson | Associate Director, Non-Academic
Programs, Macy's/DAAP Fashion Show, DAAPcamps
Michael Zaretsky | Associate Dean for Faculty
Affairs and Curriculum, Associate Professor
Lora Drew Alberto | Program Director
Craig Vogel | Associate Dean of Graduate Studies
and Research; Professor
Laura Dorl | Director of Development
Brandi Lewis | Executive Staff Assistant
Shelbie Collopy | Executive Staff Assistant
Shannon Doyle | Assistant Director
of Business Affairs
Hal Jankowski | Business Officer
Jeremy Jaskiewicz | Financial Administrator 2
Alysha Anne Wright | Senior HR Coordinator
Mychael Cornett | Senior Academic Adviser
Samantha Elizabeth Dutle | Senior Academic Adviser
Cassandra Frank | Senior Academic Adviser
Eleanor Sue Graham | Program Coordinator
for Undergraduate Recruitment
Tiffany Lynn Leazer | Associate Director,
Student Affairs
Amberly Maryo | Assistant Dean,
Student Affairs
Jaime Phipps | Senior Academic Adviser,
Student Affairs
James Berns | Manager, College Labs
Daniel Dugan | Equipment and Applications Specialist
Michael Everett | Lab Associate
Nicholas Germann | Senior Computer
& Information Analyst
John Joseph Gillespie | Computer User
Support Specialist
Daniel Kreimer | Manager, College Labs
Scott Lincoln | Director, College Labs
James Petra | Computer User Support Specialist
Aaron Rucker | DAAP Technology & Facilities
Information Technology Manager
Aaron Cowan | Program Director, DAAP Galleries
Jennifer Krivickas | Head of the Robert A. Deshon
& Karl J.Schlachter Library for Design, Architecture, Art,
and Planning
Francis Russell | Community Design Center Director,
Niehoff Urban Studio

Reviews

SAID

School of Architecture and Interior Design
University of Cincinnati

Photography Credits / **VINCENT SANSALONE**

Publications

SAID

School of Architecture and Interior Design
University of Cincinnati

Deleuze and Memorial Culture : Desire, Singular Memory and the Politics of Trauma, **Adrian Parr**, Edinburgh University Press, 2008

Deleuze and the Contemporary World, editors **Ian Buchanan** and **Adrian Parr**, Edinburgh University Press, 2006

Parametric Building Design Using Autodesk Maya, **Ming Tang**, Routledge, 2014

Architecture's Pretexts: Spaces of Translation, **Aarati Kanekar**, Routledge, 2014

Precedents in Zero-Energy Design: Architecture and Passive Design in the 2007 Solar Decathlon, **Michael Zaretsky**, Routledge, 2009

Furniture Design (1st Edition), **Jim Postell**, John Wiley & Sons Inc., 2007

Hijacking Sustainability, **Adrian Parr**, MIT Press, 2009

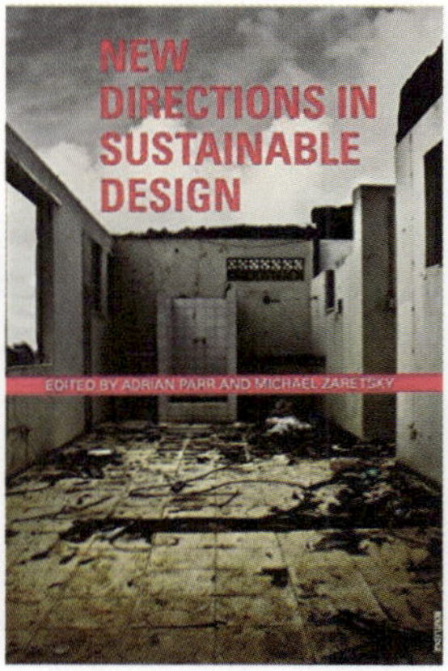

New Directions in Sustainable Design, **Adrian Parr**, Routledge, 2010

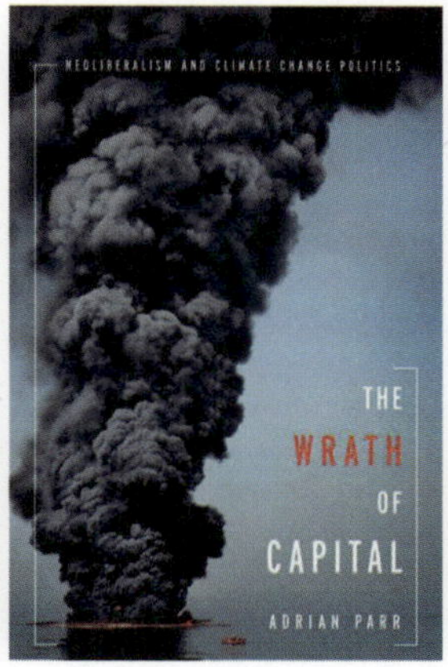

The Wrath of Capital: Neoliberalism and Climate Change Politics, **Adrian Parr,** Columbia University Press, December 2012

What Kids Should Know About Philippine Architecture, **Edson Cabalfin**, Adarna House (Manila, Philippines), 2015

Furniture Design (2nd Edition), **Jim Postell**, John Wiley & Sons Inc., 2012

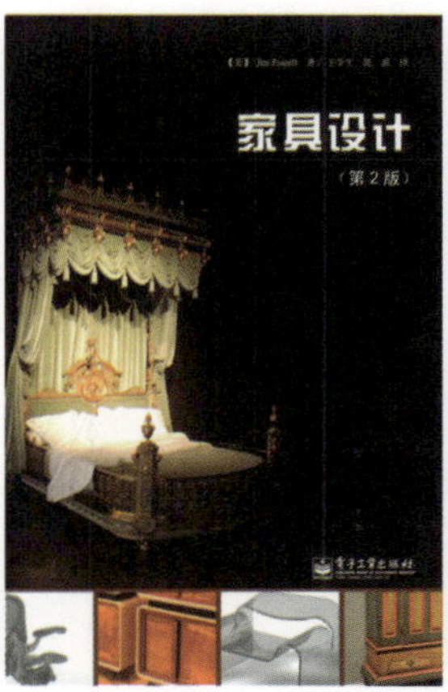

Furniture Design (Chinese edition), **Jim Postell**, John Wiley & Sons Inc./ Publishing House of Electronics Industry Beijing, 2015

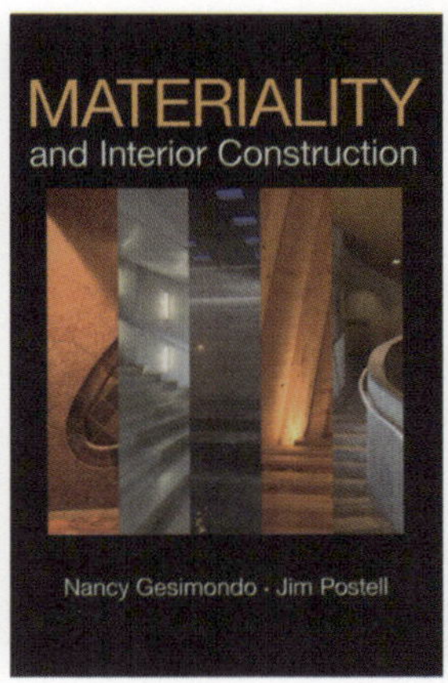

Materiality and Interior Construction, **Nancy Gesimondo** and **Jim Postell,** John Wiley & Sons Inc., 2011

50 from the 50's: Modern Architecture & Interiors in Cincinnati, **Udo Greinacher, Elizabeth Meyer, Susan Rissover, Patrick Snadon**, and **Margo Warminsky**, LuLuPress, 2008

MetroLAB

Michael Zaretsky

Public Interest Design/Build: Learning Through Making

There is no single course that can prepare students for architectural practice. Traditional studio prepares students for a specific and important set of design practices. However, some aspects of contemporary practice are rarely addressed in architecture school. Three aspects of a critical practice that a public interest design/build program addresses are a deep knowledge of implicit design opportunities afforded by the process of making, the potential for design discovery within materials and assemblies, and the embedded power of working on real projects with partners, consultants and direct community engagement.

MetroLAB is a Public Interest Design / Build program within the University of Cincinnati (UC) School of Architecture and Interior Design (SAID) in the College of Design, Architecture, Art and Planning (DAAP). MetroLAB engages students and faculty from SAID, DAAP and across UC with local, non-profit organizations and the communities they serve. Our intent is to design, construct, research and evaluate innovative projects that support the infrastructure and development of the built environment through hands-on learning and direct engagement with community members and partners.

MetroLAB was initiated by SAID Director William Williams in fall 2010, and Michael Zaretsky has led MetroLAB since that time. The first MetroLAB studio was taught in fall 2011 by Associate Professor of Practice Terry Boling. As of summer 2016, eight SAID faculty have taught MetroLAB studios. Over a dozen projects have been completed with community groups in Walnut Hills, Lower Price Hill, Over the Rhine, and Clifton, all in the Cincinnati area.

MetroLAB studio projects are usually small-scale, built projects that address needs identified by non-profit partners throughout Cincinnati. The organization identifies a need for design and construction and the MetroLAB faculty and students engage the local context, the needs of the organization and the local community. We bring innovation, community engagement and full-scale making to the process. Most studios involve an iterative series of full-scale mock-ups that are tested by the students and all other stakeholders on-site in context. This provides feedback that leads to additional prototypes and, in some cases, to permanent installations.

MetroLAB studios are offered for graduate students early in the curriculum and for undergrads later in their curriculum. These studios provide an opportunity for students to get tactile experience with materials, get to know parts of the city of Cincinnati and learn aspects of collaborative design.

MetroLAB focuses on three principles:
1. Learning Through the Process of Making
2. Applied Research and Innovation
3. Community Engagement and Impact

1. Learning Through the Process of Making
MetroLAB projects involve the unique process of learning about design through the process of making. All projects revolve around the iterative production of some built element at full-scale. In many cases, students are encouraged to build before they design. They make mock-ups of things quickly, at full-scale and allow that experience to form their design proposals. In many cases drawings are the final step instead of the first.

This prototyping process enables students to step out of the hypothetical ideas of traditional studio and come face to face with design decisions in a manner that provides an alternative, full-scale relationship to the design process.

2. Applied Design Research and Innovation
MetroLAB students engage meaningful, innovative design research in all projects. We do not rely on traditional construction methods. We seek new potential and opportunity in all forms of making. Materials are constantly tested and explored for their inherent design potential. Professor Boling often has his students produce hundreds

of examples that explore how materials can be used in ways that are not imagined, such as laminating newspaper and then sanding it to produce a powerful surface taxonomy that serves as a backdrop for poetry, as in the project "Louder Than A Bomb."

3. Community Engagement and Impact

MetroLAB projects are built within existing communities in Cincinnati. These studios incorporate input of the actual users, stakeholders and owners throughout the process. Typically, there are interactive events that are designed by the studio to get people physically engaged in this process. In some cases, the studio is actually set up on or near the site so that the students can become intimately and personally connected to the culture, context and personalities of the place where they are designing. In summer 2015, the students in the Pleasant Street Pedestrian Studio transformed a garden shed adjacent to Findlay Market into their temporary studio space. As a result, they were out on Pleasant Street nearly every day, getting to know the residents who were often found spending time on their stoops. In addition, all of our events were held on Pleasant Street. These personal interactions profoundly impacted all of the design work.

Project Types

MetroLAB projects have included exterior public spaces, interior improvements for organizations and events, exhibitions, and even a tiny house. At all scales, we avoid the traditional use of materials and focus instead on the inherent potential that is embedded within material properties.

Public Spaces

Five Points Alley and the Pleasant Street Pedestrian Project both address the improvement of outdoor public spaces. In spring and summer 2014, Terry Boling worked with the Walnut Hills Redevelopment Foundation over two semesters to learn about what that community wanted to do in Five Points Alley and then to test several different mock-ups of seating, shading, stages, and an expandable kiosk for events.

In summer 2015, Associate Professor Zaretsky worked with a group of students on a project that was sponsored by the Corporation for Findlay Market and People's Liberty. They worked with students and faculty from the School of Art and School of Planning to understand how the residents of Pleasant Street wanted to see their street improve. This ironically-named street is a four-block connection that directly links our city's public market, Findlay Market, with one of our most significant downtown parks, Washington Park. However, the street has a very high vacancy rate and with several vacant lots and many buildings standing empty. Our studio created a series of community engagement events to understand who the community is, what they like about Pleasant Street and what they would like to see. The results of the studio were a design for Cincinnati's first parklet. This was built by these students in spring 2016 and installed in summer 2016.

Interiors

In summer 2015, Professor Jim Postell and his students worked with the Seven Hills Neighborhood House in Lower Price Hill. This organization supports local youth in many ways, and they worked with Postell's group to envision a new lobby, conference room, and other improvements throughout their building. In fall 2015, Assistant Professor Stephen Slaughter and his students worked with Elementz, an Urban Arts Center in Over the Rhine (OTR) that focuses on hip-hop music and dance. Through a series of events that engaged the high school students at Elementz, they explored how the space within Elementz could be improved and could more directly express the mission and energy of the organization.

Terry Boling ran two studios that explored how materials and assemblies could change the use and experience of an interior through material innovation. In the "At Full Scale" project, students used an empty building on Republic Street in OTR as a research lab for exploration of ideas that would be useful for others attempting to renovate one of the hundreds of turn-of-the-century brick buildings in the neighborhood.

In the SAID Hallway, students were asked to transform a bland hallway in the office wing of our building into a compelling space that expressed our program. Also within our building, Jim Postell worked with a group of students to transform a storage room into a room for our PhD students with a large conference table, storage, and a kitchenette.

Exhibitions and Events

Terry Boling and his students collaborated in spring 2015

and 2016 with students and teachers of Louder Than A Bomb Cincy Youth Poetry Slam Event. The event started in Chicago and was brought to Cincinnati by the Taft Center for the Humanities. MetroLAB created elements that would support the poetry slam events including a stage, backdrop, DJ booth, and exhibition. The exhibition was presented at the event and at the Contemporary Arts Center in spring 2016.

Tiny House

In 2014, Adrienne Cassel contacted MetroLAB to see if we would be interested in designing a tiny house as a caretaker's cottage on Kamama Prairie in Adams County. The project was initiated by Michael McIntурf's studio in summer 2015 and then revised and built in spring 2016 with Adjunct Faculty Whitney Hammaker. The project involved the transformation of a twenty-foot container into an open, functional tiny house installed on the property.

Conclusion

MetroLAB studios expand our students' experience and understanding of design and the practice of architecture. This is often their first experience of a design process that results from full-scale dialogue with actual materials; it is also often the first time that they engage actual users and clients on the site where the project will be built. The results are a deep commitment and passion for these projects for the students, faculty and the communities with whom they are interacting.

TERRY BOLING / The Devil is in the Details

TERRY BOLING / Louder Than a Bomb

Five Points Alley

TERRY BOLING / Five Points Alley

Five Points Alley

Five Points Alley

MICHALE ZARETSKY / Playground Tires

TERRY BOLING / Five Points Alley

WHITNEY HAMMAKER / Tiny House

Kroger Co.

Michael Zaretsky

Kroger Co. Sponsored Studios

A sponsored studio is typically a condition where a company or corporation provides funding to support a design studio course. However, it is important to understand that the company or corporation is not hiring the faculty or students of that studio. They are not providing a product or service. The studio, under the faculty member's direction, is engaged in directed design research and specific issues that are relevant for the sponsoring company. There are many variations of the sponsored studio, and this way of working is a common model within the UC School of Architecture and Interior Design (SAID).

There are many unexpected benefits that the sponsors have discovered as a result of these experiences. When a company hires a professional firm or a consultant to do work, one of the implicit goals of the firm or consultant is that they want to make the company happy so that they will get hired again. In many cases, they are hesitant to provoke or question the company. They offer experience in a given area but may not always provide a genuine critique of the company that hired them.

Companies we have worked with value the fact that our faculty and students are extremely honest and direct in their assessments of the company and specifically the design issues that are being addressed in the sponsored studio. This honesty has been insightful and productive for our sponsors.

In addition, a firm or consultant typically includes individuals with professional experience who are, by default, older than typical graduate students. A graduate student today offers a unique perspective from the vantage point of a millennial. Every company recognizes that their future customer is the millennial, so insights from this particular user group are extremely valuable for the company.

There are several corporations that have sponsored studios with the SAID in recent years, but one of the longest standing sponsorships is with one of the most successful Cincinnati-based companies: the Kroger Corporation food retailer. Kroger is the largest food retailer in the United States with over 100 billion dollars in annual sales from its extensive array of stores types, sizes and names across the United States. Eight million people a day walk into a grocery store that is owned by Kroger. The Kroger Corporation provides relatively low-priced food for a spectrum of shoppers. We have worked directly with the Head of Design on a series of investigations into the future of food retail. In these studios, we have been able to challenge many beliefs within the corporate structure by doing extensive research in collaboration with Kroger and Dunnhumby USA (a data analysis firm), transforming data and applied research into design proposals that identify alternate directions for the future of food retail.

SAID Associate Professor Michael Zaretsky has approached these studios from the perspective of Public Interest Design (PID), a sector of design that explores the potential for design to impact communities that would not otherwise have access to design. PID is generally associated with doing work in underprivileged communities, but PID is also relevant when working with large corporations. While a company may have financial means, there is a role for public interest designers to make a case for public interest values within the tight budgets that a food retail corporation has to meet to remain profitable.

Some businesses have a profit margin that includes funding for research and development. Food retail generally works on a 1% profit margin which leaves very little opportunity for R&D. Our collaboration with a national food corporation has enabled us to engage in deep public interest design research that has impacted food retail design at a large scale.

Since 2012, faculty from the School of Architecture and Interior Design have taught six studios that were sponsored by Kroger. The Kroger Director of Design, Kenneth Pray, has been the conduit between SAID and Kroger, and several faculty and leaders within Kroger have been involved. In each case, there was a specific focus for each studio. Students addressed specific issues and provided research and case study examples to support their design research and design proposals, and studios have explored the future of different types of food retail:

The Future of the C(onvenience)-Store
The Future of Urban Grocery
The Future of Digital Grocery (co-taught with Associate Professor Edson Cabalfin)
The Future of Small Format Grocery
The Future of Natural Format Grocery

Through these five studios, a series of themes have emerged that were somewhat challenging in corporate food retail when the studios began in 2012, but are now becoming more commonly embraced in the corporate and public sectors.

Students in these studios consistently looked deeply at corporate sustainability. What was uncovered with Kroger Co. was a strong history of philanthropy that most students were unaware of. This provided important information about millennial priorities and public relations communications.

Students in these studios looked at a series of social issues such as how employees are treated, who is producing the products, what is being done with expired food which may be viable for food pantries or other uses. Students were very interested in the design of spaces available for people to eat within and around the grocery stores. They proposed many alternatives to circulation, visibility, layout and experience of seating. They also looked at opportunities to provide comfortable seating outside the building walls—on patios, decks, and roofs. Students also explored environmental issues such as the lifecycle of the products as well as the lifecycle of the building materials. They looked at site issues and parking to provide options to reduce heat island effect and create more comfortable walking and parking experiences, and many challenges to the prominent role of parking in the typical grocery store and several alternatives were explored. At a different scale, students studied and explored health issues such as the legibility of nutrition information that is available for food in the stores. This information has become much more readily in recent years and is now impacting the design of food retail stores.

There have been many tangible impacts and benefits from these studios. Through these investigations, the students have come to realize their potential public interest design role in corporate retail design.

The corporation has been impacted by a group of educated, passionate millennials who are committed to values of food equity, community engagement, food education, local food sourcing, urban gardening and other PID principles. Kroger is a respectable company that attempts to serve all members of the community, but many of these PID principles and design ideas had not been fully embraced by the company. These studios have impacted the design of stores and have also influenced the conversations within the company. The impacts have extended beyond the studios because several of our students have gone on to work for the company and have continued to positively influence projects.

Our university has benefited from the financial sponsorship as well as through the relationship with the corporation. They have now become more engaged with other projects within our College and are recognizing the untapped value of design research to influence corporations and both the public and private sectors. The influence on the shopper is significant as well. Values of food equity, food education, health and urban gardening are beginning to show up in stores across the United States.

Strategies Used Within Project Relative to the Studio Theme

1. Sponsored studios can be productive for the students, the university and the sponsor, but a PID sponsored studio must be focused on the users and the communities impacted by the industry and the stores.
2. Teach the corporation why they need to design for the customer, not the owner.
3. Utilize case study analysis and design research to identify trends and values that will impact food retail in the future.

4. As an educational entity, we have leverage and influence that no one within the company or any hired consultant could have. The students provide a unique perspective as a result of their age and experience (as Millennials), their training (as designers) and their naive honesty (they aren't shy about sharing their perspectives in front of CEOs).

Community Partners
Kroger store employees and shoppers, Uplift Solutions, Closing the Health Gap and other food and health oriented non-profits as well as members of the UC nutrition program and Allied Health program have become either financial or collaborative partners in the sponsored studio program.

Stakeholders and Affiliations
To communicate this work to a larger audience, public events were held downtown at the end of each studio to present to Kroger store employees and shoppers, those in communities that use Kroger-owned stores, UC students, and members of the community at large.

Realized Learning Objectives
1. Students understand how the design of food retail addresses demographics, food conditions and availability, economics, technology and other retail trends.
2. Students research issues of food access, food equity and other social justice issues that overlap with food.
3. Students identify specific social, technological, economic and design issues that may influence the future of food retail design.
4. Students develop specific design proposals in actual store locations. These designs will reflect an expression of a future food retail design that is driven by principles of social justice, food equity and design in the public interest.

garage
park
cafe
store

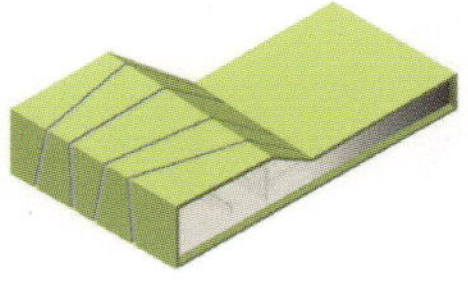

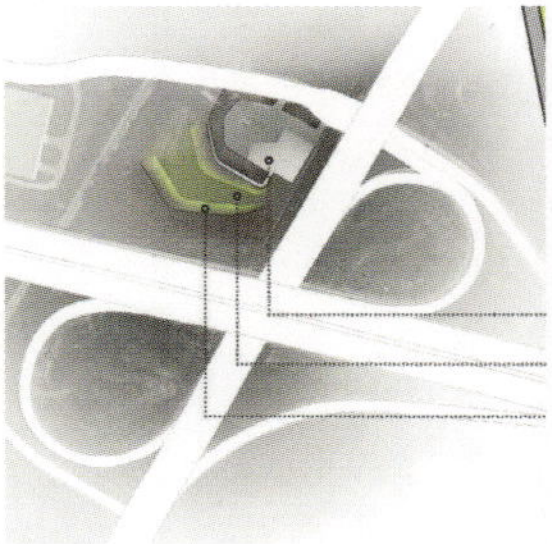

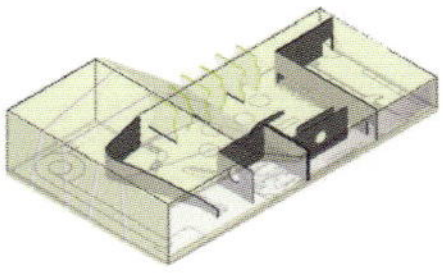

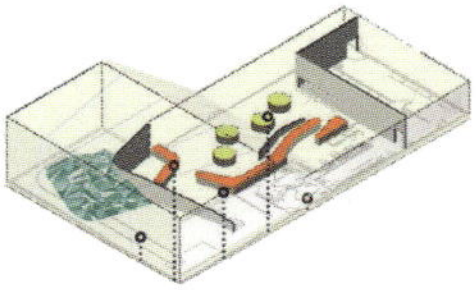

cafe
store

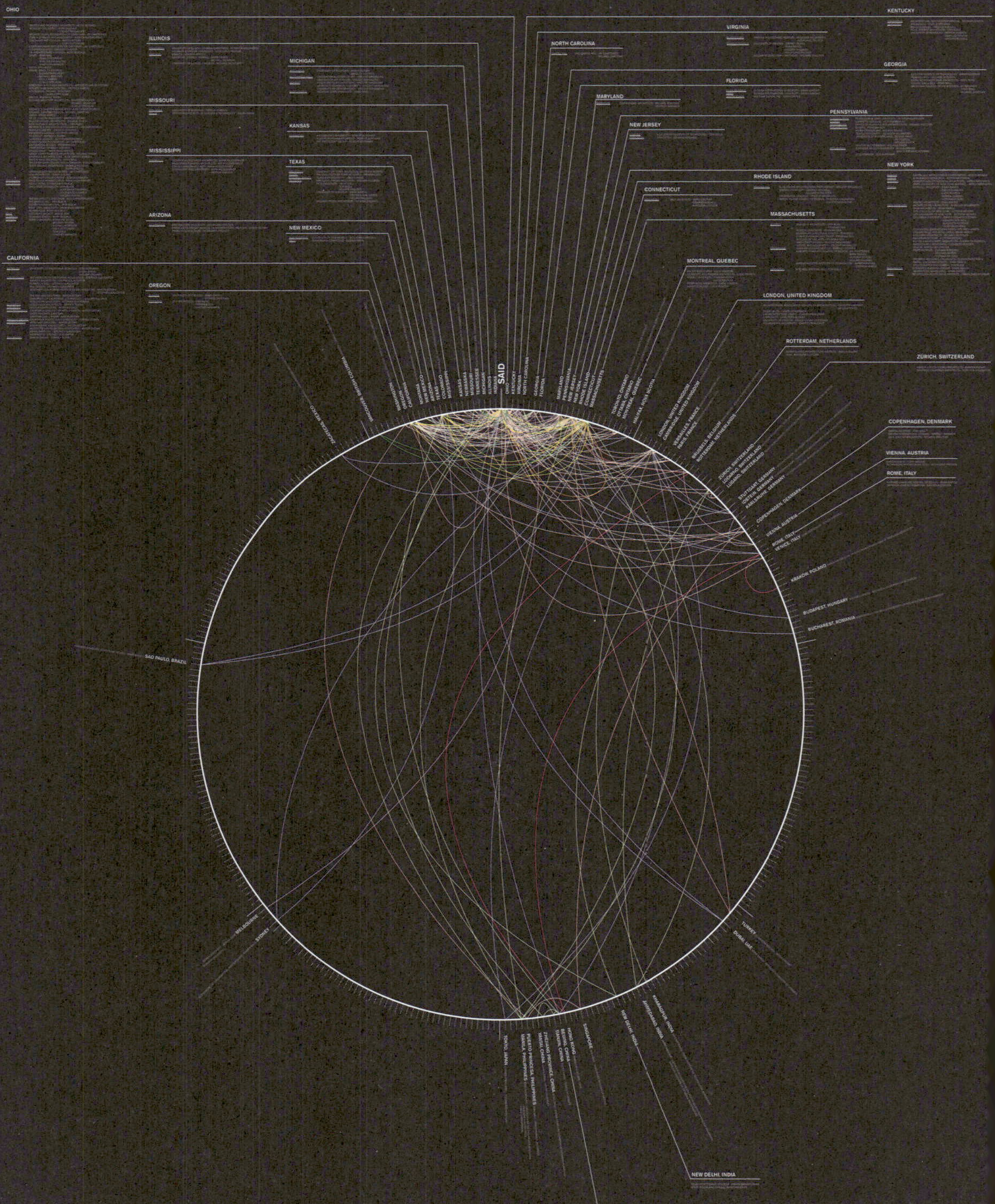

ECHOS EDITORIAL TEAM/ All Roads Lead to *SAID*

echos

TJ DUNN / Photography Credits

echos

Echos
University of Cincinnati
School of Architecture
and Interior Design

Published by
Actar Publishers, New York, Barcelona
www.actar.com

Authors
Mara Marcu

Edited by
Mara Marcu

Graphic Design
Mara Marcu with Student Editors

Student Editors: Kyle Winston, Alan Alaniz, Chas Wiederhold, Christina Tefend, Jamie Kruer, John Meyer, Anjana Sivakumar, Erin Klein, Daham Marapane, Michael Sullivan, Brady Ginn, Seher Hashmi, Gael Perichon, Farshad Khalighinejad, Kristin Moreno, and Garcia Ghislaine

Copy editing and proofreading
Gabriela Sarhos, Assoc. AIA

Printing and binding
Tiger Printing, Hong Kong

Distribution
Actar D, Inc. New York, Barcelona.

New York
440 Park Avenue South, 17th Floor
New York, NY 10016, USA
T +1 2129662207
salesnewyork@actar-d.com

Barcelona
Roca i Batlle 2-4
08023 Barcelona, Spain
T +34 933 282 183
eurosales@actar-d.com

Indexing
English ISBN: 978-1-948765-04-6
PCN: Library of Congress Control Number: 2018942687

Printed in China

Publication date: July 2018